SURNAMES

in the

UNITED STATES CENSUS

OF 1790

SURNAMES

in the

UNITED STATES CENSUS

OF 1790

An Analysis of National Origins
of the Population

AMERICAN COUNCIL OF LEARNED SOCIETIES
Report of Committee on Linguistics and National
Stocks in the Population of the United States

BALTIMORE

Genealogical Publishing Company

1969

Excerpted and Reprinted From
Annual Report of the American Historical Association
For the Year 1931
Volume I, Pages 103-441
Washington, 1932

Reprinted
Genealogical Publishing Company
Baltimore, 1969

Library of Congress Catalog Card Number 68-56110

Made in the United States of America

PUBLISHER'S PREFACE

SURNAMES IN THE UNITED STATES CENSUS OF 1790 is being reprinted in this form in order to bring this previously little known work to the attention of genealogists, historians, sociologists and others to whom it may be of interest. The work as originally published was contained in pages 103-441 of Volume I of the ANNUAL REPORT OF THE AMERICAN HISTORICAL ASSOCIATION FOR THE YEAR 1931 and consisted of various contributions in the Committee Report of the American Council of Learned Societies.

We have selected a new title for these various reports, have added a Table of Contents, but have retained the original pagination since the Index is keyed to these page numbers.

We call the reader's attention to the 35-page Bibliography appended to Annex A, pages 325-359, which, classified and annotated as it is, constitutes a valuable contribution in the study of surnames and the prevalence of the various national and linguistic stocks in the population of the United States in 1790. To date, we have reprinted over thirty odd titles, including some multi-volume sets, listed in this Bibliography. These reprints, as well as the present work, are part of our continuing program of reprinting those basic genealogical reference works which are out-of-print and in demand.

Genealogical Publishing Company

Baltimore, 1968

CONTENTS

IV. AMERICAN COUNCIL OF LEARNED SOCIETIES

REPORT OF COMMITTEE ON LINGUISTIC AND NATIONAL STOCKS IN THE POPULATION OF THE UNITED STATES

AMERICAN COUNCIL OF LEARNED SOCIETIES

REPORT OF COMMITTEE ON LINGUISTIC AND NATIONAL STOCKS IN THE POPULATION OF THE UNITED STATES

The committee of the American Council of Learned Societies on linguistic and national stocks in the population of the United States respectfully presents the following as its final report.

I. THE COMMITTEE'S PROBLEM

At the annual meeting of the council, January 29, 1927, attention was called to these facts:

1. The policy of the United States toward the immigration of aliens had been radically changed by the adoption of the national-origins plan of restricting immigration.

2. The size of the immigrant quotas allotted to the different countries under that plan would depend in part upon the attempted division of the white population of the United States in 1790 among the various national or linguistic stocks from, which it had sprung.

3. This division rested mainly upon the classification of the white heads of families enumerated at the census of 1790 according to their probable country of origin as indicated by their surnames.

4. This classification, made nearly 20 years before in a Government publication, had not been accepted by scholars as better than a first approximation to the truth.

5. The committee of three members of the Cabinet which had reported a few days before through the President to Congress, had said, " In our opinion the statistical and historical information available raises grave doubts as to the whole value of these computations (sc. of immigrant quotas) as a basis for the purposes intended."

6. The subcommittee appointed by the committee of members of the Cabinet to study the question had expressed its belief " that the results finally obtained, after such revisions as it may make within the next two or three months, will indicate the national origin of the population of the United States as nearly as may be assigned with the available data and under existing conditions," and then added that " a greater degree of accuracy could doubtless be obtained by a careful and exhaustive study of historical and genealogical records, but that is a task which might take several years for its completion and would require the assistance or cooperation of historians and experts in historical or genealogical research."

These facts almost constituted an invitation to the American Council of Learned Societies to enter upon a study which would of necessity cover a wider field than that tilled by any of its constituent societies, and the invitation became a challenge when it appeared that the chairman of the subcommittee responsible for the quotas and a critic of the Government report of 1909, who had reached widely different results, had both promised that if the committee should be appointed by the American Council of Learned Societies they would accept membership upon it.

Thereupon the chairman of the council was authorized to appoint a committee to consider the desirability of such a study. The following persons were appointed: Max Farrand, R. H. Fife, J. A. Hill, J. F. Jameson, W. F. Willcox, chairman. The committee, it will be noted, consisted of 2 statisticians, 2 historians, and 1 linguist.

The committee reported that it considered such a study desirable and feasible and recommended that funds be sought for paying the salary and expenses of an expert to work under the direction of an advisory committee in surveying the evidence, developing a plan, and estimating the cost, and the report was approved. On April 12, 1927, a further report said:

The problem on which the committee has been asked to report is the desirability of a study of the population of the United States from the standpoint of the national stocks entering into its composition. This problem has long aroused keen interest in the United States, and various efforts to solve it have been made both by individual scholars and by the Federal Government. These efforts have not yet led to an agreement in the results. On the contrary the conclusions are so far apart as to invite a reexamination of the evidence upon which they are based. The problem involves considerations and arguments which are partly historical, partly linguistic, partly statistical.

It is thus a problem not well suited for examination by a committee drawn from any one learned society. To deal with it adequately requires more time and resources than any one scholar is likely to command. On the other hand, no Government office is likely to have on its staff the trained men needed for the best results.

To illustrate the diversity in the conclusions of previous studies, we set two of them—one governmental, the other individual—side by side.

TABLE 1.—*White population of the United States distributed among its component stocks*

Stock	Governmental estimate, in 1790 [1]	Individual estimate, in 1775 [2]
English and Welsh	82.1	60
Scotch and Irish:		
Scotch_____ 7.0		
Irish_____ 1.9		
German	8.9	17–18
Dutch	5.6	11–12
French	2.5	7–8
All others	.6	[3]
	.3	[3]
Total	100.0	95–98

[1] Bureau of the Census, *A Century of Population Growth*, prepared by W. S. Rossiter, Washington, 1909.
[2] J. F. Jameson, *American Blood in 1775* (unpublished lecture).
[3] Not estimated.

Not more than a very small part of the differences in the foregoing results can be due to the slight difference in the dates for which they speak.

The committee believes that neither one of the preceding sets of proportions is supported by evidence enough to make it acceptable as more than a first approximation. It is also convinced that a careful, competent and prolonged study is likely to yield more trustworthy results than have yet been reached, and to support those results by more convincing evidence.

If the conclusions of the individual estimate already quoted should prove to be nearer the truth than the Government estimate which it aims to revise, the annual immigrant quotas from several European countries might be changed by some thousands.

Your committee recommends that an effort be made to secure a grant of $10,000 for prosecuting the inquiry, collating the extant evidence, probing for new evidence, and outlining a plan for a thorough and prolonged study if the reconnaissance survey thus provided for indicates that further work would be remunerative.

II. ORGANIZATION OF THE INQUIRY

Less than a year after it was appointed the committee presented the following report:

The work of the committee has been centered upon determining the proportions in which the white population living in 1790 within the United States as now bounded was composed of persons who, or whose ancestors, came from each of the leading European countries sending immigrants to the United States. The emphasis laid by the committee on this part of the whole problem is due to the fact that it is the question about which widely divergent opinions have been expressed by different authorities and supported by significant evidence.

The problem has been studied by the committee with the help of the above-mentioned grant which has enabled it to secure the services of Mr. Howard F. Barker and Dr. Marcus L. Hansen, the former an expert in the field of family names and indications of descent derived from them, the latter an expert in the field of the history of immigration to the United States.

Mr. Barker's revision of the evidence upon which the Government publication rested its case, that derived from the names of the heads of families in 1790, supplemented and checked by Doctor Hansen's historical studies of early migrations and of the American population in 1790, has already resulted in provisional estimates which differ not a little from those in the pioneer census publication.

Doctor Hansen has carried on historical studies parallel to these studies of family names and the committee is gratified to report that the results of the two independent lines of inquiry have tended to confirm each other.

III. LIMITATION OF STUDY TO CONDITIONS IN 1790

The committee soon after its appointment decided to restrict its inquiry to the question upon which the authorities differed most widely and upon which the training and investigation of the members of the committee enabled it best to guide the investigation. That question was: How was the white population of the United States in 1790 divided by birth or ancestry among the various national or linguistic stocks which contributed to its formation? In the course of the inquiry this question was divided into a number of subsidiary ones.

IV. POPULATION IN UNENUMERATED AREAS AND ITS CLASSIFICATION BY STOCKS

To the 3,172,444 whites reported by the census of 1790, Doctor Hansen has added 54,500 as the approximate number living in areas not then parts of the United States, like Florida and Louisiana, or in areas not actually reached by enumerators, like the Northwest Territory. The evidence for this conclusion will be found in the appendix written by Doctor Hansen. The total white population living in 1790 within the present limits of continental United States [1] was about 3,227,000.

Doctor Hansen's results on this point are brought together in the following table:

TABLE 2.—*White population in unenumerated areas classified by stocks: 1790*

Area	Total	American	French	Spanish	German
Northwest Territory	10,500	4,500	6,000		
Louisiana Purchase	20,000	2,900	12,850	2,500	1,750
Spanish United States	24,000	875		23,125	
	54,500	8,275	18,850	25,625	1,750

These districts not included by the first census contained about 1.7 per cent of the white population living in 1790 within the present boundaries of the United States.

---

[1] By continental United States is meant the area between Canada and Mexico, excluding Alaska, the Panama Canal Zone, and numerous islands recently added to the United States.

In the analysis of the remaining 98.3 per cent no class of "Americans" has been recognized. Although the figures involved are small and the probable error in their distribution is not small, yet for the sake of completeness the 8,275 "Americans" estimated by Doctor Hansen, have been distributed by assuming that they were drawn from the various national stocks in the rest of "America" according to the proportions in the population of the area of enumeration. In this way the following distribution has been made:

Spanish	25, 625
French	18, 850
English	5, 980
German	2, 280
Irish:	
Ulster	387
Free State	362
Scotch	816
Total	54, 500

V. METHOD USED IN A CENTURY OF POPULATION GROWTH [2] AND ITS SHORTCOMINGS

The work of classification was planned and directed by William S. Rossiter, chief clerk of the Bureau of the Census, and he wrote the text. The method is not completely explained in that volume or in the Census Bureau files or in the series of State reports to the interpretation of which *CPG* was devoted. The full names of the heads of families were given. Each of these families was assigned by an experienced clerk to its national stock on the evidence from the last name, surname, inherited or family name [3] of the head, but apparently without taking account of the first name or of the place of residence. Often the first name is foreign and the last name English. Such families were probably classed as English. After the names had been classified, the population of the United States was studied county by county, and the names in each assigned to the different national stocks, with a residual "all others," probably including families whose names did not indicate the national origin clearly enough to warrant the clerks in classifying them. The white population of Georgia, Kentucky, and Tennessee was classified according to the proportion in adjoining States, that of Delaware on the basis of the 1,800 returns, while that of New Jersey also received special treatment. These States included about 11 per cent of the white population.

a. After the names obviously Scotch, Irish, Dutch, French, German, Hebrew, or some other had been identified, [4] the total of these classes was subtracted from the total number of heads of families, to get the number of English names. By this procedure, all names which could not be ascribed to any of the six accepted nationalities and did not puzzle the clerk, were interpreted as English, a process which exaggerated the true number not a little.

b. The method failed to allow adequately for the continuous process by which non-English names had been modified by simplification, translation, or other processes, into forms likely to be counted as English.

c. The method was applied without considering the effect of local differences. Thus the name *Root*, which in Vermont points to an English origin but in Pennsylvania as a variant of *Roth* to a German origin, was probably treated in both States as an English name.

---

[2] Hereafter the letters *CPG* will be used to designate the volume, *A Century of Population Growth.*

[3] Hereafter in this report the word name will regularly be used as a synonym of surname or family name.

[4] *CPG*, p. 116.

d. The attempt was made to classify all names, although many gave little indication of their national origin. Thus the name *Miller* is a blend of *Millers* (English), *Millars* (Scotch), and *Muellers* (German); with the careless spelling of recorders and the changes of taste in spelling, such a group quickly became a hopeless tangle.

e. The clerks who did the classification were not trained for such a task, and those who directed them were not scholars in the fields of genealogy or history.

f. The method is a single or linear method, which affords no internal check upon its results and no indication of the margin of error to which the results are subject.

VI. REFINEMENTS OF METHOD NOW POSSIBLE

a. Attention is given only to "distinctive" names; that is, to those which point definitely to a linguistic or national stock. Examples of these "distinctive" names are *Hall* (English,) *Robertson* (Scotch), *Murphy* (Irish), *Schneider* (German).

b. The distribution of distinctive names, or the proportion that persons with distinctive names made of the total population in several European countries from which emigrants departed, in the United States as a whole, and in its divisions has been studied. The common names in England, Scotland, and Ireland had received the attention of preceding scholars, and the results were ready for comparison with the results of studying the common names of heads of American families in 1790. These comparisons indicate that a pattern of names, that is, a fixed proportion in which the bearers of the names selected as distinctive stand to the total population, is a characteristic of a given national or linguistic stock at a certain period and that unless the stock has been disturbed by migration its pattern of family names remains comparatively permanent.[5] As a result the occurrence of names distinctive of a mother

---

[5] The committee has found little evidence on the questions whether name patterns are or are not permanent and are or are not materially influenced by mass migration where that does not result in a mixture of stocks. But if name patterns in a country change radically, the proportion of names beginning with a given letter would probably change likewise. That these proportions have not greatly changed in England in 80 years is shown by the following tabulation:

NAMES BEGINNING WITH LETTER INDICATED, IN ENGLAND AND WALES, PER 1,000

	1837–1854, 21,000,000 names	1929, 658,166 names	Difference		1837–1854, 21,000,000 names	1929, 658,166 names	Difference
M	67	72	+5	S	89	90	+1
B	110	107	−3	U, V	7	7	---------
C	79	81	+2	K	20	20	---------
W	87	85	−2	E	24	24	---------
A	31	29	−2	I, J	38	38	---------
Q, X, Z	0	1	+1	L	42	42	---------
Y	5	4	−1	D	46	46	---------
O	11	12	+1	G	48	48	---------
N	17	16	−1	P	56	56	---------
F	33	34	+1	H	95	95	---------
T	45	44	−1				
R	50	49	−1		1,000	1,000	---------

In 9 cases the changes were less than 1 in 1,000 and in 8 less than 2, in 5 cases they were 2 or more, and in only 2 of the 22 were they 3 or more. The figures indicate very little change in the English name pattern in 80 years, a period during which the population much more than doubled.

To determine how closely the American and the English name patterns of to-day agree the two are compared below:

(Footnote continued on p. 112)

country in a population largely drawn from that country measures roughly the proportion of the population coming from that source. For example, if bearers of distinctive English names were nine-tenths as large a proportion of the population in Maryland in 1790 as they were in England, it is inferred that the population of Maryland was nine-tenths English.

c. This study of distinctive names has been made for the United States as a whole, for each of the States, and for the English, Welsh, Scotch, Irish, and German stocks. A summation of these results shows how nearly they account for the whole white population.

After the central registration of births, marriages, and deaths in England and Wales, which began in 1837, had accumulated and indexed more than 20,000,000 names, William Farr published a list of the 50 names occurring most often.[6] The bearers of these names included about 18 per cent of the population. Farr pointed out that in Wales the pattern of names was different from that in England and the number of names much less, perhaps nine-tenths of the Welsh population having one or another of the 100 most common names. The study was extended a generation later by Guppy, who examined the geographical distribution and prevalence of names among the farming classes of Great Britain, especially England and Wales.[7] Farr's pioneer work was imitated a few years later in Scotland[8] and in the next generation in Ireland.[9]

With this aid the name patterns characteristic of the four areas have been ascertained; using these as a basis the proportion of names in each of the American States and in the whole country in 1790, which were derived from England, Wales, Scotland, and Ireland, has been estimated.

An illustration will make the argument clearer. After a study of the distribution of Scotch names 17, including *Bruce, Duncan, Munro,* and *Ross,* were selected as distinctive. Bearers of these 17 distinctive Scotch names were about one-twelfth as large a proportion of the population in the United States in 1790 as they were in Scotland in 1860. It is inferred that the Scotch by birth

---

(Footnote 5 continued from p. 111)

NAMES BEGINNING WITH LETTER INDICATED, PER 1,000

Letter	England and Wales, 1929	United States, recent	Differ-ence	Letter	England and Wales, 1929	United States, recent	Differ-ence
K	20	42	−21	U, V	7	14	−7
M	72	93	−21	L	42	49	−7
W	85	65	+20	A	29	32	−5
H	95	80	+15	O	12	15	−3
S	90	104	−14	N	16	19	−3
T	44	31	+13	F	34	37	−3
P	56	43	+13	R	49	47	+2
I, J	38	28	+10	E	24	23	+1
C	81	72	+9	G	48	49	−1
B	107	99	+8	Y	5	5	0
Q, X, Z	0	7	−7	D	46	46	0

In England and Wales the average change of distribution in nearly three generations has been 1 name in 1,000, the average difference in distribution between recent English and American names is more than 8 in 1,000.

[6] Wm. Farr, Vital Statistics, 545–550, from *Sixteenth Annual Report,* pp. XVII–XXIV.

[7] Henry B. Guppy, *Homes of Family Names in Great Britain,* London, 1890.

[8] James Stark, Nomenclature in Scotland, in *Sixth Annual Report of Registrar-General,* Edinburgh, 1864, and in *Twelfth Annual Report of Registrar-General,* Edinburgh, 1869.

[9] Robert E. Matheson, Registrar-General, *Varieties and Synonyms of Surnames and Christian Names in Ireland,* Dublin, 1890; Report on Surnames in Ireland, with notes as to Numerical Strength, Ethnology, and Distribution, Appendix to *Twenty-ninth Annual Detailed Report of Registrar-General,* Dublin, 1894.

or descent were about one-twelfth of the population of the United States. A further study of the distribution of these names within the States showed that the Scotch were about one-sixth of the population of the most Southern States and about one twenty-fourth of the population of New England, the range being from 2.2 per cent in Connecticut to 15.5 per cent in Georgia.

VII. PROPORTION OF ENGLISH DESCENT

The list of common names prepared by Farr was shortened from 50 to 30 by excluding those prevalent also in Scotland, Ireland, or other parts of Europe, or adopted by many Americans not of English origin in Anglicizing their names. Thus *Smith* as an occupational surname is common in Scotland and Ireland, but in the United States it is also a modification of *Schmidt*, and a translation of other family names. Eight other names were excluded because in the United States they are not distinctive. *Moore*, for example, in the States south of New York, is a common transformation of the German *Mohr* and the Swiss *Moor* and so has become almost useless as an index of English origin. The remaining 22 names are of two classes—the Anglican and the Cambrian—the latter being distinctive of the population of Wales and the Welsh marches, the former distinctive of the rest of England. Class I, the Anglican names, are *Robinson, Hall, Green, Turner, Cooper, Ward, Baker, Parker, Lee*, and *Carter*. Class II, Welsh or Cambrian names, are *Jones, Williams, Thomas, Evans, Roberts, Edwards, Lewis, Morris, James, Morgan, Price*, and *Phillips*. A study of the population of England and Wales in the seventeenth and eighteenth centuries shows that those counties in which Anglican names were dominant contained about 82 per cent and those in which Cambrian names were dominant about 18 per cent of the population. If in an American State Anglican names were 88 per cent as common and Cambrian names 55 per cent as common as in England, the prevalence of English-Welsh blood would be estimated as follows:

$$88 \times 0.82 \text{--} \quad 72$$
$$55 \times 0.18 \text{--} \quad 10$$
$$\overline{ 82}$$

indicating that English blood was about 72 per cent and Welsh about 10 per cent of such a population.

By methods of this sort the proportion of the population of the several States and of the United States in 1790 which originated in England or Wales has been estimated. The result is too large because it does not fully allow for the transformations of names neither Anglican nor Cambrian into names which are one or the other, a process which went on in many parts of the country. In New Jersey the proportion of English blood could not be estimated by this method because no early list has been preserved. An estimate made by "the leading authorities upon New Jersey history" and adopted in *CPG* (p. 119) as well as by Mr. Barker, agrees much better with Barker's results than with Rossiter's for neighboring States. In the following summary the results of these computations are placed beside the corresponding figures from *CPG*.

TABLE 3.—*Estimated percentage of English and Welsh stock in the white population by States: 1790*

State	According to CPG	According to Barker	State	According to CPG	According to Barker
Maine	93	60	Delaware	86	60
New Hampshire	94	61	Maryland	84	72
Vermont	95	76	Kentucky and Tennessee	83	75
Massachusetts	95	82	Virginia	85	84
Rhode Island	96	71	North Carolina	83	98
Connecticut	96	67	South Carolina	82	75
New York	78	57	Georgia	83	70
New Jersey	58	58			
Pennsylvania	59	49	United States	82	70

The net result at this stage is to reduce the estimated proportion of English blood in the white population of the United States in 1790 from 82 to not more than 70 per cent.

VIII. PROPORTION OF SCOTCH DESCENT

Stark studied Scotch names as Farr had English, and reported upon the prevalence of the most common. Farr's list of 50 includes 20 in Stark's list of 150. *Smith*, for example, is the most common name in each country. *Robertson*, unlike *Smith*, is common in Scotland and not common in England or Ireland, and so is a distinctive Scotch name. More than half of the names in Stark's list were excluded as not distinctive or as likely to be confused with similar English or American names. *Chalmers*, for example, is a common Scotch name but has often become *Chambers* in the United States. In various ways Stark's list was reduced to 48 distinctive names. With the help of Matheson's Irish study these 48 were arranged according to their prevalence in Ireland and then divided into three groups—one in which the name was less than one-eighth as common in Ireland as in Scotland, a second in which it was between one-eighth and one-fourth as common, and a third in which it was more than one-fourth as common. The names in the first of these groups are accepted as distinctive Scotch surnames. In Scotland, according to Stark, the bearers of these names were 7.63 per cent of the population; if in the United States the bearers of them were 7.63 per cent of the Scotch population there were about 35,700 Scotch families in the United States in 1790.

The same method was applied to each State. For example, in Maine there were 58 families with distinctive Scotch names; it is inferred that there were about 760 families with Scotch names of any sort or about 4.5 per cent of the population.

The results are compared with those in *CPG* in the following table:

TABLE 4.—*Estimated percentage of Scotch stock in the white population by States: 1790*

State	According to CPG	According to Barker	State	According to CPG	According to Barker
Maine	4.3	4.5	Pennsylvania	11.7	8.6
New Hampshire	4.7	6.2	Maryland	6.5	7.6
Vermont	3.0	5.1	Virginia	7.1	10.2
Massachusetts	3.6	4.4	North Carolina	11.2	11.3
Rhode Island	3.1	5.8	South Carolina	11.7	15.1
Connecticut	2.8	2.2			
New York	3.2	7.0	United States	6.7	7.9

When estimates for New Jersey, Delaware, Georgia, Kentucky, and Tennessee derived from other sources or adjoining areas are introduced, the estimate for the whole United States rises from 7.9 to 8.3 per cent.

IX. PROPORTION OF IRISH DESCENT

The population of Ireland long has used names of different types and pointing to different origins, some indigenous, others derived from England or Scotland. They may be called Celtic-Irish, English-Irish, and Scotch-Irish names. These types are distributed unevenly in Ireland and the rate of emigration to the United States from the several districts has varied. It is desirable to distinguish between the prerevolutionary emigration to the United States from what is now the Irish Free State the former Provinces of Leinster, Munster, and Connaught, and that from Ulster, now Northern Ireland. The problem is one of great complexity and only approximate results can be secured. It is a reduced replica of the problem of estimating the colonial emigration from the British Isles to the United States, the three types of surnames in Ireland occupying somewhat the same relation to the whole that they do in the larger area.

The first task is to estimate the Celtic-Irish population in the United States. Five sets of distinctive Celtic-Irish names were derived from Matheson's evidence, one for each of the four Irish Provinces and a fifth for the island as a whole, and the results from combining the first four were compared with those from the fifth.

Matheson examined the names of 105,254 children born in Ireland in 1890, and reported surnames common to five or more. The 459 names each appearing more than fifty times and embracing almost two-thirds of the births, were selected. From that list was stricken out as Anglican every name found by Guppy to be prevalent in any English county, and as Scotch every name occurring more than six times in any Scotch county. This process eliminated more than half, the remainder being presumably distinctive Celtic-Irish names. Among those excluded were 57 characteristic Anglican, 46 characteristic Scotch names, and 112 used in England and Scotland. The large number of characteristic Anglican names suggests that English-Irish were about as numerous as Scotch-Irish in Ireland.

The 212 surnames remaining were then reduced to 185 by combining names probably variants of a common original. Thus the Irish often dropped the Scotch *Mc* and compensated for it by adding a " y," the names McMahan, Mahon, and Mahony, for example, being variants. The distribution of these 185 names in the four Provinces was then examined; if more than half the births with a given surname were found in one of the four Provinces the name was classed as provincial. This yielded the following results:

Names indicating origin in—	Number of names	Percentage of population having these names
Ulster	29	7.1
Leinster	20	8.3
Munster	57	30.6
Connaught	20	7.2
More than 1 Province	59	11.7
Total	185	_____

By omitting the less common names among the 57 distinctive of Munster and the 59 distinctive of more than one Province the list was reduced to manageable proportions with the following results:

Names indicating origin in—	Number of names	Percentage of population having these names
Ulster	29	7. 1
Leinster	20	8. 3
Munster	5	10. 2
Connaught	20	7. 2
More than 1 Province	18	7. 5
Total	92	

Among the bearers of these names the two classes of Irish names were distributed as follows:

Province	Percentage of names—	
	Distinctively Irish	Not distinctively Irish
Munster	63. 8	36. 2
Leinster	50. 9	49. 1
Connaught	50. 0	50. 0
Ulster	30. 0	70. 0
Ireland	47. 6	52. 4

showing that less than half of this fraction of the Irish population had distinctive Irish names, that conditions in Ulster were different from those in the other Provinces, and that Celtic-Irish from Munster in the United States can be identified most successfully and those from Ulster least successfully by their names.

Using these lists of provincial and of general Irish names their occurrence in the United States was studied with the following results:

Heads of families bearing those names in United States: 1790

Names indicating origin in—
Ulster _____ 1, 482
Leinster _____ 567
Munster _____ 841
Connaught _____ 378
Ireland, but Province not indicated _____ 2,158

Total _____ 5, 426

In Ireland the bearers of names not distinctive of any one Province were 75.4 per 1,000; in the United States they were 4.8 per 1,000, showing that these names and presumably, therefore, other Celtic-Irish names were 6.3 per cent as prevalent in the United States as in Ireland; from which it is inferred that 6.3 per cent of the population of the United States in 1790 was of Celtic-Irish stock.

To compare this result for all Ireland with the results for the four Provinces, the following computation has been used, the figures in the last column being the result of dividing those in the second by those in the first.

Percentage of distinctive provincial names

	Irish Province	American population, 1790	Indicated per cent of Irish in United States, 1790
Ulster	3.71	0.33	8.9
Leinster	3.12	.13	4.0
Munster	3.58	.19	5.2
Connaught	1.94	.08	4.3

Distinctive Ulster names were 8.9 per cent as common in the United States as they were in Ulster. To weight the per cents in the last column each may be multiplied by the per cent that the population of that Province in 1821, the earliest date for which trustworthy figures are obtainable, made of the total population of Ireland. The results are as follows:

Ulster _____ $8.9 \times 0.294 = 2.6$
Leinster _____ $4.0 \times .258 = 1.0$
Munster _____ $5.2 \times .285 = 1.5$
Connaught _____ $4.3 \times .163 = .7$
$$\overline{1.000 \quad 5.8}$$

This computation by provinces indicates that the Celtic-Irish in the United States in 1790 were 5.8 per cent of the population or one-half of one per cent less than the 6.3 reached by treating Ireland as a unit. The main reason for the difference is believed to be that the distinctive names used for all Ireland were more representative of the population than were the distinctive names used for the Provinces. If so, the 6.3 per cent is nearer the truth than 5.8 per cent. The Celtic-Irish thus seem to have contributed about 6.3 per cent to the population of the United States in 1790.

Of the Scotch names 14 were prevalent also in Ireland. There were 3,843 families with these names in the United States; if these names had been no more common than other Scotch names there would have been only 1,480 families; the difference represents probably the result of immigration from Ireland. If all Irish had migrated to the United States at the same rate as these Scotch-Irish, 30 per cent of its population would have been of Irish stock, showing that Scotch-Irish migration was at a much higher rate than Celtic-Irish. The question is, How much did this higher rate increase the total Irish migration to the United States?

In examining the proportion of Celtic emigrants from Ulster it was estimated that if the emigration from all Ulster had been at the same rate as that from its Celtic population, it would have made about 2.6 per cent of the population of the United States, but if it had been at the same rate as that from its Scotch-Irish population it would have made about 8.9 per cent. There was a third element in the population of Ulster, the English-Irish. Their rate of emigration was probably higher than that of the Celtic-Irish but lower than that of the Scotch-Irish. If their emigration rate had been equal to that of the Celtic-Irish the total contribution of that Province to the population of the United States would have been about 5 per cent. If it had been equal to that of the Scotch-Irish, it would have been about 7 per cent. It seems probable that it lay between these two limits and that the Province of Ulster as a whole contributed about 6 per cent to the population of the United States.

These results may now be compared with those in *CPG:*

TABLE 5.—*Estimated percentage of Irish stock in the white population by States: 1790*

State	According to CPG	According to Barker		
		Total	Irish Free State (3 southern Provinces)	Ulster
Maine	1.4	11.7	3.7	8.0
New Hampshire	1.0	7.5	2.9	4.6
Vermont	0.7	5.1	1.9	5.1
Massachusetts	1.0	3.9	1.3	2.6
Rhode Island	0.7	2.8	.8	2.0
Connecticut	0.7	2.9	1.1	1.8
New York	0.8	8.1	3.0	5.1
New Jersey	7.1	9.5	3.2	6.3
Pennsylvania	2.0	14.5	3.5	11.0
Delaware	3.9	11.7	5.4	6.3
Maryland	2.4	12.3	6.5	5.8
Virginia	2.0	11.7	5.5	6.2
North Carolina	2.3	11.1	5.4	5.7
South Carolina	2.6	13.8	4.4	9.4
Georgia	2.3	15.3	3.8	11.5
Kentucky and Tennessee	2.3	12.2	5.2	7.0
United States	1.9	9.7	3.7	6.0

The analysis indicates that not far from 10 per cent of the white population of the United States in 1790 was of Irish origin, three-fifths of it from Ulster and two-fifths from what is now the Irish Free State.

X. PROPORTION OF GERMAN DESCENT

No report has been found of the distribution of German names in Germany like those British studies which gave a foundation for estimating the proportions of English, Scotch, and Irish. Another obstacle lies in the fact that German names in the United States have been much more Anglicized or otherwise transformed than Scotch or Irish names.[10] But several scholars using other evidence have estimated the amount of German stock in the United States at more than 5 per cent and not more than 12 per cent of the population. These may be accepted at the start as the limits. The massing of the German population before 1790 in Pennsylvania also makes the problem easier.

The present estimate started with the Oath of Allegiance Record of foreign immigrants arriving in Pennsylvania. From it 198 common names were selected, 63 of which were accepted as distinctively German, the others being rejected as liable to confusion with similar English, Scotch, Irish, Dutch, or French names. These 63 names included about 3,500 entries or 4.7 per cent of the 74,500 families in Pennsylvania in 1790. The list was then reduced to 32 by omitting names used by few heads of families and those with a variety of forms. The 32 included about 2,300 heads of families or 3.1 per cent of the population of Pennsylvania. Next the prevalence of these 32 German names in other States where Germans were numerous was studied. Taking the number reported in Pennsylvania as 100 per cent and allowing for more Angliciza-

---

[10] Doctor Jameson gives an illustration of three Pennsylvania sons of a German named Klein who passed the name on to their descendants in three forms: Cline, Small, and Little.

tion in Virginia and North Carolina than in Pennsylvania, as shown by detailed analyses, the ratio in other States was:

Maryland	15.4	New Jersey	9.2
New York	12.0	North Carolina	6.5
Virginia	9.5	South Carolina	2.6

To estimate the number of Germans in these States from the preceding ratios it is necessary to know the number in Pennsylvania. Mr. Barker's conclusion is that in 1790 Germans were about one-third of the population. This would make their number in Pennsylvania about 141,000 and the families about 24,800. By applying the preceding ratios to 24,800 the number of German names in each State and their proportion of the whole were computed. The results were:

TABLE 6.—*Estimated percentage of German stock in the white population by States: 1790*

State	Per cent, German	State	Per cent, German
New England	0.4	North Carolina	3.1
New York	5.5	South Carolina	2.5
New Jersey	9.2	Georgia	3.9
Pennsylvania	33.3	Kentucky and Tennessee	13.6
Delaware	1.1		
Maryland	11.7	United States	8.1
Virginia	6.3		

Applying this 8.1 per cent to the white population of the United States in 1790 an estimate of 258,000 Germans is reached. This is probably an underestimate because it takes no account of currents of German immigration independent of that to Pennsylvania and presumably characterized by somewhat different names. To find whether this 8.1 per cent is too low 13 names were selected as especially widespread and distinctive. An analysis of the prevalence of these names materially raised the estimate of the German blood in New York and the Carolinas and in this manner brought up that for the Germans in the United States from 8.1 to 8.7 per cent or from 258,000 to 277,000.

The final outcome of Mr. Barker's study of the German stock in the United States in 1790 was as follows:

TABLE 7.—*Estimated percentage of German stock in the white population by States: 1790*

State	German		State	German	
	According to CPG	According to Barker		According to CPG	According to Barker
	Per cent	Per cent		Per cent	Per cent
Maine	0.5	1.3	Delaware	0.4	1.1
New Hampshire		.4	Maryland	5.9	11.7
Vermont		.3	Virginia	4.9	6.3
Massachusetts		.3	North Carolina	2.8	4.7
Rhode Island	.1	.5	South Carolina	1.7	5.0
Connecticut		.3	Georgia	2.8	7.6
New York	.4	8.2	Kentucky and Tennessee	2.8	14.0
New Jersey	(9.2)	(9.2)			
Pennsylvania	26.1	33.3	United States	5.6	8.7

XI. NUMBER OF DUTCH DESCENT

Since the Dutch in the United States in 1790 were the descendants of the seventeenth century settlers of New Netherland, Doctor Hansen attempted first to estimate the number in the areas of original settlement, New York, New

Jersey, and Delaware. He rested his estimate for New York on the census of 1698, which gives the population by counties and for which several of the original lists have been preserved, and reached the following results:

TABLE 8.—*White population and estimated number of Dutch stock in New York colony by counties: 1698*

County	Population		County	Population	
	White	Dutch		White	Dutch
Albany	1,453	1,350	Suffolk	2,121	---------
Ulster and Dutchess	1,228	800	Kings	1,721	1,500
Orange	200	150	Queens	3,366	250
New York	4,237	2,000			
Richmond	654	300	Total	15,897	6,650
West Chester	917	300			

A reliable authority gave the population of East Jersey in 1790 as 8,000 in eight settlements, only two of which were of Dutch origin. A study of contemporary church records in these two indicates a Dutch population of about 1,000. West Jersey was almost entirely English.

For Delaware no satisfactory data are available. In 1658 the number of Dutch settlers was reported as 600, but after that date disease and migration to Maryland and Virginia greatly checked the increase of population. The Dutch in 1700 are estimated at 1,000.

This gives 8,650 in 1700 as the maximum number of Dutch in America. Assuming that this stock doubled every 25 years (which Doctor Hansen thinks unlikely), the number in 1790 would be about 120,000.

An independent analysis of the Dutch population in 1790, first in the States of original Dutch settlement, then in New England, then in the States which received the first waves of Dutch migration from New Netherland (Pennsylvania, Maryland, and Virginia), and lastly in the Southern and Southwestern States, gives a figure which agrees reasonably well with the preceding result. Most of the estimates are based upon the number of Dutch names in local registers, genealogical dictionaries, census lists, etc. The results are as follows:

TABLE 9.—*White population and estimated number of Dutch stock by States: 1790*

State	Population		State	Population	
	White	Dutch		White	Dutch
New York	314,366	55,000	Maryland	208,649	1,000
New Jersey	169,954	35,000	Virginia	442,117	1,500
Delaware	46,310	2,000	North Carolina	289,181	800
Connecticut	232,236	600	South Carolina	140,178	500
Massachusetts	373,187	600	Georgia	52,886	100
Vermont	85,072	500	Kentucky	} 93,046	} 1,000
Rhode Island	64,670	250	Tennessee		200
Maine	96,107	100			
New Hampshire	141,112	100		3,172,444	106,750
Pennsylvania	423,373	7,500			

The total is about 10 per cent less than the maximum of 120,000, which might have been derived from the Dutch stock present in the colonies about 1700. But, Doctor Hansen concluded, "There is no assurance that colonial population grew, apart from immigration, at a rate which doubled itself in 25 years. War and disease checked the growth and in the loyalist exodus after 1783 were probably several hundreds of families of Dutch descent. Therefore, the derived figure is not unreasonable. That 90,000 of them should be concentrated in a region included in the original area of Dutch colonization indicates that the Hollanders were less mobile than the majority of their colonial neighbors."

XII. NUMBER OF FRENCH DESCENT

Doctor Hansen's estimate, 53,400, is about half the number assigned to the Dutch and larger than previous estimates. He found the French stock not easily recognizable because of the conditions under which it was introduced and because of its more uniform distribution. Its numbers can not be compared with those of the British or the German. There was no mass migration. The French trickled in, not only from France, but also from Switzerland, Great Britain, Germany, and Holland, countries in which they had taken temporary refuge, and were distributed in the settlements which people from these countries had established. In the last third of the seventeenth century, when the influx of the French was at its height, the American communities along the coast were overpopulated, and frontier advance was facilitated by the defeat of the Indians and the clearer political atmosphere. The French settled in groups broke into smaller groups and following the geographical tendencies prevalent in each particular community were scattered from Maine to the Carolinas. Another cause of their dispersion was colonial hostility preventing the establishment of French colonies, and preventing also the settlement of French in certain colonies already established.

Most of these French settlers were Huguenots. Two studies have appeared which prove that in the years immediately preceding and following the Revolution, the French language and French tastes attained a vogue in American life which made necessary the presence of French professors and those who were competent to train the rising generation in the niceties of manners; and although these studies, being more interested in the results, do not attempt any numerical review, they do present evidence which explains the appearance of many scattered French names on the census rolls of 1790.

Other sources sometimes overlooked of French immigration into the United States are the West Indies, Canada, and Acadia.

TABLE 10.—*Estimated population of French stock by States: 1790*

State	Population	State	Population
Maine	1,200	Pennsylvania	7,500
New Hampshire	1,000	Maryland	2,500
Vermont	350	Virginia	6,500
Massachusetts	3,000	North Carolina	4,800
Connecticut	2,100	South Carolina	5,500
Rhode Island	500	Georgia	1,200
New York	12,000	Kentucky and Tennessee	2,000
New Jersey	4,000		
Delaware	750	Total	54,900

XIII. NUMBER OF SWEDISH DESCENT

The first Swedish settlements were established in three localities on the Delaware, now Wilmington, Del., Philadelphia, Pa., and Gloucester County, N. J. The expansion from these centers was as follows:

1. From Wilmington into Newcastle County, Del., and into Maryland.
2. From Philadelphia southwestward down the valley of the Delaware and northwestward up the valley of the Schuylkill.
3. From Gloucester County, N. J., along the river banks and the coast of the bay into Burlington, Cumberland, Salem, and Cape May Counties.

The Swedish population of the original settlements and of these expansions before 1790 was estimated by studying census lists for that year in districts where they were available, and in other districts assessment lists, lists of taxables, and company lists of the Revolution. The results are as follows:

Delaware	4,100
Maryland	950
Pennsylvania	3,325
New Jersey	6,650
	15,025

For the rest of the country Doctor Hansen has estimated a Swedish population of 6,075 in 1790, distributed as follows:

Massachusetts	75
Connecticut	25
Rhode Island	50
New York	1,500
Virginia	2,600
North Carolina	700
South Carolina	325
Georgia	300
Kentucky }	500
Tennessee }	

This yields a total of 21,100 Swedes in the United States.

XIV. CONSOLIDATION OF RESULTS

If the foregoing results were correct they would in combination account for the entire white population of the United States in 1790. But before combining them Mr. Barker's figures must be changed from per cents to totals or Doctor Hansen's from totals to per cents. The latter course has been adopted and the results appear in the following table, in which the small groups residing in the unenumerated areas and classed by Doctor Hansen as Americans, British, or Irish have been distributed according to the proportions found by Mr. Barker to prevail among the same groups residing in the enumerated areas.

TABLE 11.—*Provisional classification of the white population into their national or linguistic stocks by States: 1790*

State	English	Scotch	Irish		German	Dutch	French	Swedish	Spanish	Total of preceding
			Ulster	Free State						
Maine	60	4.5	8.0	3.7	1.3	0.1	1.2			78.8
New Hampshire	61	6.2	4.6	2.9	.4		.7			75.8
Vermont	76	5.1	3.2	1.9	.2	.6				87.0
Massachusetts	82	4.4	2.6	1.3	.3	.2	.8			91.6
Rhode Island	71	5.8	2.0	.8	.5		.8			80.9
Connecticut	67	2.2	1.8	1.1	.3	3	.1			72.8
New York	57	7.0	5.1	3.0	8.2	17.5	3.8	0.5		102.1
New Jersey	58	7.7	6.3	3.2	9.2	20.6	2.4	3.9		111.3
Pennsylvania	40	8.6	11.0	3.5	33.3	1.8	1.8	.8		100.8
Delaware	60	8.0	6.3	5.4	1.1	4.3	1.6	8.9		95.6
Maryland	72	7.6	5.8	6.5	11.7	.5	1.2	.5		105.8
Virginia	84	10.2	6.2	5.5	6.3	.3	1.5	.6		114.6
North Carolina	98	14.8	5.7	5.4	4.7	.3	1.7	.2		130.8
South Carolina	75	15.1	9.4	4.4	5.0	.4	3.9	.2		113.4
Georgia	70	15.5	11.5	3.8	7.6	.2	2.3	.6		111.5
Kentucky and Tennessee	75	10.0	7.0	5.2	14.0	1.3	2.1	.5		115.1
United States	70	8.3	6.0	3.7	8.7	3.3	2.4	.6	0.9	103.9
Northwest Territory	29.8	4.1	2.9	1.8	4.3		57.1			100.0
Spanish, United States	2.5	.3	.2	.1	.4				96.5	100.0
French, United States	11.2	1.6	1.1	.7	8.7		64.2		12.5	100.0

In Table 11 the States fall into two classes—those in which the sum of the per cents is too small and those in which it is too large. The former group includes all the New England States with Delaware, the latter includes the other nine States. The excess above 100 per cent in the latter group is due mainly to the fact that many families having surnames classed as English were of other blood. From his previous studies in this field Mr. Barker had reached a provisional opinion that about 30 per cent of white Americans to-day with English names are not of English blood. The present study throws light upon conditions in 1790 and furnishes a rough measure of the adoption of English names by other than English persons. After studying the conditions in each State separately Mr. Barker reduced the provisional per cents of English in the population outside of New England as follows:

State	English		State	English	
	Pro-visional	Revised		Pro-visional	Revised
	Per cent	*Per cent*		*Per cent*	*Per cent*
Maine	60	60	Maryland and District of Columbia	72	64.5
New Hampshire	61	61	Virginia	84	68.5
Vermont	76	76	North Carolina	98	66.0
Massachusetts	82	82	South Carolina	75	60.2
Rhode Island	71	71	Georgia	70	57.4
Connecticut	67	67	Kentucky and Tennessee	75	57.9
New York	57	52.0			
New Jersey	58	47.0	United States	70	60.9
Pennsylvania	40	35.3			
Delaware	60	60.0			

Using these revised figures for the proportion of English, and adding a column of miscellaneous, Mr. Barker's and Doctor Hansen's combined results are shown in Table 12.

Mr. Barker's conclusion that the number of Dutch in New Jersey was somewhat overestimated by Doctor Hansen derives support from the fact that several members of the New Jersey Historical Society in 1908 concluded that the Dutch were about 12.7 per cent of the 1790 population instead of 20.6, Doctor Hansen's figure; and by the further fact that if the larger figure is accepted the sum of all the stocks slightly exceeds the entire population of the State. For these reasons the average of the two results has been adopted and the Dutch set at 16.6 per cent of the population.

TABLE 12.—*Revised classification of the white population into their national or linguistic stocks by States: 1790*

State	Eng-lish	Scotch	Irish		Ger-man	Dutch	French	Swed-ish	Span-ish	Unas-signed	Total
			Ulster	Free State							
Maine	60.0	4.5	8.0	3.7	1.3	0.1	1.3			21.1	100.0
New Hampshire	61.0	6.2	4.6	2.9	.4	.1	.7			24.1	100.0
Vermont	76.0	5.1	3.2	1.9	.2	.6	.4			12.6	100.0
Massachusetts	82.0	4.4	2.6	1.3	.3	.2	.8			8.4	100.0
Rhode Island	71.0	5.8	2.0	.8	.5	.4	.8	0.1		18.6	100.0
Connecticut	67.0	2.2	1.8	1.1	.3	.3	.9			26.4	100.0
New York	52.0	7.0	5.1	3.0	8.2	17.5	3.8	.5		2.9	100.0
New Jersey	47.0	7.7	6.3	3.2	9.2	16.6	2.4	3.9		3.7	100.0
Pennsylvania	35.3	8.6	11.0	3.5	33.3	1.8	1.8	.8		3.9	100.0
Delaware	60.0	8.0	6.3	5.4	1.1	4.3	1.6	8.9		4.1	100.0
Maryland and District of Columbia	64.5	7.6	5.8	6.5	11.7	.5	1.2	.5		1.7	100.0
Virginia and West Virginia	68.5	10.2	6.2	5.5	6.3	.3	1.5	.6		.9	100.0
North Carolina	66.0	14.8	5.7	5.4	4.7	.3	1.7	.2		1.2	100.0
South Carolina	60.2	15.1	9.4	4.4	5.0	.4	3.9	.2		1.4	100.0
Georgia	57.4	15.5	11.5	3.8	7.6	.2	2.3	.6		1.1	100.0
Kentucky and Tennessee	57.9	10.0	7.0	5.2	14.0	1.3	2.2	.5		1.9	100.0
Area enumerated	60.9	8.3	6.0	3.7	8.7	3.4	1.7	.7		6.6	100.0
Northwest Territory	29.8	4.1	2.9	1.8	4.3		57.1				100.0
Spanish, United States	2.5	.3	.2	.1	.4				96.5		100.0
French, United States	11.2	1.6	1.1	.7	8.7		64.2		12.5		100.0
Continental United States	60.1	8.1	5.9	3.6	8.6	3.1	2.3	0.7	0.8	6.8	100.0

Table 12 sets forth the final results of the investigation. They are reasonably satisfactory except for the New England States, where the unexplained element is between one-twelfth and one-fourth of the population and several times as great as in other parts of the country. This difficulty Mr. Barker is unable completely to explain and students especially interested are referred to his frank discussion of the problem.

As some readers are likely to be interested in the estimated number of white persons of various stocks in the United States and the several States, as well as in the per cents, the preceding table has been transformed by multiplying the white population of each State by the per cents in Table 12 and thus Table 13 has been derived.

TABLE 13.—*Estimated number of white persons belonging to the indicated national or linguistic stocks by States: 1790*

State	White population	English	Scotch	Irish		German
				Ulster	Free State	
Maine	96,107	57,664	4,325	7,689	3,556	1,249
New Hampshire	141,112	86,078	8,749	6,491	4,092	564
Vermont	85,072	64,655	4,339	2,722	1,616	170
Massachusetts	373,187	306,013	16,420	9,703	4,851	1,120
Rhode Island	64,670	45,916	3,751	1,293	517	323
Connecticut	232,236	155,598	5,109	4,180	2,555	697
New York	314,366	163,470	22,006	16,033	9,431	25,778
New Jersey	169,954	79,878	13,087	10,707	5,439	15,636
Pennsylvania	423,373	149,451	36,410	46,571	14,818	140,983
Delaware	46,310	27,786	3,705	2,918	2,501	509
Maryland	208,649	134,579	15,857	12,102	13,562	24,412
Virginia	442,117	302,850	45,096	27,411	24,316	27,853
North Carolina	289,181	190,860	42,799	16,483	15,616	13,592
South Carolina	140,178	84,387	21,167	13,177	6,168	7,009
Georgia	52,886	30,357	8,197	6,082	2,010	4,019
Kentucky and Tennessee	93,046	53,874	9,305	6,513	4,838	13,026
Area enumerated	3,172,444	1,933,416	260,322	190,075	115,886	276,940
Northwest Territory	10,500	3,130	428	307	190	445
Spanish, United States	24,000	610	83	60	37	85
French, United States	20,000	2,240	305	220	135	1,750
Continental United States	3,226,944	1,939,396	261,138	190,662	116,248	279,220

TABLE 13.—*Estimated number of white persons belonging to the indicated national or linguistic stocks by States: 1790—Continued*

State	Dutch	French	Swedish	Spanish	Unassigned
Maine	100	1,200			20,324
New Hampshire	100	1,000			34,038
Vermont	500	350			10,720
Massachusetts	600	3,000	75		31,405
Rhode Island	250	500	50		12,070
Connecticut	600	2,100	25		61,372
New York	55,000	12,000	1,500		9,148
New Jersey	28,250	4,000	6,650		6,307
Pennsylvania	7,500	7,500	3,325		16,815
Delaware	2,000	750	4,100		2,041
Maryland	1,000	2,500	950		3,687
Virginia	1,500	6,500	2,600		3,991
North Carolina	800	4,800	700		3,531
South Carolina	500	5,500	325		1,945
Georgia	100	1,200	300		621
Kentucky and Tennessee	1,200	2,000	500		1,790
Area enumerated	100,000	54,900	21,100		219,805
Northwest Territory		6,000			
Spanish, United States				23,125	
French, United States		12,850		2,500	
Continental United States	100,000	73,750	21,100	25,625	219,805

XV. CONCLUSION

The committee believes that the following conclusions have been established as probable:

1. The study of surnames in a large population reveals the existence of name patterns which lend themselves to statistical analysis and interpretation.

2. The material so studied makes it possible to characterize a population, to distinguish one from another, and often to measure the shares which one or another stock has contributed to a mixed population.

3. How far the name patterns in a population are stable in time, and how far they change with the results of migration or of translation or of other modification of names, and with the varying rates of increase of the component stocks are questions which the committee has not sought to decide. But it believes that these name patterns are so stable through a few generations and in large currents of migration as to warrant reliance upon them in estimating the stocks in a mixed population.

4. Many inferences from this study of American and European name patterns have been supported by historical evidence regarding the currents of immigration and the spread of settlement before 1790.

5. The results are far from final. They indicate that continued study of surnames both in Europe and in the United States is likely to throw more light upon the origin and composition of the American population.

WALTER F. WILLCOX, *Chairman.*
MAX FARRAND.
ROBERT H. FIFE.
JOSEPH A. HILL.
J. FRANKLIN JAMESON.

WASHINGTON, D. C., *February 8. 1932.*

ANNEX A. NATIONAL STOCKS IN THE POPULATION OF THE UNITED STATES AS INDICATED BY SURNAMES IN THE CENSUS OF 1790

By Howard F. Barker

Chapter I

THE POPULATION OF THE UNITED STATES IN 1790

THE CENSUS OF 1790

A remarkable feature of the inauguration of the Government of the United States was the decennial census, first taken in 1790. Several colonies had previously made counts of population, but a periodic national census was a new thing, not merely for America but for the world. Great Britain followed a decade later. The chief purpose of the census was to determine the apportionment of Representatives in Congress to the several States, but it included more information than would be given by a mere count of inhabitants. It gave the names of the heads of families and classified all white males into two age groups and the colored population as free or slave. The area covered included the thirteen original States (Maine being at that time a Province of Massachusetts), Vermont and Kentucky, which had already been admitted to the Union, and Tennessee, then a Territory. Six records have been lost—those of New Jersey, Delaware, Virginia, Georgia, Kentucky, and Tennessee. The loss of the Virginia records has been partly repaired by a list of the inhabitants of 39 counties made up from State enumerations and tax lists. These 12 records have been published and indexed and are our chief source of information concerning the population of the United States in 1790. Though lacking much of the detail found in a modern scientific census, these lists of names provide us with valuable data concerning 81 per cent of that population. They offer indirect but weighty evidence about the racial strains in the American population, and act as guides and controls to historical investigation.

The descendants of the population of 1790 comprise over half of the present inhabitants of the United States. Yet less is actually known about the antecedents of this stock than about the other elements. Beginning in 1850 the census records indicate the places of birth of all foreign-born inhabitants, and there are increasingly detailed Federal records of immigration dating from 1820. Therefore, since the immigration from 1789 to 1820 was not large, a knowledge of the elements of the 1790 population is the main requirement for understanding what has heretofore been regarded as "native stock."

ORIGINAL NATIVE STOCK

What was the nature of the population of 1790? The Bureau of the Census calls it "original native stock" because it is as American as our Government. According to the record, the inhabitants of the country then numbered about 3,930,000, of whom 3,172,444 were whites. These whites were predominantly English. But to what extent is the term "English," as a designation of blood,

126

confused with the same word meaning "American" or "persons speaking only English"? To what extent is the name English misapplied to all people originating in the British Isles, who are more correctly designated as British? What numbers had the stock of New Netherland attained by 1790 and how largely was it Dutch? How numerous were the descendants of the Germans who had settled by thousands, particularly in the Middle and Southern States; of the French who had come from both France and Canada; of the small Swedish stock which had settled here six or seven generations before? Finally, what were the contributions of unorganized migration of individuals and small groups from other countries? Considering the importance of the subject, very little thought has been given to these questions, and it now seems desirable to measure as exactly as possible the contributions of the different national stocks to the original population of the United States. Such is the purpose of the following studies.

There are three fairly distinct views of the composition of the American population in Washington's time. Of widest currency is the one which may be called the "school-book" view. According to this conception the population was almost entirely English except in Pennsylvania and New York, where substantial numbers of Germans and Dutch are recognized, and except for a scattering of French, mainly Huguenots, and Irish, mainly from Ulster, who demand recognition because of their contributions to the roll of famous names. According to another view the original population of the United States was a "medley of nations." This conception—expressed by Benjamin Franklin; David Ramsay, a contemporary historian of the Revolution in South Carolina; Dr. Johann D. Schoepf, chief surgeon to the German troops in the Revolution; and Crèvecoeur, author of the well known *Letters from an American Farmer*—emphasizes the "miscellaneous and recalcitrant elements" of the population, the groups "composed of the most contradictory characters," and the "promiscuous crowd." A third view limits that part of the population classed as miscellaneous by demonstrating the existence of definite currents of immigration from particular countries which have not received sufficient recognition.

None of these viewpoints is unbiased. But a general idea of the composition of the population is useful in approaching a detailed quantitative study of its elements. Various racial and linguistic strains have already been investigated. One can hardly say that the English have been studied as a stock. They figure as administrators or vaguely as "the people," so that the numbers of English have commonly been estimated by subtracting the elements of other blood. Bearing in mind that the stocks were somewhat fused, it is nevertheless permissible to accept the general notion that the English were the dominant stock, the Germans and Irish next in importance, the Dutch and Scotch next, along with the Welsh (if the Welsh are to be distinguished from the English); last in point of numbers were the French and the German-speaking Swiss and Austrians. This rough grouping will be made more precise by the results of detailed analysis.

In approaching the analysis of the original native stock one must acknowledge that a number of factors bear on the problem. For one thing, the population of 1790 was not *homogeneous* throughout the whole area; districts present different mixtures. This initial conception should also recognize that a large part of the population had been in the country from four to seven generations and was not conscious of national antecedents. It should not attempt inferences as to population from the lives of leaders nor from the names of towns and landmarks. It should not disregard the effects of wars nor of the routes over water and land which bore traffic, sometimes in one direction only, sometimes in two, nor of certain well-known currents of secondary migration, proceeding not only westward but also northward into the outlying parts of New England and southward up the valley of Virginia. Finally, it should make allowance for the less tangible changes in the population caused by infusion and diffusion. Infusion finds illustration in the fact that of the first 200 white men and women married in the Dutch Reformed Church of New Amsterdam only about half came from Holland or were born under the Dutch flag. An example of diffusion is to be seen in Felt's record for Massachusetts in 1777. which shows that of the male population 16 years or more of age, somewhat more than 1 per cent were classed as "strangers." In this connection the comment of Suessmilch is also to the point:

Compared with France and Spain, England has an advantage in welcoming foreigners into the colonies and giving them by naturalization all the rights of natives.[1]

In short, the investigator must take into account all the more readily distinguishable forces bearing on the composition of the population of 1790. The impartial measuring of these factors constitutes a difficult and complex problem.

APPROACH TO ANALYSIS OF POPULATION

The methods of inquiry used for the analysis of a modern census are not of much use in dealing with the census of 1790. As noted above, several studies of particular elements in the population have been made, and some excellent work has been accomplished by means of a great variety of methods and often a curious compounding of them. For example, the number of Germans was estimated on the basis of the sales of spelling books and subscriptions to periodicals. Estimates have often been made in terms of "racial" settlements or church congregations of particular denominations, supplemented by rather indefinite allowances for individuals not connected with these institutions. There emerge, however, three main methods of inquiry, which may be classed as genealogical, historical (though in a broad sense all three methods are historical), and nomenclatural. None is adequate in itself, but each offers important contributions. The following observations indicate the strength and the weakness of each.

GENEALOGICAL INQUIRY

The genealogical method is based on the study of individuals, and thus, while it is useful in dealing with limited portions of the population, it has great disadvantages when applied to the population as a whole.

How much examination of records would be necessary to obtain a representative picture of the antecedents of a section of population would depend mainly on the length of residence of the population in America. Generally, the older the families the easier it is to obtain information on a given number of persons. Evidently the later the migration the greater the number of distinct family groups to be studied to account for a sample population of given size. The volume of work necessary for a complete survey may be somewhat roughly estimated. If the immigrants came on the average in groups of 10, related by family ties, and at a mean date of 1715, three generations before 1790, such a family would contain about 80 persons. This would mean that nearly 40,000 such family groups would need to be investigated before the survey of the entire white population in 1790 was completed. Inasmuch as both of the

---

[1] *Göttliche Ordnung*, ed. 1761, vol. 2, p. 189.

assumptions above minimize the problem of grouping the records, a complete survey would require stupendous labor.

In the second place, genealogical records are incomplete, and those which exist are not representative of the whole population. Most available genealogical material deals with persons and families of relative importance. The student of population must examine not individuals or families who distinguished themselves but rather the less colorful and more truly representative masses.

HISTORICAL INQUIRY

There are two methods of inquiry into population called historical, that of " specific settlement " and that of " county analysis." These methods reverse each other; that is, the method of specific settlement, beginning with the settlement of a stock in certain regions, traces migration from these centers, while that of county analysis, beginning with the population of a limited area—a parish, a town, or a county—attempts to determine the ancestry of that population by means of local history. In other words, the method of specific settlement inquires into the posterity of a given population group, while that of county analysis inquires into the ancestry of such a group. Both methods provide important information; the latter, if executed with proper perspective and an intimate familiarity with local conditions, can produce excellent results, such as the analysis prepared by William Nelson for the classification of the population of New Jersey in *A Century of Population Growth.*

Yet both the historical methods have disadvantages. The method of specific settlements overlooks the effects of infiltration of individuals and small groups. The settlements with which the historian is concerned were not closed groups; migration went on all the time between them, and perhaps the greater part of it was the movement of individuals rather than of groups. Sons left home; soldiers stayed where the march left them; sailors where the voyage took them. In view, then, of a degree of mixture in the original settlements and a slow stirring about in the following years, the calculation of ancestry in terms of original immigrants is apt to be misleading. Especially is this true in dealing with districts near navigation routes, where traffic was busiest.

In using county analysis it must be remembered that people with several generations of American ancestry were commonly thought of as natives and were not known by their original stock. This method is apt to overemphasize institutional groupings, having no technique for detecting temporary affiliations with churches or other institutions, affiliations which, because they were matters of convenience rather than of tradition, offer no reliable evidence as to national stocks.

Historical inquiry seldom confines itself to either of the two methods described above; it usually combines them, emphasizing one or the other and making supplementary use of genealogical and nomenclatural evidence.

NOMENCLATURAL INQUIRY

There are three methods of employing family names as evidence of origin. The first classifies all names according to nationality. It was used in the only attempt, so far as I know, to analyze the whole population, namely, in the chapters on nationality in *A Century of Population Growth.*[2] The findings of this work were based on a classification of all the family names in the 1790 records. This pioneer study, involving the distribution of nearly half a mil-

---

[2] Pp. 116–124, 227–273. Hereafter this title will be cited as *CPG.*

lion families with 27,000 different names, deserves great credit, but its conclusions are based on an inadequate method. It draws inferences from many names which are worthless as indexes of nationality. For example, how shall one say how many *Millers* in the 1790 census were really *Millers*, and how many were properly Scotch or Irish *Millars* or German *Muellers?* And of the real *Millers*, how many were English, and how many were Scotch or Irish? This method becomes badly involved in dealing with names introduced from two or more countries, particularly those common to England, Scotland, and Ireland; also with those which in America took the place of other similar names, leaving no evidence of the national origin of the families which bore them.

Any codification of names "is obviously in the nature of an indication of blood, or what may be termed nationality strain, since it takes no account of the actual place of birth or parentage of the individual, or of the length of time which the bearers of the name may have been absent from the mother country. The ancestors of the bearer of an Irish or Dutch name may have arrived in the first shipload of immigrants who landed on the shores of Virginia, Manhattan, or New England, so that at the time of the First Census the descendants enumerated possessed few or none of the characteristics of the nationality indicated. On the other hand, the individual may have arrived in the United States alone or with his family but a few weeks prior to the enumeration." [3]

A second and better method of nomenclatural inquiry, instead of distributing all the names in the records, uses only those of recognizable national origins. It bases its conclusions only upon the occurrence of non-English names, because English names often superseded analagous forms. By determining the frequency of names clearly indicating different national stocks, one can estimate the relative number of people of non-English origin. This method calculates the German population, for instance, by means of the frequencies of such names as *Schneider, Schwartz, Hess, Hahn, Bischoff,* and *Beyer*.

Interpretation of recognizably national names has been discussed by Doctor Jameson in an unprinted lecture from which I am permitted to quote:

> Yet it might seem that persons of German and other non-British blood might be securely detected by their surnames, and that the proportions of such might readily be discovered by running through long lists of names and noting which were German or French or of other linguistic character. We have, indeed, this recourse at our disposal, but to suppose that it enables us to compute the full tale of non-English population is quite beside the mark. It is to make no allowance for the inveterate desire of those who must make their living among English-speaking persons to modify these strange patronymics into something rational and intelligible.

It is difficult to transform an enumeration of patently non-English names into a trustworthy measure of a given stock. Correlated historical research and statistical information concerning ratios of name frequencies (the availability of which will be discussed later) can be evoked to supplement this method; but ultimately the validity of the conclusions reached will depend on the nationalities of the names considered and the degree of change they have undergone in America. In general, names of recognizable national origin are rather unsatisfactory for statistical purposes because there are among them many whose usage has been considerably reduced by translation and adaptation. The clearly German names just mentioned will illustrate this point. An enumeration of the bearers of these names would include all the *Schneiders*, because in this case variants could be identified; but the German *Beyers* would be con-

---

[3] *CPG*, p 116.

fused with the Scotch *Byers* and the German *Bischoffs* with the English *Bishops*. Furthermore, we do not know how often the name *Hays* has supplanted *Hess* nor how often *Schwartz* has been translated to *Black*.

A third and still better method of nomenclatural inquiry limits still more the names which are used. From the recognizable names with which the second method concerns itself, a selection is made of those which may be called "distinctive." A distinctive surname is one pointing clearly to a definite origin, having wide currency and clearly recognizable form, and little liable to changes which may disguise its origin. The definition does not exclude variations in form unless they take the appearance of other names. *Hall* and *Parker*, for instance, are distinctive among English surnames; *McLeod* and *Robertson* among Scotch, *Murphy* and *Doherty* among Irish, *Schneider* and *Stauffer* among German. The bearers of such names may be regarded as statistical units; the third nomenclatural method of population analysis, with which we are particularly concerned, makes use of these units.

This method ascertains the prevalence of national stocks by measuring as groups the bearers of distinctive surnames, and then, on the basis of the proportions these groups bear to the total population, determining the relative prevalence of the national stocks which they represent. It is simply illustrated in the following quotation from Oscar Kuhns on the distribution of Pennsylvania Germans in the nineteenth century:

Such distinctively Pennsylvania German names as *Hoover, Garver, Landis, Brubaker, Stauffer, Bowman, Funck, Lick,* and *Yerkes* scattered all over the West tell the story of the part played by their bearers in the early part of the century in the conquest of the West.[4]

Professor Kuhn's statement does not provide a perfect illustration of identification by distinctive names, because he has not selected his names on the basis of importance, and also because he has chosen one (*Bowman*) which is not distinctive, but a rather common English name; but the implications in his statement hold, that it is usual to look for evidence of ancestry in names which retain distinctive national characteristics, and that historians, in estimating the contribution of a stock, commonly center their attention on the individuals bearing names peculiar to that stock and yet of frequent occurrence. So far as possible the names employed as indicators should be of wide currency because familiarity insures against misconstruction and corruption.

The aim of this inquiry is to estimate the national and linguistic contributions to the 1790 population of the several States and the country as a whole. The system of investigation used follows the line suggested in Professor Kuhn's statement; that is, the frequency ratios of distinctive surnames are used as a basis from which to calculate the prevalence of the various national stocks. It is essentially the same method as that used in the business forecasts familiar to economists and business men. Selected surnames are employed for reckoning the levels of population stocks much as the sales of selected commodities are used to determine levels of prosperity and business activity.

A conspicuous merit of this method is that its findings have a control within themselves as effective as the external control of general history. It balances analysis and synthesis; for the whole population is analyzed by means of the full list of family heads, yet the proportion of each stock is built up by a study of the ratios of name occurrence. Since the appraisal of each stock is made on a separate basis, to show the ratio of that stock to the whole population, the accuracy of the independent appraisals for any area can be controlled by their sum, which should approach 100 per cent. Furthermore the appraisal

---

[4] *German and Swiss Settlements in Pennsylvania*, p. 60.

of each stock is based not on one index but on several, since the bearers of each distinctive name offer a separate indication of the prevalence of the parent stock. Any really significant contribution is thus confidently assigned a rating within narrow limits.

Because of the many complications produced by the mixture of stocks and individual adaptations, it is not possible in every case to obtain a final estimate by one series of calculations. In such instances the preliminary interpretations of the evidence are adjusted on the basis of historical inquiry, statistical restatement, and deductive reasoning. Certain stocks, for example, were so meagerly represented in some regions and the population in some areas was so small that the evidence provided by names must be adjusted to conform to the peculiarities of settlement revealed by historical research. Again, some stocks were composed of elements so distinct as to require study of differential rates of migration or at least some revision of general statistics. Finally, the lack of data on the original importance of the characteristic names of some substocks and on the population for which the census of 1790 was lost, requires the use of deductive reasoning as a guide or aid to the formal computation by the method of distinctive surnames.

Evidence other than that offered by surnames is used chiefly for qualifying the conclusions drawn from nomenclatural evidence, which is considered the most satisfactory and comprehensive. The procedure will be to set forth the principles governing the interpretation of nomenclatural evidence, to make methodical inquiries leading up to quantitative results, to test these results in various ways, and finally to reach a conclusion concerning the contribution of the several stocks.

Chapter II

INTERPRETATION OF THE CURRENCY OF NAMES

At the end of the foregoing chapter the three elementary types of nomenclatural inference were briefly described. It is now desirable to outline the general subject of nomenclatural indications of origins.

DEFINITIONS OF NAMES

Evn in its limited application to persons the term "name" has several meanings. A name may designate an individual. However, it is more commonly employed with the significance of a proper name. In this sense, names are of two sorts: Christian names and surnames. Christian names (also called "baptismal," "given," and "fore" names) are sometimes useful in an inquiry into the ancestry of an individual, at least as supplementary evidence or in dealing with a stock of fairly recent migration. But in general, Christian names are of little value for our purpose, first because many of them are cosmopolitan, and second because there is no telling what motive led to the selection of a particular baptismal name. If we assume that the name was handed down in the family, we still do not know whether it was on the paternal or the maternal side.

In this inquiry surnames are our main concern. A name is called a surname when applied not to individuals but to family groups. As such, it is often regarded as a "family name," thus giving the impression that the name belongs to the family, whereas the more correct notion is that the name is assigned to the family by society for its own convenience, more or less as parents assign a baptismal name to a child. Surnames can be classified on the basis of occurrence as rare or common—if proper names can properly be called common—and the use of any particular surname is here to be thought of in terms of the number of people to whom society has assigned it.

The term "surname" may be used with or without allowance for variations in spelling. This is an important distinction, and the principle governing the grouping of names must be clearly understood. Unless grouping has a purpose, we should concur in the principle laid down by William Farr, whose contribution to nomenclatural science will be discussed presently, of reckoning every form of a surname, however slightly it may differ from others, as a separate surname.

Farr holds that it is not usual to regard diverse forms as representing one name only, "nor would their bearers probably all concur in admitting the common origin of the several variations." On the other hand, we must admit that odd forms often have significance only when related to more familiar ones, and that the term "name" can properly have a generic meaning. In the generic sense, names are headings for variants of common origin. As will be seen, the assembling of American variants of names requires great care because the mixed antecedents of many specific names and the blending of name groups make it difficult to distinguish fundamental from accidental similarities. When it is necessary to combine American names into groups,

133

these groups must be defined by listing all variants included in them—a procedure which has been followed in this study, although the details are not reproduced here.

SURNAMES AS INDEXES OF PATERNITY

The fact that surnames are inherited gives them value as indexes of origin. Their hereditary nature is subject to exceptions, of course, since they undergo change; but whether modified or not, they are under the control of society and are designations of the male lines of descent. Consequently the analysis of a population based on surnames refers directly only to the male line; but it can be assumed that the feminine population had the same origin as the masculine, that the maiden names which disappear in any generation showed the same proportions of various types as the names which replaced them; and that the intermarriages between two stocks counterbalanced each other. Applied to the American Colonies, this assumption is justified, since there is no indication of significant variation in the proportion of the sexes in the leading stocks.

SOURCES OF FORMS

The 1790 records do not list only original or immigrant names but show also names developed in America. Some of the original surnames have been superseded by these new forms and others by similar immigrant names. It is therefore necessary to note some general principles applying to both the classification of immigrant names and the interpretation of American forms in terms of them, in order to understand lists in which the two types are mingled.

An entry in the 1790 record for a particular form does not necessarily indicate that the name goes back to an immigrant ancestor, and is therefore a European name. Changes may have taken place in the form since the arrival of the ancestor, or there may have been other departures from hereditary usage. For example, at a later period the family names of negroes were largely adopted from the whites with whom they were associated.

Of the changes undergone by names, there are two principal types, the imitative and the adaptive. Besides these there is an indeterminate class. Imitative changes arise from comparison of names and are commonly called changes by analogy. The comparison involved is usually one of form, but sometimes the analogy is based upon meaning. Examples of the first kind of imitative change are the formers *Caylor* and *Baylor*, where the German *Koehler* and *Beiler*, respectively, were altered by analogy with *Taylor*. Imitative changes frequently cause familiar forms to replace strange ones; as, for example, *Grove* for *Graf* by analogy of sound, *Carpenter* for *Zimmerman* by analogy of meaning, and *Smith* for *Schmidt* by analogy of both.

Adaptive changes result from purely American habits of speech; they are largely adaptations of spelling to pronunciation, simplifications of pronunciation, or both. Thus *Slaymaker* is a variant of *Schleiermacher*, and *Balsgrove* of *Pfalzgraf*. These are purely linguistic changes, and are not based, like those in the first class, upon a comparison of surnames as such.

The third, or undeterminate, class of changes is of comparatively small importance. Concerning them Ernest Weekley says:

In 1790 one is struck by the prevalence of crude and grotesque nicknames, often obvious perversions of foreign names, but frequently, no doubt, deliberately assumed by or conferred on men who had cut even the surnominal tie with Europe.[1]

---

[1] *Surnames*, reprinted, N. Y., 1927, pp. 8–9.

Weekley especially notices the crudity of some of the names, but what he says is not markedly different from Farr's remarks, in a paper to be discussed later, on names in English registers:

Some of the terms which swell the list are so odd and even ridiculous that it is difficult to assign any satisfactory reason for their assumption in the first instance as family names, unless, indeed, as has been conjectured, they were nicknames or sobriquets which neither the first bearers nor their posterity could avoid.

It is indeed difficult to understand how various odd names came into being, but they may generally be considered offshoots of the established nomenclature such as the biologists call "sports." Names do not arise spontaneously nor do they exist without relationship to other names. All new names are formed on some kind of pattern, because the imagination always has a pattern in perception. Many new formations were drawn from the nickname idiom, an original source of names; but a large proportion of them are misconstructions of standard names, possibly misspellings by marshals of the census. Thus *Lunch* appears to have been intended for *Lantz*, and *Boils* for *Boyles*. In general people choosing new names had little choice, for names are commonly assigned rather than assumed. The number of surnames of indeterminate source can therefore be steadily reduced by detailed inquiry.

In tracing an immigrant name, one may find entries in the census of 1790 both for the original form and for a number of variants. Conversely, in analyzing the 1790 records, one must distinguish between forms supported by full heredity and forms developed in America; the latter may or may not readily disclose the European antecedent. The difficulty is that many American names are capable of diverse interpretations, and many European originals were common to several countries.

SOURCES OF FREQUENCIES OF NAMES

We now turn from forms of names to their frequencies; that is, to their occurrences relative either to the population of the United States or to the total of some national stock. The frequency of a name is its representation relative to a total. Its currency is its frequency at a stated place and time; in this work the term applies to the United States in 1790. The following remarks on the interpretation of currency demand the tentative classification of name forms as "immigrant" and "American," two categories which are not mutually exclusive.

Even an immigrant name may have had several origins; such names range in geographical background from narrowly local to broadly cosmopolitan. Many of them originated in single countries or principalities or even smaller areas. Generally, localization meant limitation of numbers, yet many of the commonest names in colonial America came from single countries. On the other hand, many names of varying frequencies, including some generally thought of as characteristic of one country, were shared by several, sometimes in two or more linguistic areas. *Smith*, for example, often considered an English name, and actually the commonest in English usage, is also the most largely used name in Scotland and very common in Ireland. *Anderson* has long been used in the whole British Isles, as well as in Sweden and elsewhere in the neighborhood of the North Sea and the Baltic. It is therefore always necessary to examine the possibility that the American bearers of such a name may have mixed antecedents.

The bearers of one surname may be heterogeneous not only because of diverse immigrant origins but also because of its substitution for still other names. Thus *Smith* is British on three counts, German by substitution for *Schmidt*, French by substitution for *Le Fevre*, and even more cosmopolitan because of its replacement of sundry other names.

Sometimes names of apparently clear origin require some adjustment before being assigned. *Somerset*, for instance, seems clearly enough of English origin, yet there was at least one German of the name in the country at about the time we are considering, for William Kingdom makes mention of " a German of the name of Somerset." [2]

A name developed in America is sometimes traceable to more than one original. An instance is provided by the name *Doty*, which in New England was apparently borne mainly by the descendants of a man first known as *Doten*,[3] while in the South it seems to have been most commonly an abbreviation of *Doherty*.

When one considers the variety of interpretations that can be made of entries in the 1790 records, one is convinced of the undesirability of classifying names entry by entry. When a name may indicate any one of several origins, it is often impossible to assign an individual bearer of it to a stock, without a genealogical inventory. Alternatives, therefore, can be properly handled only by " factoring " or prorating. Considered as individual entries, the chances are equal that a Campbell, for example, is Scotch or Irish; and it is five to two that a Cunningham is Irish rather than Scotch. Since the minute examination of township and county lists as a means of gaging the probabilities is out of the question, the procedure is to use the alphabetic index of State records and subdivide the total numbers of Campbells and Cunninghams according to one's knowledge of the general proportions.

Both heredity and evolution must be taken into account in interpreting the number of bearers of a name in the 1790 census. A high frequency usually indicates common usage among immigrants, but in many instances it is explained by early immigration and multiplication through several generations or by American favor. Paucity of bearers of a name may ordinarily be explained as the result of slight representation among immigrants, but disfavor may also have reduced its use. Thus the frequency of *Huber* in the Pennsylvania census shows clearly a German element in the population, but does not indicate the full measure because the name was replaced by *Hoover, Hover*, and other forms.

This brief survey of the elements to be considered in the interpretation of frequencies demonstrates the need of selecting the evidence to be used in a nomenclatural inquiry. Attention must be centered upon the names and name groups which are most nearly immigrant in character and least the results of transformation. Of the continually evolving mixture of immigrant nomenclatures the investigator must locate those parts which are relatively constant.

NAMES WITH STRIKING CURRENCY

Attention is now directed to some of the names most numerously represented in the census of 1790. The main body of a nomenclature is in the names of high frequency, and perspective is obtained by first examining these statistically, rather than by minute attention to individual forms.

The following table contains in four columns the surnames borne by at least one in 500 of the heads of families in the four most populous States for which the 1790 record is preserved. This table indicates that though there

---

[2] *America and the British Colonies.* London, 1820, p. 29.
[3] Savage's Dictionary, II, 61.

were fundamental similarities in nomenclature throughout the country, some names show wide variation of frequency in different regions. It suggests also that whatever significance names may have it is the common names which deserve the most attention. So many people bore such names as these that an explanation of their currency will account for the origin of large blocks of the population.

TABLE 1.—*Surnames attaining a representation of upwards of 1 in 500 in the 1790 records of four States*

[The numerals shown are the numbers of bearers of the name per 100,000 of white population]

Massachusetts (130 families or more recorded)	New York (109 families or more recorded)	Pennsylvania (149 families or more recorded)	North Carolina (105 families or more recorded)
Adams, 497. Allen, 563.	Allen, 314.	Anderson, 213.	Alexander, 226. Allen, 291.
Baker, 397. Bates, 208. Briggs, 291. Brown, 865.	Baker, 304. Brown, 744.	Brown, 578.	Baker, 249. Bell, 266. Brown, 643.
Chase, 236. Clark, 592. Coffin, 204. Cole, 205. Cook, 235. Curtis, 225.	Carpenter, 270. Clark, 260. Cook, 229.	Clark, 234.	Campbell, 217. Carter, 247. Clark, 272. Cox, 278.
Davis, 553.	Davis, 372.	Davis, 431.	Davis, 748.
Ellis, 222.		Evans, 216.	Edwards, 251. Ellis, 200.
Foster, 544. French, 251. Fuller, 291.		Fisher, 259.	
Gardner, 259. Green, 308.	Green, 336.		Green, 255.
Hall, 380. Hill, 305. Howard, 241. Hunt, 227.	Horton, 202. Hunt, 218.		Hall, 342. Harris, 390. Hill, 346.
Johnson, 420. Jones, 445.	Johnson, 297. Jones, 385.	Johnson, 205. Johnston, 310. Jones, 397.	Jackson, 304. Johnson, 289. Johnston, 516. Jones, 1,084.
King, 231.	King, 205.		King, 278.
Leonard, 235. Lewis, 241. Lincoln, 218.	Lawrence, 224. Lewis, 281.	Lewis, 204. Long, 268.	Lee, 219. Lewis, 325.
Miller, 212. Morse, 365.	Miller, 651. Moore, 202.	Martin, 311. Miller, 1,047. Moore, 395. Moyer, 211.	Martin, 323. Miller, 291. Moore, 561. Morgan, 225. Morris, 228.

TABLE 1.—*Surnames attaining a representation of upwards of 1 in 500 in the 1790 records of four States*—Continued

[The numerals shown are the numbers of bearers of the name per 100,000 of white population]

Massachusetts (130 families or more recorded)	New York (109 families or more recorded)	Pennsylvania (149 families or more recorded)	North Carolina (105 families or more recorded)
Parker, 426. Peirce, 346. Perkins, 233. Phillips, 236. Pratt, 356.	Palmer, 257.		Parker, 384. Powell, 249. Price, 211.
Reed, 383. Rice, 340. Richardson, 386. Robinson, 201. Rogers, 305. Russell, 274.	Rogers, 220.	Reed, 262. Roberts, 205.	Roberts, 205. Rogers, 259.
Shaw, 251. Smith, 1,581. Snow, 277. Stone, 319.	Smith, 1,810.	Scott, 236. Smith, 1,129. Stewart, 211.	Sanders, 215. Scott, 204. Smith, 1,383.
Taylor, 330. Thayer, 316. Thomas, 222. Turner, 202.	Taylor, 297. Thompson, 218.	Taylor, 268. Thomas, 313. Thompson, 274.	Taylor, 548. Thomas, 268. Thompson, 255. Turner, 257.
Walker, 282. Wheeler, 307. White, 590. Whitney, 241. Williams, 460. Wood, 458. Wright, 304.	Weeks, 200. White, 301. Williams, 380. Wood, 451. Wright, 259.	Walker, 208. Weaver, 252. White, 271. Williams, 321. Wilson, 370.	Walker, 320. Ward, 280. Watson, 202. White, 512. Williams, 1,016. Wilson, 445. Wood, 217. Wright, 219.
		Young, 317.	

Questions are immediately suggested by the similarities and dissimilarities appearing in these lists. The constant eminence of certain names offers occasion for studying the similarities of population groups, while the absence of other names from some of the lists leads one to ascertain whether they had little currency in these States or whether they narrowly missed classification among the names of highest currency. It is natural to ask why there were so few names listed under New York and Pennsylvania as compared with the other two States. The antecedents of these populations were mixed to such a degree that only the most favored names attained the designated currency (1 in 500), and consequently attention is drawn for the most part to names shared by two or more stocks. Perhaps the lists appear English to a surprising degree. If so, it is partly because the English stock was the only one present in sufficient proportions to give its characteristic names high currency and partly because many of the names are only nominally English. Not only were they common among the Scotch and Irish but they were also used by other stocks. In the Pennsylvania lists, for example, many of them were used by Germans, *Fisher* being substituted for *Fischer*, *Long* for *Lang*, and *Weaver* for *Weber*.

PATTERN OF NAMES AS A SOCIAL CHARACTERISTIC

Names such as the foregoing were of such general use that their numbers were little affected by the rates of reproduction in particular families. The people who bore them are not to be thought of as families, but rather as population groups capable by their size of representing the average in vitality, number of children, etc., of the larger groups to which they belong. Name frequencies are therefore significant in that they are subject to general laws such as control the growth of population.

Evidently one should be slow to assume blood relationships among the bearers of any surname. This stands as a warning to untrained students of history who are quick to think people of one name "all descended from" a certain immigrant. This error is most likely to affect the interpretation of names in dealing with those supposed to be peculiar to certain areas. *Adams* is such a one, occurring only among the Massachusetts names in the table above. This does demonstrate that it had a special advantage in New England, but the very number of persons bearing it in one State shows that they could scarcely have been related. Furthermore, it was common throughout the country, though nowhere to such a degree as in Massachusetts. Massachusetts shows 324 heads of families named *Adams;* New York, 94; Pennsylvania, 115; and North Carolina, 104.

The repetition of a name is thus to be explained in terms of society rather than it terms of a family. This is most evidently true of names of the highest frequency, but it will appear later than many of even the rarest names are not spasmodic, but occur in regular though slight reflection of their frequency in the original homes of the stocks bearing them. Admitting that numbers insure impartiality, it is practicable to assume that the fortunes of families have only an incidental relation to the currencies of names, especially since the lists we are dealing with are made up largely of the bearers of common names. On this point *CPG* says:

The tendency of the population at that period to group under surnames of frequent occurrence is indicated by the fact that 11,934 names represented less than 1 per cent of the white population, 11,742 represented 15.7 per cent, and the remaining 3,661 names specified in Table III represented 83.8 per cent.[4]

In examining common names, therefore, we are justified in looking for a certain stability of occurrence. Those whose distribution appears to be haphazard are almost invariably of small numbers. The distribution of moderately common names was doubtless somewhat influenced by the fortunes of particular families and individuals, yet regularized by the fairly large numbers of families bearing them.

Although comparative nomenclature is not concerned primarily with families, there is some advantage in thinking of the population for a moment in terms of specific settlers and their families, in order to consider what evidence names can offer concerning the character of the populations of the several States.

INTERRELATIONS OF THE POPULATIONS OF THE STATES

In an examination of the indexes of the State lists one is impressed by the interrelationships among them. To be sure, there are always names of moderate frequency in individual States which do not appear in others, but there is invariably a general continuity. The spread of particular families is illustrated by the number of *Custis* households. This surname, associated with that of Washington, was probably a purely family designation, yet the Custises

---

[4] P. 115, *CPG* reports a total of 27,337 surnames.

were not confined to one narrow area. Nine *Custis* families were recorded in New York, three in Virginia (besides one *Custus*), and one each in Pennsylvania, Maryland, and North Carolina (besides one more *Custus* in Maryland).

New York, because of its Dutch settlements, is the outstanding instance of a State containing a large element of separate origin from the rest of the country. Yet there are few name groups peculiar to the State. Materials for comparison are collected in Table 111 of *CPG*, which sets forth important names and some, though not all, of their variants. This table shows that there were in fact names peculiar to New York, such as *Blauvelt, Bogardus, Bradt, Burtis, Clute, Groat, Groesbeck, Hasbrouck, Houghtalen, Onderdunk, Polhemus.* Certain names beginning with *Van* appear also to occur only in New York, simply because variants without the prefix have not been assembled in the table. But many surnames commonly associated with New York alone were merely centered there. The following cases illustrate a not uncommon type of distribution.

There were 23 *Brinckerhoff* households in New York, 8 in Pennsylvania, and 1 in South Carolina; *Brundage*, New York 36, Connecticut 3, Pennsylvania 2, Vermont and Massachusetts 1 each; *(Van) Buskirk*, New York 27, Pennsylvania 15, Maryland 1; *Conklin*, New York 195, Pennsylvania 6, Maine, Vermont, Massachusetts, and North Carolina, 1 each; *Countryman*, New York 13, Pennsylvania 6, South Carolina 2, Virginia 1; *Halstead*, New York 57, Virginia 5, Pennsylvania 4. Probably all these names indicate family groups. Some more numerously represented names give even clearer evidence of interrelation among the States. *Bennet* and *Livingston*, names commonly associated with New York, are shown to be by no means peculiar to that area. There were 143 *Bennets* listed in New York,[5] partly through the special influence of the elder Bennet, an Englishman who early settled in New Netherland; but the name had a total of 713 entries, with not fewer than 22 in any State. The *Livingstons* also were centered in New York, with 54 entries there, but the remainder of the 117 were scattered through 9 other States. Many other names, such as *Romine, Rose, Rouse, Rowe*, and *Rowley*, were more numerously represented in New York than elsewhere, but were nevertheless links between most of the country and the old world.

At the other extreme from a "family" name such as *Custis* is *Smith*, the most noncommittal of all. Consider its distribution throughout the country as a whole. Even though, as was suggested above, *Smith* is often a name developed in America, the following figures show the joint origins of the populations in the several States:

TABLE 2.—*Proportions of Smiths per 10,000 of population*

Connecticut	189	South Carolina	147
New York	180	North Carolina	138
Vermont	172	Maryland	119
Massachusetts	159	Pennsylvania	113
Rhode Island	156	Virginia	112
New Hampshire	149	Maine	112

In view of the evidence presented by names ranging from rare to highly common, it is apparent that the State populations are not to be treated as separate units, but as interrelated parts of the whole population of the country, showing no marked discontinuity. Thus the concept of original settlements with sharp outlines is untenable, and we can not determine, from a knowledge of the original immigrant populations of Virginia, New York, and Massachusetts, who lived there in 1790.

---

[5] *CPG*, p. 229.

DISTRIBUTION OF NAMES AND FAMILIES

In the last section it was pointed out that names presumably borne by blood relatives are usually found scattered over several States. When we turn to names not predominantly " family " names, still more extensive connections between the States are to be expected. Therefore it is reasonable to assume that the bearers of moderately common names in any one State are not to be thought of as clear-cut family clusters, but rather as the nuclei of various family groups, together with fragments of groups centered elsewhere. Families bearing common names can not, of course, be readily distinguished from each other; nevertheless they presumably spread about in the same way as those families which can be more clearly traced. The bearers of common names can therefore be considered as representing families well intermingled.

The intermingling of families under one name may be illustrated by reference to *Adams*, a name generally associated with New England alone. It is probable that most descendants of the early New England Adamses were living there in 1790, but that some of them had scattered. A Massachusetts family of the name may have had a branch in Connecticut, which in turn may have had an offshoot in that part of Pennsylvania settled from Connecticut. Another family of Adamses settling in the same State may have expanded to Maine. Still another may have been represented in the Cape May settlements of New Jersey, which were largely of New England stock. While these New England families were spreading other Adamses in other States were doing the same. Unrelated families bearing the name were living in New York and Virginia, and by 1790 some of these had contributed to the roll of Adamses in the New England States. Consequently groups of bearers of any name, *Adams* or another, deny the value of analysis by specific settlement. The interconnections of groups of bearers of a name having been established, questions present themselves as to the origins of the many families which composed these large groups. We are particularly concerned with determining whether the name frequencies of Europe can throw any light on the origins of the more common American names; and if so, whether the same principles can be applied to the interpretation of names of lower frequency. Fortunately European nomenclature has been examined statistically, so that there is available a considerable body of data on the name frequencies among the populations from which the American settlers were drawn. The following sections are devoted to a survey of the most important of these studies.

AUTHORITATIVE STUDIES OF EUROPEAN USAGE

The first students of comparative family nomenclature were George Graham,[6] Registrar General for England and Wales in the 1850's, and William Farr.[7]

---

[6] Maj. George Graham, second son of Sir James Graham, first Baronet of Netherby, Carlisle, entered the East India Co.'s service and retired as major (First India Regiment) in 1831, having been military secretary in Bombay 1828–1830; private secretary to his brother, Sir James Graham, Secretary of State; Registrar General of births, deaths, and marriages for England and Wales, 1842–1879. He died May 20, 1888, in London. His tenure of office as Registrar General covered the census of 1851, 1861, and 1871, and he was responsible for the publication of the annual reports each year. The actual compilation of the report on nomenclature in England and Wales was the work of Dr. William Farr, statistical superintendent in the general registrar office at that time. (Information by W. J. Cook, Esq., for the Registrar General.)

[7] William Farr, 1807–1883, statistician. From 1837 to 1879 in the Registrar General's office; assistant commissioner for the census of 1851 and 1861, and commissioner for that of 1871, writing most of the reports on the three; author of many papers on general statistics and on life tables for insurance. (Information available in encyclopedias.)

Farr was the first to raise questions concerning the number and range of family names and to answer them, at least in part, by the examination of large lists. He provides us with data on the variety of names current in England and Wales in the middle of the last century. He noted the peculiarities of the nomenclatures of Wales and Cornwall and described the usages in other parts of the country. He paid special attention to the commoner English names, examined the occurrences in a combined record of over 2,500,000 entries, and made a table of the 50 leading names and their frequencies, estimating the numbers of their bearers in England and Wales in 1853. He observed that one could ascertain " with tolerable certainty the relative numbers of the adherents of each." He raised but did not answer questions about the history of the relative numbers and about the details of local distribution.

The next authority, in point of time, is Robert Stark, physician in the office of the Registrar General for Scotland in the 1860's.[8] He prepared a table of the 50 leading names of that country in 1861, compared it with Farr's, and surveyed their distribution. This was followed two years later by another study extended to cover 150 names or groups of names, which accounted for practically half the population of Scotland. In this investigation he studied rather carefully the relative frequencies of various names and devoted considerable attention to the varieties of distribution.

The occurrence of names was next examined by Albert Heintze,[9] a German etymologist, who published in 1882 Die Deutschen Familiennamen. He studied the history, distribution, and relative frequency of leading German names and types of names. He was the first thorough student of geographical distribution. He based his observations on the enlistment records of 1870–71 and regularly studied names in the light of their frequency, but unfortunately did not present any tables of the numbers observed.

In 1890 Henry B. Guppy[10] published his Homes of Family Names in Great Britain, which unlike the works of Farr and Stark, was an unofficial inquiry. His object was not to specify leading names but to investigate the nomenclature of the masses in relation to geography. He set out to inquire whether there was regularity in the apparently indiscriminate distribution of surnames

---

[8] Dr. Robert Stark was the first superintendent of statistics in the office of the Registrar General for Scotland, being appointed to that position in 1855. He held the appointment for nearly 20 years, resigning in 1874. He died in 1890. Doctor Stark was a doctor of medicine of Edinburgh University, a fellow of the Royal College of Physicians of Edinburgh, a licentiate of the Royal College of Surgeons of Edinburgh, and a fellow of the Royal Scottish Society of Arts. In addition to being the author of various official reports he contributed many articles to medical journals and also wrote on a variety of other subjects. (Information supplied by J. C. Dunlop, Esq., Registrar General for Scotland.)

[9] Albert Heintze, 1831–1906, was professor (Oberlehrer) at the Gymnasium in Stolp, Pomerania, for many years, apparently to the age of 75, and was reputed to have been a devoted teacher and an energetic, painstaking scholar. Die deutschen Familien-Namen, geschichtlich, geographisch, sprachlich, was first published in 1882 (Halle); second edition, 1903. After his death his friend Cascorbi published the third edition (enlarged from the original author's notes) in 1908, the fourth in 1914, and the fifth in 1922 (enlarged and revised). Heintze also published Deutscher Sprachhort, ein Stil und Wörterbuch, Leipzig 1899–1900, also Gut Deutsch, Eine Anleitung zur Vermeidung der häufigsten Verstösse gegen den guten Sprachgebrauch etc., sixth edition, Berlin, 1895, also an essay (1877) on the medieval poem Gregorius auf dem Steine. (Information by A. B. Faust, Cornell.)

[10] Henry Brougham Guppy, 1854–1926, naturalist. Traveled extensively first as a surgeon in the Royal Navy (1876–1885) and later as a botanist, specializing on plant-dispersal and littoral fauna. Gold medalist, Linnean Society, 1917. Published only the one book on names, his other publications dealing with the natural history of the Solomon Islands, Hawaii, Fiji, West Indies, and Azores. (Who's Who, 1926.)

over Great Britain, and concluded that there was actually an orderly arrangement.[11] This opinion was reached first by attention to the usage of the settled farming population, and second by concentration on names exceeding an established minimum frequency. Eliminating rare usage heightened the focus, and disregarding the city populations enabled him to ascertain the *original homes* of the names and the character of their distribution at the opening of the industrial era. He gives details on the occurrence of some 4,000 English names, expresses their numbers in percentages of the farming groups in the counties, and characterizes generally the nomenclatures of the counties of England and Scotland in terms of names classified according to distribution and frequency. In his classification according to distribution he found that of the 4,100 names of not uncommon use in England and Wales about 2,400 were local in single counties. Seventeen of the names occurred in over three-quarters of the counties, 51 in over half but not more than three-quarters, and 134 in at least a quarter but not more than a half. The remaining names of the 4,100 occurred originally in small districts ranging in extent from two to nine counties.

Like Heintze he studied companionships among names, but from the point of view of the ecologist rather than from that of the specialist in dialects. His attention, moreover, was centered upon specific names rather than on types. It is also to be noted that he discovered systematic supplementary and complementary usages, showing similar names occurring together (supplementary) and in different places (complementary). His study of Scotch nomenclature was intended primarily to give perspective on usage in the border counties.

The greatest investigator in the field is Sir Robert Matheson, assistant Registrar General for Ireland in the 1890's.[12] Starting with the fundamentals, he has covered the field thoroughly. It was his intention to tabulate the outstanding names and groups of names in Irish usage after the manner of Farr and Stark, but this work was delayed for some years by the necessity of preparing a codification of the variants and synonyms of Irish names. Having made this, he analyzed the frequencies of names in the Irish birth records of 1890, covering about 105,000 entries. From this analysis he not only determined upon the leading Irish names and established their ratios but worked out in detail the distributions and group relationships of all but the rare names in the Irish records. His contribution is the more impressive in that Irish nomenclature, in some respects more complicated than those of Great Britain and Germany, had had comparatively little study, whereas the other outstanding investigators mentioned were able to profit by the earlier work of etymologists and to set forth their mathematical findings in the light of previous philological observations. Despite the disadvantages against which he had to work, Matheson's record of Irish usage is exemplary for the purposes of comparative study.

All the above-mentioned authorities examined the relationships of names, noting the total numbers of different forms appearing in the records and characterizing to some extent the whole nomenclatures of the several countries. All except Farr observed the natural groupings of names, Matheson in particular making an elaborate codification of Irish nomenclature which

---

[11] *Homes of Family Names in Great Britain*, pp. 5, 6.
[12] Right Hon. Sir Robert Edwin Matheson 1845–1926, barrister-at-law. Entered the General Registration office, Dublin, in 1877, as secretary; assistant, 1879–1900; Commissioner of Irish Census 1881, 1891, 1901, Registrar General 1900–1909. Publications other than on names, treating Irish marriage laws; injuries to farm crops; housing of people in Ireland. (*Who's Who,* 1926.)

shows relationships in derivation and relative numbers. Matheson and Guppy extended their studies to cover all names of more than rare occurrence, and reassembled their data to show varying usages in counties and districts. Less is known about the natural groupings and local occurrences of Scotch names than of English and Irish, but some notes on local conditions are provided by Stark and Guppy.

In all the populations studied there was found a great range of frequencies, although some nomenclatures showed more variety than others. In every case a comparatively small number of names accounted for a substantial part or the population. In England, for example, although Farr estimated that some 35,000 different names were in use, 50 of them accounted collectively for 18 per cent of the population. Scotland shows less variety in nomenclature than England; according to Stark, only about 7,000 different forms were current. Stark's statement, however, is not as reliable as Farr's, since he was less precise in the definition of specific forms. His observation, allowing for some variability in spelling, was that the 50 most common names accounted for approximately 30 per cent of the population of Scotland. In his second study he found that 150 names were borne by 47 per cent of the population. It is therefore evident that the common names are important not only individually but collectively, and that those of rarer occurrence, even when combined, account for a small part of the population.

Fortunately the studies made by the British registrars can be considered essentially accurate in their statements of frequency ratings. To control his findings, Farr compared records of different periods and used the frequencies of *Smith* and *Jones* as specimens. He noted some irregularities in the occurrence of common names in specific records, even when comparatively large numbers were involved; yet he felt he was able to ascertain the relative numbers with "tolerable certainty." An anonymous commentator writing in the *Cornhill Magazine* in 1868 [13] examined the dependability of Farr's figures, and inquired somewhat into the constancy of occurrence of leading names. His observations indicate that the proportions of bearers of specific names are somewhat variable, but that a number of common names taken together provide reliable data. Stark, like Farr, criticized his own figures, and observed that his first conclusions concerning numbers and relative frequencies were strikingly confirmed by subsequent inquiry. Although Matheson commented in detail upon the unreliability of Irish spelling and upon changes in usage during the nineteenth century, his study gives the impression that the frequencies of common Irish names grouped according to their roots constitute significant data.

COMPARATIVE STUDY OF FREQUENCIES

In approaching the comparative study of frequencies in Europe and America we must bear in mind that many names of infrequent occurrence in Europe were not represented at all in colonial America. This fact does not invalidate the evidence offered by all names, but it does draw attention to the difference, for statistical purposes, between rare and common names. The latter provide the investigator with the most useful material.

Both Farr and Stark compared the frequencies of common names in a number of records. Farr, comparing several annual records of birth first with each other and then with records of marriages and deaths, found that the proportions of bearers of the common names remained fairly constant

[13] Vol. 17, pp. 405–420.

through all the records, but that the total number of names varied according to the size of the registers. His comparisons indicated that about 35,000 different names were used in England and Wales. One register of 157,000 entries showed almost exactly 25,000 different surnames; another of 118,000 entries showed nearly 21,000 surnames. The two contained 32,818 different names, of which only 13,201 were common to both. These fluctuations are the result of competition of the rarer names in the limited cumulation. The greater the frequency of a name, the more certain it was to be represented in the annual registers and the more constant was its proportion.

Farr compared the occurrences of the 50 most common surnames in 9 quarterly indexes of births, 8 of deaths, and 8 of marriages, and satisfied himself that their relative numbers were dependably constant.[14] Thus it appears that such a record as Farr's, dealing only with common names, can be confidently relied on as a basis for comparative study; the same can be said of Stark's, which, though more extensive, deals with names of high frequency. The data provided by Matheson and Guppy on less common names must necessarily be used with greater caution. The evidential value of rare names is lessened by the fact that their representation in limited lists is fortuitous.

Conclusions based upon comparisons with European usage, however, are useless for our purpose, unless the proportions of common names remained fairly constant over a long period of time. The authorities referred to above studied the nomenclature of the nineteenth century, and the immigrants into whose origins we are inquiring left Europe during the seventeenth and eighteenth centuries. Farr himself asked, "Do these common names hold the same rank in point of numbers which they had at first or have some of them spread and multiplied more rapidly than others?"[15] After careful examination of the problem, I believe that one may depend upon the constancy of occurrence of the leading English and Welsh names throughout the seventeenth, eighteenth, and nineteenth centuries, if care is taken to avoid a few which underwent modifications in spelling.

Though a study of the history of English and Welsh nomenclature shows the former to be more constant in its pattern, the Welsh names transmitted to America as shown in the census of 1790 follow very closely the proportions observed by Farr. It is possible to study the transference of Welsh names very effectively because of their relatively limited area of origin; they are not, like English names, subject to the irregularities which go with a wider geographical distribution. Since the American records of 1790 agree substantially in the frequencies of common Welsh names with Farr's observations in the nineteenth century, and since the proportions of common English names are known to be more constant than those of the Welsh, it is safe to assume that the features of both nomenclatures have been fairly constant since the seventeenth century.

The same can not be said of Irish usage. Family nomenclature there was in the process of formation when migration to America began, and it is only recently that even the most common Irish names attained established spellings. Matheson's record of 1890 does not represent the usage of earlier generations in Ireland as far as individual surnames are concerned. It does, however, show the proportions of groups of names etymologically allied. These groups,

---

[14] Sixteenth Annual Report of the Registrar General. London, 1856, p. xx.
[15] p. xix.

formed about elemental names or roots, can be considered constant functions of Irish population.

Scotch nomenclature is of an intermediate character between the English and the Irish. It contains some names of established spelling and constant frequency; others, used as clan designations, are variable in spelling, and can be considered constant functions only when the variants are grouped.

Any comparison of American and European frequencies must take account of the Americanization of foreign names. All names, even English, underwent modification in America, those least common and least natural to English speech generally suffering the greatest change. Consequently only Welsh and English names can be relied on to preserve their original forms in America. After Welsh and English follow, in order of increasing susceptibility to change, Scotch, Irish, and German names; other non-British forms were subject to the greatest modification of all. The acceptance of English standards was due in part to the maturity of the English nomenclature and in part to the large numbers of Englishmen in the colonies.

The question may be raised whether class migration would lessen the value of the comparison of frequencies in American and European usage. Along with the common belief that names are connected with family strains there is the idea that names are stratified socially, and that American nomenclature may not therefore be a true reflection of the nomenclature of the original homes of immigrants. This objection is indeed applicable to rare names, the bearers of which may belong to limited classes; but it does not affect common names, which by their numbers and wide geographical distribution are shown to be functions of the masses. Guppy [16] examined carefully the occurrences of English names of all degrees of commonness, and found that they were not to be classified according to social position. Hence, even though one believe that America was settled largely by people without property, he may still expect to find the familiar European names represented in about the same proportions in America as in Europe.

GEOGRAPHICAL ORIGINS

The authoritative studies mentioned, supplemented by some etymological data, enable us to determine the origins of names on the basis of established frequencies. Since the British authorities take account of political divisions, it is possible to assign names on the basis of frequencies not only to the three main divisions of the British Isles but to some extent to counties. Information can thus be gained concerning the origins of British names within limited areas. Continental names, on the other hand, can be treated only in linguistic divisions. In these studies the English, Scotch, and Irish elements of the population will be presented on the basis of national origins, [17] but the German stock is to be understood as of German-speaking origin, without distinguishing Germans from Austrians and Swiss. I do not examine the occurrence of Dutch and French names for the purposes of this report; such information as I now have would not permit the determination of specific national origins.

---

[16] *Homes of Family Names in Great Britain*, pp. 9, 10.

[17] These estimates refer, of course, to blood strains, as was indicated in the quotation from *CPG* introducing the consideration of nomenclatural methods of inquiry; they do not indicate the immediate provenance of immigrants. Some families, for example, may have spent a considerable time, even several generations, in Canada or the West Indies before arriving in the area we know as the United States.

REFLECTION OF FREQUENCIES IN NOMENCLATURE

In general the nomenclature of a country peopled by immigration reflects the nomenclatural characteristics of the original home of the population, the frequencies of names in the new country bearing a definite relation to those in the parent area. Thus the American colonies, settled by immigration from many areas, used a composite nomenclatural system which reflected the usages of several European sources of immigration. Notice that the various areas from which names were brought to America are not necessarily whole countries. Emigration from a populous country, for example, may have proceeded at different rates and under different circumstances from its several parts; in such a case it is necessary to consider separately the reflected nomenclatures of these parts.

The reflection of frequencies is the foundation of the interpretation of American nomenclature. Tentatively, at any rate, the frequent and regular occurrence of a name in the 1790 lists, compared with its occurrence in its native European area, is to be considered indicative of the proportion of its stock to the whole population. Other explanations of currency may be found, which will affect the final selection of names constituting clear evidences of origin, but the first step is to examine the regular frequencies in the country as a whole and in the several States, leaving the irregularities and fortuitous occurrences for later consideration.

American nomenclature has been described as a composite, but it is a composite which has undergone modification in America. This modification of names is the chief factor preventing the perfect reflection of European frequencies. Before going further it is necessary to look for a moment at the general process of Americanization of immigrant names.

AMERICAN NOMENCLATURE AS A MODIFIED COMPOSITE

In the mixture of nomenclatures found in colonial America evolution was more lively than in the more homogeneous systems of European countries. Aside from the general fact that any new nomenclatural pattern is unstable and dynamic, there were two chief reasons for the greater evolutionary vigor of surnames in America. First, when specific surnames were imported from more than one European country they gained by their combination a numerical advantage which they had not had in their several original homes. For example, though the pattern of American names was largely English, it was not narrowly so; names like *Smith, Taylor, Brown, Johnson,* and *Wilson,* because they were common all over the British Isles, are more conspicuous in America than *Jones, Hall* and *Parker,* which are characteristically English and not British. In the second place, many non-English names were introduced, especially in the eighteenth century, which were immediately subjected to change and adapted to American speech.

Three phases are to be observed in the evolution of American nomenclature. To begin with, it was a mixture or composite of European nomenclatures. Second, this mixture became a blend; that is, the various elements of the original mixture were fused, and there was a partial disappearance of foreign forms. The third and final phase is the modification of the blend by the adaptation of names to American speech and the pattern of American nomenclature.

Though these phases are distinguishable, it is nevertheless necessary to remember that the processes of mixing, blending, and adapting all went on together. The result was a nomenclature essentially a mixture but adapted as a whole to American society.

A SECTION OF THE CENSUS

For the sake of concrete illustration, let us now examine a section of a State list on the basis of reflected frequencies and of the development of an American nomenclature. In the following statement, a portion of the Pennsylvania census is analyzed and a preliminary interpretation of name currency is made in the light of (1) data provided by Graham, Stark, Matheson, and Guppy; (2) usage observed in the records of arrivals in Pennsylvania: (3) data provided by Heintze on German names and by Kuhns on the Pennsylvania German; and (4) supplementary reference to county directories of Scotland and military rosters of France. In this statement each name is followed by a letter in parentheses, denoting the frequency of its occurrence: *a*, indicates that the name was used by 1 or more in every 1,000 of the heads of families in the Pennsylvania census; *b*, from 1 in every 2,000 to 1 in every 1,000; *c*, from 1 in every 4,000 to 1 in every 2,000; and *d*, 1 in every 8,000 to 1 in every 4,000. In terms of number of entries, these designations have the following meanings: *a*, 74 entries or more; *b*, 37 to 73; *c*, 18 to 36; *d*, 9 to 17. Names used by fewer than one family head in 8,000 are passed over to heighten the focus.

ILLUSTRATIVE INTERPRETATION OF A SECTION OF A STATE LIST, CENSUS OF 1790

All the names in the Pennsylvania index with more than eight entries from *Ro-* to the end of *R*

ROAD (*b*)—Transliteration or "English spelling" of *Roth*—a highly common German name.

ROADS (*c*)—Americanization of the above in *-s*. Also an English name peculiar to Bucks. Version of the English names *Rhodes* and *Rhoades*.

ROAN (*d*)—Irish have this spelling and also *Rowan*, *Roughan*, and *Rohan*. Given names indicate German antecedents. German origin unknown.

ROBB (*c*)—A Scotch and Irish name. Highly common among Scots. Occasionally for *Raub*, a rare German name.

ROBERTS (*a*)—Predominantly English but somewhat cosmopolitan. Was prevalent in three-fourths of England and Wales; original ratio 1 in 235 English. May have replaced the uncommon English *Probert*, Scotch *McRobert* or Irish *McRoberts*. This name of low frequency among Scots or Irish, but both used *Robert*, capable of Americanization to this form. There was a rare German surname of this spelling and the moderately common name of *Ruppert*. *Robert* was a highly common French name.

ROBERTSON (*c*)—A leading Scotch name. Original Scotch ratio over 1 per 100. Occasionally Irish and English. English antecedents limited to extreme northern counties. In Pennsylvania probably includes some members of a family of the early Swedes named *Robertsson*. Some loss in natural ratio by variability. (See *Robeson*.)

ROBESON (*b*)—Variant of Scotch *Robertson* and possibly of English *Robson*. The latter was prevalent in five counties of England and occasional in Scotland but did not become a common Pennsylvania name (only one entry).

ROBINS (*d*)—A local (4 county) English name. Americanization of *Robin* and possibly *Robinet*, moderately common French names.

ROBINSON (*a*)—Predominantly English. Prevalent in three-fourths of England; original ratio 1 in 276 of English. Significant Irish use. Rare in Scotland. Not so cosmopolitan but more Irish than *Roberts*. Some loss in natural ratio by variability. (See *Robison*.)

ROBISON (*b*)—American version of the above.

RODE (*d*)—A German name. Version of German *Roth, Rohde,* and *Rhode,* the first of which was highly common among Germans.

RODERMEL (*d*)—German *Rothaermel.*

RODGERS (*c*)—A rare English name (rather peculiar to Derby); companion to *Rogers.* A common Irish name. The Scots had the name *Rodger.* Compare *Rogers.* To the extent the "*d*" is significant this name derived first from Derby, secondly from Ireland and thirdly from Scotland (for *Rodger*). Pennsylvanians to this day are prone to "spell *Rogers* with a *d.*"

RODRUCK (*d*)—German *Rothrock.* Probably ultimately becomes *Roderick* but this was a Celtic given name and not a surname.

ROGERS (*b*)—A name prevalent in five-eighths of England. Outside of Pennsylvania has tended to replace *Rodgers.* A common Irish name, somewhat more so than *Rodgers.* Americanization of *Roger* and *Rodger,* not uncommon Scotch names. Americanization of the moderately common French *Roger.*

ROOD (*d*)—German *Roth* (see *Root*). Also an English name peculiar to Somerset.

ROOP (*c*)—German *Rupp* and *Rapp,* especially the former which was moderately common.

ROOT (*d*)—Given names suggest this was another variant of the German *Roth.* Elsewhere it must have been more commonly the Essex name (*Root*) or the Lincolnshire *Wroot.*

ROSE (*b*)—English with cosmopolitan additions. Prevalent in over a quarter of England. Not uncommon in Scotland. Occasional in Ireland. American version of English *Roose* and *Rowse,* Cornish names. A rare German name but may be for the more common *Ross* (significance disregarded as was common).

ROSS (*a*)—Predominantly Scotch. A leading Scotch name; original Scotch ratio about 7 per 1,000. Not uncommon in Ireland. No more use in England than such forms as *Roose, Rowse* and *Russ,* all "county" names. A moderately common German name. May have occasionally been used for the French *Rossi.*

ROTH (*d*)—The German *Roth* with the silent "*h*" retained and probably given enunciation. Version of English *Wroth,* a peculiar Devonshire name. There was also a German name *Rath* which this may represent.

ROUGH (*d*)—Possibly Scotch. More likely for German *Rauch* and *Rauh*—particularly the former, common in German immigration. *Rauch* proved a distinctly inconvenient American name and became variously *Rough, Rock, Rook,* etc. This form was by analogy with *Dough-erty, McLough-lin,* etc., but the new form was misinterpreted and the pronunciation "*ruf*" acquired.

ROW (*c*)—Given names indicate this was for the common German *Rau* and *Rauh.* European frequencies indicate it may also have represented the English name of the spelling, the English *Rowe* and *Roe,* and the French *Roux.* German in Pennsylvania; cosmopolitan in the country as a whole. Pronounced to rhyme with either "*how*" or "*snow.*"

ROWAN (*d*)—An Irish name as were also *Roughan* and *Ruane* which it may have replaced.

ROWLAND (*c*)—A local English name (occurring in 3 counties). Occasional in Ireland. Version of German *Roland* and French *Rolland.*

ROYER (*c*)—A Huguenot name.

RUDOLPH (*d*)—Highly common among German arrivals in Pennsylvania. Had the original variant *Rudolf.*

RUDY (*c*)—The German, or more properly Swiss, *Rudi.* (No occurrence is noted for an Irish name *Ruddy.*)

RUE (*d*)—French *Delarue*. Possibly also for *Roux* and *Leroux*. Of the three, original frequency must ultimately have given *Roux* the greatest influence on American nomenclature, but in what form is unknown.

RULE (*d*)—*Ruhl*, a moderately common German name.

RUMMELL (*d*)—German for *Rummel*, *Rommel*, *Rumpel*—none originally especially common. The double "*l*" was an Americanization.

RUSH (*b*)—The German name *Rusch*, but not an uncommon English and Irish name. German emphasis here.

RUSSEL (*c*)—Mainly for the British *Russell* which was a leading Scotch name, prevalent in over a quarter of England and common in Ireland. The single "*l*" was uncommon there except in Scotland. Version of German *Ruesel* and *Reitzel* and French *Roussel*. Cosmopolitan with Scotch emphasis; less English than the next.

RUSSELL (*c*)—Interpretation similar to *Russel* but more strongly British, particularly English.

RUTH (*d*)—A common German name and related to *Roth*. Occasionally Irish, as there was such an Irish name.

RUTTER (*c*)—A name prevalent in about an eighth of England. Version of German *Reuter*.

RYAN (*c*)—A leading Irish name especially characteristic of Munster. Seldom the version of the rare German names *Rein* and *Rhein*.

The above interpretative experiment shows something of what may be gained by consideration of European frequencies and by classification of the American names by commonness. It reveals that surnames as indicators of origin of population range from those which may be fairly surely interpreted, through those which show potentialities possibly measurable, to others too complex for consideration. Evidently we shall now be interested in principles for selection of evidence and for control of interpretation of names subject to mixed influences.

FREQUENCIES OF NAMES IN CAUSAL RELATIONS

This section of the Pennsylvania census gives an idea of the many elements which went into the formation of American nomenclature. At first sight, the very number of factors to be reckoned with seems to prevent the determination of origins by means of surnames. In fact, if the entries are taken singly, it is often quite impossible to tell which of a number of interpretations is the right one; but by examining them collectively one can estimate the force of the various factors operating, and interpret as a statistical unit a large number of entries which could not be interpreted individually. The relationships of frequencies in European nomenclatures also contribute to the recognition of the forces at work in America. The examination and comparison of name frequencies lead to the conception of nomenclature as the result of definite causes or combinations of causes in an orderly and determinable relation to each other. Yet surnames are not all equally useful as indicators of origin. Some can be surely interpreted, others afford evidence under careful analysis, and others are too complex for consideration. Therefore it is necessary to make a selection of names to be used as indicators; also to set down the principles governing such a selection, as well as those underlying the interpretation of the names of a mixed nomenclature.

Taking American nomenclature as it has been described above, a blend of nomenclatures modified by adaptation, the investigator determines the contribution of each European element by working backwards through the stages of its evolution. That is, he must first examine the adaptive changes that have occurred in order to eliminate the American forms and reveal the blend of European nomenclatures with which he is to work. Next, by studying the process of blending, he will arrive at a view of the mixture underlying it. Finally, since many of the names comprising it are of indeterminate origin, he must clear away confusion in the mixture of immigrant names itself. Thus he arrives at his end by the process of removing several layers of wrapping. This is the procedure in actual investigation; the next section will view the structure of nomenclature in the reverse order, that is to say in the historical order of its evolution.

THE CAUSES OF NAME FREQUENCIES VIEWED HISTORICALLY

Since the nomenclature of each American State is fundamentally a combination of European nomenclatures, it is important to know the nature of the sampling which brought European names to this country. If surnames are to be relied upon as evidence of origin, the sampling of European nomenclature must be thoroughly representative; or, if not, it must be possible to measure the irregularities and to balance them against one another. The quantity of immigration, and the time during which it occurred, both have an important bearing on the representation of a European nomenclature. Representation is also conditioned by migration from limited districts or from certain social groups.

Of these the most important factor is the quantity of migration. If it involved only a few people, fortuitous representation of names is to be expected. The greater the numbers, evidently the more extensive the sampling and the more regular the representation of names. But the total quantity is the sum of annual totals, spread over a period of years. While the annual totals may exhibit peculiarities, in a long period of migration these irregularities may be balanced, and a representative sampling of the nomenclature be attained. Such a migration as that of the English, for example, operating in large numbers over a long period, produced a reliable sampling of one European nomenclature. When, however, migration brought considerable numbers for a few years and then was suspended, as was the case with the English in New England, the sampling must have shown definitely the peculiarities of the movements during those few years. Students of European migration, impressed with the peculiarities of movements during short periods, may be inclined to doubt that migration effectively samples a population. But upon testing the results of two centuries of immigration, as revealed in the records of 1790, they will observe that the peculiarities of separate influxes of short duration have been balanced and absorbed, so that the total commonly shows ratios of usage clearly reflecting European ratios.

A thorough reflection of European frequencies is not to be expected unless migration was regularized both regionally and socially. For this reason it is best sought by comparison with a fairly restricted European area. A large territory may be inaccurately represented when taken as a whole, on account of emigration from certain districts therein, and the consequent emphasis upon local surnames. The smaller subdivisions, however, must be large enough to have distinctive surnames of sufficient frequency to make them statistically useful.

In addition to the regional complication, there was in some instances a social one which we call factional emigration. In such a case one element of a composite population was mainly active in migration. This is illustrated by the migration of Scotch-Irish, who, despite several generations of residence in Ireland, constituted a stock separate from the Irish.

After surnames had been introduced to America by immigrants they were subject to the imitative and adaptive changes which have been described.

These developments may be rationalized, though not so readily as the factors controlling the introduction of names. Modifications of the type called imitative largely effected the blends in nomenclature. Names of a certain type in one system often influenced names in another, thus producing forms which replaced original immigrant names. For example, many German names in *-li, -lein,* and *-lich* were changed by analogy with English and Irish names in *-ley* and *-ly.* Other imitative changes were caused not by similarities between certain types, but rather by the association of particular names. The change of the German *Jung,* for instance, to *Young* was the result of the high frequency of both names and domination by the latter. Similarly the increased use of *Allen* was due to association with the Scotch *Allan,* the Dutch *Van Allen,* and the German *Alein.* Changes of the adaptive type constitute the last disguise of the original nomenclatures. Though adaptation was more widespread in its operation, it was less destructive of the original name patterns than analogy; it worked in accordance with known phonetic laws to adapt foreign names to American speech. On the whole, Americanization was an essentially regular process, operating by the interaction of names and by phonetic evolution.

The interplay of mixing, blending, and adaptation was affected by special conditions in various States. A high degree of mixture tended to stimulate blending but actually retarded adaptation. The dominance of one stock, such as the English in most States, produced one-sided nomenclatural developments; and when the predominant stock also dictated the language, the interaction of names and their adaptation to the language were closely linked. The records of New York and Pennsylvania, where the dominant stocks were not originally English speaking, offer some interesting examples of the way a mixture reacts on subsequent developments.

The Pennsylvania census, from which a section was chosen for preliminary examination, probably comes the nearest of all to showing the original mixture of nomenclatures, because the great mixture of stocks in that State, and the fact that it was fairly recent, prevented in some measure the adaptation of names. In a population representing several nationalities, the pressure of Americanization is less great than in more homogeneous groups. Somewhat similar degrees of mixture retarded the adaptation of names to American speech in Maryland and New York. The States in the extreme north and south, Maine and South Carolina, also display fairly clear mixtures of European nomenclatures because the migrations which peopled these regions were of comparatively late date. Thus the date of immigration and the degree of mixture both have an effect upon the amount of adaptation undergone by the original immigrant names.

It is in New England that the reflection of European frequencies is least apparent. Here two problems are involved, the first of which is genealogical. Since there were probably about 5,000 heads of families in New England by 1650, each of them represented in the records of 1790 by an average of 15 entries, the actual lines of descent of these people must be studied in conjunction with the interpretation of subsequent mixture. The second problem dealing with the peculiarities of this area is sociological. The original settlers bore an extraordinary proportion of names not in common use abroad, and during the first years in America their names developed an unusual number of variants. Even English names, which are commonly quite stable, underwent numerous modifications, so that the oddities of New England nomenclature constitute a separate problem, suggesting the need of an inventory of the early settlers and a catalogue of their descendants. In spite of the work of Savage, Dexter, Holmes, and others there remain gaps in this field.

It would be an interesting inquiry to ascertain the social cause of the many variants of New England names. Ordinarily as a population of mixed antecedents becomes fused, its nomenclature is gradually simplified; the more familiar names increase in frequency, and variants tend to disappear. In New England this simplification seems not to have occurred until after many of the leading names had developed a number of forms.

In the following sections are presented various classifications of specific names, in the light of which distinctive names will be chosen as reliable indicators of origin.

TYPES OF NAMES—COMMON AND UNCOMMON

A most important classification of names distinguishes them as common and uncommon. This is, of course, a flexible distinction, which may be applied as the occasion demands. One system of definition is used in the excerpt quoted above from the Pennsylvania census, where the criterion is percentage of population. This method may be more useful in dealing with frequencies within one list than in comparing separate State lists, because, as was seen in the lists of leading names in the four most populous States, specific names do not attain such high frequencies against the background of a mixed population as they do when the population is homogeneous. We look among common names for evidence of origins. Since not all common names yield clear testimony, it is necessary to make a selection from among them. There is no danger that the material to be considered will be unduly limited by selection, for there are plenty of names to choose from. The population of 1790 was concentrated under comparatively few of the 27,000 names in the records; yet about 3,600 were required to account for 85 per cent of the population. Even when these forms are assembled into groups, there are still many groups available from which to select.

From the concept of reflected ratios proceeds another useful classification of names on the basis of frequency. A surname may be potentially common or uncommon as well as actually so. Thus a name of high frequency in a European source of immigration was potentially common in America, whether it was actually so or not. Since the actual commonness of a name in the census of 1790 is sometimes due to a combination of causes, its potential commonness is useful as a test for the validity of names as indicators. Some common European names are found to reflect in American usage their original frequency, but it does not follow that all their companion names were represented in the same way. For example, we shall find that among Welsh names *Jones* shows a frequency in America about in accordance with those of associated names. But *Davis*, a name of similar origin, occurred much more frequently, and *Davies* much less frequently, than the theory of reflected frequency would lead us to expect, apparently because American usage confused the two, preferring the former. *Moore*, a leading English name, might be expected to show about the same frequency as *Lee* and *Parker*. As a matter of fact, it attained much greater numbers, especially in Pennsylvania and States to the south; the apparent irregularity is accounted for by the fact that *Moore* became the American version of the German *Mohr* and the Swiss *Moor*.

Though names of high frequency in the American records are most useful, those of slight representation also yield information, chiefly of a negative sort. That *Murphy* and *Sullivan*, for instance, were not among the highly common American names tends to demonstrate that the Celtic-Irish were not a large element of the population; that *Robertson*, *M'Leod*, and *M'Kenzie* were only moderately common indicates that the purely Scotch element was not large;

the comparative rarity of certain important Scotch names, such as *Chalmers* and *McInnes*, suggests that the districts of Scotland to which they were peculiar made but little contribution to American population.

TYPES OF NAMES BY ANTECEDENTS

A classification of names by antecedents must first eliminate names which were developed in America and those which superseded immigrant names. Names actually introduced by immigrants may then be classified as of simple or mixed geographical origin. This classification is made by comparison of the schedules of the registrars and other authorities on the nomenclatures of European countries. The classification of names according to antecedents is not so simple as it looks; the investigator has need of a thorough familiarity with the usages of the important contributory countries, with the varieties of all names of importance, and with the tendencies of their evolution.

In classifying names by antecedents it is necessary to distinguish between "joint usage" and "by-usage." By-usage is usage not accounted for by the known patterns of European nomenclature; it is occasional and accidental, being made up of the inevitable exceptions to the general rule. When a name is called distinctive of any region, it is not to be thought that every person so designated can be traced to that region, but merely that the occurrence of the name elsewhere is so slight and so irregular as to be without significance. Joint usage, on the other hand, is regular and measurable; when the collateral usage of a name is proved to be more than sporadic, it is to be considered joint usage. Off-hand, for example, one might think of *Kieffer* and *Lehmann* as German names, as indeed they are; but they are not distinctive, since their occurrence in France is sufficient to constitute joint usage. Although there is room for doubt concerning some incidental usages, it is practicable to classify names by specific (or simple) and mixed antecedents.

Sometimes in a doubtful case it is possible to invoke the original companionships of names as indicators of their origin. For example, the name *Thomas* is of very uncertain origin, because it is common in a number of European areas. But if it is found that a large number of Thomases were invariably associated with a large number of Joneses, Williamses, and Morgans it is quite certain that immigration from Wales and southwestern England was almost solely responsible for the currency of the name, since it was in that section that all four names were originally associated.

TYPES OF NAMES ACCORDING TO COMPANIONSHIPS

Criticism of companionships constitutes one form of the study of relative occurrences. Names may be classified as of normal or abnormal ratios in relation with those which are generally associated with them. Sometimes they will show in the American records relative frequencies about the same as those noted abroad, but commonly some of them will exhibit abnormally high frequencies, and others abnormally low, in relation to their companion names. Such exceptional frequencies demand explanation. One would like to know why *Lewis*, which seems to be an English name of Welsh type, was commonly represented in the American States on a scale out of proportion to related names, and why *Evans*, coming from a similar geographic background, was generally of abnormally low frequency.

Some abnormal ratios of associated names can be explained by means of regional emigration. The data available on European frequencies make possible a number of observations concerning regional irregularities in migration.

It happens, for example, that the leading English names treated by Farr fall into two classes—those generally distributed over the country, though not especially numerous in the Southwest, and those whose numbers are derived from extremely high frequency in the Southwest, particularly in Wales. The relative occurrences of the names so classified demonstrate that there was a difference in the scales of migration from the two parts of the country. Such an observation helps our knowledge of companionships and of contacts with definite European areas.

The drafting and redrafting of lists of companion names is essential to the selection of nomenclatural evidence of origin. Equipped with lists of associated names, the investigator is prepared to make an intensive study of relative occurrences.

TYPES OF NAMES ACCORDING TO FAVOR

The classification of names according to favor cuts across that by original companionships. It recognizes three types, marked by American favor, disfavor, and neutrality. Such a classification is important, because it helps explain ratios of representation which might be wrongly attributed to special features of immigration. In general, names chosen as indicators of origin should be of the neutral type; this is not always necessary, however, since once the grounds of favor and disfavor are understood, names of the two types can be selected in such a way that they will counterbalance each other.

Among the names studied by Farr there are illustrations of the operation of American favor and disfavor. *Davis* and *Moore*, already spoken of, were popular names; *Davies, Bennett, Hughes,* and *Griffiths* were in disfavor. Both sets are therefore avoided as indicators of English blood.

Favor and disfavor are unstable. *Bennett* and *Hughes*, for example, were in temporary disfavor at the time of the first census, having developed a large number of variants, not all of which were of immigrant origin, thus causing the natural English forms to appear in low ratio. Americans subsequently returned to the English usage in spelling these names.[18] The unpopularity of *Griffiths*, on the other hand, has become permanent. The usual American form is *Griffith*, but a number of other variants have been evolved.[19]

Whether or not immigrant names attained neutrality in respect to American favor and disfavor depended largely on their appropriateness to the English language. But even this generalization admits of exceptions, because there were names in use in English-speaking countries not natural to the English language, while others current in non-English-speaking countries, when removed from their original environments, readily passed as English. From the standpoint of the linguistic control on favor, names may be divided into four classes: (1) Those which, having originated in the British Isles, are strictly English in form; (2) those which, having originated in the British Isles, have been accepted in the English language; (3) those which, though of non-British origin, are not unnatural in form to the English language; and (4) those which originated in non-English-speaking countries and are foreign to the English language in form. Those of the second class, largely of Celtic and Gaelic origin, and those of the fourth class, often failed to attain currency in America on account of their form.

In connection with this classification, the great importance of the interaction of specific names should be noted. The relation of *Moore* and *Mohr* is such a

---

[18] *Bennett* now shows a normal ratio in relation to its companion names. (See Hall, Parker & Co., Surnames, *Am. Speech,* Vol. I, pp. 596–607.)

[19] See Surnames in *-is* in *Am. Speech,* Vol. 2, pp. 316–318.

case; *Mohr* was superseded by *Moore* not because it was inappropriate to English, but simply because it was the less appropriate of the two forms. Such instances of favor resulting from the concurrent use of two names are actually more important than those based purely on the general principle just laid down. The interaction of similar names often created or disguised whole groups of names, while the general principles of favor and disfavor usually brought about the adaptation of details of form. As was said in connection with the names *Young* and *Allen*, the increase and decrease of usage are to be interpreted in terms of the interplay of frequencies as well as in the light of phonetic evolution.

NAMES SELECTED AS EVIDENCE OF ORIGINS

These classifications support the thesis that some names are much more effective indicators of origins than others. Many have been passed over because of the complexity of their antecedents. This does not mean that they are to be disregarded, but rather that their currencies are to be considered as sidelights on the interpretation of more dependable names. Lists of all sorts of names indicate the total number of people to be accounted for; but only lists of selected distinctive names give direct evidence of origin.

DISTINCTIVE NAMES AND GROUPS

The term "distinctive name" was introduced in the preceding chapter and defined as a surname pointing clearly to a definite origin, having wide currency and a clearly recognizable form. That a distinctive surname must have a permanency of form does not mean that it may have no variants in American usage, but merely that it must be free from the operation of American favor or disfavor. In dealing with English names we shall define them in accordance with Farr's principle, which recognizes no variability in spelling. In other cases we shall treat names in groups and trace outstanding forms with their variants from Europe to America. Naturally the selection of English names is much more exacting on this account; despite the strict limitation there is a considerable number of common English names left for examination.

Of the 50 English names which Farr designated as outstanding 8 are eliminated on account of the complications introduced by American favor and disfavor, such as were illustrated in the discussion of *Davis, Moore, Bennett, Hughes*, and *Griffiths*. The following 20 names are passed over because they are of mixed antecedents: *Smith, Taylor, Brown, Johnson, Wilson, Wright, Wood, Thompson, Walker, White, Jackson, Hill, Clark, Martin, King, Allen, Clarke, Cook, Shaw*, and *Watson*. The list is given here because it is necessary to recognize that the large occurrence of these names in American records tends to exaggerate the English contributions to American population. Any laxity in accepting, as distinctive, names which are really of mixed antecedents would bias the conclusions. Especially must this point be stressed in dealing with English names because it is precisely this disregard of the distinction between English and British, and between English and English-looking, which has caused so many investigators to underestimate the non-English stocks in our population.

Since favor and disfavor did not affect the American use of most English names and their variants, it is possible to treat the English names according to Farr's principle, and anticipate the same degree of variation in American usage as in English. Not so, however, with the non-English names; for since these stocks were often minorities, and the names unfamiliar, various adaptations and interpretations were sometimes made. Such names are therefore assembled in groups comprising the different American modifications; thus is avoided the bias which would be inevitable if we were to deal only in rigidly defined specific names. The term distinctive can thus be applied not only to names, but to groups of names.

NAME GROUPS

A name group is an assemblage of names on the basis of derivation and origin. We are primarily concerned with the identification of groups involving neither mixed geographical antecedents nor American blend forms. The fundamental idea in the grouping of names is to assemble around certain names of frequent use other forms which may be considered modifications of them.

The study of the grouping of names is primarily etymological. A few notes from the registrars will indicate the principles upon which they worked. Farr, though he did not assemble variants in groups, recognized the common origins of many names, since he pointed out that diversity was largely the result of " disregard of uniformity and precision in the mode of spelling." He held that the number of English surnames had been greatly increased by slight orthographical variations as well as by other corruptions. This is true, of course; but related names often differ in more than orthography. They have frequently undergone organic changes, such as the addition or dropping of a syllable or the substitution of one sound for another. After Farr, Stark treated names in groups whenever he believed they were fundamentally related. The footnote to his first table of leading Scotch names reads as follows: " The different spellings are included in the above surnames—as Thompsons along with the Thomsons—but in every case the Scottish spelling of the name is given, as they very greatly preponderate in the Scottish indices. The different modes of writing the Highland names, M' or Mac, can not even be regarded as a difference in spelling." This was a rather indefinite stand, which ignored the necessity of exact definition of variants. Somewhat more precision, though still not enough, was shown in Stark's second paper, where he designated with an asterisk those names which in his opinion had a variety of spellings.

Not until Matheson did the grouping of names become scientific. Probably because his material demanded linguistic study, Matheson was careful to specify every form which he included in a given group. He did not always give the frequencies of all the variants, but he was careful to show that of the leading form in relation to the others. Thus he noted that the spelling *Kelly* occurred in 1,238 of the 1,242 entries under that heading.

There are two especially important reasons why Matheson's codification should be taken as the model for all American studies of nomenclature. First, unless a name used as a group heading is precisely defined, it is without value as a statistical term. To say that a certain name, variants included, is highly common is to make a statement so vague as to be of little use; in order to understand the group we must know how much variation is involved in terms of the number of forms and their relative frequencies. Another reason demanding stipulation of the forms composing a group is found in the peculiar complexity of American nomenclature. In dealing with American names, grouping informs us immediately only of apparent similarities; one must investigate further in order to distinguish between variants and resemblants.

An endeavor to obtain naturalness in the grouping of names calls attention to the great difference between the nomenclature of a homogeneous population and that of a mixture such as the American. In the former case, when there is no great foreign influence brought to bear on it, the nomenclature evolves a definite structure, made up, as it were, of a number of lesser nomenclatures, each consisting of one or more common forms and their variants. But when the antecedents of a population are mixed, questions arise as to the size of the name groups to be recognized. Such was Matheson's experience when he came to work over Irish usage. There, for example, the use of prefixes introduces a problem. The apparently natural grouping of prefixed names may be contradicted by that of those without prefixes. Thus it is a matter of opinion or convenience whether *Connell*, *O'Connell*, and *M'Connell* are classified as headings of three separate groups or as belonging in one only. There is even greater uncertainty in the codification of American names because of the mixture of antecedents and the resultant variability accompanying the process of Americanization.

It is essential to the codification of American nomenclature to recognize two kinds of grouping, one of which deals in "surnouns" and the other in "aggregates." Surnouns are groups of names made up of forms closely related in both etymology and geographical background. Frequently they exhibit no great amount of joint usage, and can therefore be classed as of simple origin in American usage. For example, *Sullivan* and its variants appearing in the records of 1790 may be grouped as a surnoun, such forms as *Sulivan*, *Sullaven*, *Sullivant*, and *Sylivant* being readily recognized and as certainly Irish as *Sullivan* itself. There are, however, parts of American nomenclature where surnouns can not be distinguished because original name groups have coalesced. In such cases, the resultant groups are known as aggregates. An example is provided in the section quoted from the Pennsylvania census. Two variants of the German *Roth* are *Road* and *Root*. But *Root* is an English name, common in Essex. Furthermore, the form *Road*, of German origin, developed the variants *Roads* and *Rhoades*, which merge with variants of the English *Rhodes*, even though of entirely independent origin. The recognition of an aggregate such as this puts an end to codification.

To sum up, the two kinds of groups in American nomenclature are surnouns— those containing forms of definable origin, ordinarily with a single frequently used form as a nucleus; and aggregates—those containing a number of nuclei of diverse origins.

CODIFICATION OF AMERICAN NAMES

The codification of American names is facilitated by observing frequencies. Rare names may be disposed of quickly, both as regards their antecedents and the confusion resulting from aggregation. Guided by relative frequencies, one can resolve a large portion of American names into surnouns. All forms of high frequency are potentially group headings, to be outlined with other forms only on the basis of demonstrable relationship. Rare forms, particularly those of American coinage, may ordinarily be identified with the most nearly similar immigrant names. A consistent following of this practice enables one generally to avoid mistakes, except such as may be considered to balance each other.

Although the grouping of names involves etymology, the observations of etymologists are not particularly useful for our purpose, because their emphasis on original derivations of names organizes a nomenclature into a collection of a few highly complex groups of great antiquity. This complication can be avoided by considering only contemporary conditions. In the grouping of names current in 1790, it is quite unnecessary to recognize relationships which were obsolescent by the time migration to America began. There is no more need of tracing eighteenth-century family names back to their common medieval originals than of recognizing *an* and *one* as one word.   Guppy's studies demonstrate that forms of common etymological origin were often definitely localized in separate parts of England and that others of separate origin had become confused.   The codification of names should therefore be concerned with the associations actually prevailing in the seventeenth and eighteenth centuries, and recognized by the people involved in the migration to America.   Observation of the ways in which analogy worked will give us an insight into these associations.   Aggregates of names developed in America were due chiefly to confusion, so that intermediate forms grew up between moderately similar names, and closely similar names tended to replace each other.   The process of change by analogy was aided by the fact that uniformity and accuracy in spelling were not considered such important matters in the eighteenth century as they are now.   The problem is to determine as far as possible what distinctions in names were clearly drawn by the people of 1790.

Not only time but place should be considered in the codification of American nomenclature.   If, for example, there is a question as to the origin of a particular name apparently English, yet of only limited geographical distribution in England, there is good reason for seeking an explanation of it as a modification of some more broadly distributed continental name.   *Root*, for example, is logically to be interpreted throughout the South as a variant of *Roth* rather than as the Essex name.

This introduces the tentative interpretation of names according to the area of their occurrence in America.   Forms occurring throughout the whole country must obviously be explained in terms of antecedents or forces common to all the States, but those showing localization or gradations of distribution may be variously interpreted.   Some of them are really distinct names; some are local Americanizations of immigrant forms, and some which from the point of view of a local nomenclature may be considered surnouns are nevertheless aggregates in relation to American nomenclatures as a whole.   *Hoff* and its variant *Huff* illustrate the last of these classes.   At first sight it would appear that *Hoff* and *Huff* should be recognized as clearly of German origin, yet it is found that they were current chiefly in the South and practically disappeared in New England, where *Hough* was common.   Evidently in such a case we are dealing with an aggregate having the nuclei *Hoff* in the South and *Hough* in the North.   Local evolution was probably determined by the predominant forms, so that some people of English antecedents in the South bore apparently German names, while the situation was reversed in New England.[20]

Such an instance shows that the trend of nomenclatural evolution varies in different areas according to the population.   It is therefore important in the preliminary study of names of specific origin to observe the local conditions in the different States, in order to find out in what ways the names under consideration were likely to change, and whether they were subject to the influence of analogous names of different antecedents.   Had the English Roots, for example, been very numerous in the regions where the German Roths settled, *Root* would have become a still more common name with the addition of German usage.   As it was, the Roths settled among English who had no names of great frequency similar to theirs, and *Roth*, finding no definite pattern for imitation, evolved into a dozen different forms.

After examining local situations for possible confusion of names such as has been illustrated, and eliminating nondistinctive names, it is my practice to define name groups for the country as a whole.   If no special difficulties are encountered in any one region, I then establish a definite standard for the

---

[20] *Cf.* Tables 63 and 64.

group. For example, the form *Money* is included in the Irish *Mooney* group, since it is a genuine variant and should be classed with *Mooney* in considering the country as a whole, even though the name *Money*, found in Rhode Island, was derived from the French *le Moyne*.[21] The slight error thus introduced in the delimitation of the group is compensated by the exclusion of the rare names in *Mun-*, such as *Munnie*, of uncertain origin.

To sum up, we may say that the codification of American names is possible largely because of the limitation of the mixture involved. To this mixture we can apply our knowledge of the relationships found in European usage, taking into consideration the factors of time and geography. We encounter many name groups, called aggregates, which are so complex as to defy analysis for origins; others, known as surnouns, are useful as indicators of the antecedents of their bearers, with some exceptions on account of joint usage. Having eliminated the aggregates, we next center our attention on the surnouns deriving from the country under consideration. Of these a few are rejected because of joint usage in the final selection of evidence. Those surnouns finally chosen as indicators are tested on the basis of unity, coherence, and mass. That is, they must be of common derivation; their forms must be closely and recognizably related; and they must show a degree of frequency sufficient to insure them against misinterpretation on account of unfamiliarity. A schedule of distinctive surnouns having been established, it remains to obtain from their occurrence an average effectively indicating how much the stock they represent contributed to the American population. This brings us to the determination of various ratios of occurrence.

RELATIVE OCCURRENCES OF NAMES

Occurrences are relative in two ways; for the frequency of a name may be compared with that of another name, or there may be a comparison of the occurrences of the same name in America and in its original European home. In the first kind of comparison one might note that the Joneses were about half again as numerous in England and Wales as the Williamses, and then find out whether this proportion was reproduced in the American records. Such comparison as this, dealing as it does with the implied companionships of names, is useful as a test of geographical classification, sometimes revealing that names of a generally similar geographical background must be subclassified by smaller areas. It shows, for example, that there were probably different rates of migration from the different Provinces of Germany. It also tests the purity with which European nomenclatures were reproduced in America. If, in observing the relative occurrences of certain names of the same background, it is found that some are abnormally represented, it may be inferred that something beside heredity has effected its American frequency. It gives a clue to the fact that *Moore* did not remain an English-American name with some Irish by-usage, but gained new usage from other sources.

The second kind of comparison, to which the first may be incidental, is the basis of our actual measurement of the different stocks. It will be convenient here to introduce and explain another term used in the analysis of American nomenclature.

RECURRENCE OF NAMES

The term "recurrence," signifying "occurrence again," denotes particularly the occurrence of a name in a colony as a function of its occurrence in a European area.

---

[21] *Rhode Island Historical Tracts*, No. 5, p. 26.

Naturally the comparison of occurrences, to be effective, must be made on the basis of large lists, the larger the better. The ratios determined by the registrars, because the records they used were so extensive, can be counted authentic. Other things being equal, recurrences in the country as a whole afford a better basis for comparison than do those in the several States. Yet some of the States were sufficiently populous to make the occurrences of names in their censuses mass phenomena. The State lists of Pennsylvania, Massachusetts, New York, and North Carolina contain more than 50,000 entries each. Four others—those of Connecticut, Maryland, South Carolina, and New Hampshire—contain upwards of 20,000 entries. The Virginia record used in place of the census has nearly 40,000. These numbers are sufficient to show the common names in proportions little, if at all, influenced by fortuitous developments. The interpretation of recurrences in Maine, Vermont, and Rhode Island must be more cautious because of the comparatively small numbers involved. Although the object of these studies is to determine the antecedents of the American population as a whole, much interest attaches to the analyses of the several State populations. Furthermore, with the aid of separate State determinations we can gain knowledge of the population of adjoining States whose records have been lost.

One of the many advantages of nomenclatural inquiry is that each distinctive name offers separate evidence concerning the contribution of its parent stock. Nevertheless, the indicators are ordinarily to be arranged in classes in order that the finding may be based upon recurrences of substantial measure. A class of names obviously provides a broader base for calculation than a single name, though it should be viewed not as a unit but as a composite itself susceptible to analysis. The terms "class" and "group" must be carefully distinguished. A group is an assemblage of names having similar etymological origin; a class is an assemblage on the basis of a common geographical origin. The arrangement of names in geographical classes is to be distinguished from the general sorting used in *CPG*, also known as classification.

The simplest way to derive the rate of recurrence of a class of names is in percentages of the respective populations. Suppose, for example, that the bearers of a certain class of names comprised 6 per cent of the population of England and that the names accounted for 4 per cent of the population of America. Then, since four is two-thirds of six, the ratio would indicate the English origin of two-thirds of the American population. Such a class rating provides a comparatively simple index of relationships. For it to be reliable, however, each name in the class must have sufficient numbers to warrant individual attention. The class established for such calculation must be definitely homogeneous, and the class rating must be obtained by averaging a series of unit ratings. To continue with the example, let us suppose that in the class of names constituting 6 per cent of the population of England there were three, each of which constituted six-tenths of 1 per cent of the population. When these names were transmitted to America they may not all have shown exactly the ratio anticipated, namely four-tenths of 1 per cent. One may have constituted five-tenths of 1 per cent of the American population, another four-tenths, and the third three-tenths. While two or the three names deviated from the expected ratio, yet the three make an average of four-tenths of 1 per cent, and the class measurement would be considered typical of the unit measurements. Evidently it is necessary to take care that the measurement of a class of names is typical of the measurements of its component units.

While this system of measurement by percentages is readily understandable and useful for the interpretation of class recurrences, it is not the best means of handling individual recurrences. A better method for separate names is described in the next section.

FACTORS OF RECURRENCE AND THEIR INTERPRETATION

Recurrences of names can also be stated in numbers obtained by division. These numbers are here called factors. They are obtained by comparing the number of heads of families of a certain name in an American area and in the country from which the name was introduced. Thus one can view the factors of recurrence in the several States as parts of the factors for the whole country. If, for example, there were a hundred times as many people of a certain surname in England as there were in America, 0.01 would be the factor of recurrence of that name.

A further advantage of factors of recurrence is that they facilitate the criticism of companionships along with the determination of class ratings. Detailed calculation of a number of companion names might show certain deviations, clearly revealed by their factors of recurrence, as, for example, 0.009, 0.010, 0.013, etc.

Factors are particularly useful in showing how thoroughly migration sampled a population. Evidently if names of similar origin show essentially like factors of recurrence, it may be assumed that random sampling produced a nomenclature reflecting fairly accurately the frequencies of the European area concerned. It does not, of course, indicate that migration effected random sampling continuously, but merely that in the long run it produced in America a definite reflection of the European nomenclature.

On the other hand, wide discrepancies among factors of recurrence suggest irregularities of some sort in the numbers or periods of migration. If care has been exercised in the classification of names and in the avoidance of names affected by American favor and disfavor, the comparison of such factors may provide reliable evidence of regional or factional migration sufficient to distort the American reflection of European usage.

The separate scrutiny of the recurrences of a class of names may raise certain problems concerning the determination of their average. When the factors are widely dispersed, different methods of obtaining averages, such as the use of arithmetic means and of medians, may produce different results. While the high and low factors of a class will in some cases nicely balance each other, often they produce a lack of balance which demands investigation. Thus statistical criticism is necessary to determine whether widely dispersed factors produce a significant class average.

Even when factors of recurrence are in close agreement, it is still possible that distortion has taken place in the reflection of the European nomenclature. There still may be bias traceable to American favor or disfavor. Since English names in particular were favored in the growth of American nomenclature, their apparent recurrence in an American area is to be considered as somewhat exaggerating the representation of English stock there. Scotch and Irish names on the whole were little subject to bias, those few which were in disfavor being compensated for by others slightly favored. German names, however, were at a disadvantage in America; even the most careful selection of distinctive names can not escape some understatement of German representation. The occurrence of German names, however, will be measured not by their occurrence in Germany but by basic numbers established in Pennsylvania; consequently this possibility of bias is reduced to a minimum.

The recurrences of a class of names ordinarily show some dispersion, and it is always interesting and sometimes useful to look for explanations of the high and low factors. High factors usually indicate that people of the name migrated at an early date or in especially large numbers. They may also be accounted for by joint usage or American favor. Low factors of recurrence, usually the result of late migration or migration in small numbers, may also be explained by American disfavor, or by the fact that the names in question were localized in an area which did not contribute much to migration. Thus in the study of English names it will be found that *Parker* and *Baker* were particularly well represented in the American records. The high factor of *Parker* is probably the result of the early immigration of large numbers of people bearing the name, particularly into New England. The high factor of *Baker* is partly attributable to the same cause, but is also caused by the substitution of the name for moderately common Teutonic names of the same meaning. Also among English names *Cooper* and *Robinson* will be found to have low factors. I find no definite explanation of the underrepresentation of *Cooper;* it may be that the name was peculiar to a part of England not numerously represented in migration. The same explanation may possibly serve for *Robinson*, but it is more probable that the low factor in this case was due to the American use of *Robison* in place of the original form. The investigation of specific recurrences may lead to extensive inquiries. In the present study they are examined only to the extent necessary to insure the proper selection and classification of the names used as indicators of origin.

The classification of names has been a most exacting part of these studies. It constitutes the stage of definition of units in which the more apparently statistical work of measuring relationships has its foundation. Since specific names or groups are not to be implicitly relied on as indicators of the proportions of their antecedent stocks, I have been particularly careful to marshal names and name groups in classes in such a way as to balance the inevitable variables.

CHAPTER III

EVIDENCE OF ENGLISH CONTRIBUTIONS TO 1790 AMERICA

This estimate of English contributions to the American population of 1790 is based on the relative American occurrences of leading names of known ratio in England.

RECORDS AVAILABLE FOR COMPARISON

This study rests on a comparison of Graham and Farr's record [1] of the 50 most commonly used surnames in England and Wales as deduced from indexes of the registers of birth, deaths, and marriages and the estimated population in 1853, with records of American usage. The American data are the indexes to the census records for 1790 covering the 11 States of Maine (treated separately in that census as a Province of Massachusetts), New Hampshire, Vermont, Massachusetts, Rhode Island, Connecticut, New York, Pennsylvania, Maryland, North Carolina, and South Carolina; and the index to the special tax record for Virginia compiled by the Bureau of the Census from returns of the State enumerations made in 1782–1785 covering 38 counties. The date of the Virginia record is near enough to that of the 1790 census to afford legitimate comparison, but as the compilation accounts for only about half the population of Virginia, the constituent elements of the population may not be fully apparent in the name uses shown there.

These 12 American records reveal the number of American bearers of the leading English names listed by Farr, and comparison of their proportions with those of the bearers of the same names in England and Wales gives a basis for estimation of the number of English in the American population of 1790.

Five other States or districts on or near the Atlantic seaboard were covered by the census of 1790, but the records for these were lost and no complete record on the currency of names of that period in New Jersey, Delaware, Georgia, Kentucky, or Tennessee is known to exist. Interpolation for these areas is made after the States of record have been studied.

METHOD OF COMPARISON

The measurement of the English contribution to American population is accomplished (1) by determining from Farr's tabulation the leading names available from the European standpoint as indicators of English origin, and (2) by comparing American usage with the selected part of Farr's record. Survey of European usage discards 20 names from Farr's list, and examination of American usage eliminates 8 others. The remaining 22 names are subjected to several different methods of comparison in order to picture the composition of the population as a whole, but calculations for all comparisons are made by the same general method, each including comparison of Farr's record with the 12 American records and with summaries of these covering the whole area of record as well as separate large parts of it.

---

[1] Sixteenth Annual Report of the Registrar General, London, 1856, p. xxiii et seq.

164

Appraisal of the English elements in these several populations is based on the relative occurrences of the selected leading names, in accordance with the thesis that English bearers of common names in a substantial immigration were in a constant proportion to bearers of less common names. It is maintained that if the number of English-American bearers is known, the size of the English element in the American population can be calculated; but while American bearers can be identified, the number of English-Americans can only be approximated because of complicating factors. Pure recurrence of the selected names is not found because the functional relationship between American and English ratios was disturbed by changes in the names and by irregularities in sampling. Although original bearers of these names were almost entirely within England, yet by-usage existed; and because the settlement of America was dominated by the English, their names gained through American favor, so that the number of bearers of English names in America in 1790 was augmented by other Americans of non-English paternity. Hence these measurements yield maxima showing the proportions of the population that may have been English, although the actual proportions were probably somewhat less.

In order to present quickly a general view of the English contribution to the population, the recurrence of English names in the several States and in the whole area of record will first be surveyed with as little attention as possible to detail. The conclusions thus arrived at will be tentative, and subject to considerable modification in the light of a detailed scrutiny. In the detailed calculations the aim is to set forth first the facts concerning the American occurrence of leading English names, then the conclusions drawn from these facts as quantitative data, and finally notes on those conclusions based on data viewed as qualitative. No attempt is made to calculate the actual proportion of English within the maxima derived until the study of other stocks provides some perspective on Anglicization.

SELECTION OF EVIDENCE

In making up a list of names to be used as evidence, 20 of the 50 English leading names are discarded at the outset, because they are British rather than distinctively English. Of the remaining 30, 8 more are rejected as a result of an examination of their American usage. The details of this selection will be reviewed later; for the purpose of the preliminary calculation it is sufficient to say that 22 names have been selected as valid indicators of the proportion of English in the American population of 1790.

To take a very simple instance of the calculation from recurrences, we observe that the bearers of these 22 names amount to 8.01 per cent of the population of England and Wales. According to the theory of recurrence, then, the proportion of the population of an American area bearing these names, compared with the 8.01 per cent of the population of England and Wales, indicates what part of the total population of the American area in question is of English and Welsh origin. Thus, the bearers of these 22 names constitute 4.95 per cent of the population of South Carolina. Since 4.95 is 62 per cent of 8.01, the off-hand indication is that 62 per cent of the population of South Carolina is of English or Welsh origin. Similarly, the bearers of these 22 names constitute 5.24 per cent of the population of Maryland, indicating that the parent stock represented by these names amounts to 65 per cent of the population.

The 22 names upon which these calculations are based do not form a homogeneous class, but fall into two general divisions. One of these, Class I, may be designated as Anglican. The bearers of these names were found nearly all over England and in Wales. Most of them were numerously represented in half the English counties, and four in over three-fourths. To this group belong the following names: *Robinson, Hall, Green, Turner, Cooper, Ward, Baker, Parker, Lee*, and *Carter*.

Te remaining 12 names forming Class II, *Jones, Williams, Thomas, Evans, Roberts, Edwards, Lewis, Morris, James, Morgan, Price*, and *Phillips*, we shall call Cambrian. The bearers of these names, though found throughout England, were concentrated chiefly in Wales and some half-dozen counties bordering on Wales. A peculiarity of Welsh nomenclature must be noted in this connection. Farr remarked: "The contribution of Wales to the number of surnames * * * is very small in proportion to its population. Perhaps nine-tenths of our countrymen in the principality could be mustered under less than 100 different surnames; and while in England there is no redundancy of surnames, there is obviously a paucity of distinctive appellatives in Wales, where the frequency of such names as *Jones, Williams, Davies, Evans*, and others, almost defeats the primary object of a name, which is to distinguish an individual from the mass."

As a consequence of the relative paucity of Welsh surnames, the 12 indicators which we have classed as Cambrian gained high ratios in original English use, even though the population which they represented was only a minority. It is therefore necessary to determine upon a proper weighting for the two classes of names.

Study of the distribution of bearers of these two types of nomenclature indicates that Anglicans were four and a half times the number of Cambrians, hence the measures of recurrence of Anglican names are four and a half times as significant as those of Cambrian names. A weighted average is derived by taking nine-elevenths of the proportion of English indicated by American usage of Anglican names and adding two-elevenths of the proportion indicated by American usage of Cambrian names. For example, if the heads of American families used 88 per cent as much of Anglican and 55 per cent of Cambrian surnames as the English, the population would have been 82 per cent English in origin as follows:

$$88 \times 9/11 \text{ is } 72$$
$$55 \times 2/11 \text{ is } 10$$
$$\overline{11/11 \text{ is } 82}$$

This calculation deals with the two classes without consideration of the peculiarities of the several indicators; in actual practice this simplicity can not be attained. However, approximately the same measures for English contributions to the several States are obtained by the simplified as by more detailed calculation, provided there are eliminated from the names in each class in each area those showing the highest and the lowest ratios of usage, as most out of line with companion names. Distortion of class measurements by exceptional influences of certain names will be considered later, but to avoid the confusion of the principal irregularities in the ratios of these names in specific areas, information is given at this point concerning names of abnormally high or low representation in the particular States or areas.

The term "abnormal recurrence" is used in Tables 3 and 4, following, to indicate the remarkably high or low measure of representation which caused the rejection of specific names as indicators of English population in a definite area, and may or may not disclose irregular relationship between English-American and English population. If the exceptional American frequency was produced by irregular migration, recurrence is truly abnormal; but if by deviation in spelling, by adoption, or by some other feature of favor, recurrence is confused with favor. Hence "abnormal recurrence" is used here to mean either recurrence irregularly derived or somewhat disguised by variable usages. Ratios of the numbers or bearers of these names in the American records and in the original English record are compared, and in each list the occurrences of the two names at the extremes of high and low relative representation are set in parentheses to show that their exceptional measures of recurrence debar them as indicators of English origins in the area noted.

Table 3 states the listings of English names of both Class I and II in the 12 American records, in declining order of their importance in England, an order not consistently reflected in American figures. Column 1 gives the totals for the whole area of record, column 2 for New England, and column 3 for the remaining area of record. Table 4 states the listings for Class I and II names in the several States of record.

TABLE 3.—*Listings of leading English surnames in the area of record and two sections of the area*

[Parentheses denote abnormal recurrence in the region]

	Area of record	New England	Remaining area of record
CLASS I			
Robinson	[1] (780)	358	[1] (422)
Hall	1, 484	814	670
Green	1, 124	505	619
Turner	759	280	479
Cooper	574	[1] (123)	451
Ward	700	257	443
Baker	1, 157	494	[2] (633)
Parker	[2] (1, 120)	[2] (583)	537
Lee	653	243	410
Carter	669	240	429
CLASS II			
Jones	2, 610	737	1, 873
Williams	2, 257	730	1, 527
Thomas	1, 147	351	796
Evans	[1] (572)	[1] (115)	[1] (457)
Roberts	763	237	526
Edwards	543	128	415
Lewis	[2] (1, 194)	[2] (490)	[2] (704)
Morris	492	74	418
James	421	91	330
Morgan	568	199	369
Price	466	47	419
Phillips	560	251	309

[1] American ratio exceptionally low compared with English.
[2] American ratio exceptionally high compared with English.

TABLE 4.—*Listings of leading English surnames in the several States of record, 1790*

[Parentheses denote abnormal recurrence in the State]

CLASS I

Name	Maine	New Hampshire	Vermont	Massachusetts	Rhode Island	Connecticut
Robinson	44	43	52	131	21	67
Hall	63	124	70	248	62	(247)
Green	30	61	41	201	(107)	65
Turner	29	(17)	23	132	14	65
Cooper	12	20	(6)	(42)	13	(30)
Ward	17	26	17	122	9	66
Baker	39	40	45	259	43	68
Parker	(47)	(95)	(70)	(278)	15	78
Lee	(6)	11	24	99	10	93
Carter	23	40	14	94	(6)	63

Name	New York	Pennsylvania	Maryland	Virginia	North Carolina	South Carolina
Robinson	(60)	113	74	105	(50)	(20)
Hall	105	103	109	127	180	46
Green	183	84	87	69	134	62
Turner	70	40	84	88	135	62
Cooper	84	108	(53)	(50)	103	53
Ward	100	(32)	51	73	147	40
Baker	(166)	(146)	(96)	86	131	38
Parker	66	77	49	88	(202)	55
Lee	65	58	48	66	115	58
Carter	33	34	39	(137)	130	(56)

CLASS II

Name	Maine	New Hampshire	Vermont	Massachusetts	Rhode Island	Connecticut
Jones	89	106	59	290	20	173
Williams	37	52	55	300	57	229
Thomas	45	32	28	145	19	82
Evans	[1] 9	[1] 35	[1] 18	[1](30)	6	[1](17)
Roberts	35	(63)	25	38	12	64
Edwards	6	9	1	57	14	41
Lewis	(36)	24	(43)	157	(65)	(165)
Morris	4	(2)	5	27	(2)	34
James	5	12	2	29	28	15
Morgan	5	14	16	70	2	92
Price	(2)	3	(0)	23	7	12
Phillips	12	16	16	(154)	24	29

See footnote at end of table.

TABLE 4.—*Listings of leading English surnames in the several States of record, 1790*—Continued

CLASS II—Continued

Name	New York	Pennsyl-vania	Maryland	Virginia	North Carolina	South Carolina
Jones	210	296	243	359	570	195
Williams	207	239	170	229	(534)	148
Thomas	72	233	147	131	141	72
Evans	[1](28)	161	64	(66)	(86)	52
Roberts	54	153	59	80	108	72
Edwards	47	(66)	(26)	99	132	45
Lewis	(153)	(152)	49	(127)	171	52
Morris	40	110	45	66	121	36
James	25	67	40	67	94	37
Morgan	48	70	40	50	118	(43)
Price	33	63	(117)	66	111	29
Phillips	86	67	23	50	68	(15)

[1] Adjusted for misspellings: Actual numbers, spelled *Evans*, were Maine, 6; New Hampshire, 29; Vermont, 12; Massachusetts, 21; Connecticut, 10; and New York, 20.

GENERAL VIEW OF CONTRIBUTIONS OF ENGLISH

A general view of English contributions to American population as a whole and in parts may now be set forth, estimated according to the simple form of calculation. The percentage which bearers of the selected typical names in each class in an area constituted of the total number of heads of families in that area is determined and then compared with the corresponding figure for the original ratio.

For example, Table 5 shows Class I in Maryland made up of the eight names other than *Baker* and *Cooper* which in this State were respectively highly prevalent and strikingly uncommon. The remaining Class I names covered 1.655 per cent of the heads of families in this State, while in England their bearers constituted 2.151 per cent. The Maryland ratio being 77 per cent of the normal English ratio indicates that if all English had been represented in the State in ratios of bearers of Class I names, the English would have constituted 77 per cent of the population.

Table 5a shows Class II in Maryland made up of the 10 names other than *Price*, highest, and *Edwards*, lowest. The remaining Class II names covered 2.692 per cent of the heads of families in the State, while in England their bearers constituted 4.840 per cent, thus giving Maryland 56 per cent Cambrian representation, and indicating that had all other English names been represented in this State on the same scale the proportion of English would have been 56 per cent.

Hence, to determine the proportions of English in Maryland, the readings of 77 per cent Anglicans and 56 per cent Cambrians are combined, the resulting weighting of the two figures in the 9-and-2 ratio obtaining 73 per cent maximum English contribution to the population of Maryland.

Tables 5 and 5a show the representation of Anglicans and Cambrians as indicated by Class I and Class II names respectively, according to the simple form of calculation; also computations for the States and for the area of record and its principal divisions, as in the Maryland reading. In both tables the figures in column 4 denotes the proportions of English indicated if all were of the type of nomenclature designated.

TABLE 5.—*Calculation of representation of English in the States on the basis of recurrence of Class I surnames as defined by the exclusions noted*

| State | Names excluded as of abnormal recurrence in the State or area | Bearers of Class I surnames typical of the State or area | | Representation of English [1] |
		In England and Wales, 1853	In the State, 1790	
		Per cent	*Per cent*	*Per cent*
Maine	Parker, Lee	2. 248	1. 510	67. 2
New Hampshire	Parker, Turner	2. 133	1. 515	71. 0
Vermont	Parker, Cooper	2. 176	1. 910	87. 8
Massachusetts	do	2. 176	1. 971	90. 6
Rhode Island	Green, Carter	2. 147	1. 679	78. 2
Connecticut	Hall, Cooper	2. 060	1. 389	67. 4
New York	Baker, Robinson	2. 052	1. 294	63. 1
Pennsylvania	Baker, Ward	2. 166	. 828	38. 2
Maryland	Baker, Cooper	2. 151	1. 655	76. 9
Virginia	Carter, Cooper	2. 207	1. 862	84. 4
North Carolina	Parker, Robinson	2. 077	2. 045	98. 5
South Carolina	Carter, Robinson	2. 108	1. 594	75. 6
New England	Parker, Cooper	2. 176	1. 843	84. 7
Remaining area of record	Baker, Robinson	2. 052	1. 453	70. 8
Area of record	do	2. 077	1. 578	76. 0

[1] Were all other English names represented in the State or area on the same scale as the class of leading names here dealt with, the percentage of English would have been that here stated.

TABLE 5a.—*Calculation of representation of English in the States on the basis of recurrence of Class II surnames as defined by the exclusions noted*

| State | Names excluded as of abnormal recurrence in the State or area | Bearers of Class II surnames typical of the State or area | | Representation of English [1] |
		In England and Wales, 1853	In the State, 1790	
		Per cent	*Per cent*	*Per cent*
Maine	Lewis, Price	4. 841	1. 451	30. 0
New Hampshire	Roberts, Morris	4. 700	1. 258	26. 8
Vermont	Lewis, Price	4. 841	1. 503	31. 0
Massachusetts	Phillips, Evans	4. 651	1. 742	37. 5
Rhode Island	Lewis, Morris	4. 811	1. 697	35. 3
Connecticut	Lewis, Evans	4. 542	1. 895	41. 7
New York	do	4. 542	1. 507	33. 2
Pennsylvania	Lewis, Edwards	4. 731	1. 958	41. 4
Maryland	Price, Edwards	4. 840	2. 692	55. 6
Virginia	Lewis, Evans	4. 542	3. 174	69. 9
North Carolina	Williams, Evans	3. 988	3. 109	78. 0
South Carolina	Morgan, Phillips	4. 938	2. 841	57. 6
New England	Lewis, Evans	4. 542	1. 643	36. 2
Remaining area of record	do	4. 542	2. 512	55. 3
Area of record	do	4. 542	2. 178	48. 0

[1] Were all other English names represented in the State or area on the same scale as the class of leading names here dealt with, the percentage of English would have been that here stated.

The importance of classification into Classes I and II, and the separate study of their figures, is emphasized in the readings of Table 6. For example, the estimated proportion of English in Maryland, as shown in this table and in the illustrative calculation above, is 73 per cent; compare this with the 65 per cent obtained by rough calculation, without classification, in the foregoing section. In the same way, South Carolina in the formal calculation in Table 6 shows an English ratio of 72 per cent, as against the 62 per cent obtained by rough calculation.

Table 6 gives, in columns 1 and 2 respectively, the separate readings of Class I and II names in each State of record, in New England, in the remaining area of record, and in the whole area of record; column 3 combines these figures by the 9-and-2 weighting to show approximate maximum English contributions to populations; approximate, because different methods of averaging give somewhat different results, and maximum because the averages are somewhat biased by non-English use of the names whose frequencies are basic to the measurements.

TABLE 6.—*Calculation of the indicated maxima for contributions of English to the population of the States of record, 1790, by combining the readings of Classes I and II surnames*

[All figures are percentages of population.]

	Representation of English indicated by names of class		
	Class I [1]	Class II [1]	Class I and II combined [2]
Maine_____	67. 2	30. 0	60. 4
New Hampshire_____	71. 0	26. 8	63. 0
Vermont_____	87. 8	31. 0	77. 5
Massachusetts_____	90. 6	37. 5	81. 0
Rhode Island_____	78. 2	35. 3	70. 4
Connecticut_____	67. 4	41. 7	62. 7
New York_____	63. 1	33. 2	57. 7
Pennsylvania_____	38. 2	41. 4	38. 8
Maryland_____	76. 9	55. 6	73. 0
Virginia_____	84. 4	69. 9	81. 8
North Carolina_____	98. 5	78. 0	94. 8
South Carolina_____	75. 6	57. 6	72. 3
New England_____	84. 7	36. 2	75. 9
Remaining area of record_____	70. 8	55. 3	68. 0
Area of record_____	76. 0	48. 0	70. 9

[1] These 2 columns represent hypothetical conditions, assuming the two classes of names to be fully representative.
[2] This column, treating the 2 classes of names in proper significance, gives the measures of English population indicated by the ratios of use of leading English names.

The separation of Class I and II names derives its greatest importance not from the fact that the two classes represent two types of nomenclature, but because they ordinarily show markedly different rates of prevalence. To make clear the 9-and-2 weighting and to disclose the almost constant underrepresentation of Cambrians, Table 7 is introduced here to show the relative contributions of the two classes.

The figures for Maine, for example, have shown that if all English in that State were represented on the plane of Anglicans, the English contribution would have been 67.2 per cent, while if by Cambrians it would have been 30.0 per cent. But combine these figures in the 9-and-2 weighting which accords Anglicans four and a half times the significance of Cambrians, and the 67.2 per cent reading for Anglicans indicates that they constituted 55.0 per cent or less of the population, this being nine-elevenths of 67.2; while the 30 per cent reading for Cambrians indicates that they constituted 5.4 per cent or less, this being two-elevenths of 30 per cent; the two together giving 60.4 per cent as the indicated total English contribution to the population of Maine. This intermediate step in weighting is shown in Table 7 where the figures for the States and areas of record are set down in columns 1 and 2 as for two distinct stocks, and the ratio between the two classes is shown in column 3.

TABLE 7.—*Indicated contributions of English of two types of nomenclature to the population of the States of record and comparison of the indicated contributions*

| | Estimated maxima for per-centages of population of— | | Ratio of Cambrian to Anglican [1] |
	Anglican type	Cambrian type	
			Per cent
Maine	55. 0	5. 4	9. 8
New Hampshire	58. 1	4. 9	8. 4
Vermont	71. 8	5. 6	7. 8
Massachusetts	74. 1	6. 8	9. 2
Rhode Island	64. 0	6. 4	10. 0
Connecticut	55. 2	7. 6	13. 8
New York	51. 6	6. 0	11. 6
Pennsylvania	31. 2	7. 5	24. 0
Maryland	62. 9	10. 1	16. 1
Virginia	69. 0	12. 7	18. 4
North Carolina	80. 6	14. 2	17. 6
South Carolina	61. 8	10. 5	17. 0
New England	69. 3	6. 6	9. 5
Remaining area of record	57. 9	10. 0	17. 3
Area of record	62. 2	8. 7	14. 0

[1] Potential ratio 22.2 per cent.

SUMMARY OF ENGLISH CONTRIBUTIONS (SIMPLE CALCULATION)

Briefly summing the findings of the simpler form of calculation, it is noted that the 22 indicators of English contributions to 1790 American population prevailed in the American States on a scale of seven-tenths the occurrence they would have had in England. These names are divided into two classes: Anglicans representing normal varied nomenclature through England; and Cambrians, largely concentrated in Wales and Southwest England; the two showing marked difference in their rates of prevalence. Estimation of all English on Anglican and Cambrian bases of 76 and 48 per cent respectively, assuming no non-English usage in either class, derives 71 per cent total English contribution to American population.

Measures of recurrence show Cambrians represented in the area of record in the ratio of 14 per cent of the Anglicans, instead of in the proportion of two-ninths of the Anglicans as predicated by original conditions in England. Viewing the differentiation of class as a matter of type of name, with mingling of the two classes in the motherland, suggests factional migration with Cambrian reluctance to move; but as Cambrians concentrated chiefly in Wales and Southwest England, geographic interpretation indicates that migration showed a disproportionate drift of English from parts of the country other than Wales and the Welsh border.

As illustrated by the preceding calculation, the main investigation was based on the thesis that the ratio of bearers of English names in the American area to that of bearers in England approximates the proportion of English-Americans in the American area. Comparison of Farr's record of occurrences of leading English surnames with their measures in the American records was supplemented by study of Guppy's material on distribution of original bearers.

Farr defined surnames by reckoning each separately, however slight the difference in spelling; hence the indicators chosen for this study were only those names which maintained constant forms in American usage. Each of these names represents its group, variable spellings being viewed as used in constant ratio to these principal forms. Actual proportionate usage of the important names is never constant within the group, but occurrences of the varying forms show frequent close approximation to constancy. For example, among the 22 indicators some could only be spelled in one way, such as *Carter* and *Parker*. Others introduce irregularities, such as *Phillips*, which shows local irregularities in the use of the double *l*. And *Evans* has a noticeable increase in variable spelling where it was least familiar; in this one instance adjustment for misspellings is made. American versions which have changed some group constructions prevent the use of some names as indicators, for lack of data on occurrences of these variants in England.

In order to be available as an indicator, a name must meet three requirements: First, it must be distinctively English, not broadly British; secondly, the surname group to which it belongs must have been carried over into American nomenclature without admixture from other sources; and thirdly, it must have preserved its English spelling in America.

Comparison of Farr's report for England and Wales with Stark's for Scotland and Matheson's for Ireland divides the 50 leading English names into three main classes: British, Anglican, Cambrian.

The British class consists of 20 names familiar in England, but commonly used also by Scotch and Irish, and although introduced into America chiefly by the English, deriving American usage assignable only to mixed British antecedents.

Anglican and Cambrian classes include the remaining 30 names. Anglican names, together with a great variety of others characteristic of English nomenclature, prevailed in England, with declining force in the southwest and in Wales; and in this latter area the Cambrians centered, with scattered distribution throughout other parts of England.

The definition of Cambrian names depends not upon the area of their occurrence, for they are found throughout England, but upon the area in which they attain a marked degree of frequency. To determine this area use was made of Guppy's study, based upon the occurrences of names among rural populations, in which it is possible to discern the original provenience of surnames which have become mingled in the great cities since the industrialization of England. Roughly speaking, this area comprised Wales and the southwestern part of England, from Somerset and Hampshire as far north as Cheshire. The Cambrian names had some prevalence in Cornwall and Devon, but generally speaking these two counties had a distinctive nomenclature of their own.

The area of concentration for Cambrian names comprised Wales, Monmouth, Gloucester, Shropshire, and Hereford. In this region the people may be deemed to have been almost entirely of Welsh nomenclature. The intensive character of the usage of the 12 most distinctive Cambrian names is disclosed by the fact that, in Guppy's observation, their bearers constituted the following percentages of the original population: Wales, 40 per cent; Monmouth, 34 per cent; Shropshire, 18 per cent; Hereford, 17 per cent; and Gloucester, 6 per cent. The secondary area for the prevalence of these names and the type of nomenclature which they represent comprised Cheshire, Cornwall, Devon, Hampshire, Somerset, Staffordshire, Warwick, Wiltshire, and Worcester.

Of the 12 names finally retained as Cambrian indicators, the following 7 were found by Guppy to occur at a rate of more than 7 per 10,000 in more than half the county units into which he divided the country: *Edwards, James, Jones, Morris, Phillips, Roberts,* and *Williams.* It should be noted that the 40 county units referred to in connection with Guppy are not all separate counties. Some of them are combinations, as Rutland combined with Leicestershire and Westmoreland with Cumberland.

As already observed the Cambrian names gained markedly lower measures of recurrence in America than did the Anglican. Some, however, rather regularly showed occurrence on a better scale than others. One unfamiliar with the original situation could not distinguish by measures of recurrence what names were specially well represented Cambrian-Anglican names and which were poorly represented Anglican names. A question will arise particularly as to the proper classification of *Lewis.* This name so continually showed the highest measure of recurrence of any name which we classify as Cambrian that it seems well to specify its original distribution. According to Guppy, a picture of the original localization of the bearers of *Lewis* is obtained from the following figures showing the numbers of bearers of the name per 10,000 in the county units as he defines them: Monmouth, 400; South Wales, 330; Hereford, 168; North Wales, 150; Shropshire, 100; Wiltshire, 80; Cheshire, 57; Worcester, 56; Gloucester, 25; Hampshire, 21; Berkshire, 20; Warwick, 18; Norfolk, 17; Devon, 13; Somerset, 11; Staffordshire, 10; Yorkshire (West Riding), 7. This discloses that the *Lewises* were originally scattered over 17 of Guppy's county units but found their principal numbers in the 8 first mentioned. Converting Guppy's percentages to absolute numbers shows that over eight-tenths of the *Lewises* were in these eight localities and that, indeed, nearly three-fourths of them were in Wales, Monmouth, Shropshire, and Hereford. This is a fairly typical Cambrian distribution—a good illustration, and determinative of the classification of *Lewis.*

Table 8 presents these three classifications of the leading English names,[2] and shows the Anglican class determined by elimination. Column 1 lists the 20 names significant in other parts of the United Kingdom, hence not distinctively English; column 2 the 17 names originally concentrated in and near Wales; column 3 the remaining 13 names distinctively Anglican and representative of normal varied English nemenclature. Four of these last had Irish by-usage, but American occurrences indicate this insufficient to modify their definition as distinctively Anglican.

---

[2] Taken with some revisions from the author's paper on English surnames, Hall, Parker & Co., Surnames, *Am. Speech,* August, 1926, Vol. I, No. 11, pp. 596–607.

TABLE 8.—*Classification of the 50 surnames of greatest usage in England and Wales, 1853*

British		Cambrian		Anglican	
Position	Surname	Position	Surname	Position	Surname
1	Smith	2	Jones	12	Robinson [2]
4	Taylor	3	Williams	16	Hall
6	Brown	5	Davies	17	Green
10	Johnson [1]	7	Thomas	23	Turner
11	Wilson	8	Evans	28	Cooper
13	Wright	9	Roberts	29	Harrison
14	Wood	19	Hughes [2]	30	Ward [2]
15	Thompson [1]	20	Edwards	33	Baker
18	Walker	21	Lewis	39	Moore [2]
22	White	26	Harris [3]	40	Parker
24	Jackson	32	Davis [3]	46	Bennett
25	Hill	34	Morris	47	Lee [3]
27	Clark	35	James	50	Carter
31	Martin	37	Morgan		
36	King	43	Price		
38	Allen	44	Phillips		
41	Clarke	49	Griffiths		
42	Cook				
45	Shaw				
48	Watson				

[1] Neither Johnson nor Thompson strong in Scotland but allied with Johnston and Thomson from British-American view point.
[2] Irish usage also.
[3] Welsh in origin but early of broad distribution in England.

Anglican:[3] The 30 names which European usage indicates distinctively English are reduced to 22 by irregularities in American reproduction.

Three Anglican names—*Harrison, Moore, Bennett*—are withdrawn. *Harrison* was not represented in American nomenclature on the scale indicated by the currency of companion names, offering a contrast to *Harris* which achieved undue frequency in usage.

Moore[4] replaced German forms of similar sound, such as *Mohr*, particularly in the South; it was greatly affected by variable spelling in Great Britain; and in America, gained ascendency over *Moor* and *More* and even over the Scotch *Muir.*

Bennett is used to-day by English-Americans in about the same ratio as in Farr's England, but in 1790 its American spelling was not dependable. The 12 American records list heads of families totaling 378 *Bennet*, 249 *Bennett*, 36 *Bennit*, and 49 *Bennitt.*

The 10 names—*Robinson, Hall, Green, Turner, Cooper, Ward, Baker, Parker, Lee, Carter*—were leaders in the nomenclature of England proper and are therefore adjudged Anglican, called Class I, and used to determine the representation of the main English element.

Cambrian: Five of the 17 Cambrian names are withdrawn: *Davies* and *Davis*, not recognized as separate in American usage; *Harris*[3][5] indistinguishable from *Harrison; Hughes*, because of variable spelling; *Griffiths*, not established in American usage, giving way to variants[5] of simple pronunciation.

[3] Hall, Parker & Co., *Surnames, Am. Speech*, August, 1926. Vol. I, No. 11, pp. 596–607.
[4] Our Leading Surnames, *Am. Speech*, June, 1926. Vol. I, No. 9, pp. 470–477.
[5] Surnames in -is, *Am. Speech*, April, 1927. Vol. II, No. 7, pp. 316–318.

Both *Davis*[3,4,5] and *Harris*[3,5] were of irregular distribution, from the standpoint of differentiation of the two types of English names. *Davis* was properly the English version of the Welsh *Davies* which it replaced almost entirely in America. Guppy reported occurrence for *Harris* in over three-fourths of England and Wales, an abnormal distribution for a Cambrian name, and it was also decidedly popularized in America.

Evans is retained among the 12 typical Cambrian names, but only with allowance for misspellings and inaccurate recording as *Evens* or *Evins*. Its principal currency was from Pennsylvania southward. From New York northward, where it suffered a marked degree of misspelling, the actual count is 104 *Evans* among 168 of this surnoun. But since 85 per cent (428 among 501) of heads of families in the south, where the surnoun was familiar, were recorded *Evans* rather than *Evens* or *Evins*, it may be considered that 85 per cent of the heads of families in the north were properly *Evans* also, so that *Evans* is reckoned at 143 instead of 104 in that area. Even after this adjustment it has the lowest measure of relative usage in the Cambrian class.

The twelve names—*Jones*,[4] *Williams*,[4] *Thomas, Evans, Roberts, Edwards, Lewis*,[5] *Morris*,[5] *James, Morgan, Price, Phillips*—whose bearers were originally in Wales and some half dozen English counties bordering it, with scattered usage throught England, are recognized as Cambrian and called Class II.

READINGS OF THE SPECIFIC NAMES

To utilize with greater accuracy the evidence afforded by English names, we shall now examine the occurrences of the individual names. As an aid to comparisons, the American occurrences of names are expressed in terms of the numbers of English families to which they are appropriate. These figures are computed by application of English ratios to the number of bearers among heads of families in an American record. By dividing the number of American family entries[6] by the number of such entries per thousand English, one arrives at a modified factor of recurrence which, since it is derived from a ratio per thousand, is to be read in thousands. The number of English-American families indicated by the factor of recurrence is therefore determined simply by moving the decimal point three places to the right.

For example, Farr estimated 39,100 bearers of *Parker* in a population of 18,404,421, or original occurrence of 2.12 per thousand; the 12 American records for 1790 list 1,120 heads of families named *Parker;* dividing 1,120 by 2.12 gives a factor of recurrence of 528.3 disclosing that *Parker* prevailed in the American area at a rate natural to 528,300 English families. Essentially the same result is obtained with the approximate multiplier in Farr's Table XIX. Using the multiplier 471 in that table, the American Parkers are found to be appropriate to 527,520 English families, an estimate somewhat less accurate than that obtained by the factoring method because the multiplier 471 is the nearest whole number.

Table 9 shows the ratios of bearers of the 22 indicators in England and Wales.

---

[3] Hall, Parker & Co., Surnames, *Am. Speech*, August, 1926. Vol. I, No. 11, pp. 596–607.
[4] Our Leading Surnames, *Am. Speech*, June, 1926. Vol. I, No. 9, pp. 470–477.
[5] Surnames in -is, *Am. Speech*, April, 1927. Vol. II, No. 7, pp. 316–318.
[6] Population in terms of families averages 5.6 persons per family. (*CPG* Table 44.)

TABLE 9.—*Proportion of persons in England and Wales bearing the under-mentioned common surnames*

Anglican Surnames	Of the entire population, 1 in—	Cambrian Surnames	Of the entire population, 1 in—
Baker	422	Edwards	316
Carter	551	Evans	198
Cooper	380	James	427
Green	310	Jones	76
Hall	305	Lewis	318
Lee	523	Morgan	449
Parker	471	Morris	424
Robinson	276	Phillips	486
Turner	327	Price	486
Ward	402	Roberts	235
		Thomas	196
		Williams	115

Table 10 lists the absolute and relative occurrences of both Class I and Class II names in England and Wales in 1853, and in the American area of record in 1790, the names in each class arrayed according to the size of English-American population which their numbers denote. The same process of calculation is applied later to obtain measures of recurrence for separate parts of the American area, particularly the individual States.

TABLE 10.—*Absolute and relative occurrence of leading English surnames in England and Wales in 1853 and the American area of record in 1790*

Surname	Bearers in England and Wales, 1853 [1]	Number per 1,000 England and Wales, 1853	Number of listings in 12 censuses United States of America, 1790 [2]	Number of English families to which the American occurrence is natural [3]
CLASS I				
Parker	39, 100	2. 12	1, 120	528, 300
Baker	43, 600	2. 37	1, 157	488, 190
Hall	60, 400	3. 28	1, 484	452, 440
Carter	33, 400	1. 81	669	369, 610
Green	59, 400	3. 23	1, 124	347, 990
Lee	35, 200	1. 91	653	341, 880
Ward	45, 700	2. 48	700	282, 260
Turner	56, 300	3. 06	759	248, 040
Cooper	48, 400	2. 63	574	218, 250
Robinson	66, 700	3. 62	780	215, 470
CLASS II				
Lewis	58, 000	3. 15	1, 149	379, 050
Phillips	37, 900	2. 06	560	271, 840
Williams	159, 900	8. 69	2, 257	259, 720
Morgan	41, 000	2. 23	568	254, 720
Price	37, 900	2. 06	466	226, 210
Thomas	94, 000	5. 11	1, 147	224, 460
Morris	43, 400	2. 36	492	208, 470
Jones	242, 100	13. 15	2, 610	198, 480
James	43, 100	2. 34	421	179, 910
Roberts	78, 400	4. 26	763	179, 110
Edwards	58, 100	3. 16	543	171, 840
Evans	93, 000	5. 05	[4] 572	113, 270

[1] In a population of 18,404,421.
[2] Heads of families indexed in a record of 451,120 families.
[3] These values for total English representation are obtained from the ratios of the occurrences in column 3 (United States) to those in column 2 (England and Wales).
[4] In the instance of this name, there is an adjustment for misspellings which slightly increases the total of listings.

DIVERGENCE OF THE RECURRENCE MEASURES IN THE COUNTRY AS A WHOLE

Interpretation of factors for specific names tests the relative representation in an American area by English standards of companionship. Perfect reflection of English nomenclature in an area would show the same factor for all of Farr's names; the more divergent the factors, the more distorted the reflection. Since there are several different measures for the size of the English-American element intermingled with others in the American area, it is necessary to determine which measure is the best.

Comparison of the factors for specific names offers evidence on the irregularities in the transmittal of names not obtained in the simplified calculation. It illuminates though it does not necessarily solve the problem of distinguishing these irregularities from modifications of usage by favor and by the complications of non-English usage. This leads to the important question of what measures of occurence shall be considered typical.

Anglican names show much divergence in readings. Contrast *Parker* and *Robinson*, whose American occurrences were respectively at rates indicating 528,300 and 215,470 English families in the United States, the other selected names of Class I ranging between these extremes. Figures so divergent make it difficult to determine the plane of English representation toward which they tend. A median of 344,930 is obtained by arranging the names in order of their strength, as shown in Table 10, and ascertaining a measurement halfway between that of *Green*, lowest of the top five, and that of *Lee*, highest of the bottom five. Another average would be gained by simply totaling the readings and dividing by 10. This is not done because the study carried to the separate states discloses it an ineffective process. In obtaining arithmetic means it becomes the policy to eliminate the highest and lowest names and average the others, giving in this instance a mean of 343,580. The conformity of these two averages is an indication that had the Anglican rate applied to all English the stock would have been represented by 344,000 families.

Cambrian names also show a wide range of readings, spreading from the recurrence of *Lewis*, at a rate indicating 379,050 English families, to that of *Evans*, at a rate indicating 113,270. The 12 readings show a median of 216,460; and eliminating *Lewis* and *Evans*, as of abnormal high and low usage respectively, results in an arithmetic mean of 217,480. Contrast this approximate 217,000 families indicated by the Cambrians with the 344,000 indicated by the Anglicans.

RECURRENCES IN NEW ENGLAND CONTRASTED WITH THOSE IN THE REMAINING AREA OF RECORD

Further examination of the American records reveals that divergent national measurements are mainly chargeable to New England, yet stressing that distinction is modified by observation of conditions in New York as much like those in New England as like those in the States southward. Dividing the country into two parts shows measures of recurrence in the area other than New England in much better conformity than in the country as a whole, reminding one of the concept of reflected frequencies. Separate State records show that certain circumstances produced conformity of rates of recurrence, while other conditions whose nature is yet to be learned resulted in divergence.

Interpretation of New England origins is confused by the discrepancy between the large number of English-looking names and the low ratios for leading English names. That familiar English surnames were not nearly so widely used in New England as might be expected in a population commonly thought 90 per cent English is established by preliminary recurrence tests of Farr's names, showing that English did not exceed 81 per cent in any New England State and had an average much lower than that in the States in this region, on the whole constituting not more than 75 per cent of New England population. In contrast, percentages estimated by CPG analysts on the basis of superficial character of name forms are as follows: Maine, 93; New Hampshire, 94; Vermont and Massachusetts, 95; Rhode Island and Connecticut, 96.

It is unlikely that extended inquiry with more names available as indicators would reveal an English contribution of more than 75 per cent. Of the 173,130 families listed [1] in the census of 1790 for New England, 90 per cent is 155,820; and of the 22 indicators, only 5 showed occurrence appropriate to English population of this size. (See Table 11.) Yet three names had higher ratios than in the motherland, though not necessarily higher than in specific parts of England; *Parker* on a scale natural to 275,000 families, *Hall* to 248,170, and *Baker* to 208,440. Two other names had frequencies closely appropriate to 90 per cent: *Green*, with a rate natural to 156,350, and *Lewis* to 155,560. Only three other names—*Carter, Lee, Phillips*—had recurrences even fairly appropriate to 90 per cent.

High ratios of such names as *Parker, Hall,* and *Baker* were due largely to low Cambrian representation. (Table 7.) Had there been no Cambrians in New England, Anglican names would have tended to prevail in ratios eleven-ninths of those natural to England as a whole. But Cambrian representation being half the relative proportion which perfect English sampling would have given, Anglicans showed ratios one-ninth more than Farr records.

Since, therefore, the low average ratio of currency of leading English names is assured, the problem of how the comparatively small number of their bearers could have been accompanied by so many others with apparently English names resolves itself into the conclusion that names labeled English by CPG analysts were English in form only, their evident English characteristics explained by Anglicization, using the word broadly to convey both original extended usage and acquired usage in English-speaking America.

Three types of Anglicization influenced New England nomenclature. Many names commonly called English had early British by-usage, particularly in lowland Scotland and in Ulster and Leinster in Ireland. Others were the replacements of non-English appellations, adapted to the dominant nomenclature, in consequence of the heterogeneity and irregularity of settlement of non-English which made it difficult to preserve European standards. Still other names are thought to have arisen through the seafaring activities of New Englanders who kept contact with various parts of Europe, with the fishing banks and with the West Indies, continually taking new men into service from different ports. The nationalities of these men and the names they acquired on shipboard are not studied here, but that many New England settlers gained their names and their knowledge of English at sea is a fair inference from the irregularities of local nomenclature showing crude imitation of English patterns.

The process of Anglicization was peculiar in that it seems to have favored English-looking forms rather than English names. Anglicization usually implies not only development of new names on English patterns, but voluntary usage of English names: some names remodeled, others first experimented with and then shortly standardized in simple forms, and others replaced directly by more familiar ones. But the 1790 records for New England do not show any marked standardization, and this inclination toward diversified nomenclature bears on the low ratio of familiar English names.

---

[1] As shown by the alphabetic indexes.

Divergence of recurrence measures caused by regional origins of the English has been discussed; disparity between measures of currency for Anglican and Cambrian names indicates marked difference in the rate of migration from Wales and southwest England and that from the remainder of the country; but that the home area was not limited is shown by the considerable variation in representation of different names in the several New England States. Determination of regional origins by study of recurrences is prevented by the fact that the indicative Anglican names had original bearers in many English counties, but did not have identical distribution in the motherland, and consequently were irregularly affected by varying local rates of migration that gave certain names unusual representation. Thus *Parker*, *Hall*, and *Baker* gained good representation in most of the migration to New England, while *Robinson*, *Turner*, and *Cooper* seldom accompanied them. But although *Parker* had the highest measure of recurrence in the area as a whole, *Green* had a relative representation four times as great in Rhode Island, and *Hall* more than twice as great in Connecticut. (See Table 13.) Weaknesses showed even more irregularity. *Cooper*, least represented Anglican name in New England as a whole, was also least familiar locally in three States. But *Lee* was subnormal in Maine, *Turner* in New Hampshire, and *Carter* in Rhode Island. Among Cambrian names there was also decided variation in representation. *Lewis* (see Table 12) had the greatest measure of recurrence in four States, but *Roberts* the greatest in New Hampshire, and *Phillips* in Massachusetts and Connecticut. All this points to even but nevertheless diversified streams of English migration to the several parts of New England.

Quantity and timing of migration also influenced measures of representation. About 5,000 families reached New England before the Puritan period in England, when political changes turned the English migration largely to other parts of the new world. And while infiltration during the last half of the seventeenth century may have been steady enough to account for considerable numbers of persons who were in the area in 1790, the ultimate New England nomenclature was strongly affected by the name patterns in the great single wave of immigration in the 1630's and 1640's. Many English names, such as *Sawyer* and *Libby*, obtained good currency in New England, even though they were uncommon if not rare in the motherland. All of the names which found representation in the movement were more or less influenced by rates of reproduction of their bearers, thus partly accounting for divergent recurrence measures of companion names in New England. Leading English names, therefore, failed to attain in New England those impartial measures of currency which they developed in the parts of the country not dominated by the Puritans.

Table 11 presents the abnormal conditions in New England in contrast to the better conformity obtaining in the remaining area of record, for both Class I and Class II names. The upper half of the table shows that dispersion of the measures of recurrence of Anglican names was much greater in New England than in the remaining area of record. It shows that *Parker*, with the highest representation in New England, prevailed on a scale suitable to an English population more than five times that indicated by *Cooper* with the lowest representation; and great spread also between *Hall*, second highest, and *Turner*, second lowest. But in the remaining area of record it shows that *Baker*, highest, prevailed on a scale not quite three times that of *Robinson*, lowest; and the spread between *Parker* and *Turner*, respectively, second from top and bottom in this column, was correspondingly less.

The lower half of Table 11 shows that Cambrian names also had a wide range in scale of recurrence in New England, despite the fact that they were drawn from a limited area in England and Wales. But dispersion was much less in the remaining area of record. *Lewis* and *Evans* were respectively the high and low names in both parts of the country, but the rate of prevalence of *Lewis* in New England was over seven times that of *Evans*, while in the remaining area it was only a little more than twice as great.

TABLE 11.—*English population indicated by the recurrences of specified names in New England and the remaining area of record*

[Population stated in terms of families]

New England		Remaining Area of Record	
Surnames	English population indicated by the recurrence of name	Surnames	English population indicated by the recurrence of name
Class I			
Parker	(275, 000)	Baker	(279, 750)
Hall	248, 170	Parker	253, 300
Baker	208, 440	Carter	237, 010
Green	156, 350	Lee	214, 650
Carter	132, 600	Hall	204, 270
Lee	127, 230	Green	191, 640
Ward	103, 630	Ward	178, 630
Robinson	98, 900	Cooper	171, 480
Turner	91, 500	Turner	156, 540
Cooper	(46, 770)	Robinson	(116, 570)
Average after parentheses.[1]	145, 850	Average after parentheses.[1]	200, 940
Median	129, 920	Median	197, 960
Class II			
Lewis	(155, 560)	Lewis	(223, 490)
Phillips	121, 840	Price	203, 390
Morgan	89, 240	Morris	177, 110
Williams	84, 000	Williams	175, 720
Thomas	68, 690	Morgan	165, 470
Jones	56, 050	Thomas	155, 770
Roberts	55, 630	Phillips	150, 000
Edwards	40, 510	Jones	142, 430
James	38, 890	James	141, 020
Morris	31, 360	Edwards	131, 330
Price	22, 820	Roberts	123, 480
Evans	(22, 770)	Evans	(90, 500)
Average after parentheses.[1]	60, 900	Average after parentheses.[1]	156, 570
Median	55, 840	Median	152, 880

[1] Arithmetic average (mean) after exclusions marked by parentheses.

RECURRENCE OF NAMES AS SOCIAL PHENOMENA

Reflected nomenclatural frequencies in a colony obtain only when numbers and uniformity or variability of migration afford random sampling. Whether frequency patterns have been reproduced is determined by comparing factors of recurrence. The closer the conformity of factors the more probable is it that these factors offer evidence of migration rates little disguised by voluntary usage of names. Certain is it that this conformity denotes representative Old World sampling.

Detailed examination of recurrences of the selected English names discloses areas where their currencies were clearly reflective of Old World patterns. It discloses other areas where dispersion of factors of recurrence demands critical examination.

Discordant measures of recurrence do not necessarily point to irregularities in migration, for high frequency may be the result of voluntary use and low frequency of voluntary disuse. The former is more susceptible to proof than the latter and also a more likely development in the instance of dominant English names.

The data at hand on English names afford just enough evidence of preferential use to enable the designation, by contrast, of irregularities probably due to limited or erratic migration. The influence of variability of migrations, annual quantities, and geographical and social controls can not be identified here; but calculation based on a greater number of names—particularly those of less extensive original distribution—together with studies of periods prior to 1790, might reveal much about the special features of migration. At present we can at least determine what part of the American area was peopled by representative English migration, and what part was peopled by migration which brought large numbers of certain names to the disadvantage of others.

Comparison of measures of recurrence is important for modifying estimates of the maximum proportions of English in the American area of record, but still more important in that it affords actual illustrations of reflected frequencies, offering convincing proof that frequencies of common names are not accidental but spring from well differentiated causes, presenting measures of recurrence which advance the formulation of principles for orderly study of comparative nomenclature, and throwing light on the antecedents and attitudes of the American people.

In surveying occurrences as social phenomena, it is noted that Cambrian names were from a more definite area of the motherland and that their recurrences, in consequence, were not so likely to be influenced by regional conditions as were those of Anglican names. But surname nomenclature developed more slowly in Wales than in England and it is probable that many Welsh did not have true surnames, particularly in the early days of their migration.

Farr[8] remarks this feature of Welsh nomenclature:

In Wales, however, the surnames if *surnames* they can be called, do not present the same variety, most of them having been formed in a simple manner from the Christian or forename of the father in the genitive case, a *son* being understood. Thus Evan's son became *Evans;* John's son, *Jones,* etc. Others were derived from the father's name coalesced with a form of the word *ap* or *hab* (son of), by which Hugh ap Howell became *Powell,* Evan ap Hugh became *Pugh,* and in like manner were formed nearly all the Welsh surnames beginning with the letters "B" and "P." Hereditary surnames were not in use even amongst the gentry of Wales until the time of Henry VIII, nor were they generally established until a much later period; indeed, at the present day they can scarcely be said to be adopted amongst the lower classes in the wilder districts, where, as the marriage registers show, the Christian name of the father still frequently becomes the patronymic of the son in the manner just described.

Thus some of the Welsh did not transmit their names to their sons and grandsons. But while Welsh nomenclature was not settled in the eighteenth century, its coordination with a fixed system of given names maintained practically the same scheme of nomenclature from one generation to the other, even though individuals did not inherit names as the surname system con-

---

[8] P. XVII.

templates; and the relative usage of the different family names remained fairly constant and in definite ratio because drawn from a limited selection of given names whose choice was fixed by custom. What change there was in this nomenclature can be described as a rotation rather than a trend. For this study of social phonomena, therefore, the advantage of the Cambrian names in being from a fairly limited area of the motherland is only partly offset by the disadvantage of this patronymic feature.

RECURRENCES OF CAMBRIAN NAMES IN THE SEPARATE STATES

Table 12 shows measures of occurrence of Cambrian names in the several States of record, beginning in the south where conditions most reflected those abroad.

In the area from South Carolina to Pennsylvania the ideal of reflected frequency was almost realized. South Carolina is characteristic in showing the more commonly used names prevailing at rates only moderately higher than those less commonly used. Eliminating *Morgan* and *Phillips* *as* having the highest and lowest relative measures of occurrence, the remaining measures are in good conformity. The readings which may be considered normal to the class ranged from that of *Williams* on a scale natural to 17,000 English families down to *Evans* natural to 10,000, and the average is readily ascertained as approximately 15,000. Percentage ratings on the basis of 15,000 as 100 per cent bring out the conformity of recurrences: *Morgan* 128, *Williams* 113, *Roberts* 112, *Lewis* 110, *James* 105, *Morris* 101, *Jones* 99, *Edwards* 95, *Thomas* 94, *Price* 94, *Evans* 68, *Phillips* 48.

The definite reflection of frequency in this area offers convincing evidence that currencies of names are functionally related to conditions in the motherland. Inasmuch as this reproduction of Cambrian nomenclature denotes a connection extending over more than two centuries—since migration began early in the seventeenth and Farr's analysis was made after the middle of the nineteenth—the similarity of rankings is impressive. The evidence, therefore, is that notwithstanding Welsh changing of patronymics, a fairly constant use of comparatively inflexible patterns persisted both in the motherland and in America over this long period. This goes far to answer Farr's query, raised after his tabulation was prepared, " Do these common names hold the same rank in point of numbers which they had at first, or have some of them spread and multiplied more rapidly than others? "

It does not follow, however, that a like reproduction of Old World standards marked American usage in the north. From New York through New England dispersion of readings indicates complicating variables, such as irregularities in migration or deviation from European standards of spelling or from Welsh standards in choice of patronymics, and distortion accompanying this dispersion makes it difficult to determine proper averages of the measures of relative currency.

In New York the system of establishing an arithmetic mean by discarding the highest and lowest names gives an arithmetic mean of 18,840 English families, a figure appreciably higher than the median of 16,000. This is a significant discrepancy.

In New England there was an irregularity in the reproduction of ratios even greater than in New York, the frequencies of names being so disturbed as to confuse the understanding of their interrelations. Although in New York, *Phillips* with the highest currency that may be considered normal prevailed on a plane only a little more than four times that of *James*, the corresponding low name; in Connecticut, *Morgan*, the highest normal name, had a measure seven times that of *Price*, the lowest.

However, since names of the Cambrian class in five States show comparatively good conformity in measures of recurrence and give significant averages, we can approximate from averages of the measures of recurrence in the other States the measures of the English-American populations involved.

TABLE 12.—*Recurrence of Cambrian names in specified States*

[Indicated population stated in terms of families]

SOUTH CAROLINA

Name	English population indicated by the recurrence of the name	Name	English population indicated by the recurrence of the name
Morgan	(19, 280)	Thomas	14, 090
Williams	17, 030	Price	14, 080
Roberts	16, 900	Evans	10, 300
Lewis	16, 510	Phillips	(7, 280)
James	15, 810		
Morris	15, 250	Average after parentheses.	14, 900
Jones	14, 830		
Edwards	14, 240	Median	15, 040

NORTH CAROLINA

Williams	(61, 450)	Phillips	33, 010
Lewis	54, 290	Thomas	27, 590
Price	53, 880	Roberts	25, 350
Morgan	52, 910	Evans	(17, 030)
Morris	51, 270		
Jones	43, 350	Average after parentheses.	42, 360
Edwards	41, 770		
James	40, 170	Median	42, 560

VIRGINIA

Lewis	(40, 320)	Phillips	24, 270
Price	32, 040	Morgan	22, 420
Edwards	31, 330	Roberts	18, 780
James	28, 630	Evans	(13, 070)
Morris	27, 970		
Jones	27, 300	Average after parentheses.	26, 470
Williams	26, 350		
Thomas	25, 640	Median	26, 820

MARYLAND

Price	(56, 800)	Roberts	13, 850
Thomas	28, 770	Evans	12, 670
Williams	19, 560	Phillips	11, 170
Morris	19, 070	Edwards	(8, 230)
Jones	18, 480		
Morgan	17, 940	Average after parentheses.	17, 420
James	17, 090		
Lewis	15, 560	Median	17, 520

TABLE 12.—*Recurrence of Cambrian names in specified States*—Continued

[Indicated population stated in terms of families

PENNSYLVANIA

Name	English population indicated by the recurrence of the name	Name	English population indicated by the recurrence of the name
Lewis	(48, 250)	James	28, 630
Morris	46, 610	Williams	27, 500
Thomas	45, 600	Jones	22, 510
Roberts	35, 920	Edwards	(20, 890)
Phillips	32, 520		
Evans	31, 880	Average after parentheses	33, 310
Morgan	31, 390		
Price	30, 580	Median	31, 640

NEW YORK

Lewis	(48, 570)	Thomas	14, 090
Phillips	41, 750	Roberts	12, 680
Williams	23, 820	James	10, 680
Morgan	21, 520	Evans	(5, 540)
Morris	16, 950		
Price	16, 020	Average after parentheses	18, 840
Jones	15, 970		
Edwards	14, 870	Median	16, 000

CONNECTICUT

Lewis	(52, 380)	Edwards	12, 970
Morgan	41, 260	James	6, 410
Williams	26, 350	Price	5, 830
Thomas	16, 050	Evans	(3, 370)
Roberts	15, 020		
Morris	14, 410	Average after parentheses	16, 550
Phillips	14, 080		
Jones	13, 160	Median	14, 240

RHODE ISLAND

Lewis	(20, 630)	Jones	1, 520
James	11, 970	Evans	1, 190
Phillips	11, 650	Morgan	900
Williams	6, 560	Morris	(850)
Edwards	4, 430		
Thomas	3, 720	Average after parentheses	4, 820
Price	3, 400		
Roberts	2, 820	Median	3, 560

TABLE 12.—*Recurrence of Cambrian names in specified States*—Continued

MASSACHUSETTS

Name	English population indicated by the recurrence of the name	Name	English population indicated by the recurrence of the name
Phillips	(74, 760)	Morris	11, 440
Lewis	49, 840	Price	11, 170
Williams	34, 520	Roberts	8, 920
Morgan	31, 390	Evans	(5, 940)
Thomas	28, 380		
Jones	22, 050	Average after parentheses	22, 810
Edwards	18, 040		
James	12, 390	Median	20, 040

VERMONT

Lewis	(13, 650)	Morris	2, 120
Phillips	7, 770	James	850
Morgan	7, 170	Edwards	320
Williams	6, 330	Price	(000)
Roberts	5, 870		
Thomas	5, 480	Average after parentheses	4, 400
Jones	4, 490		
Evans	3, 560	Median	4, 980

NEW HAMPSHIRE

Roberts	(14, 790)	James	5, 130
Jones	8, 060	Edwards	2, 850
Phillips	7, 770	Price	1, 460
Lewis	7, 620	Morris	(850)
Evans	6, 930		
Morgan	6, 280	Average after parentheses	5, 830
Thomas	6, 260		
Williams	5, 980	Median	6, 270

MAINE

Lewis	(11, 430)	Edwards	1, 900
Thomas	8, 810	Evans	1, 780
Roberts	8, 220	Morris	1, 690
Jones	6, 770	Price	(970)
Phillips	5, 830		
Williams	4, 260	Average after parentheses	4, 360
Morgan	2, 240		
James	2, 140	Median	3, 250

RECURRENCES OF ANGLICAN NAMES IN THE SEPARATE STATES

Anglican names, like Cambrian, show rather good conformity in the South and divergent measures northward, but with some irregularities in the Carolinas and with the more striking irregularities beginning in Pennsylvania.

Anglican readings are generally more difficult to express in averages, but even in New England Anglican dispersion is less than Cambrian.

In Rhode Island a marked difficulty is encountered where *Green* had extra-ordinary currency and both *Hall* and *Baker* much higher prevalence than the other names. Excluding *Green*, highest, and *Carter*, lowest, the arithmetic average indicates that had all English been of the Anglican type the maximum English contribution to population would have been 8,500 families, while the median, intermediate between readings for *Robinson* and *Lee*, indicates a maximum of only 5,500, a discrepancy perhaps attributable to the small population of Rhode Island, which scarcely permits valid measurement of rates of recurrence.

North Carolina shows that American usage of Anglican names was not entirely chargeable to English heredity, several names occurring there in higher ratio than normal in England. The index of the 1790 census shows 52,560 families in North Carolina, but the names from *Parker* to *Hall* in Table 13 point to even greater English-American numbers and possibly indicate that the State's population was largely drawn from parts of England where these names were particularly common. This only partly explains the situation, however, for the apparent recurrences of these names did not greatly exceed those of the other Anglican names, nor even those of the Cambrian names. Occurrences of Anglican names point to a contribution of between 53,000 and 55,000 families, and those of Cambrian names to about 42,000. Interpreting these combined measures according to the relative importance of the two types of nomenclature in the motherland, the entire population of North Carolina was apparently English-American, the arithmetic mean showing that the scale of occurrence of these names was one natural to a population 98 per cent English, while the median indicates a full 100 per cent.

This striking evidence of extraordinary local usage of the leading English names leads to investigation which discloses that, far from being almost wholly English, North Carolina's population contained a substantial element with non-English names, *CPG* recognizing 17 per cent, which would mean that English stock accounted for less than 83 per cent of the population. The tendency of the *CPG* classification to understate the non-English is recognized in the report of Doctor Hill and his committee to the Secretaries of State, Commerce and Labor, February 15, 1928:

It was to be expected that whatever error there might be in this classification would be in the direction of an overstatement of the English element in the population, because that was the dominant element in most parts of the United States at that period, and for that reason the name changes would naturally be in the direction of the Anglicization of names of non-English origin. Moreover, there would be a natural and justifiable tendency on the part of the classifiers to assign to the dominant element in the population all names not clearly of other origin.

Supposing, then, that the dominant English element in North Carolina was indeed 83 per cent of the population, it is clear that the leading English names within the realms of English-American nomenclature were used disproportionately to the rarer and less common names. Non-English usage of English names did not uniformly strengthen the whole structure of English nomenclature, but emphasized certain parts of it. Consequently appraisal by the usage of common names tends to overestimation.

Hence observations of these radical conditions in North Carolina reconcile the two principles revealed, that the measures of the apparent recurrence of leading English names exaggerate the contributions of English blood,[9] while

---

[9] *How We Got Our Surnames, Am. Speech,* Oct., 1928. Vol. IV, No. 1, pp. 48–53.

the usage of non-English names minimizes the contributions of non-English stocks. The keenest discernment of non-English names touched up in letter and syllable to imitate English models still fails to identify all non-English people, because some of them acquired by adoption the most English of English names. Leading names of England had a standing in English-American nomenclature even higher than that abroad, mainly because of their preferential use by persons of other antecedents. Part of this disturbance may have come from discontinuance of old English names, resulting in internal changes in the transplanted nomenclature, but most of it arose through the adjustment of name structure to fit the requirements of a mixed people. English-American nomenclature therefore not only failed to coincide exactly with English-American population, but extended beyond it.

While this investigation of adoptive usage was occasioned here by the occurrence of certain Anglican names in North Carolina, the principles developed apply equally to the readings of Cambrian names, and the fullness of their application in other states will be considered later.

Table 13 details the measures of occurrence of Anglican names in the several States of record.

TABLE 13.—*Recurrence of Anglican names in specified States*

[Indicated population stated in terms of families]

SOUTH CAROLINA

Name	English population indicated by the recurrence of the name	Name	English population indicated by the recurrence of the name
Carter	(30, 940)	Baker	16, 030
Lee	30, 370	Hall	14, 020
Parker	25, 940	Robinson	(5, 520)
Turner	20, 260		
Cooper	20, 150	Average after parentheses	20, 260
Green	19, 200		
Ward	16, 130	Median	19, 680

NORTH CAROLINA

Parker	(95, 280)	Green	41, 490
Carter	71, 820	Cooper	39, 160
Lee	60, 210	Robinson	(13, 810)
Ward	59, 270		
Baker	55, 270	Average after parentheses	53, 280
Hall	54, 880		
Turner	44, 120	Median	55, 080

VIRGINIA

Carter	(75, 690)	Turner	28, 760
Parker	41, 510	Green	21, 360
Hall	38, 720	Cooper	(19, 010)
Baker	36, 290		
Lee	34, 550	Average after parentheses	32, 460
Ward	29, 440		
Robinson	29, 010	Median	32, 000

TABLE 13.—*Recurrence of Anglican names in specified States*—Continued

[Indicated population stated in terms of families]

MARYLAND

Name	English population indicated by the recurrence of the name	Name	English population indicated by the recurrence of the name
Baker	(40, 510)	Ward	20, 560
Hall	33, 230	Robinson	20, 440
Turner	27, 450	Cooper	(20, 150)
Green	26, 930		
Lee	25, 130	Average after parentheses	24, 800
Parker	23, 110		
Carter	21, 550	Median	24, 120

PENNSYLVANIA

Name	English population	Name	English population
Baker	(61, 600)	Carter	18, 780
Cooper	41, 060	Turner	13, 070
Parker	36, 320	Ward	(12, 900)
Hall	31, 400		
Robinson	31, 210	Average after parentheses	28, 530
Lee	30, 370		
Green	26, 010	Median	30, 790

NEW YORK

Name	English population	Name	English population
Baker	(70, 040)	Turner	22, 880
Green	56, 660	Carter	18, 230
Ward	40, 320	Robinson	(16, 570)
Lee	34, 030		
Hall	32, 010	Average after parentheses	33, 400
Cooper	31, 940		
Parker	31, 130	Median	31, 980

CONNECTICUT

Name	English population	Name	English population
Hall	(75, 300)	Green	20, 120
Lee	48, 690	Robinson	18, 510
Parker	36, 790	Cooper	(11, 410)
Carter	34, 810		
Baker	28, 690	Average after parentheses	29, 430
Ward	26, 610		
Turner	21, 240	Median	27, 650

RHODE ISLAND

Name	English population	Name	English population
Green	(33, 130)	Turner	4, 580
Hall	18, 900	Ward	3, 630
Baker	18, 140	Carter	(3, 310)
Parker	7, 080		
Robinson	5, 800	Average after parentheses	8, 540
Lee	5, 240		
Cooper	4, 940	Median	5, 520

TABLE 13.—*Recurrence of Anglican names in specified States*—Continued

[Indicated population stated in terms of families]

MASSACHUSETTS

Name	English population indicated by the recurrence of the name	Name	English population indicated by the recurrence of the name
Parker	(131, 130)	Turner	43, 140
Baker	109, 280	Robinson	36, 190
Hall	75, 610	Cooper	(15, 970)
Green	62, 230		
Carter	51, 930	Average after parentheses	59, 550
Lee	51, 830		
Ward	49, 190	Median	51, 880

VERMONT

Parker	(33, 020)	Turner	7, 520
Hall	21, 340	Ward	6, 850
Baker	18, 990	Cooper	(2, 280)
Robinson	14, 360		
Green	12, 690	Average after parentheses	12, 670
Lee	12, 570		
Carter	7, 730	Median	12, 630

NEW HAMPSHIRE

Parker	(44, 810)	Cooper	7, 600
Hall	37, 800	Lee	5, 760
Carter	22, 100	Turner	(5, 560)
Green	18, 890		
Baker	16, 880	Average after parentheses	16, 420
Robinson	11, 880		
Ward	10, 480	Median	14, 380

MAINE

Parker	(22, 170)	Ward	6, 850
Hall	19, 210	Cooper	4, 560
Baker	16, 460	Lee	(3, 140)
Carter	12, 710		
Robinson	12, 150	Average after parentheses	11, 340
Turner	9, 480		
Green	9, 290	Median	10, 820

INFLUENCE OF REGIONAL MIGRATION

Examination of occurrences of Anglican and Cambrian names separately draws attention to the influence of regional migration on the currency of names, for had the two classes been considered as one, a wide range of measures of recurrence would have been strikingly apparent. This classification by type accounts for much of the dispersion of factors and practically amounts to a differentiation of geographical origin, suggesting that a greater number of names—particularly those of various restricted geographical origins—would secure additional evidence of the difference in rates of migration from different parts of England and Wales.

Had there been no regional or factional migration of English and no disturbance of the recurrences of the leading English names, column 3 in Table 7 would show a constant ratio of 22.2 per cent, the proportion of 2 Cambrians to 9 Anglicans. But the much lower figures shown for every State except Pennsylvania indicate a disproportionate drift of Anglicans to America. Only in Pennsylvania did the Cambrian type contribute its expected proportion to the stream of English immigrants. Cambrian under-representation elsewhere indicates that ordinarily the Cambrian faction was only about two-thirds as much inclined to move as was the Anglican faction; but since the Cambrians were largely concentrated in Wales and some half dozen near-by English counties, here is evidence of regional migration also. Evidently the urge to migration in Wales and the southwest was less strong than in the rest of the country.

In the States from Pennsylvania southward, where the best conformity of factors in the two classes obtained, there was also rather close similarity in the measures of English representation of each class; so that separation into the two classes adds little information on English content of population in that region. But without it very low measures of English representation would be derived for New York and New England. For this area we must be on our guard against overemphasizing the low recurrence of Cambrian names.

AVERAGING THE MEASURES OF RECURRENCE OF NAMES AS CLASSIFIED

Though certain expressions may be construed as typical of class measurements, subject to recognition of the bias introduced by non-English usage, there still remains a further step in averaging before maximum English contributions are appraised. To complete the statement of averages of indicated contributions to the States of record, comparisons will be made between the results by classes according to the three methods used and then the basis of combination or weighting will be critically examined.

Besides the arithmetic means and the medians obtained in the detailed examination of recurrences, averages have been obtained by simplified calculation. This, it should now be noted, gives results which are weighted arithmetic means. The arithmetic means subsequently determined are of the uniform weight type commonly called " simple averages." These three types of averages are now to be contrasted.

From the purely statistical standpoint, median measurements are more nearly typical and probably convey more accurately the measures of the origins revealed in the classes of names, but they have certain disadvantages in demonstration not shared by arithmetic means. "Average" as ordinarily used signifies "arithmetic mean." Recurrences of individual names indicate that arithmetic means are unduly biased if derived from the measures of recurrence of all names in the classes, since there is usually some lack of symmetry in the arrangement of factors; but the simple process of discarding the highest and lowest factor in each class, for each area, enables us to determine typical recurrences as arithmetic means.

Even though the simplified calculation took advantage of detail in the specification of names to be considered normal it produced means which the statistician will recognize as reacting strongly to exceptional readings within class groupings. Its advantage of achieving results at a stroke is, therefore, offset by susceptibility to distortion. The arithmetic means subsequently determined are more dependable because their calculation treats all the names except the extremes as uniformly valid indicators.

Final summaries will contrast results from the three forms of average. For the sake of continuity, simplified and detailed calculations will be distinguished, and the two types of arithmetic means will be recognized by reference to the calculation, the term "arithmetic mean" being used solely in connection with the latter calculation.

Compilation of these figures shows that each method gives a somewhat different result when estimates are made for the separate States and added together than when directly obtained for larger areas. Results from simplified and detailed calculation of arithmetic means are closely similar, but results from medians tend to lower estimates of English content in the population and also show greater discrepancy between estimates by direct calculation for larger areas and those by total of estimates for the separate States.

In addition to obtaining average recurrences of Anglican and Cambrian names by classes by one or the other of the methods just compared, it is necessary to make one more step in averaging before estimates of maximum contributions of English stock as a whole are obtained. This is the combining of Anglican and Cambrian readings heretofore spoken of as weighting and accomplished in 9-and-2 ratio which gives Anglican names four and a half times the significance of Cambrian names.

As Cambrian names were less commonly used, final measurements of maximum English representation would be considerably changed by alteration of this weighting; increased weighting would reduce estimates for English, particularly in the north, where *Jones* and its companions were much less common than *Parker* and its companions. Arguments may be advanced both for higher and lower weighting, those for the former being possibly stronger.

No good reason appears against the 2-in-11 weighting as unduly emphasizing Cambrian names, except that their American usage attained an average of only 14 per cent relative to Anglican names, instead of 22 per cent. This may be thought to indicate that English population did not contain Cambrians in the ratio calculated. It has been seen that New England was chiefly responsible for the low recurrence measure for Welsh names; since historians agree that New Englanders originated mainly in eastern parts of England, while Cambrians were concentrated in the west and southwest, the latter would naturally be meagerly represented in the New England area.

Bearers of the 22 names available as indicators in Farr's list collectively constituted 8 per cent of English in the population, in which the 12 Cambrian names had much greater importance, their bearers constituting 5.36 per cent of Farr's population, while the 10 Anglican constituted but 2.65 per cent. Outstanding Cambrian names also had a greater original average frequency, 0.447 per cent, as against Anglican 0.265 per cent of the population of England. Guppy's data on distribution disclose early representation of Cambrians both in east coast and north midland counties as well as in southern and midland England, 7 of the 12 indicators having significant frequencies in over half of the county units.

These may all be strong reasons for thinking Anglican nomenclature not originally four and a half times as extensively used as Cambrian, and that a 2-in-11 allowance for Cambrian stock is insufficient.

But the 2-and-9 weighting deduced from Guppy's data on prevalence originally concentrated in or near Wales is coordinate with information on the population of the English counties in the eighteenth century.

The English census of 1841 [10] shows the estimated population of England and Wales by counties in 1630, 1670, and 1700, and the application of Guppy's percentages to these estimates or to their average confirms the observation that

---

[10] Introduction, pp. 36, 37.

people with Cambrian nomenclature originally constituted approximately two-elevenths of the population of the dual domain. Differences in ratios obtained for different periods are partly explained by the shifting of population. During the eighteenth and nineteenth centuries a continual increase in regions becoming industrial centers caused declining ratios in Wales and near-by English counties. Emigration was greater from other areas than from the Cambrian territory, and it is probable that the relative importance of this nomenclature in the motherland is somewhat greater now than in the eighteenth century. Variations considered, it seems that its ratio to the total population during the period of emigration prior to 1790 is satisfactorily calculated as two-elevenths, or 18.2 per cent.

CONTENT OF INDEXES

Alphabetic indexes prepared in late years furnish the data used in this study concerning the. numbers of families bearing the indicator names. On the basis of the totals in these are computed the ratios of indicated numbers of English families which determine maximum English contributions to population.

Differences between several totals for population are to be noted. Table 14 compares (1) the count of names of family heads covered by alphabetic indexes, (2) the number of families classified by *CPG* analysts, and (3) the census totals as originally tabulated, reference being to recapitulations in the introductions to index volumes. The alphabetic indexes on which the present study is based are found at the back of the index volumes. The total number of families alphabetically indexed was 451,120, of which 173,130 were in New England and 277,990 in the remaining area of record.

The number of recognized entries for a particular name and the total number for all names in a record are defined as noted in the footnotes to this table. In most instances, the listings indexed agree closely with census figures and doubtless present an accurate picture of name usages of the people. But the alphabetic list for North Carolina shows several thousand more heads of families than were available to the *CPG* analysts, names from tax lists seeming to have been added since that tabulation. Also the record for Virginia, derived from tax lists of the decade prior to 1790, covered only about half as many people as the population of that State in the year of the First Census.

TABLE 14.—*Schedule of the number of families covered by the alphabetic indexes classified by name in A Century of Population Growth and accounted for by tabulations of local population*

	Alphabetic index actually covers [1]	Families classified by name CPG [2]	Total families pp. 9–10, indexes
Maine	17, 020	16, 972	17, 098
New Mampshire	24, 090	23, 982	24, 080
Vermont	14, 970	14, 969	14, 983
Massachusetts	65, 230	65, 149	65, 779
Rhode Island	11, 140	10, 854	11, 306
Connecticut	40, 680	40, 457	40, 878
New York	54, 540	54, 190	54, 884
Pennsylvania	74, 510	73, 323	72, 371
Maryland	32, 690	32, 012	33, 554
Virginia [3]	37, 710	38, 245	(4)
North Carolina	52, 560	48, 021	57, 827
South Carolina	25, 980	25, 552	26, 185

[1] Heads of families other than those shown by given names only, inserted only for cross reference, or marked Indian, Negro, mulatto, black, darky, free, minor, or abbreviations thereof (as F. M. and F. N.).
[2] C. P. G., Table 44.
[3] Partial record from tax lists; data incomplete.
[4] Not set forth.

ESTIMATED ENGLISH CONTRIBUTIONS TO STATE POPULATIONS

Estimates by arithmetic means and by medians, for apparent percentages of English in the states separately, in New England, in the remaining area of record, and in the total area of record, are shown in Table 15.

The course of each method of calculation is well illustrated in the figures for Maine. Arithmetic averaging for Maine has indicated 11,340[11] English families if the whole stock were represented in ratio to bearers of leading Anglican names, and 4,360[12] if of leading Cambrian names. Nine-elevenths of the first figure and two-elevenths of the second give, respectively, 9,280 Anglicans and 790 Cambrians, a total of 10,070 English families in Maine. Medians have indicated 10,820 English families in Maine if the whole stock were represented in ratio to bearers of leading Anglican names, and 3,250 if of leading Cambrian names. Nine-elevenths of the first figure and two-elevenths of the second give, respectively, 8,850 Anglicans and 590 Cambrians, a total of 9,440 English families in Maine.

Comparison of these two totals discloses both the strength and weakness of the methods of calculation. Table 15 contrasts the maxima of the two processes in columns 1 and 2 with the totals of families indexed in column 3, and lists the percentages of population obtained by each method in columns 4 and 5. But since separate measures for the Anglican and Cambrian classifications are not shown in this table, it is important to note that most of the divergence in the indicated measures of English stock is traceable to that in the indicated measures of Anglican stock. Attention has already been called to the remarkable percentage for English in North Carolina, noted in this table, and how it illustrates adoptive and other nomenclatural influences.

TABLE 15.—*Estimates of maximum percentages of English in population obtained from the numbers of families indicated by the recurrences of leading English names*

	Estimated maxima for numbers of English families obtained as—		Total families indexed	Percentages derived for maximum contributions of English to population	
	Arithmetic means	Medians		Arithmetic means	Medians
Maine	10,070	9,440	17,020	59.2	55.5
New Hampshire	14,490	12,840	24,090	60.1	53.3
Vermont	11,240	11,240	14,970	75.1	75.1
Massachusetts	52,870	46,090	65,230	81.1	70.7
Rhode Island	7,870	5,170	11,140	70.6	46.4
Connecticut	27,090	25,210	40,680	66.6	62.0
New York	30,760	29,080	54,540	56.4	53.3
Pennsylvania	29,390	30,940	74,510	39.4	41.5
Maryland	23,460	22,920	32,690	71.8	70.1
Virginia	31,370	31,060	37,710	83.2	82.4
North Carolina	51,290	52,810	52,560	97.6	100.5
South Carolina	19,290	18,830	25,980	74.2	72.5
By addition:					
New England	123,630	109,990	173,130	71.4	63.5
Remaining area of record	185,560	185,640	277,990	66.8	66.8
Area of record	309,190	295,630	451,120	68.5	65.5
By direct calculation:					
New England	130,400	116,450	173,130	75.3	67.3
Remaining area of record	192,880	189,770	277,990	69.4	68.3
Area of record	320,650	321,580	451,120	71.1	71.3
By calculation and addition, area of record	323,280	306,220	451,120	71.7	67.9

[11] Table 13.
[12] Table 12.

COMPARISON OF ESTIMATES OF ENGLISH CONTRIBUTIONS

Table 16 compares maximum English contributions in the several States, in New England, in the remaining area of record, and in the whole area of record, by percentages derived through the three processes of interpretation—simplified calculation, arithmetic means, medians.

The simplified calculation for the area of record and for its principal parts by addition has not heretofore been shown. This table now shows results of adding estimated maxima for the several States, as well as calculation of maxima for the larger areas direct from recurrence of names in their records.

Results from simplified calculation are very like those obtained from arithmetic means, some differences being occasioned by the fact that the former method does not treat all names as uniformly valid indicators. Results from medians are ordinarily lower, with rather poor internal coordination.

TABLE 16.—*Percentages derived for maximum contributions of English to population of specified areas of the United States in 1790 by three processes of averaging measures of recurrence of leading English names*

| | Simplified calculation | Detailed calculations | |
		Arithmetic means	Medians
Maine	60. 4	59. 2	55. 5
New Hampshire	63. 0	60. 1	53. 3
Vermont	77. 5	75. 1	75. 1
Massachusetts	81. 0	81. 1	70. 7
Rhode Island	70. 4	70. 6	46. 4
Connecticut	62. 7	66. 6	62. 0
New York	57. 7	56. 4	53. 3
Pennsylvania	38. 8	39. 4	41. 5
Maryland	73. 0	71. 4	70. 1
Virginia	81. 8	83. 2	82. 4
North Carolina	94. 8	97. 6	100. 5
South Carolina	72. 3	74. 2	72. 5
By additon:			
New England	71. 2	71. 4	63. 5
Remaining area of record	66. 1	66. 8	66. 8
Area of record	68. 0	68. 5	65. 5
By direct calculation:			
New England	75. 9	75. 3	67. 3
Remaining area of record	68. 0	69. 4	68. 3
Area of record	70. 9	71. 1	71. 3
By calculation and addition; Area of record	71. 0	71. 7	67. 9

CRITICISM OF READINGS

Anticipation that the study of relative usage of leading English names would gage the maximum English in the separate States and in the larger areas of record is defeated by finding these measurements only roughly approximate. The figures obtained by the several methods of calculation differ and also fail to show coordination when summarized, figures for the larger areas invariably giving higher ratings by direct calculation than by totaling calculations for the separate States.

Discrepancies are due mainly to the ups and downs of specific names in local records; some variations may be traced to geographical background, some to local preference, a number to varying degrees of non-English usage, and others probably to the fluctuations of family fortunes.

It is more difficult to make sound estimates for the smaller States, those for Rhode Island, Maine, New Hampshire, and Vermont particularly being derived from comparatively small numbers of listings related to no very large populations. It is questioned, indeed, whether any State had a population large enough completely to free recurrences from the influence of specific families. Even in the more populous States the numbers of bearers of specific names reflect variation in rates of reproduction of families, as, for example, *Price* in Maryland and *Carter* in Virginia.

" Estimated maxima " for English contributions are so designated because they are derived from currency measures of names not used solely by the English. Attention is again drawn to the striking example of North Carolina, the rate of currency there indicating the whole population English despite the manifestly non-English names of a large percentage, and demonstrating not only a simplification of nomenclature which increased the familiarity of familiar names, but also non-English usage of English names in substantial proportions. The currency of Farr's names in North Carolina overstates the State's actual English element by at least 20 per cent, for appraisal of overstatement is coordinated with *CPG* classification of 17 per cent usage of various names there as non-English, and as the non-English must have been greater than that disclosed in *CPG*, the local discount applicable to the readings of Farr's names must be more than 17 per cent. Though this measurement is not held valid for other States, it does point to the progressive advantages of the leading English names. Since the pattern of English-American names was essentially the same in all the States from Pennsylvania southward, marked overstatement in North Carolina predicates a like exaggeration in this whole middle and southern region.

How closely the indicated English contributions derived from averages of recurrences conformed to actual numbers of English in the other States of record—New York, and those in New England—can not be determined, since in that area there was both more irregularity in occurrences and consequently more dispersion of factors admitting the possibility that designated maxima may understate English contributions. But in general they may be considered exaggerated, because in these States, as in the southern, the leading English names were subject to non-English usage drawn from by-usage and from imitation.

Maximum English contributions may be set forth by comparing the summaries obtained through the several methods of calculation and selecting the highest; this reveals that in the area of record, which comprised 11 specified States and half of Virginia, the English were not responsible for more than 72 per cent of the population. In New England, English contributions did not exceed 76 per cent, and in the remaining area of record the percentage, lowered by the low proportions in Pennsylvania, may be stated as 69 per cent.

LOCAL LIMITS OF ENGLISH CONTRIBUTIONS

Because of discrepancies, conclusions from the preceding data as to English contributions to individual states are drawn with difficulty. In order that estimates for the states accord essentially with those for the whole area of record and for its principal parts, it is necessary to interpret state calculations somewhat liberally. The following figures are from the series by detailed calculation of arithmetic means, which is rather consistently highest.

Maximum percentage of English-American population

Maine	60	New York	57
New Hampshire	61	Pennsylvania	40
Vermont	76	Maryland	72
Massachusetts	82	Virginia	84
Rhode Island	71	North Carolina	98
Connecticut	67	South Carolina	75

There are a few instances of substantial disagreement between the three sets of estimates and in these instances preceding data possibly point to larger contributions of English, as follows: New Hampshire, 63; Vermont, 78; New York, 58; Pennsylvania, 42.

THE STATES VIEWED AS A SERIES

Analysis discloses that English contributions to State populations of 1790 formed a series with no marked break, the remarkable consistency of per-centages indicating American population at that time a coherent whole, the State populations more fully related than is at once apparent. The series may be graphically presented as an M, the high points in Massachusetts and North Carolina, the low point in Pennsylvania. The English population of Maine was possibly 60 per cent, New Hampshire and Vermont showing ratios intermediate between that and 82 per cent in Massachusetts, with gradual decline to 40 per cent in Pennsylvania, then increasing to a climax of 98 per cent in North Carolina. The rise in the proportion of English from Pennsylvania to North Carolina was probably not so sharp as the maximum calculations would suggest, because of non-English use of the more familiar names. South Carolina showed a lower rating for English contributions than North Carolina, probably indicating that settlements in the extreme south were increasingly mixed and that the proportion of English in Georgia was correspondingly lower than in South Carolina.

Cambrian proportions were unaffected by the total number of English. (See Table 7.) Indeed Cambrians were relatively most numerous in Pennsylvania where the whole stock was most poorly represented, the line of their ratios tending to form a series with a single high point in that State, though with some irregularities in rise and fall. The proportion of Cambrians relative to Angli-cans was higher in Maine than in New Hampshire and Vermont—its lowest measurements—but increased through Massachusetts to Connecticut, fell slightly in New York, reached its highest point in Pennsylvania and declined steadily though not markedly to the southern limit of the area of record, with slight irregularity in Maryland and Virginia partly explained by incomplete data for the latter. Although less consistent than that of the possible proportions of English as a whole, the Cambrian series supports the conclusion that there was no marked discontinuity in the settlements along the Atlantic seaboard. Tracing these relationships makes possible a fair interpolation for the States for which the records of 1790 are missing.

INTERPOLATION FOR STATES OF MISSING RECORDS

The five areas containing parts of the main body of the population in 1790 for which records of names of that date are missing are New Jersey, Delaware, Georgia, Kentucky, and Tennessee; to these may be added Virginia, estimates for which are based on the State tax lists of a few years earlier.

The orderly progression in percentages for maximum English contributions to populations suggests that conditions in the areas not covered by the available records may be estimated by studying those of neighboring States. The steady decline from Massachusetts to Pennsylvania suggests that the English proportion in New Jersey was intermediate between that of New York and that of Pennsylvania. New Jersey's close contacts with neighboring States, and particularly with the urban groups of New York and Philadelphia—contemporary statement had it that the State was tapped like a cask at both ends by removals to the two cities—together with travel across the State, tended to make New Jersey population more a national sample than a derivative of the local early settlements. Replacements followed removals and there is little doubt that the proportion of English was intermediary between that in eastern Pennsylvania and in parts of New York comprising the lower Hudson Valley and Long Island. Assuming 57 per cent English contribution in New York and 40 per cent in Pennsylvania, interpolation for New Jersey gives something more than 50 per cent.

Rather than set down our own approximate figure, we use the estimate prepared for CPG [13] by Mr. William Nelson, the corresponding secretary of the New Jersey Historical Society, in consultation with Dr. Austin Scott of New Brunswick, N. J., and Dr. E. S. Sharpe, president of the Salem County Historical Society. This represents a painstaking estimate by leading authorities.

Mr. Nelson computes the population of English in New Jersey as 58 per cent. It is highly significant that this estimate coordinates closely with figures we know apply to maximum proportions of English. Mr. Nelson's estimate is based on an analysis of county populations in terms of settlements and subsequent internal migration. That he arrives at a higher figure for the proportions of English in New Jersey than we might have obtained by the use of lists of names, indicates that his method tends to attribute to the English a fair proportion of Americanized English-speaking persons of unknown origin. It suggests that such computations are even more likely to overstate the proportions of English than calculation based on the recurrences of family names.

Delaware's established administrative relations with Pennsylvania, and the fact that it is bounded on two sides by Maryland, suggests that the composition of the State was closely related to that of these neighboring States. It is unlikely that Delaware contained a greater proportion of English than either Maryland or Pennsylvania, as estimated in CPG, [14] particularly as both Wilmington and Newcastle were active ports and common landing places for immigration in colonial days; nevertheless, interpolation for Delaware can only approximate conditions as a whole, since they were quite unrelated to those in western Pennsylvania and western Maryland. In some respects, Delaware's relationships with New Jersey were closer than with Pennsylvania. A maximum estimate of 60 per cent English in Delaware appears to be sound when compared with the maximum proportions of English in the neighboring States: 58 per cent in New Jersey, 40 per cent in Pennsylvania, and 72 per cent in Maryland.

Before interpolating for the remaining States in this area, it is well to recall that conditions in Virginia were determinative of those in the whole South, even though only about half of its population was covered by the tax list. Because Virginia had the largest white population of all the States, we must not be too sure of the representativeness of the substitute record. Nevertheless the available material does not yet indicate reason to distrust it. The estimate of 84 per cent English in Virginia accords with figures derived for Maryland and North Carolina, and since analysis for the latter shows decided

[13] P. 119.
[14] Pp. 116–121.

overstatement of English there, the percentage estimated for its northern neighbor may be accepted as a satisfactory maximum.

The population of Georgia, Kentucky, and the district which subsequently became Tennessee were estimated in *CPG*[15] on the basis of North Carolina's English proportions, but those findings are rendered ineffective by the disclosure of gradations in the proportions along the Atlantic seaboard. Since it is known that people from Pennsylvania, Maryland, Virginia, and North Carolina migrated to the territory south of the Ohio River, each of these neighboring States contributed to the population of Kentucky and Tennessee. No information defines the bounds of the principal contributory areas within these States nor the measures of their contributions, but it is inferred that the population of this trans-Appalachian territory of Kentucky and Tennessee together was derived in about equal proportions from the western parts of these four States to the east, and the arithmetic average of 75 per cent English for this area is advanced as a fair measure of the maximum English in the unit of Kentucky and Tennessee.

Georgia was settled at a late date and its population increased by secondary migration whose composition was probably about that of the Carolinas through which most of it flowed. From North Carolina southward the settlements reflected the trend in the immigration of the eighteenth century. The opening of South Carolina did not progress rapidly until after 1750 when settlements in Georgia began to constitute a southern bulwark. It is fair to assume, therefore, that the population of South Carolina was intermediary between that of North Carolina and that of Georgia, hence the estimate of 70 per cent maximum English proportion in Georgia is deduced.

The foregoing interpolations for the areas of missing records, combined with the figures from the several States for which records have been preserved, indicate that the total English contribution did not exceed 70 per cent, or a population of 2,207,760 out of a total of 3,172,444.

SUPPLEMENTAL USE OF LEADING ENGLISH NAMES

Logical study of English contributions includes investigation of the discount applying to estimated proportions in order to derive actual measures, and of the varying scale of non-English use of English names throughout the country.

Overstatement arises partly from original usage of names in countries other than England, partly from acquired usage in America. Ordinarily in determining nationality on the basis of name uses, by-usage is a more potent cause of error than acquired usage. In this study the inaccuracies arising from by-usage are minimized by careful selection of indicators; the second factor— voluntary, imitative, preferential, or acquired use—is probably more important to our calculations.

Several of the names employed as distinctively English are known to have had some usage in other countries. Matheson gives data on all names of more than rare usage in Ireland (see Table 56), and mentions all of these names as finding some bearers there. Only three of them—*Robinson*, *Ward*, *Lee*—are thought to have been used by Irish-Americans in any appreciable numbers, and comparison with Farr's scale of ratios failing to show high measures of American currency indicates either that Irish by-usage accounted for few heads of families in the 1790 records, or else that this by-usage can not be detected by the liberal standards of class occurrence.

---

[15] P. 121.

None of the names used in this study as distinctively English is reported by the Scotch registrar to have been common in Scotland. He specifically states that Jones, the second most commonly used name in England, was "nowhere" in Scotland, and that Robinson was almost entirely replaced by Robertson. But Guppy shows four English indicators—*Hall, Turner, Edwards,* and *Philips* (one "*l*")—frequently used by Scots, hence they must be rated moderately common among this nationality. Names used in the northern countries of England commonly found bearers among Lowland Scots, though *Edwards* and *Philips* did not pass into Scotland in this way but were independently derived from the names in use prior to the development of the surname system. *Hall* possibly gained Scotch usage through emphasis in northern England, as it was common in both Northumberland and Cumberland. *Turner* probably passed over to Scotland by contacts along the western coast, as it was familiar in Cumberland but not in Northumberland. *Robinson* was common in both of the northern counties of England, but was not favored in Scotland. *Green, Lee,* and *Parker* were common names in Northumberland, and may have had bearers among Scots coming to America from the Berwick and Roxburgh regions adjoining Northumberland.

Acquired usage is more difficult to identify than by-usage, and is determined more by the character of Anglicization, than by its degree. The two main phases of Anglicization, remodeling of non-English names and adoption of standard English forms, proceeded together, but local American usage showed differences in their relative emphasis. In the north, particularly in New England, much revision of names occurred without a corresponding measure of adoption of standardized English forms in place of other names. In the South, especially in North Carolina, simplification was an important factor in Anglicization and actively led to marked voluntary usage and hence to standardization of leading English names.

Every State accorded some special favor to most of the distinctively English names; only a few were in disfavor, *Robinson* occasionally giving way to *Robison,* and *Phillips* to *Philips*—two changes deemed unnatural to English-American nomenclature. But on the whole, developments followed the natural and universal tendency toward increased use of the more familiar forms.

The tendency of marshals of the census to interpret rare forms according to their knowledge of familiar ones increased the ratio of use of common names. Since they could not have been familiar with all of the authentic forms, they must have interpreted some names closely similar to familiar names in forms such as are here used as indicators.

Adoption of English names was not uniform in degree in the several parts of the country, but was affected locally by the character of mixed nationalities, by toleration or the lack of it, and by education. Generally speaking the greater the need for English as a common language, the greater the Anglicization of family nomenclature. But local mixtures of heredities which might have effected changes in names can not be read from the totals in State records. Where there was a large non-British element, as in Pennsylvania and New York, there were many segregated communities almost uninfluenced by Anglicization. But in New England there was little segregation and as a result great modification of names. Toleration of diverse antecedents would perpetuate strange names while its absence would force unfamiliar names into old patterns. Education should have kept down the tide of Anglicization in the north as compared with the plantation country, as the greater its scope the more developed the reverence for ancestral spellings and forms of surnames. Despite these generalizations, the local measures of voluntary use of leading English names can not be determined by deduction.

The list following sets forth actualities and probabilities for non-English use of leading English names, based chiefly on a study of the nomenclatural patterns in the several States and on careful comparison with name frequencies of the several countries furnishing migration to colonial America. By-usage can not be very surely ascertained, and all statements concerning it are dependent on European records of original association of names. Statements on voluntary usage are gathered partly from genealogical readings and partly from observation of offsetting decline in the use of other names. Observations on the inadequate representation in 1790 of non-British names known to have been previously numerous are based especially on comparison with the *Oath of Allegiance Records* of arrivals in the Province of Pennsylvania, and with many available marriage records in Dutch and German churches. Developments of marked significance in one locality may have been quite unimportant elsewhere. Complications and contradictions abound and constitute a promising field for further research.

BAKER—Exceptionally familiar throughout area of record in 1790, doubtless augmented by highly common Dutch, Flemish, and German names of like meaning, with decided advantage in New York and Pennsylvania where it usually replaced *Bekker*, *deBekker*, and *Becker*. Scotch *Baxter* had same meaning, but remained distinct.

CARTER—The principal voluntary use of *Carter* must have been as an Anglicization of *McCarty*. A few listings are regularly found for *McCarter*. The name sometimes replaces French *Cartier* and *Chartier*. Some authorities hold that the Mayflower family of *Carter* were originally *Cartier*. The remarkable frequency of the name in Virginia is doubtless due in part to the spread of the well-known *Carter* family.

COOPER—Lack of representation in migration accounts for dearth in America in 1790 and to-day. Used as a translation for *Boettcher* and other names of like meaning; also a transliteration of *Kupfer*.

EDWARDS—Confined to central and southern England, with northern limit in Cheshire; and to Scotland north of the Forth and the Clyde. Scant non-English usage in America, but occasionally replaced French *Evrard*.

EVANS—Relative weakness in 1790 was not due to increased forms in *B*, such as *Bevan*, which were rare in 1790 records. Understatement by misspelling is allowed for in this study.

GREEN—Original by-usage among Scotch. Translation for fairly common German *Gruen*. Benefits from its evident meaning are not great unless the large colonies of *Green* in Rhode Island and New York were of mixed origins. No exceptional currency from Pennsylvania southward.

HALL [15]—Small numbers in southern and central Scotland. No evidence of being a translation. High frequency in New England benefiting from companship of *Hale*. *Holl* in Pennsylvania represented moderately common German name.

JAMES—Slight evidence of scattered European usage. Not recognized in America as translation of *Jacobs*, a common American name then, though not now.

JONES—The frequency of this name has not been increased as much by translation and other changes as has that of the other great Cambrian leader, *Williams*. It is not commonly recognized as meaning "*Johns*," but like *Johns* it may have been used occasionally as a transliteration of the German *Tschantz*. *Jonnes* and *Jons* suggest transition from common French *Jean* which did not gain place in America. *Jones*, though not unknown in Scotland, had in 1863 a frequency of only about 50 per 100,000 (Stark).

---

[15] See Note 3, p. 175.

LEE—Prevalent in Northumberland and western England, with Scotch by-usage and incidental Irish usage. The frequencies of *Lee* in the 1790 records are about normal for a leading English name. In addition to the Irish, it was probably borne by people of miscellaneous original names, such as Scandinavian *Lie*, and English *Lea*, *Leigh*. The latter are companion names of western England, disappearing in America.

LEWIS—This name had remarkable frequency in the 1790 records. Its main gain was probably from the French for it is known as the English version of the French *Louis*. Possibly Scots will the found under this name, particularly if from the Isle of Lewis, but it is not reported as a Scotch name.

MORGAN—A few Germans may be looked for under this name. However, *Morgan* was not a common German name. *Morgenthaler* found the interpretation *Morgandollar*, and because of its length was possibly occasionally abbreviated to *Morgan*.

MORRIS—Increased by German *Moritz*, and less by French *Maurice* and *Moreau*. Weak in New England where it was probably sometimes replaced by common *Morse;* elsewhere it was above Cambrian norm.

PARKER—Prevalent in Northumberland; hence probably had Scotch by-usage. Remarkable frequency in New England. No common transitions benefiting it are known, but all common American names gained early benefits by abrupt and sometimes unaccountable transitions. May be abbreviation of common *Parkhurst*. In and about Delaware it may have helped to replace Swedish *Parchon*, which disappeared.

PHILLIPS—Substantial voluntary usage traceable to decline of cognate *Philip*, *Philippe*, and *Philips*. *Philip* was a moderately common surname for "foreigners," especially Germans; French *Philippe* also common; and Scotch *Philips* known. Remarkable familiarity in Massachusetts and New York in 1790 probably due to these transliterations. Especially characteristic of the north, with possible French-Canadian adoption of the form, but scarcely free from voluntary usage in any State.

PRICE—Strong in South, where Welsh probably preferred it to variant *Rice* which Germans adopted in place of common *Reiss*, etc.; yet Germans also replaced *Preuss*, *Preiss*, etc., with *Price*.

ROBERTS—Probably had special favor among Welsh-Americans, as *Probert*, the variant in *P* (corresponding to *Pugh* for *Hughes*, and *Pritchard* for *Richards*, etc.) was little used. *Roberts* had original German usage, and also substituted for *Ruppert*, *Ruprecht*, etc. Natural successor to *Robert*, originally a common name for French and occasional for Scots and Irish. Probably gained from Scotch *McRobert* and Irish *McRoberts*, as the dropped prefix and added *s* were both characteristic of Americanization. The Delaware Swedish family of *Robertsson* may have added to numbers of *Roberts* by dropping *-son* as did the *Gustafssons* (*Justice*) and *Martenssons* (*Morton*). (Cp., p. 148.)

ROBINSON—Fair Irish, scant Scotch usage. Weakness probably due to variable spelling. *Robison* is an American offshoot. *Robinson* or *Robins* may have replaced French *Robinet* which did not thrive. (Cp., p. 148.)

THOMAS—Varied origins other than English. Highly common among Germans and French and "foreigners" arriving in Pennsylvania. Probably replaced *Thomasson* and *Thomos* among early Swedish settlers.

TURNER—Original Scotch by-usage from Dumfries to Glasgow. Moderate German usage. Americanization of common French *Tournier*.

WARD—Surprisingly weak leading English name in 1790. Irish by-usage. German usage by progressive changes of *Wirtz* (*Werts*) and *Wirth* (*Werd*). May have occasionally replaced *vanWart*, as the Dutch commonly dropped the preposition.

WILLIAMS—Substantial voluntary usage. Often replaced north-of-England *Williamson;* German *Wilhelm*, highly common in eighteenth century arrivals, but survived by only a few score entries of the spelling in 1790 records; French *Guillaume* and *Guillemin;* and Dutch *Willemse*, which disappeared.

SUMMARY

The rather orderly representation of leading English names in American nomenclature is disclosed by comparing measures of American usage with measures of frequency in the motherland. Marked similarities in rates of frequency are noted particularly in the South; the general constancy of English nomenclatural standards during more than two centuries is fairly well established by this comparison of American usages derived from seventeenth and eighteenth century immigration with English usages recorded in the middle of the nineteenth century; and the repetition of many original English characteristics in the American patterns demonstrates that reflected frequencies offer an ideal standard for testing irregularities of immigration.

Maximum English measures in the several States, based on comparison of recurrences of the leading English names, reveal progressive relationships between States: All the estimates are summed up in the statement that not more than 70 per cent of the American population were of English blood. The following table presents details of this appraisal.

TABLE 17.—*Estimated maxima for numbers and proportions of English in the white population of the United States, 1790*

	White population	Percentage possibly English	Number possibly English
Maine	96, 107	60	57, 660
New Hampshire	141, 112	61	86, 080
Vermont	85, 072	76	64, 650
Massachusetts	· 373, 187	82	306, 010
Rhode Island	64, 670	71	45, 920
Connecticut	232, 236	67	155, 600
New York	314, 366	57	179, 190
New Jersey	169, 954	58	98, 570
Pennsylvania	423, 373	40	169, 350
Delaware	46, 310	60	27, 790
Maryland	208, 649	72	150, 230
Kentucky and Tennessee	93, 046	75	69, 780
Virginia	442, 117	84	371, 380
North Carolina	289, 181	98	283, 400
South Carolina	140, 178	75	105, 130
Georgia	52, 886	70	37, 020
United States	3, 172, 444	70	2, 207, 760

Gradations in indicated English proportions show an ascending line from Maine to a peak of 82 per cent in Massachusetts, steady decline to 40 per cent in Pennsylvania, another rise to 98 per cent in North Carolina, and a final drop in Georgia to 70 per cent, close to the average for the whole country. The areas of Massachusetts and North Carolina are conspicuous as having dominant English nomenclature and a good majority of English population.

The degree to which non-English usage of English names in the north contributed to overstatement of English proportions there is not yet determined. In North Carolina, however, we find that *CPG* recognizes 17 per cent of the population as bearing non-English names. This, in addition to the fact that the method used in *CPG* can not fully account for the non-English, indicates that our present appraisal decidedly exaggerates the numbers of English in the southern part of the country. The estimate of 70 per cent in the whole country is therefore to be reduced to allow for the incidental use of English names.

For detailed study the leading English names are divided into two classes: Anglicans, leaders in the normal varied English nomenclature; and Cambrians, whose original frequency was gained through striking repetition in Wales and southwest England where nomenclature was little varied. The two classes show widely different distribution. Anglican names were largely used in the Carolinas, Virginia, Maryland, Massachusetts, and Vermont; and least used in Pennsylvania.

Cambrian names attained a high peak in North Carolina, declined gradually northward, were strongly uncommon in New York, peculiarly unfamiliar north of Rhode Island. On the whole they showed only about two-thirds of their old-world ratio to Anglican names, comparison with which reveal Cambrians relatively strongest in Pennsylvania where they were not much below their North Carolina maximum, and where Anglican names had their poorest representation.

Class measures of currency definitely reflect English ratios in the South. Dispersion begins among Anglicans in Pennsylvania and becomes more marked for both classes northward. Readings of this dispersion indicate that the English (including the Welsh) in the States from Pennsylvania southward were of diversified origins and fairly impartially represented the several parts of the motherland; while northward, in New York and New England, certain regions of the motherland were represented to the disadvantage of others, thus pointing out that migration to New York and New England was of specialized type.

Analysis shows that English representation was not so large as commonly thought. Measures derived from interpretation of names are with difficulty brought down to the bedrock of English paternity. American names have an appearance that connotes English antecedents, but it springs only partly from English heredity and is rather largely the result of English speech. The English had no great majority in most States and were in the minority in one or more.

Comparison of American and English nomenclature, based chiefly on measures of American currency of leading English names, deduces that the former was Angloid or near-English and reveals three types. An area in the South, of which North Carolina was the center, showed familiar names introduced by the English in high favor; records for this area show many names remodeled to English forms, but not nearly so many as the currency of standard English forms would suggest. An area in the North, with Massachusetts as its center, showed nomenclature of English pattern but with imitations that changed parts of names without transcribing them entirely; English-looking names were in wide use, but standardized English forms were not proportionately represented. The third type was in Pennsylvania and New York, and again in the extreme northern and southern States, where the non-English element was substantial, and, until 1790, so apparent that modifications were not so evident.

Consideration of the situation revealed in this analysis heightens appreciation of English culture and its power of assimilation and its ability to guide and direct a mixed population.

Discussing the individualistic struggles on the American frontier as contrasted with the oppressive conformity of American life, Frederic L. Paxson[16] says "It is a nice question whether the equalitarian or the individualistic forces were the weightier." This study of American usage of leading English names shows equalitarian forces dominant in the movement westward from the south-

---

[16] *History of the American Frontier*, New York. 1924. P. 251.

ern seaboard, the records for these States showing common adoption of names already made familiar by others and the people satisfied to be labeled with standarized designations. But in the North, it shows the people much more individualistic; indeed it may be suspected that they sometimes devised new spellings merely to avoid having the same names as other people.

This study of English contributions is weakened by being based on names too few, too prominent, and, in the case of the Anglicans, too bare of details. Although collectively they represent a substantial sample of English population, averages could be more accurately tested if more names were available. Their wide use by the English made them outstanding when American nomenclature was in its formative period, and they were so popularized as unavoidably to bias findings derived from relative occurrences. They give only a bare outline of Anglican representation, leaving considerable doubt as to whether irregularities in representation were due to regional migration or to some other factor. Guppy treats English names much more extensively than does Farr, but unfortunately his measures of occurrence are not coordinate with any definite schedule of population. It is to be hoped that some future investigation will provide us with analyses of the occurrence of names in eighteenth-century England, on the lines of Matheson's study of Irish usages, so that the details of the English contribution may be more adequately ascertained.

Chapter IV

CONTRIBUTION OF SCOTS TO 1790 AMERICA

THE NON-ENGLISH

Each nationality presents different problems, but the study of the Scotch discovers features common to other non-English groups, while some of the difficulties encountered in the study of the English recur in changed guise. The task of distinguishing between evidence of English blood and results of English influence becomes an inquiry into the separate phases of Anglicization.

The Scots, as Britishers, might seem to offer no complication of adjustment to English influence, nor of Anglicization of name. But the Scots were a distinct people, and even the Lowlanders, close neighbors of the English along the natural boundary of the river Tweed and the Cheviot Hills, reacted strongly to actual intermingling, while the Highlanders were almost a strange people and had decided adjustments to make.

In order, therefore, to recognize Scotch names despite their Anglicization, we turn to the distinctive non-English names, fortresses marking the boundaries broken through by Anglicization. Changes of names did not ordinarily efface the Scotch pattern, although two instances appear where the Scotch names *Chalmers* and *Turnbull* were replaced by the English forms *Chambers* and *Trimble*.

Anglicization in America was not a new development but a transplanted process centuries old in the British Isles and acquiring fresh vigor in the New World. Thus it is hard to distinguish between the interaction of names in the mixed nomenclature, the general reaction to common speech, and the momentum of both these forces at migration. Original by-usage colored American usage, and the Scotch name odd or difficult in the new environment was supplanted by an English one already in occasional use among the Scotch or at least familiar to them. Adopted usage of English names occurs where other Britishers were numerous, as in North Carolina, where a little by-usage gave rise to considerable imitative usage.

THE BRITISH COMPOSITE

Examination of the affinity between English, Scotch, and Irish is necessarily included in the appraisal of independent Scotch contributions, since inquiry into the origins of the 1790 population is based on both linguistic and geographical classification, and the Lowland Scotch constitute a geographical subdivision of the English-speaking stock.

Distinguishing the Scotch from other Britishers requires attention to four special themes—aggregation of broadly British names; anticipation that the total Scots in America exceeded those of recognizably Scotch surnames; consideration of Scotch names other than those bearing the characteristic *Mc;* and liberality in selecting distinctive Scotch names.

Original frequency and not preconception of characteristic forms determines the identity of Scotch names; Lowland names, even though they lack the extreme distinctiveness of Highland names, must have place among the indicators;

and by-usage among the English can not be guarded against stringently since it but balances the English influence in the American nomenclature pattern. In spite of these considerations, there is necessity for relying largely in this pioneer study on distinctive Highland names as indicators of Scotch blood.

Joint usage can not be studied here, other than in its most obvious bearings, as in the overlap of Scotch nomenclature into northern Ireland. But many of the most characteristic Lowland names were used also in northern England and in parts of Ireland, and this lack of distinctive Lowland nomenclature prevents full recognition of its contributions. Investigation reveals few leading Scotch names that were not used in Ireland, but a study of these names develops a list which may be called distinctively "Scotch"; other lists, comprising shared names, are known as "Scotch-Irish." The establishment of norms of recurrence of Scotch names will permit classification of American usage of Scotch-Irish names as Scotch and Irish and offer a basis for information on the distinct contributions of each to American population.

GROUP TREATMENT OF SCOTCH NAMES

Only the English were numerous enough in the American colonies to maintain old-world standards in name spelling; hence irregularities in spelling necessitate treating non-English names differently from English ones.

Scotch names were not ordinarily as much modified as Irish, nor nearly so much as Continental names. A study of them is much aided by the records of 1861 and 1863 by Dr. James Stark, assistant to the Scotch registrar. These records facilitate the study of the Scotch more than Farr's aided in the study of the English, since Stark includes a larger number of names and a greater proportion of the population. (Farr listed 50 names whose bearers constituted 18 per cent of the English population, while Stark gave 150 names with bearers numbering practically half the population of Scotland.) But Stark adds nothing to our knowledge of the development of names under American influence. He treated of variations in spelling but did not give details of such variability, nor can these be fully supplied by data from directories and genealogies, for few studies have been made of the evolution of names in colonial America.

Comparison with Scotch directories of to-day, with their lists of identical names and few variations in spelling, reveals the marked variability of these names in the 1790 record. For example, the American forms of *Fraser*, *Buchanan*, and *McPherson* are striking modifications and corruptions, and some surnouns show derivatives which almost replace the original forms, as *Southerland* for *Sutherland*, and *McCloud* for *McLeod*.

This variability in Scotch names in America in 1790 but illustrates a general characteristic of non-English nomenclature and provides a field for introducing the systematic group treatment of all non-English names in which the variants are assembled around the parent forms. In determining non-English contributions to population, attention is concentrated on groups of surnoun type, and the indicators must be names that were distinctive in European usage and remained so through the variations that marked the blend of nomenclatures in America.

The Distinctive Name System.

The necessity for grouping Scotch appellations and the availability of many names as potential indicators, dictate a complete statement of the distinctive name system.

This formality will provide landmarks for guidance and criticism of the Scotch study and those to follow. The system is basically correct in measuring stocks in terms of recognizable parts but would fail if its statistical units were not selected and defined with care, because names are not always strictly hereditary. Admitted gaps in data need not prevent formulation of an ideal procedure giving rules for selection, group definition and mensuration, determining foreign nomenclatural influence in the American nomenclature of 1790. The suggested method for measuring the contributions of a stock by the evidence of its name uses consists of the following steps:

1. To survey the usage of names in the mother country at the mean time of emigration, observing general features of nomenclature.

2. To characterize this nomenclature in terms of definite important groups of names determined by a two-fold study of relative frequency of particular names, and of precision in grouping them.

3. To determine the distinctiveness of these groups by (a) observing what forms have almost the whole body of their European usage in the country under consideration, and (b) classifying the original groups according to their structure and content under European conditions so as to specify those with content practically limited to forms peculiar to the country. This is the specification of immediate distinctiveness.

4. To test further this tentative list and eliminate those not ultimately distinctive. This is the test of permanence of form and of grouping in American nomenclature and should restrict the list to names which so maintain identity in America that the number of their bearers can be considered indicative of specific origin.

5. To define these name groups by their ratios of usage abroad by means of data on frequency of names in the foreign country at the mean time of emigration. For this there should be information on the names outstanding in foreign usage, their relationships to supplemental names, and the proportions of bearers of the name groups, as codified, in the Old World stock.

6. To note American bearers of these surnouns by following their evolution through modifications in American usage, and describing the changing groups in terms of numbers of bearers of recognized forms, and thereupon study the observed distribution.

7. To estimate totals of persons of the origin under consideration from the ratios of currency of the distinctive surnouns, viewed in the light of the proportions of population bearing these surnouns in the mother country.

Both this step and the preceding one should employ internal checks on the calculations, for these are special virtues of nomenclatural comparison. Both the estimating of relative numbers in step 6 and this one of estimating absolute numbers on the basis of ratios may and should employ classification of data for comparison of readings.

8. To criticize these findings by historical and other syntheses. Findings are obtained without detailed examination of the history of settlement by people of the origin under consideration, but should be capable of verification by historical inquiry; and though based on numbers bearing certain names of limited usage, should produce estimates properly accounting for total populations in American areas.

This method of tracing the evolution of nomenclature falls, then, into three subdivisions: Survey of the foreign nomenclature as a whole, first in its European and then in its American background, with a resulting tentative list of distinctive name groups; following these groups through their changes as they become American, selecting those which preserve their integrity in American usage; and accurately defining the groups and measuring their usage in the mother country and in America, to establish the total contribution to American nomenclature on the basis of the specific contributions distinguished.

Dr. James Stark, assistant to the Scottish registrar, in his second report on names (1863), stated the frequencies of the 150 names or name groups most largely used in his country. Comparison of his schedule with records of English usage disposes of more than half as not distinctively Scotch. Some of the others are unavailable as indicators of Scotch antecendents because of confusion in America. Scrutiny of European and American usage finally leaves 45 names as either rather definitely Scotch or Scotch-Irish. Comparison of Stark's schedule of the occurrence of these 45 in Scotland with Matheson's for occurrence in Ireland enables classifying them with respect to their relative distribution east and west of the North Channel. Arrayed in order of their relative occurrence in the two British countries, these 45 names fall into three classes.

Class I. Practically no Irish usage recorded: *M'Leod*, *Munro*, *M'Pherson*, *M'Kinnon*, *M'Laren*, *Robertson*, *M'Intosh*, *Sutherland*, *M'Kenzie*, *Bruce*, *M'Gregor*, *Cameron*, *Fraser*, *Duncan*, *Ritchie*, *Ross*, *Buchanan*.

Class II. Substantial Irish usage: *Christie*, *M'Donald*, *Donaldson*, *Ramsay*, *Robb*, *M'Farlane*, *M'Intyre*, *Morrison*, *Murdoch*, *Tait*, *Rankin*, *Baxter*, *Jamieson*, *Forsyth*.

Class III. Names with original numbers in Ireland approaching or exceeding those in Scotland: *Ferguson*, *Campbell*, *Findlay*, *Black*, *Gordon*, *M'Dougall* (with *M'Dowell*), *Moffat*, *Maxwell*, *Blair*, *Craig*, *Orr*, *Cumming*, *Boyd*, *Cunningham*.

American names are assembled under these names as group headings practically as is illustrated by Table 111 of *A Century of Population Growth*. From the American usage of the names in Class I this study establishes the representation of Scots, and from Class III, in comparison with normal measures of representation of Scots, a subsequent study measures the presence in America of Irish with names originating in Scotland.

The 17 names in Class I are viewed as distinctively Scotch. Treated as group headings, they show 2,725 entries in the twelve 1790 records, an average of about 160 apiece, with a range from *Robertson* 506 and *Ross* 439 down to *M'Kinnon* and *M'Laren*, 32 apiece. Relative to usage among Scots, *Buchanan*, *Ross*, and *Bruce* were most numerously represented and *M'Kenzie*, *Cameron*, *and M'Kinnon* least numerously.

From the relative numbers of American users, it appears that Scots were responsible for 7.9 per cent of the population in the area of record in 1790. Interpolating for the States for which record is missing, 8.3 per cent is obtained for the contribution of Scots to the white population as a whole. It is significant to note that the names indicate 7.0 per cent Scots in New York, and 8.6 per cent in Pennsylvania, whereas the figure derived by the historian William Nelson for the intermediate State of New Jersey is 7.7 per cent. The indicated percentages of Scots run approximately 15 per cent in the Carolinas, 10 per cent in Virginia, between 7 and 9 per cent in the States from Maryland to New York, and at an average of 4.3 per cent in New England. The relative occurrences of the several name groups being in good conformity the representation of Scots is satisfactorily established as 8 per cent. This is more likely an overstatement than an understatement.

Class III names become available as indicators of class origin in Ireland. These names invariably show substantially more American usage than is explained by the norms of recurrence developed by Class I. This excess of currency is attributed to Scotch-Irish origin. Their measures are taken up after those of more typical Irish names in a succeeding chapter. The currency of Class II names might be tested in similar fashion but this has not been undertaken.

THE BASIC SCOTCH RECORD

Doctor Stark's first report, 1861, commented on general features of Scotch nomenclature and compared his list of 50 leading Scotch names with those reported by Farr for England. The second report is a test of the first and has the further merit of extending the statement of frequencies to cover the 150 names most used in Scotland. It gives valuable detail on geographical antecedents of the names, but erroneously characterizes more than half of the 150 as peculiar to Scotland. Stark's comment on immigration indicates that the bearers of native names were less numerous among the people of Scotland in 1863 than among true Scots. Although Stark designated some names as variable in spelling, no information was given on the frequency of variants relative to that of dominant forms.

The reader may gain a picture of Scotch nomenclature from the text of Stark's second report, dated 1863.[1]

" In the sixth detailed report, applicable to the registers of 1860, a few pages were devoted to the subject of Scottish nomenclature; and among other particulars, a classified list was given of the 50 most common surnames in Scotland, as deduced from the general indices to the registers of births, deaths, and marriages for the years 1855, 1856, and 1858, which embrace upwards of 609,000 names. The annexed Table LVI exhibits the result of a similar but much less extended investigation in the general index to the birth registers only for the year 1863, which embraces upwards of 109,000 names, and it is satisfactory to find that the conclusions arrived at in the former report are strikingly confirmed by the subsequent and more limited inquiry. No fewer than 47 of the 50 surnames specified in that report again appear, and although their relative position and estimated number in the population are in several instances somewhat different, the general similarity of the two lists is very remarkable. The three surnames contained in the former list which do not occur in the annexed table are *Black, Sutherland,* and *Gibson,* in lieu of which we have *M'Intosh, Russell, and Gordon.* In both lists the nine strongest surnames are the same, viz., *Smith, M'Donald, Brown, Thomson, Robertson, Stewart, Campbell, Wilson,* and *Anderson,* the only difference in their order being that Thomson and Robertson change places—their respective numbers, however, in both lists, being strikingly similar. As stated in the former report, the surname of *Smith* is *facile princeps* on both sides of the border; but it is somewhat curious to find that *Jones,* which occupies the second place in England, is " nowhere " in Scotland, seeing that the number of births under that surname in Scotland during 1863 was only 54, indicating a population of little more than 1,500 persons.

---

[1] There are some additional sources: Guppy's chapters on Scotch names and his data on distribution and frequency of names in England, both contained in his *Homes of Family Names in Great Britain;* James B. Johnston's *The Scottish Macs* (Paisley, 1922, 65 pp.) ; Alex Macbain's *Personal Names and Surnames of the Town of Inverness* (Inverness, 1895, 105 pp.) ; and numerous books on Scotch clans and life in particular parts of Scotland, which, however, seldom treat of emigration.

"TABLE LVI.—*The 50 most common surnames in Scotland, as ascertained from the general index to the birth registers for the year 1863*

Surnames	Number in index	Estimated number in entire population in 1863	Surnames	Number in index	Estimated number in entire population in 1863
*Smith	1,581	44,268	Watson	536	15,008
*M'Donald	1,308	36,624	Walker	523	14,644
*Brown	1,209	33,852	Taylor	517	14,476
*Thomson	1,117	31,276	M'Leod	513	14,364
Robertson	1,116	31,248	*Ferguson	473	13,244
*Stewart	1,095	30,660	Duncan	463	12,964
Campbell	1,079	30,212	Gray	456	12,768
Wilson	1,048	29,344	Davidson	451	12,628
Anderson	949	26,572	Hunter	438	12,264
Scott	803	22,484	Hamilton	430	12,040
*Miller	767	21,476	*Kerr	419	11,732
M'Kenzie	764	21,392	Grant	408	11,424
*Reid	706	19,768	M'Intosh	408	11,424
Ross	680	19,040	*Graham	401	11,228
M'Kay	669	18,732	*White	399	11,172
*Johnston	644	18,032	*Allan	390	10,920
*Murray	640	17,920	*Simpson	383	10,724
*Clark	638	17,864	M'Gregor	373	10,444
*Paterson	635	17,780	*Munro	369	10,332
Young	629	17,612	Sinclair	367	10,276
*Fraser	627	17,556	Bell	362	10,136
*M'Lean	602	16,856	Martin	360	10,080
Henderson	590	16,520	*Russell	342	9,576
Mitchell	578	16,184	Gordon	340	9,520
*Morrison	562	15,736			
Cameron	548	15,344	Total	31,705	887,740

"NOTE.—The surnames indicated by an asterisk in Tables LVI and LVII occur under 2 or more different spellings.

"Notwithstanding the large accession of Irish and other immigrants, several of our most common Scottish surnames still very decidedly predominate in certain parts of the country. Thus we find from the general index already refered to, that of the 3,856 births in the five clans of *M'Donald, M'Kenzie, M'Kay, M'Lean,* and *M'Leod,* during the year 1863, no fewer than 1,300 occurred in the counties of Ross and Cromarty and Inverness, indicating a population of 36,400. The *M'Donalds* appear to be strongest in Inverness-shire, where they constitute about 8,000 of the population, their estimated number in Ross and Cromarty being 4,670, and in Argyllshire little more than 2,000. The *M'Kenzies* are most numerous in Ross and Cromarty, where they considerably exceed 6,000, their strength in Inverness-shire being only about 1,900. The *M'Kays* preponderate in Caithness and Sutherland (cir. 4,000), and the *M'Leods* in Ross and Cromarty (cir. 5,350); while the *M'Leans* are pretty equally divided among the three counties of Argyll, Ross and Cromarty, and Inverness, where they collectively amount to about 6,450. Nearly one-third (124) of the *M'Intosh* births occurred in the counties of Inverness, Elgin, Nairn, and Banff, indicating a population of 3,470; while the most numerous section of the *M'Gregors* appears to be in Perthshire, where they amount to upward of 1,400.

"The *Robertsons* preponderate in the shires of Perth and Forfar, in which they are about equally strong, constituting in these two counties a population of 6,200. The *Stewarts* are strongest in Perthshire, where they amount to about 3,500; while their estimated number in Argyllshire is under 700, and in Galloway (Kirkcudbright and Wigtown) only 360. They are, however, pretty numerous in the counties of Renfew and Ayr, where they contribute about 2,800 to the population. The *Campbells* appear to amount to nearly 2,000 in Argyllshire, and to about 1,450 in Perthshire, their estimated number in the city of Glasgow being upwards of 6,000.

"About one-half of the 50 surnames in the preceding table do not appear to prevail in any particular counties. A few of these, such as *Anderson, Ferguson, Duncan, and Davidson*, may perhaps be regarded as more peculiarly Scottish patronymics, but it is believed that most of them are of frequent occurrence on both sides of the Tweed. No fewer than 11 of them are to be found among the 50 most common surnames in England, as specified in the Sixteenth Annual Report of the Registrar-General of England, viz, *Smith, Brown, Thomson* (*Thompson*), *Wilson, Clark, Watson, Walker, Taylor, White, Allan* (*Allen*), and *Martin*.

"The following is a list of other surnames in Table LVI, which appear to preponderate in certain parts of the country, with their estimated numbers in the different counties in which they most extensively prevail:

Scott_____ Roxburgh and Selkirk, 2,900. Forfar, 2,150.
Ross_____ Ross and Cromarty, 3,600.
Johnston___ Dumfries, 1,700.
Murray_____ Dumfries and Roxburgh, 1,230. Elgin and Banff, 920. Perth, 560.
Fraser_____ Inverness, 4,300.
Cameron___ Argyll, 2,460. Inverness, 1,300. Perth, 1,300.
Hunter_____ Stirling and Clackmannan, 1,600. Ayr, 1,100. Fife, 1,100. Perth, 300.
Hamilton__ Lanark, 5,800 (of whom nearly one-half are in the city of Glasgow). Renfrew and Ayr, 2,800.
Kerr_____ Renfrew and Ayr, 2,700. Berwick, 280. Roxburgh, 170.
Grant_____ Elgin, Nairn, and Banff, 3,000. Inverness, 1,300.
Graham____ Dumfries, 800. Perth, 420. City of Glasgow, 1,960.
Munro_____ Ross and Cromarty, 2,000. Inverness, 650.
Sinclair____ Orkney and Shetland, 1,350. Caithness, 1,250.
Bell_____ Dumfries and Roxburgh, 2,000.
Gordon____ Aberdeen, 2,000. Elgin, Nairn, and Banff, 1,500.

"Table LVII, exhibits a classified list of the 100 surnames next in order, as ascertained from the general index to the birth registers of 1863. The two tables thus embrace the 150 most common surnames in Scotland, which contributed upwards of 52,000 births in the year 1863, and appear to be represented by no fewer than 1,457,176 persons (47 per cent), or within 93,000 of the half of the entire population. In other words, it is probably not far short of the truth to state that every second person in Scotland bears one or other of these 150 surnames, the total estimated number of surnames in Scotland being about 6.800. * * *

"TABLE *LVII.—Continuation of Table LVI showing the 100 surnames in Scotland next in order to those specified in Table LVI, as ascertained from the general index to the birth registers for the year 1863*

Surnames	Number in index	Estimated number in entire population in 1863	Surnames	Number in index	Estimated number in entire population in 1863
Black	339	9, 492	Boyd	186	5, 208
Sutherland	334	9, 352	*M'Ewan	185	5, 180
M'Farlane	330	9, 240	*Rodger	185	5, 180
Gibson	326	9, 128	*Paton	180	5, 040
*Stevenson	326	9, 128	Rae	176	4, 928
M'Millan	320	8, 960	Bain	176	4, 928
Wallace	317	8, 776	M'Rae	175	4, 900
M'Pherson	316	8, 848	*Hutchison	175	4, 900
*Milne	304	8, 512	Alexander	173	4, 844
Muir	301	8, 428	Ramsay	172	4, 816
M'Intyre	300	8, 400	Weir	167	4, 676
Marshall	290	8, 120	*Nicolson	165	4, 620
Watt	279	7, 812	Turnbull	163	4, 564
Kennedy	276	7, 728	Tait	162	4, 536
Craig	271	7, 588	*Rankin	162	4, 536
*Crawford	264	7, 392	Boyle	162	4, 536
*Kelly	259	7, 252	*Cumming	162	4, 536
M'Lachlan	259	7, 252	*M'Neil	161	4, 508
*Nicol	258	7, 224	Chalmers	157	4, 396
Wright	255	7, 140	Jack	154	4, 312
*Dickson	253	7, 084	Murphy	154	4, 312
M'Dougall	252	7, 056	Lawson	153	4, 284
Ritchie	252	7, 056	*Sim	153	4, 284
Bruce	241	6, 748	Dick	152	4, 256
*Findlay	241	6, 748	Moffat	152	4, 256
Cunningham	238	6, 664	Blair	151	4, 228
Williamson	238	6, 664	Cairns	151	4, 228
*Jamieson	230	6, 440	*Steel	151	4, 228
Douglas	229	6, 412	M'Innes	150	4, 200
Christie	229	6, 412	King	150	4, 200
*Matheson	228	6, 384	Murdoch	149	4, 172
*Laing	228	6, 384	*Sharp	148	4, 144
Wood	228	6, 384	Adam	147	4, 116
Forbes	225	6, 300	Forrest	145	4, 060
*Hendry	223	6, 244	Baird	144	4, 032
M'Kinnon	220	6, 160	Jackson	144	4, 032
*Gardner	219	6, 132	*Low	143	4, 004
*Burns	218	6, 104	Hogg	142	3, 976
*Irvine	215	6, 020	Forsyth	142	3, 976
*Aitken	214	5, 992	Cook	141	3, 948
Lindsay	211	5, 908	*M'Guire	141	3, 948
Fleming	211	5, 908	Baxter	140	3, 920
Donaldson	208	5, 824	Hill	140	3, 920
Buchanan	205	5, 740	Barclay	135	3, 780
M'Laren	205	5, 740	*Inglis	134	3, 752
*Stephen	205	5, 740	Orr	133	3, 724
M'Kie	198	5, 544	Robb	133	3, 724
Currie	197	5, 516	Strachan	133	3, 724
Shaw	193	5, 404	Maxwell	133	3, 724
Hay	191	5, 348			
*Neilson	186	5, 208	Total	20, 337	569, 436

"NOTE—The surnames indicated by an asterisk in Table LVI and LVII occur under 2 or more different spellings."

TESTING THE DISTINCTIVENESS OF SCOTCH NAMES

Comparison of Scotch usage with that of England and Ireland reveals lack of distinctiveness for a number of names which Stark termed Scotch; and further study shows some names were shared with other people. Some instances of miscellaneous British usage discovered in genealogical records were not reported by the usual authorities.

In the following presentation of the tests for distinctiveness it has not been thought necessary to report separately the result of European and American studies as the European comparisons generally signal American confusion resulting from the disappearance of fine distinctions.

The gutterals *ch* and *gh* and the prefix *Mc* require special attention in the search for variants. These gutterals were commonly replaced in America by *sk*, *f*, or *th*, resulting in apparently different names. The prefix *Mc* demands attention because the Scots sometimes had supplementary names with and without it and, while less inclined than the Irish to discard prefixes, showed a tendency in America to drop this syllable. In a number of instances this abbreviation produced names very like the English.

Details of the eliminations in the process of selecting Scotch indicators emphasize the extensive interrelationships between Scotch and other British nomenclatures, and prove that the differentiation of English, Scotch, and Irish antecedents by name classification, as attempted in *CPG*, is impracticable, since many characteristic Scotch names were common in other countries.

SCOTCH NAMES DISTINGUISHED FROM ENGLISH

The selection of distinctive names was begun by examination of English usage. In 20 instances Farr provided the evidence of generality, that number of leading Scotch names being among the 50 most common in England. Generally Guppy's information on distribution in England was the basis for elimination as not distinctive.

If the list of distinctive Scotch names were limited to those which had no similar or identical forms in England, the result at best would be a few Highland names. Since indicators must include both Highland and Lowland names, it was held essential to retain some known to have had English usage. Comparison with English usage excluded all names which Guppy cited as occurring in more than two English counties,[2] but not those he reported as occurring in one or two counties. This liberality in classification is a factor for overstatement of Scotch antecedents, possibly overcome by other features in the calculation.

The overlap of English and Scotch nomenclature helps to explain the common overestimate of English proportions in the American colonies, many names ordinarily called English being really British. Remembering that many of these names became popularized on introduction into America and acquired bearers who were not British, it is still more evident that the designation " English " must always rest on analysis of usage.

The test for English usage leads to three main sets of eliminations, (1) names native to more than two counties of England but having practically no alternative forms in English usage; (2) names occurring in England in the

---

[2] Guppy treated England and Wales in 41 units, ordinarily recognizing county boundaries, but with some mergers, and a division of Yorkshire. Of these Middlesex may generally be disregarded because of scant detail.

usual Scotch forms and also represented in English nomenclature by fairly simi-
lar forms; (3) names not designated distinctively Scotch because there are
English names but slightly different. These three together eliminate 76 of
Stark's 150 leading Scotch names. Other eliminations, based on evidence of
English usage noted in sources other than Guppy, are shown in another section.

Table 18 contains 28 Scotch names commonly used in England, 11 of which are
in Farr's list of 50 leading English names. Among them are *Anderson, Bell,
Gibson, Graham, Hunter, Lawson, Marshall, Miller, Russell, Scott, Williamson,*
and *Young* usually thought of as English names but which may not have been
more emphasized by the English than by the Scotch. On the other hand, five
names—*Alexander, Crawford, Douglas, Grant,* and *Henderson*—were native
to so few countries in England that, in popular expression, they may be called
Scotch.

TABLE 18.—*Leading Scotch names commonly used by English*

Name	Entries in Scotch index	English counties in which native ⊗	Name	Entries in Scotch index	English counties in which native ⊗
Alexander	173	4	Lawson	153	6
Anderson	949	7	Marshall	290	6
Bell	362	13	*Miller	767	13
*Brown	1,209	[1] 40	*Russell	342	12
*Crawford	264	3	Scott	803	18
Douglas	229	3	Shaw	193	[1] 14
Gibson	326	11	*Smith	1,581	[1] 41
*Graham	401	5	Taylor	517	[1] 39
Grant	408	3	Walker	523	[1] 28
Henderson	590	3	Watson	536	[1] 24
Hill	140	[1] 28	*White	399	[1] 33
Hunter	438	7	Williamson	238	12
Jackson	144	[1] 29	Wright	255	[1] 31
King	150	[1] 28	Young	629	28

⊗ According to Guppy.
* Including variants per Stark.
[1] See Table 8 for position among English leading names.

Table 19 accounts for elimination of 21 of Stark's names. It covers those
represented in England both by the same and by other names or forms. One
column shows the number of counties for which Guppy reports native English
usage of the specific forms, and another details English usage of other names
or forms. There are several instances of the Scotch form occurring in only
one English county: *Allan, Hogg,* and *Stewart* in Northumberland; *Hay* in
Lincolnshire; and *Johnston* and *Sim* (with *Simm*) in the unit of Cumberland
and Westmoreland.

TABLE 19.—*Names highly common in Scotland and also occurring in England with related forms*

[Including some, as Allan, Johnston, and Reid, which may be considered Scotch complements of English names]

Name	Entries in Scotch index	Number of English counties in which the Scotch form is reported ⊗	Notes on other English names and the number of counties in which reported ⊗
*Allan	390	1	Allen, 32.[1]
*Clark	638	[1] 36	Clark with Clarke, 36.
Cook	141	32	Cook with Cooke, 32.
Davidson	451	5	Davidson with Davison, 5.
Gardner	219	16	Gardiner with Gardner, 16.
Gray	456	16	Grey, 2.
Hay	191	1	Hayes, 7.
Hogg	142	1	Hodge, 3.
*Johnston	644	1	Johnson, 32.[1]
Martin	360	[1] 32	Martyn, 1 (Cornwall). Marten, 1 (Kent).
Mitchell	578	23	Michell, 1 (Cornwall).
*Reid	706	2	Read, 17; Reed, 15.
*Sharp	148	14	Sharp with Sharpe, 14.
*Sim	153	1	Sims, 5; Simm, 1.
*Simpson	383	15	Simson, 1 (Essex).
*Steel	151	5	Steel with Steele, 5.
*Stevenson	326	14	Stephenson with Stevenson, 14.
*Stewart	1,095	1	Steward, 3; Stuart, 1.
Wallace	317	3	Wallis, 9.
Wilson	1,048	[1] 30	Willson, 1 (Huntingdon).
Wood	228	[1] 27	Woods, 7.

⊗ According to Guppy.
* Including variants per Stark.
[1] See Table 8 for position among leading English names.

Table 20 accounts for the elimination of 27 more names none of which is reported used by the English in exactly the Scotch form. Invariably a slight change in spelling by Scotch-Americans or English-Americans produces confusion in the interpretation of American records. The American tendency to add *s* was well defined, and the names *Adam, Aitken, Bain, Dick, Rodger, Stephen,* and *Watt* in this list differ from the English forms only through its lack. *Hay* and *Sim* present a like situation in the preceding list.

TABLE 20.—*Leading Scotch names not distinctively Scotch-American because of the existence of English names but slightly different*

Name	Entries in Scotch index	Notes on English names with number of counties in which reported ⊗
Adam	147	Adams, 22.
*Aitken	214	Atkins, Adkins, 11.
Bain	176	Baines, Baynes, 7.
Baird	144	Beard, 7.
Currie	197	Curry, 2; Cory, 2.
Dick	152	Dicks, 1 (Somerset); Dix, 1 (Norfolk); Deck, 1 (Suffolk); Deeks, 2.

⊗ According to Guppy.
* Including variants per Stark.

TABLE 20.—*Leading Scotch names not distinctively Scotch-American because of the existence of English names but slightly different*—Continued

Name	Entries in Scotch index	Notes on English names with number of counties in which reported ⊗
*Dickson	253	Dixon, 13 (rarely Dickson).
*Hutchison	175	Hutchinson, 8.
*Inglis	134	Ingall and Ingle, 1 (Lincoln); English (surname) 4.
*Kerr	419	Carr, 9.
*Laing	228	Lain, 1 (Norfolk); Lang, 1 (Devon).
*Low	143	Lowe, 9.
M'Kay	669	Kay, Kaye, 3.
M'Kie	198	Key, 5.
*M'Lean	602	Lane 16, Lain, 1 (Norfolk).
*M'Neil	161	Neal, Neale, 12.
M'Rae. (See Rae.)	175	Ray, 1 (Essex); Rea, Reay, 3.
Muir	301	Moore, 29; Moor, 1 (York, N. & E. R.).
*Neilson	186	Nelson, 7.
Nicol	258	Nichol, 2; Nicholls, Nichols, 17; occasionally Nicols, Nickels, and Nickolls, also Nicholas and Nickless.
*Nicolson	165	Nicholson, 9.
*Paterson	635	Patterson, 2; Pattison, 3.
Rae	176	Ray, 1 (Essex); Rea, Reay, 3.
*Rodger	185	Rogers, 25; Rodgers, 1 (Derby).
*Stephen	205	Stevens, Stephens, 21.
*Thomson	1, 117	Thompson, 27.[1]
Watt	279	Watts, 14.

⊗ According to Guppy.

* Including variants per Stark.

[1] See Table 8 for position among leading English names.

OTHER NAMES NOT DISTINCTIVELY SCOTCH

In addition to the above, 26 names were eliminated, for sundry reasons, from the list of indicators of Scotch blood. Their exclusion was based on clan records and genealogies indicating more use in England than Guppy's record disclosed, or on preliminary investigation of American occurrences disclosing coincidences that involved them in aggregative American usage.

The following notes illustrate two important phases in any study of sources of names, namely, irregularities and companionships. A preparatory scrutiny of American usage of the 74 names determined on as possible indicators in Stark's list discovered some with numbers too great, too few, or too irregular to be accounted for on the basis of companionship. In some instances these *irregularities* were due to usage by people who had names so alike that they finally used these names instead of their own. In others it happened that names rare in Europe early gained a foothold in America and acquired remarkable numbers, the descendants of a few individuals producing considerable irregularities in the scheme of American nomenclature. These latter instances neither demonstrate nor deny the rule, but simply mark the exceptions inevitable in any field of human activity and necessitate a study of American currency so that what were truly family lines will not be given general significance.

No test of origins is more effective than the examination of *companionships*. Records are never available for all of the American bearers of a particular name, and the most conclusive evidence concerning the sources of American currency is drawn from a comparative study of frequencies. If a name is to be rated as of particular origin, its standing in American currency, compared with other names which were its original companions in that place of origin, must reflect old-world relationships in frequency. Hence names presumably Scotch must be labeled exceptional if their usage was one-fifth as much or five times as much as a preliminary study of Scotch-American usage indicates it should be. Excessive American currency probably indicates that these names were introduced from European localities other than those under consideration, and slight currency suggests that Americans replaced them with new forms or that their introduction was hindered by some special factor.

The test of companionship ultimately disposed of three names not eliminated at this point. European data indicates *Forbes* as a distinctively Scotch name, but formal examination of American usage will show American currency so great as to demonstrate that the name must have had sources besides Scotland. Similarly, in the study of Scotch-Irish names, *Paton* will prove to have had such great currency as to presuppose British rather than merely Scotch-Irish antecedents; while *M'Innes* will reveal such slight usage as to intimate that its American numbers were not functionally related to original numbers in Scotland and Ireland.

The following paragraphs detail nomenclatural relationships of 22 Scotch appellations whose American currency could not be interpreted without disproportionate study; also of four other names—*Boyle, Kelly, M'Guire,* and *Murphy*—included in Stark's list but actually Irish (having gained their numbers in Scotland by migration during the nineteenth century). *Burns* will be noted to have become the American interpretation of a number of names, particularly the Irish *Byrne,* originally quite unrelated. Six names—*Cairns, Irvine, M'Ewan, M'Lachlan, M'Millan,* and *Milne*—show marked degrees of confusion with other names, and draw attention to American aggregates.

BARCLAY—Subject to confusion with *Berkeley,* a rare English name which became markedly important in America through early introduction. Guppy did not report names of this pattern as even locally common in England. Matheson showed *Barclay* and *Berkeley* as separate names, both rare, in Ireland.

BOYLE—Scarcely represented in the county directory of Scotland, hence not native. A leading Ulster name carried to Scotland in numbers by migration during the middle of the nineteenth century.

BURNS—Greatly popularized in America. The popularity of this name, combined with the American tendencies to add *s* and spell phonetically, largely accounts for the rarity in American rosters of the important Leinster name *Byrne,* whose potential currency was that of *Doyle,* its companion in Leinster. *Burns* probably also replaced the less important Irish appellation *Beirne* and covered some Swiss from *Bern. Burns* was of strictly local use in England.

CAIRNS.—American usage makes an aggregate of variants of this name and those of the Irish *Kearns,* the German *Kern* and the English *Karn.* The American tendency to add -*s* is again important. *Cairns* itself was known in only one county in England and *Karn* was local to Surrey. Both *Kearns* and *Cairns* were fairly common in Ireland. *Kern* was highly common among German immigrants. (Oath of Allegiance Record.)

CHALMERS—American usage of this name was almost *nil.* It appears to have been replaced by *Chambers.* Anderson reports *Chalmers* and *Chambers* as synonymous. (Wm. Anderson, *Genealogy and Surnames,* Edinburgh, 1865.) Aside from one entry for *Chalmor* and one for *Chalmer,* the only entries in the 1790 records identifiable as *Chalmers* are in the South Carolina census: *Chalmers,* 6, and *Chalmbers,* 3. The dominant *Chambers* was native to 10 English counties.

FLEMING—Seems to have been more important in England than indicated by Guppy. (John R. Magrath, *The Flemings of Oxford*, Oxford, 1904.) It is important to note that usage of *Fleming* as a surname is only an indirect result of Flemish settlement in the United Kingdom. It would naturally gain usage as a family designation where Flemish provincials were exceptional. Guppy reported it as native only to Cumberland and Westmoreland.

FORREST—French and Walloon settlers in America commonly bore the names *Deforest* and *de Forrest*. In England *Forrest* was common only in Lancashire.

HAMILTON—Not a common name in England, yet too familiar to be designated non-English. Guppy did not report it but noted *Hambleton* as native to Staffordshire. Phelps reported a Leicester line of *Hamiltons*. (James A. Phelps, *The Hamilton Family in America*, New York, 1913. This title contains one of those ridiculous instances of the misuse of the term " family " as applied to the bearers of a common name.) The American bearers of the name must have been largely Scotch and Irish, but commonly English and sometimes properly *Hambletons*.

HENDRY—Note the Teutonic *Hendrichs* and *Hendryx*, the English *Hendy*, also the possibility of occurrence in abbreviation of names like *Hendrichson*.

IRVINE—A fine illustration of an aggregate in American nomenclature. *Irvine* itself was not English but *Irving* occurred in two English counties. In Ireland both *Irwin* and *Irvine* were common, and were supplemented by *Ervine* and *Erwin* in small numbers. Further, Faust reports *Erwin* (vol. I, p. 291) as a Pennsylvania-German name. The American bearers of *Erwin*, however, seldom had Teutonic baptismal names. In the complex American group, Irish bearers are excessive for a good study of Scotch origins.

JACK—Subject to confusion with the French *Jacques* and the English *Jacks*. The latter is reported as native only to Salop.

KELLY—Native to Cornwall and Devonshire, England. Gained its numbers in Stark's record by movement of Irish eastward, but may have been a rare Scotch name. It is the second most common name in Ireland where it scarcely had the variant *Kelley*, which is characteristic of American nomenclature.

KENNEDY—Clouded in America by usage of names on the order of *Canada*. *CPG* analysts were unable to subclassify 32 forms of the *Kennedy-Canada* pattern.

LINDSAY—Variety of English names on this pattern. (John W. Linzee, *The Lindeseie and Limesi Families of Great Britain*, 2 vols., Boston, 1917.) Diversity of English forms possibly accounts for Guppy's reporting none common in even one county.

M'EWAN—Forms an aggregate with the variants of the important Irish name *McKeown*, which was of unstable spelling. English name *Evans* sometimes considered a translation of some of these forms.

M'GUIRE—Carried to Scotland by the Irish. No usage in the county directory of native Scotch families.

M'LACHLAN—Overshadowed by Irish *McLaughlin* and *McLoughlin*. Numerous variations on this pattern in the 1790 records, but almost never this form. Entries for *Claflin*, *McGlothlin*, *Loughlin*, and all forms which are promising variants, do not number enough bearers properly to reflect both Irish and Scotch antecedents. Superficially indicates that the true *M'Lachlan* clan sent few numbers to colonial America.

M'MILLAN—MILNE—Inextricably confused with each other and other names in America. With the prefix they blend with the Irish *McMullan*. Irish had also common name *Mullan* (variable spelling) ; French had *Mullen* and *Moulin*. The most common 1790 names on the general pattern were *McMullen*, *McMillan*, and *Millens*. Probably such *Milnes* as there were among the colonials used either *s* or *Mc*, or both. Prefix was usually subject to disuse, but there are other groups which show reverse tendency, as this seems to.

MATHESON—Guppy reported *Madison* native to Durham and Lincolnshire, and *Mattison* local to Yorkshire; also occasional English use of *Mathison, Matterson, Matteson* and *Matson.* Rare in Ireland. Occurrence in 1790 record erratic. A striking feature was 74 entries for *Mathewson* in the little State of Rhode Island.

MURPHY—The most common Irish name, neither English nor properly Scotch.

MURRAY—Subject to confusion with French *Maury,* and German *Maurer.*

SINCLAIR—Originally Norman, but modern bearers are largely Scotch. Nowhere common in England, but covered a number of families or family branches there. (Thomas Sinclair. *The Sinclairs of England,* London, 1887.) Some usage in almost all European countries. (Leonard A. Morrison, *The History of the Sinclair Family in Europe and America,* Boston, 1896.) Bearers other than Scotch are more prominent than numerous.

STRACHAN—When the surname system was taking shape, this name had various forms such as *Straquhan, Strathauchin,* and *Strauchin.* (Memorials of the Scottish Families *Strachan* and *Wise,* Edinburgh 1877.) In America the name seems to have been lost between *Stratton* and *Strawn.* The origin of *Strawn,* earlier *Strawchen,* seems unknown. (*Old Richland Families,* Norristown, Pa., 1898.) *Stratton* not investigated, but it is pointed out that the Gaelic *ch* occasionally becomes *th* or *t,* and that *Strachan* originally had variants containing *th.*

TURNBULL—Affected, like *Strachan,* by a pattern for imitation accidentally found in America; or like *Chalmers,* by an English pattern. American usage runs to *Trimble,* occasionally to *Trumbull.* Guppy reported *Turnbull* but not *Trimble.* Whatever its origin, *Trimble* was the directing agent in this segment of nomenclature.

WEIR—The English have *Were* and *Ware,* originally local to Devonshire; and *Warr,* local to Buckinghamshire. New Amsterdam Dutch used *Van der Weir.* And there was also *De la Warr* (original of *Delaware*).

NAMES SHARED WITH THE IRISH

Comparison with formal records of English usage eliminated more than half of Stark's names from those potentially distinctive, and further comparisons made a number of others unavailable as indicators of Scotch antecedents because of confusion with various names in America. This preliminary scrutiny of European and American usage finally left but 48 names rather definitely Scotch. Comparison of these 48 names in Scotland with Matheson's record for occurrence in Ireland shows their relative distribution east and west of the North Channel.

In Table 21 the 48 names remaining to be tested are shown in the order of their distinctiveness tested by scarcity of bearers in Ireland.

This table, based on Stark's and Matheson's data on original frequency, compares relative numbers of bearers in Ireland with those in Scotland, rating the names accordingly. Column 1 shows the number of entries Stark noted for each name in the Scotch register of 1863, in a total of over 109,000. As he observed that the population of Scotland then was not purely Scotch, it is practical to view these entries as the number per 100,000 Scots. Column 2 shows the number of entries found by Matheson in the Irish birth register of 1890, totaling 105,000. Because of the difference in dates it is practical to speak of these as approximately the number among 100,000 Irish. Column 3 shows the ratios between these two sets of numbers. The ratios are purely arbitrary but enable arraying the names according to their representation in Ireland. Since the population of Ireland was greater than that of Scotland, the proportion of Irish bearers relative to Scotch was greater than these figures indicate.

The notes at the right supplementing the figures in the Irish column are made possible by Matheson's details on the frequency of names in Ireland.

Names are viewed in groups; the most common form in each is followed by an improper fraction, with a numerator indicating the number of Irish entries assembled under it as a group heading, and a denominator the number of the specific spelling. Thus "*Frazer 41/27*" indicates that the Irish ordinarily spelled the name with *z* and that of 41 entries of this general type 27 were *Frazer;* others in the group are indicated by the improper fraction to have used a different spelling, and it happens that all used *Fraser*. Notes calling attention to names which, in the writer's opinion, were not related to the Scotch names and were distinguishable from them in American usage are preceded by the word "also." In the absence of the word "also," the names cited are considered to have been actually Scotch names or their derivatives or names so similar that they must be viewed as closely related in American usage. Matheson's fine distinctions, such as the recognition of separate *McFarland* and *McFarlane* groups (without variation in the former "group") must be disregarded. In this study the two fall under the heading *McFarland*, making a group constituting 58 per 100,000 of Irish.

TABLE 21.—*Scotch names in the order of distinctiveness tested by uncommonness in Ireland*

Scotch name viewed as key name for group	Number per 100,000 Scots [1]	Number per 100,000 Irish [2]	Ratio of numbers	Notes on Irish groups and other names
M'Leod	513	----	------	
Munroe	*369	------	------	
M'Pherson	316	------	------	
M'Kinnon	220	------	------	
M'Laren	205	------	------	
Robertson	1,116	18	0.02	
M'Intosh	408	7	.02	
Sutherland	334	6	.02	
M'Kenzie	764	*22	.03	McKenzie, 22/21.
Bruce	241	7	.03	
M'Gregor	373	*16	.04	McGregor, 16/14.
Cameron	548	30	.06	
Fraser	*627	*41	.07	Frazer, 41/27, including Fraser 14.
Duncan	463	*41	.09	Duncan, 41/35, also Donegan, 31/23.
Forbes	225	*22	.10	Forbes 22/20.
Ritchie	252	*24	.10	Ritchie 24/23.
Ross	680	73	.11	
Buchanan	205	*24	.12	Buchanan 24/20; also Bohan 30/27; Bohane 5; Bogan 12/7.
Christie	229	*33	.14	Christy 17, Christie 16.
M'Donald	*1,308	*191	.15	McDonald 191/173; also Donald 6.
Donaldson	208	33	.16	
Ramsay	173	*28	.16	Ramsay 16, Ramsey 12.
Robb	133	21	.16	
McFarland	330	*58	.18	McFarland 46; McFarlane 12/7.
M'Intyre	300	*58	.19	McIntyre 58/42.
Morrison	562	*111	.20	Morrison 111/93.
Murdoch	149	*30	.20	Murdock 18, Murdoch 12.
Tait	162	36	.22	Tate, 36/25, including Tait, 10.
Rankin	*162	36	.22	
Baxter	140	31	.22	

[1] Entries in Scottish register for 1863, total 109,000, per Stark. Asterisk indicates variability in spelling recognized by Stark other than alternative use of *Mc* and *Mac*, when prefix occurs; variants are not specified.
[2] Entries in birth record of Ireland, 1890, total 105,000, as tabulated by Matheson. Asterisk indicates variable spelling accounted for at right. Matheson used the notation *Mc* for the prefix which Stark wrote *M'*. Variability in Irish spellings was much greater earlier in the century; Matheson's book of variants often shows variants for names not variable in 1890.
*Including known variants.

TABLE 21.—*Scotch names in the order of distinctiveness tested by uncommonness in Ireland*—Continued

Scotch name viewed as key name for group	Number per 100,000 Scots	Number per 100,000 Irish	Ratio of numbers	Notes on Irish groups and other names
Jamieson	*230	*52	0. 23	Jamison 52/24 including Jameson 20 and Jamieson 7.
Forsyth	142	*33	. 23	Forsythe 33/29.
Ferguson	473	*133	. 28	Ferguson 133/130; also Fergus 8.
Campbell	1, 079	349	. 32	Also Gamble 40/38.
Findlay	*241	*76	. 32	Finlay 76/69.
Paton	*180	*60	. 33	Patton 60/49 including Patten 10.
Black	339	116	. 34	
Gordon	340	*122	. 36	Gordon, 122/118.
M'Dougall	252	*91	. 36	McDowell, 91/89.
Moffat	152	*68	. 45	Moffett, 68/12, including Moffat, 11; Moffatt 11; Moffet, 10; Moffitt, 11; Moffit, 7.
Maxwell	133	68	. 51	
Blair	151	78	. 52	
Craig	271	*150	. 55	Craig 120; Creagh 17; Cregg 13.
Orr	133	73	. 55	
Cumming	*162	*131	. 75	Cummins 77; Cummings, 20/10; Commins, 20/17; Commons, 14/13.
Boyd	186	*55	. 83	Boyd 155/154.
M'Innes	150	*128	. 85	McGuinness 128/47.
Cunningham	238	*215	. 90	Cunningham 215/202.

*Including known variants.

The above tabulation indicates that distinctiveness of Scotch names must be construed relative to Irish usage and its modifications. Consideration of the very different conditions obtaining in the eighteenth century modifies these findings, but it is warrantable to accept them as an essentially accurate rating of the relationships of Scotch and Irish usage. Nonusage in Ireland is not demonstrated by absence of an entry in the Irish column as the minimum Matheson noted was five births. While his accuracy for 1890 is unquestioned, it is possible that names only slightly used in Ireland varied in the degrees of their representation in annual records, and likewise that once there were bearers of such names in Ireland.

DISTINCTIVELY SCOTCH NAMES DISTINGUISHED FROM SCOTCH-IRISH

Examination of the list of 48 names as arrayed in order of relative Irish usage indicated the desirability of recognizing three classes, only about a third being sufficiently free from Irish usage to be construed as distinctive, and another third, the names beginning with *Campbell*, being definitely the joint property of Scotland and Ireland. By these standards, the names from *M'Leod* to *Buchanan* in Table 21, were established as distinctively Scotch, or, in contrast to the others, as Class I. Those from *Christie* to *Forsyth* become Class II—Scotch names having substantial Irish usage. Those from *Ferguson* to *Cunningham* become Class III—names Scotch in origin but with usage in Ireland approaching or exceeding that in Scotland.[3]

---

[3] In popular expression, certain of the names heretofore eliminated may be added to the above classes—*Matheson, Chalmers, Sinclair,* and *Strachan* are distinctively Scotch with qualification. *Hamilton, Fleming, Cairns, Irvine,* and *M'Lachlan* might be entered in Class III as Scotch-Irish, except for the unusual situations previously noted.

The status of the name *Matheson* is instructive of the accidents of history. The Irish registrar had a Scotch name, the English registrar a name the joint property of England and Scotland (Table 18), and the Scottish registrar a name not common in his country but indeed cosmopolitan.

These studies completed the classification of leading Scotch names into seven classes; 3 related to English usage, 1 showing miscellaneous relationships, 2 defined relative to Irish usage, and 1 recognized as distinctively Scotch. The examination of Scotch contributions to American population was continued through the agency of the names thus identified as most nearly distinctive.

DEFINITION OF DISTINCTIVE GROUPS

For the Scots, as for all stocks not English, the inquiry must be concerned with relative representation of surnoun groups in America and abroad. Immediate emphasis falls upon the definition of the selected names as designations subject to some variation. The process of "definition" is that of determining the proper variants of names under Old World and American conditions. Both the recent statement of the ideal method of inquiry and the consideration of codification in Chapter II showed the importance of definition.

The inquiry next considered (1) just what Stark's tabulation of Scotch frequencies in 1863 means for the time when migration to colonial America was taking place, and (2) what American names should be recognized as resulting from the transmittal of the selected names to the New World. While Stark's report noted variation in his time for only a part of the names, a general study of nomenclature reveals that practically all of the names were variable in earlier times and became increasingly so on introduction into America.

Examination of the American record to learn what names lie within the groups represented in Stark's tabulation indicated that variability arose largely from (1) the migration of the Scots before Scotch nomenclature had crystallized into its modern form, (2) insufficient numbers of Scots in America to maintain Old World standards for spelling, and (3) the inaccuracy of the American marshals of the census in recording. Circumstances affecting Scotch nomenclature in the seventeenth and eighteenth centuries can not be discussed here; but as the clan organization was destroyed and the Highlanders modernized only about the middle of the eighteenth century, discretion was necessarily applied to identifying the earlier forms of clan names. While the Highlanders early recognized clan designations as surnames, standardization of spelling was slow in developing. A low state of literacy in Scotland also naturally occasioned various forms of names. In tracing the evolution in America of names already variable in the mother country it is important to remember that Americans of that time often spelled phonetically, losing some features of Scotch orthography in the process. Highland names generally were more modified than Lowland, but invariably the modification depended a good deal on familiarity with Scotch nomenclature in American localities.

A study of the forms resulting from the census taking would presumably show that while the marshals were guided in spelling by the better educated citizens, they were responsible for various forms which would not have occurred had the individuals made their own entries, and, further, that they were often left to develop their own versions when the head of the family was not sure of the spelling of his own name. Such misconstruction and crudity are typified by two illustrations: Very commonly the marshals wrote the given name *Angus* as *Anguish;* and ordinarily the surname *Sutherland* as *Southerland*—an enlightening bit of evidence, since no true Briton would confuse the name *Sutherland*, drawn from one of the most northerly counties in Scotland, with the mere sound of the word *southern*. *Southerland* is unintentional humor, but the marshals did better when they wrote *Forthsides* for *Forsyth.*

The sources consulted in this matter of variants and versions of Scotch names included Giles's directories of Scotland, Guppy's study of Scotch nomenclature, Matheson's two publications on forms of names in Ireland, and certain clan records and genealogical publications. But the determining of the forms to be recognized as variants or versions was based mainly on criticism of Table III, *CPG*, which shows the more common names in the census arranged in groups based on resemblance and often presenting a fairly satisfactory codification by origin.

Many of the selected names had English or Irish by-usage, and possibly some of the American forms assigned to the groups were really English or Irish variants. Inevitably the process of codifying American names leads to the formation of some groups which include persons of nationality other than the one being considered at the moment. The definition of the Scotch names involves a general tendency toward overstatement and one strong tendency toward understatement, the latter being that disuse of the prefix *Mc* frequently prevents full identification of variants.

Following is a statement of details of Scotch-American usage as disclosed by the Class I names, with considerable detail given to illustrate the general process of definition:

BRUCE—135 entries for *Bruce*, 11 miscellaneous such as *Bruse* and *Bruze*. *Brewis* (Virginia) excluded, since known as a Northumberland name.

BUCHANAN—Defined approximately as in Table 111, *CPG*. *Buch-* is often *Buck-*, and *-anan* shows various interpretations. Names of the pattern, *Bohannon*, are construed as hybrids of this name and the Irish *Bohan;* only *Buhannon* included here. Two-syllable names avoided as probably cognate with Irish *Bohan, Bohane, Bogan.* The usage of questionable names was only scattering.

CAMERON—Scant representation, and everything on the *Cam-r-n* pattern is accepted, including four *Camron*.

DUNCAN—Group limited to 2-syllable names in *Dun-*. *Dunkin* is principal variant. Variants must be distinguished from those of Irish *Donegan*.

FORBES—Difficult to define because of occurrence of *Fobes* (Massachusetts), *Forbus, Forbush,* and *Furbush* in fair numbers. *Fobes* ignored here; others construed as variants.

FRASER—The 19 forms in Table 111, *CPG*, are accepted here, as are five other entries in *Fre-*, all in Pennsylvania. Dominant American form *Frazier* is suggestive of Irish influence. Highly variable in American usage even to-day; diversity in 1790 record may be accounted for by slight modifications of pronunciation with recognition of some usage not Scotch.

M'GREGOR—Group probably weakened by loss of prefix. Several entries for *McGregory* are included, a modification tending toward the favored English *Gregory*. Eight entries without prefix may be considered Scotch—for example, *Grigger*. Definition here more liberal than in *CPG*.

M'INTOSH—Accepted practically as in *CPG*. Principal form is *McIntosh* rather than *Mackintosh*, lately more familiar. Forms without prefix would still be distinctive, but none seems to have been developed.

M'KENZIE—Highly variable; spelling and perhaps pronunciation imitate English *Kinsey*. Names without prefix excluded. The American group is formed around *McKinsey*.

M'KINNON—Scant representation, but possibly difficult to identify. Suggests influence of Irish *McKinny* from which it is distinguished here. Contrast infrequency of *McKinnon* with frequency of *McKinny*. Definition here more liberal than in *CPG*, and includes small numbers of *McCannon* and *McHonnen*. Forms without prefix excluded because of presence of English *Kenyon*.

M'LAREN—Scant representation, or marked blending with Irish *McCleary;* entries for *McClary* excluded here because it may have been intended for either name. The 32 entries identified as *M'Laren* include 19 in North Carolina, of which 17 were *McLerran*, one *McClaran*, and one *McClaren*. Pennsylvania shows five entries, all different and all involving *McC.*

M'LEOD—The 135 entries include 80 in North Carolina, of which 64 are *McLeod* and 13 *McCloud*, the latter illustrating the usual tendency in misspelling. This group is a good example of misconstruction increasing as local frequency decreases. *McC's* numerous, and *McClouds* in almost every State; but only five entries for *McLeod* other than those in North Carolina. Names without prefix excluded here. Comparison of currency of *M'Leod* and variants as defined, with that of companion names, indicates variants are not fully identified.

McPHERSON—Includes forms in Table 111, *CPG;* also six entries for *Farson* (associated with six for *McFarson*) in New Hampshire. Forms without prefix beginning with *P* excluded, because of English *Pearson, Peirson* and *Pierson. McPherson* dominant by virtue of numbers from Maryland south; otherwise forms in *McF*, especially *McFarson*, were usual.

MUNRO—Six spellings, combinations of *Mun-* and *Mon-* with *-ro, -roe,* and *-row;* single entries for *MnRow* [sic] and *Menroe, Munroe* dominant, but *Mon-* forms rather common in South and in New York. In 1790 Americans had not yet turned toward *Monroe* which now has several. times the frequency of all other forms together.

RITCHIE—Comprises 7 forms in *Rich-* and *Ritch-*, as in *CPG.* The 110 entries in the 12 indexes include 61 in Pennsylvania where the format is *Richey* 35, *-ie* 3, *-y* 4; and *Ritchey* 11, *-ie* 7, *-y* 1.

ROBERTSON—Limited to 7 forms. The 506 accepted entries include *Robertson* 351, *Roberson* 94, *Robeson*, 44 *Robason* 13, *and* miscellaneous 4. Although definition is more stringent than *CPG's*, it is still possibly too liberal, because of association with English *Robinson* and *Robson.* The most questionable entries are those for *Robeson*, found almost entirely in Pennsylvania (38) and North Carolina.

Ross—Only this exact form accepted. Influenced through by-usage of English, Irish, and Germans, and some voluntary usage. (See notes on Pennsylvania names in R-, *Chapter II*, p. 149.)

SUTHERLAND—Largely *South-*, sometimes *Soth-*, and sometimes *-lin.* Good illustrations of American unawareness of derivations.

AMERICAN USAGE OF SCOTCH NAMES

Tables 22 and 22a set forth the numbers of heads of families identified as bearers of the selected Scotch names in the 1790 records, the side heads being the group headings as already defined, arranged in the order of their importance in Scotland. Table 22 covers the New England States, and Table 22a the States remaining in the area of record, with totals by States and by surnouns, and a special set of totals omitting the name *Forbes* as showing such great currency that it can not be construed distinctively Scotch.

TABLE 22.—*Heads of families of selected Scotch names in New England, 1790*

Names [1]	Maine	New Hamp- shire	Vermont	Massa- chusetts	Rhode Island	Con- necticut	Total
Robertson	16	38	5	21	------	22	102
M'Kenzie	4	3	------	2	3	2	14
Ross	21	12	9	49	17	8	116
Fraser	2	2	5	10	3	7	29
Cameron	------	1	------	1	------	1	3

[1] In order of importance in Scotland.

TABLE 22.—*Heads of families of selected Scotch names in New England, 1790*—Continued

Names	Maine	New Hampshire	Vermont	Massachusetts	Rhode Island	Connecticut	Total
M'Leod	1	3	1	5	1	------	11
Duncan	2	17	6	8	1	6	40
M'Intosh	4	6	3	8	------	3	24
M'Gregor	1	4	1	2	1	2	11
Munro	1	7	7	63	23	15	116
Sutherland	1	------	6	1	------	1	9
M'Pherson	2	12	1	4	------	1	20
Ritchie	1	3	1	2	------	------	7
Bruce	1	4	9	45	------	1	60
Forbes	20	2	6	66	------	18	112
M'Kinnon	1	1	------	------	------	------	2
M'Laren	------	1	2	------	------	------	3
Buchanan	------	------	------	------	------	------	2
Total (18)	78	116	64	287	49	87	681
Total omitting Forbes	58	114	58	221	49	69	569

TABLE 22a.—*Heads of families of selected Scotch names in the remaining area of record, 1790*

Names [1]	New York	Pennsylvania	Maryland	Virginia	North Carolina	South Carolina	Total
Robertson	42	58	28	99	108	69	404
M'Kenzie	13	22	13	6	30	19	103
Ross	43	111	30	36	65	38	323
Fraser	26	37	25	18	43	32	181
Cameron	16	15	1	9	23	16	80
M'Leod	9	25	3	3	80	4	124
Duncan	16	51	17	19	41	39	183
M'Intosh	12	4	4	9	24	9	62
M'Gregor	8	17	7	4	9	4	49
Munro	28	6	6	9	21	7	77
Sutherland	35	8	4	19	22	4	92
M'Pherson	10	7	18	11	37	16	99
Ritchie	4	61	6	11	8	13	103
Bruce	6	8	10	33	21	8	86
Forbes	25	19	5	13	35	7	104
M'Kinnon	6	1	1	------	22	------	30
M'Laren	2	5	1	------	19	2	29
Buchanan	16	53	16	7	20	19	131
Total (18)	317	508	195	306	628	306	2,260
Total omitting Forbes	292	489	190	293	593	299	2,156

[1] In order of importance in Scotland.

RELATIVE AMERICAN OCCURRENCE OF SCOTCH NAMES

In the interpretation of the significance of the occurrence of Scotch names which follows, elementary steps are brought out so as to simplify understanding of the complete sequence.

In the measurement of recurrences of Scotch names, the entries observed by Stark in a total of 109,000 are construed as the ratio per 100,000 native Scots, an adjustment to allow for the " large accession of Irish and other immigrants " in Scotland prior to 1863. This adjustment of the data now has greater importance than it had in Table 21 where only approximation was necessary. As a result of employing the convenient round figure Scotch stock is rated at 92 per cent of the measures otherwise obtainable, but in the author's opinion is not thereby understated.

Table 23 measures the recurrences of the selected Scotch names in the area of record, by comparing the numbers of heads of families in 1790 United States with ratios per 100,000 Scots, and deriving the total numbers of Scotch-American families indicated by the usage of each name. This type of calculation may be illustrated by the surnoun *Robertson* for which there were 506 entries in the American record, resulting from a Scotch ratio of 11.16 per thousand. Dividing 506 by 11.16 shows a scale of occurrence in America natural to slightly more than 45,000 Scotch families, the factor of recurrence being 45.3.

The measures of indicated Scotch population range between 14,000 and 65,000 Scotch families, exclusive of the reading from *Forbes* which has been noted as entirely out of ratio with the other names in this list; its abnormality is demonstrated here and in Table 24, and the name is then dropped from the list of indicators.

TABLE 23.—*Recurrence of selected Scotch names in the 1790 records*

	Scots per 100,000, 1863	Heads of families United States, 1790	Number of Scotch-American families indicated by the recurrence of the name
Robertson	1, 116	506	45, 300
M'Kenzie	764	117	15, 300
Ross	680	439	64, 600
Fraser	627	210	33, 500
Camerson	548	83	15, 100
M'Leod	513	135	26, 300
Duncan	463	223	48, 200
M'Intosh	408	86	21, 100
M'Gregor	373	60	16, 100
Munro	369	193	52, 300
Sutherland	334	101	30, 200
M'Pherson	316	119	37, 700
Ritchie	252	110	43, 700
Bruce	241	146	60, 600
Forbes	225	216	96, 000
M'Kinnon	220	32	14, 500
M'Laren	205	32	15, 600
Buchanan	205	133	64, 900
Total (18)	7, 859	2, 941	37, 400
Total, omitting Forbes	7, 634	2, 725	35, 700

Table 24 lists the selected Scotch names in the order of the total numbers of Scotch-American families which they indicate for the area of record. It brings out clearly the abnormality of *Forbes*. The arithmetic average occurrence of 17 other names indicates 35,700 Scotch-American families, very nearly the same as the median measurement of the 18 names. When *Forbes* is eliminated, the median becomes 33,500, indicating that arithmetic averages overstate the proportion of Scots.

This table discloses two important points concerning measurements of rates of migration obtained from a study of Scotch names; the low position of the *Mc* names, and the intangibility of regional influences. That the Highland clans with names involving the prefix " Mac " had less than average representation is not clearly indicated because of disguise frequently accompanying loss of the prefix. The low standing of *McKinnon* may have a special explanation. Examination of American usage indicates a surprising number of Americans named *McKinney*, which may generally be thought of as Irish, yet it may be that Scots adopted an Irish pattern in this instance.

Regional origins of the Scotch are not immediately disclosed by these figures. For example, a contradiction is noted in the readings of *Ross*, *M'Kenzie* and *M'Leod*, names reported by Stark to have had their principal center in the counties of Ross and Cromarty. The recurrence of *Ross* tends to show that this area was largely represented in American migration, an inference denied by the measurements of its companions *M'Leod* and *M'Kenzie*. This may be explained by the popularization of the name *Ross* in America and by some lack of favor for the other two names, both of which were easily misinterpreted, one because of its pronunciation (McCloud), the other by the dominating presence of the English name *Kinsey*. Aside from the considerations of favor and disfavor for names in America, the shortness of this list makes it unsuitable for tracing local origins.

TABLE 24.—*Scotch names arrayed by recurrence in the area of record*

Name	Number of Scotch-American families indicated by the recurrence of the name as defined	Name	Number of Scotch-American families indicated by the recurrence of the name as defined
Forbes	96, 000	M'Leod	26, 300
Buchanan	64, 900	M'Intosh	21, 100
Ross	64, 600	M'Gregor	16, 100
Bruce	60, 600	M'Laren	15, 600
Munro	52, 300	M'Kenzie	15, 300
Duncan	48, 300	Cameron	15, 100
Robertson	45, 300	M'Kinnon	14, 500
Ritchie	43, 700	18 collectively	37, 400
M'Pherson	37, 700	17 collectively, omitting	
Fraser	33, 500	Forbes	35, 700
Sutherland	30, 200	Median of 17	33, 500

SCOTCH CONTRIBUTIONS TO POPULATION IN TERMS OF FAMILIES

Table 25 carries out the determination of Scotch-American families by States. It shows in column 1 the collective numbers of heads of families bearing the specified names in each State in the area of record, ranging from 49 in Rhode Island to 593 in North Carolina. Column 2 shows the indicated totals of Scotch families. The figures by States range from 640 in Rhode Island to 7,770 in North Carolina, the total for the country being approximately 35,700. Percentage contributions to population will be determined by another calculation in the next table. The estimates of the numbers of Scotch-American families shown in Table 25 will prove useful in the analysis of American usage of names shared by the Scotch and Irish, to be examined in Chapter VI.

TABLE 25.—*Contributions of Scots to American population, 1790, in terms of families indicated by the numbers of heads of families 17 specified names*[1]

Areas	Heads of families census of 1790 United States listed under 17 names[2]	Number of Scotch families indicated by the collective recurrence of the names	Areas	Heads of families census of 1790, United States listed under 17 names[3]	Number of Scotch families indicated by the collective recurrence of the names
Maine_____	58	760	Maryland_____	190	2,490
New Hampshire___	114	1,490	Virginia[3]_____	293	3,840
Vermont_____	58	760	North Carolina___	593	7,770
Massachusetts_____	221	2,890	South Carolina___	299	3,920
Rhode Island_____	49	640	Area of record:		
Connecticut_____	69	900	By direct cal-		
New York_____	292	3,820	culation____	2,725	35,700
Pennsylvania_____	489	6,410	By addition__	2,725	35,690

[1] Whose bearers are estimated from Stark to constitute 76.34 per 1,000 among Scots.
[2] For detail by specific name see Tables 22 and 22a.
[3] Partial record only.

PERCENTAGE CONTRIBUTIONS OF SCOTS TO POPULATION

Table 26 shows the calculation of the percentage contributions of Scots to population in the area of record in 1790, following the plan used in Table 5 in the study of the English, with the difference that while in the English study of recurrences the names were tested in each State and certain names designated as of abnormal ratio so that each State had a special list of indicators, in Table 26 the same list of indicators is used in each State.

Column 1 shows the total number of heads of families in the alphabetic indexes of the census of 1790, column 2 accounts for 2,725 families bearing one or another of the 17 distinctively Scotch names, and column 3 gives the ratios in number per thousand. The area of record shows 451,000 families containing 2,725 bearing the specified names. Hence the names were used by six per 1,000. Among Scots they were borne by 76 persons per thousand, thus indicating that in the area of record Scots constituted slightly less than 8 per cent of the population. (6.04 divided by 76.34 gives 0.079.) Column 4 shows the percentage contributions of Scots to the several States of record. While these figures directly concern the Scotch they indirectly throw light on the general composition of the population, particularly the possible distribution of the English.

TABLE 26.—*Calculation of percentage contributions of Scots to population in the area of record, 1790*

	Total, heads of families indexed, Census of 1790	Heads of families listed under 17 Scotch names [1]	Number per thousand listed under these names	Indicated percentage of contribution of Scots to population [2]
Area of record	451, 120	2, 725	6. 04	7. 9
Maine	17, 020	58	3. 41	4. 5
New Hampshire	24, 090	114	4. 73	6. 2
Vermont	14, 970	58	3. 87	5. 1
Massachusetts	65, 230	221	3. 39	4. 4
Rhode Island	11, 140	49	4. 40	5. 8
Connecticut	40, 680	69	1. 70	2. 2
New York	54, 540	292	5. 35	7. 0
Pennsylvania	74, 510	489	6. 56	8. 6
Maryland	32, 690	190	5. 81	7. 6
Virginia	37, 710	293	7. 77	10. 2
North Carolina	52, 560	593	11. 28	14. 8
South Carolina	25, 980	299	11. 51	15. 1

[1] Whose bearers constitute 76.34 per 1,000 among Scots.
[2] Determined from the ratio of the proportion in column 3 to the original Scotch proportion of 76.34 per 1,000.

The indicated proportions of Scots in the States of record have a seried relationship which confirms the working hypothesis of close connections between adjoining States. In New England the proportions of the stock declined in all directions from New Hampshire. Along the seaboard, Connecticut provided the low point from which there was an almost continuous rise in proportions southward. This graduation indicates the probable conditions in States of lost records.

For New Jersey an estimate of 7.7 per cent is adopted from Nelson (*CPG*, pp. 119–121) because of the conformity of his findings with the foregoing readings for adjoining States (New York, 7.0; Pennsylvania, 8.6).

INTERPOLATION FOR STATES OF MISSING RECORDS

Conditions in the small unit of population in Delaware can be gaged by the figures for the adjoining States—Maryland 7.6, New Jersey 7.7, Pennsylvania 8.6 percentages all close to 8 per cent, which is adopted here as an approximate figure for the Scotch in Delaware.

Kentucky and Tennessee derived their population mainly from States to the east, chiefly Pennsylvania, Maryland, Virginia, and North Carolina. Assuming these four States contributed about equally to the population of less than 100,000 in these two districts treated here as a unit, the proportion of Scotch is found to have been about 10 per cent.

Georgia, the most southerly State, must have had the highest proportion of Scotch, there being a definite increase in ratios from Connecticut to North Carolina and some further gain in South Carolina. This suggests an estimate of 15.5 per cent for Scotch contributions to Georgia's population.

SUMMARY

Table 27 details the estimated numbers and proportions of Scotch in the white population of the United States in 1790, by States and in total, with subtotals for New England. Column 1 shows population totals, column 2 percentages, and column 3 absolute numbers of Scotch in these totals. Column 4 indicates the geographical distribution of Scotch in percentages of their total of 263,330.

This estimate of numbers and distribution fairly certainly indicates that almost two-thirds of the Scotch were in the five States of Virginia, North Carolina, Pennsylvania, New York, and South Carolina, named in the order of their importance. Particularly large numbers of the Scotch were in Virginia (17 per cent), North Carolina (16 per cent), and Pennsylvania (14 per cent) ; and about one-sixth of the stock was in New England. Relative to total white population the stock is estimated as 8.3 per cent.

TABLE 27.—*Estimated numbers and proportions of Scots in the white population of the United States, 1790*

	White population	Per cent Scotch	Number Scotch	Geographical distribution (per cent)
United States	3, 172, 444	8. 3	263, 330	100. 0
Maine	96, 107	4. 5	4, 320	1. 6
New Hampshire	141, 112	6. 2	8, 750	3. 3
Vermont	85, 072	5. 1	4, 340	1. 7
Massachusetts	373, 187	4. 4	16, 420	6. 3
Rhode Island	64, 670	5. 8	3, 750	1. 4
Connecticut	232, 236	2. 2	5, 110	1. 9
New England	(992, 384)	(4. 3)	(42,690)	(16. 2)
New York	314, 366	7. 0	25, 010	9. 5
New Jersey	169, 954	7. 7	13, 090	-5. 0
Pennsylvania	423, 373	8. 6	36, 410	13. 9
Delaware	46, 310	8. 0	3, 700	1. 4
Maryland	208, 649	7. 6	15, 860	6. 0
Kentucky and Tennessee	93, 046	10. 0	9, 300	3. 5
Virginia	442, 117	10. 2	45, 100	17. 2
North Carolina	289, 181	14. 8	42, 800	16. 3
South Carolina	140, 178	15. 1	21, 170	8. 0
Georgia	52, 886	15. 5	8, 200	3. 1

Chapter V

CONTRIBUTIONS OF THE CELTIC IRISH TO 1790 AMERICA

Although the study of the Irish contribution to American population bears a general resemblance to that of the Scotch, there is considerable difference, largely because the data on Irish names are more complete and the demands upon the investigator more exacting. The information on Irish nomenclature permits giving much attention to the classification of names with the object of ascertaining regional origins. This permits a determination of the total Irish by a combination of estimates for the Provinces so that less emphasis is placed on names generally representative of the Irish than was the case with the Scots. The northern Irish occupy a commanding position in this study, corresponding to the Lowland Scots in the previous one. Like them they display a nomenclature of such diversity that its recurrence can be fully interpreted only by consideration of usage not fully distinctive. What makes the present study exacting is that the Irish contained substocks which not only had different types of names, sometimes names hardly peculiar to their motherland, but also showed independent rates of migration. This means that the cleavage of the people must be reflected in analyses by regions or Provinces and by substocks.

SOURCES

The principal materials for this study are the report on nomenclature of the Irish in 1890, by Sir Robert Matheson, then assistant registrar-general for Ireland; a supplementary report by Matheson on variants and synonyms of Irish names (Dublin, 1890); the American indexes compiled from returns of the census of 1790; and Table 111 in *CPG*, showing the principal name forms in use in America in 1790. Attention was also given to many authorities on etymology, local American history, and genealogy for information or suggestions on the origin of names not immediately identified as variants of Irish roots.

OUTLINE OF THE IRISH STUDY

Matheson's report is the chief European reference, but as it was made substantially more than a century after the mean date of emigration to colonial America, it imposes the necessity of allowing for evolution in Irish nomenclature and for adjustment in the Irish population during that period. Evolution of Irish nomenclature during the eighteenth and nineteenth centuries involves consideration of the development and decline of forms. The effects of their rise and fall are offset by grouping, and difficulties in accurate definition of groups are largely avoided by class treatment leading to average measures of occurrence. The problem of the flux of population within Ireland from the time of the mean date of migration down to 1890 is treated by balancing, weighting, and averaging the recurrence measures of groups and classes of names. Only arithmetic averages are used, the essential agreement between totals of figures for provincial origins and those for currency of names of general background in Ireland implying that the use of medians would not radically affect the findings.

232

The evidence on Irish nomenclature permits classifying the names with the object of tracing regional migration and determining total Irish by coordinating estimates for the provinces. Like the Lowland Scotch, the northern Irish have such diversity of nomenclature that interpretation of its currency includes consideration of usage other than of the distinctive names, but the latter necessarily form the basis of this study, since while not thoroughly representative of the people as a whole, they are thoroughly Irish.

This study was designed to determine Irish proportions in the United States in 1790 by original Provinces and as far as possible to designate these proportions in each State. But as these contributions can not be fully measured on the basis of usage of the distinctive names, it is necessary to determine what contribution is disclosed by American currency of peculiarly Irish names, and then to what extent findings for the several Provinces must be adjusted to allow for factional migration of Irish with names not peculiar to that nationality.

Matheson's information on the occurrence of names in Ireland is so extensive that virtually half of this study is given to the classification of names by their original geographical background. Common names in Ireland are classified as distinctive or otherwise; the distinctive names are then classified by area of principal usage, and five sets of these are given comparative study. Four are of names distinctive of the four Provinces—Leinster, Munster, Ulster, Connaught—and support studies to determine provincial representation, summarized to estimate the total number of Irish in America. This summary is then compared with findings obtained from measuring American usage of names of general antecedents in Ireland, which provides a control to prevent radical misinterpretation of the indicators, guard against serious errors in calculation of provincial proportions, and afford a check on the proportion of Irish in America.

In view of all these considerations, the present chapter is concerned with Irish contributions to American population had all Irish migrated at the rate of the native faction with peculiarly Irish names, here called Celtic to distinguish them from the English-Irish and the Scotch-Irish. A later chapter will study the migration rates of the three Irish factions forming the stock as a whole.

METHOD

The evidence concerning Irish names is formally treated in a series of 12 steps suggested by the wealth of nomenclatural detail and the varied aspects of the subject, the separate steps evolving naturally through the distinct phases developed in the successive treatments of the material, an adaptation of the ideal distinctive name system outlined in Chapter IV.

The plan has two main divisions, treating European classification and American usage. The first division comprises the recasting of Matheson's material in five steps: Abstracting common Irish names; preliminary sorting to eliminate the nondistinctive; refining group arrangements and segregating distinctive groups; classifying the peculiarly Irish groups according to geographical background; and selecting indicators of provincial and general Irish antecedents. The line between original and ultimate distinctiveness is not sharply drawn since the overlapping of English and Scotch nomenclatures into Ireland makes the tests of original peculiarity quite comprehensive.

The evidence both on provincial Irish names and on those of general antecedents in Ireland points to an Irish contribution of about 6 per cent to American population had all factions been represented in ratio to those with distinctive Irish names. The provincial findings and the control findings are enough alike superficially to admit the assumption that they cover the evidence, but closer observation reveals a larger Irish representation in the country, explained by sharp factional cleavage in the Irish population. The measurements here nevertheless definitely indicate the contributions of the main body of population in the motherland, and particularly its relative distribution along the Atlantic seaboard.

The second division is opened with the establishment of American usage, beginning with step 6 and carried through steps 7 and 8. Interpretation of Irish contributions takes form in step 9 where American usage of the selected Irish surnouns is compiled. Step 10 gives a preliminary statement of the method of coordinating provincial ratings brought out further in step 11, and step 12 completes the compilation of Celtic representation in total and by Provinces. The last four steps together interpret the relative occurrences of distinctive Irish names in America in terms of contributions by Provinces to the States of record, make interpolation for the States of missing records to complete the ratings and finally check the coordination of the several sets of findings.

CLASSIFICATION OF IRISH BY SURNAMES

Matheson's record of surnames in common use in Ireland in 1890 gives the number and distribution of births recorded under all names (as he defines them) having five or more entries in the birth registry of that year. He treats certain odd spellings and some names of minor use as variants, and lists separately the names without prefixes. For names in common use, the total number of births in the registry gives a satisfactory measure of the total bearers in the population.

Step 1 made an abstract of all names in Matheson's record showing 50 or more births. They will be referred to as common names. As there were 105,254 births in that year (1890), the minimum frequency of these names was practically 1 per 2,000. A total of 459 names covering 66,525 births appeared in this abstract, indicating that names in common use in Ireland accounted for upward of 63 per cent of the population; but as some names of minor use were so like common ones as to be hardly distinguishable, they are here combined with those they most resemble, this change resulting in the abstract covering 64.7 per cent of all births.

Step 2 separated distinctive Irish names from those of significant use outside of Ireland, and those very closely similar to names used by other nationalities. American records revealed further instances of confusion between variants of different names, and the ultimate list of names of common use in Ireland but not peculiar to it totaled 247, showing that more than half of the 459 names in common use in Ireland were not distinctively Irish.

The test of significant use in England[1] was established usage in at least one county; that in Scotland was seven listings in the Scotland County Directory.[2] Many Irish names show a few listings in the Scotch directory—*Murphy* has four—but seven listings or more demonstrate established usage in Scotland.

The national origin of 32 of the names construed as not distinctively Irish probably would not be questioned aboard, but their variants can not be readily distinguished from names of other antecedents in America. A few like *Darcy*

---

[1] Guppy, *Homes of Family Names in Great Britain*, London, 1890.
[2] Giles, *Scotland County Directory*, 1902.

and *Devine* were French in form; the remainder were similar to other British names.   Also among the exclusions are 215 names of mixed British antecedents, the classification of which suggests some interesting questions about contributions of Scotch and English to Irish blood; 112 were used in Scotland and England; 57 in England but not in Scotland, and 46 in Scotland but not in England; indicating that in distinguishing the Irish the Scotch-Irish are no more of a problem than the English-Irish.

Table 28 shows a specimen page of the author's record of common names not distinctively Irish; also the general form of the data concerning Irish usage. Two instances of the author's simplification of Matheson's codification appear on this page; *Keany* under *Keane*, and *Carney* under *Kearney*.   Treated separately by Matheson, these two rare names show less than 50 births and hence are not included independently in this abstract but because of their resemblance to names more commonly used are added to other groups, just as Matheson combined *Johnston* and *Johnstone*.

The six columns of figures in this table show numbers of births recorded in Ireland in 1890.   Column " T " lists the total births recorded under each surname as defined by Matheson; columns " L," " M," " U," " C," the recorded births in the four Provinces—Leinster, Munster, Ulster, and Connaught, and by inference the distribution of bearers; column " sp.," the numbers of entries under different spellings if several were grouped together, also births not specifically designated and here denoted by " var." (variant).   Comparison of the first two columns shows the degree of late nineteenth century variability in the surname group.

The remarks at the right in the table are merely suggestive.   Surnames showing significant use in Scotland and England are marked " S," and " E," respectively.   Since Matheson combined variants with outstanding names, these designations invariably mean that Irish variants are not distinctively Irish, and commonly mean that the names themselves had other than Irish use.   The remarks concerning *Keane* and *Kearney* illustrate possible confusion of variants. The forms *Kane* and *Keane* not only resemble each other and English names, but *Keane* is often pronounced *Kane* by the Irish.   Slight variations in the pronunciation of *Kearney* associate it with both Irish *Carney* and English *Corney*.

TABLE 28.—*Specimen page of list of names of common use in Ireland but not distinctively Irish*

[Births, Ireland, 1890]

Name or name group	sp.	T	L	M	U	C	Remarks
Comparison, 1 per 1,000.	105	105	26	26	37	16	
Jackson_____	100	101	20	12	60	9	S. E.
Var_____	1						
Jamison_____	24	52	10	1	41	____	S. E.
Jameson_____	20						
Jamieson_____	7						
Var_____	1						
Jennings_____	61	63	6	11	12	34	E.
Var_____	2						
Johnson_____	____	58	18	21	16	3	S. E. English prefer Johnson; Scots, Johnston.
Johnston_____	320	341	43	4	281	13	S. E.
Johnstone____	21						

TABLE 28.—*Specimen page of list of names of common use in Ireland but not distinctively Irish*—Continued

Name or name group	sp.	T	L	M	U	C	Remarks
Jones_____	_____	152	60	38	45	9	S. E.
Jordan_____	91	98	36	10	21	31	E.
Var_____	7						
Joyce_____	_____	164	15	17	1	131	E.
Kane_____	175	190	57	10	96	27	E. See Keane.
Var_____	15						
Keane_____	185	202	13	113	6	70	E. English Keen, Keene.
Var_____	17						
Keany_____	(18)	(33)	(1)	____	(8)	(24)	
Var_____	(15)						
Kearney_____	137	147	50	31	45	21	E. English Carne, Corney, Karn.
Var_____	10						
Carney_____	48	(49)	(7)	(4)	(8)	(30)	
Var_____	1						
Kelly_____	1,238	1,242	435	211	267	329	S. E. 16 Kellys are found in Scottish directory; also original use in Cornwall and Devon.
Var_____	4						
Kennedy_____	436	446	123	149	112	62	S.
Var_____	10						
Kerr_____	_____	142	12	2	123	5	S.
King_____	_____	203	43	47	51	62	S. E.

Step 3 simplified Matheson's codification by reducing the headings in the abstract from 459 to 428 through combining related and similar names into surname units, defining name groups to obviate subtle distinctions in determining their content in American usage. For example, *Mahon, McMahon,* and *Mahony,* are combined because of identity of root form; the prefix was frequently discarded in the eighteenth century and the Irish often added " y " in such cases. In the same way, the similarity of *McDonagh* (without prefix) *Donohoe* and *Donoghue,* dictated that they be viewed as one variable designation.

Recoding did not cover names used by others than the Irish, since many of them derived their original or usual forms outside of Ireland, but did add some names to the list of those not distinctively Irish. For example, significant use of *Connell* and *McConnell* in Scotland indicated that *Connolly, Conneely,* and *O'Connell* could not be retained as distinctive Irish names. The new codification shows 212 peculiarly Irish surnames assembled into 185 name groups, hereafter to be called surnouns or merely names.

CLASSIFICATION OF IRISH NAME GROUPS

Step 4 classified distinctive Irish names by geographical antecedents. Distribution of births recorded under the 185 surnouns was subjected to application of a rule to define localization in a province. In general, if a surnoun showed more than half of its use in a province it was held local to that province. This rule treats Ulster somewhat liberally, because at the time of

Matheson's record that province had about 35 per cent of the population of the country. Non-Irish names were so common in Ulster that a more rigorous rule would restrict its indicators to names so weak as not to be characteristic of the province. For Connaught the rule was liberalized. As few common names showed definite localization there, the list of names local to Connaught was allowed to include names with only 40 per cent of their bearers in the Province.

Classification of the 185 distinctive Irish surnouns by geographical background showed the following numbers for the Provinces: Leinster 20, Munster 57, Ulster 29, Connaught 20. The remaining 59 distinctive names were without localized usage and hence are available as general indicators.

Table 29 shows the percentages of population comprised by these names.

TABLE 29.—*Names available as Irish indicators*

For—	Number of names	Importance of bearers in corresponding population	For—	Number of names	Importance of bearers in corresponding population
		Per cent			*Per cent*
Ireland generally	59	11. 7	Munster	57	30. 6
			Ulster	29	7. 1
Leinster	20	8. 3	Connaught	20	7. 2

Step 5 completed the selection of surnouns suitable as indicators on the basis of degree and locality of original occurrence. There being a limitation in the number having majorities of users in Leinster and Ulster and the number measuring up to a liberal interpretation of the localization rule for Connaught, obviously consistency did not require the use of all names available for Munster, nor for Ireland generally. Hence surnouns of localized Munster use and those of general Irish use were arrayed for restriction of the indicators.

Munster surnouns showed five with very great usage, accounting together for 10.2 per cent of the population of that Province, their bearers having numbers comparable to those of surnouns in the other provincial lists.

Names for Ireland as a whole fell into three groups: 18 showing 200 or more births; 22 showing from 100 to 199; 19 showing 50 to 99. Those in the first group constituted 7.5 per cent of the population of the whole country, thus providing a class sufficiently large to use as a control on provincial determinations.

Table 30 shows the number and percentage importance of the selected names in the country as a whole and in the several Provinces.

TABLE 30.—*Importance of selected Irish names*

Names chosen as indicators for—	Number of surnouns composing class	Importance—	
		In population designated	In total population
		Per cent	*Per cent*
Ireland generally	18	7. 5	7. 5
Leinster	20	8. 3	3. 1
Munster	5	10. 2	3. 6
Ulster	29	7. 1	3. 7
Connaught	20	7. 2	1. 9

That the classes of names to be used as indicative of provincial emigration are representative of their Provinces is shown by measurement of the original concentration of each class in its own Province, in the following percentages for number of bearers in the Province at reference: Leinster 67.2, Munster 69.6, Ulster 67.5, Connaught 55.4.

Table 31 shows the composition of these classes of distinctive Irish names.

TABLE 31.—*Composition of classes of distinctively Irish names regarded as indicative of particular origins*

Character of class	Name designating the group	Related common and minor names and principal variants
Leading names of general Irish antecedents (200 births or more registered).	Brady_____	
	Brennan_____	Brannan, Brannon.
	Burke_____	Bourke.
	Carroll_____	O'Carroll, McCarroll.
	Dolan_____	Dillon, Dowling, Doolan, Doolin.
	Fitzpatrick_____	
	Flanagan_____	
	Flynn_____	O'Flynn.
	Kenny_____	Kenna, McKenna, McKinney.
	Lynch_____	
	McDonagh_____	Donohoe, Donoghue, Donaghy.
	McGrath_____	Magrath, McGraw.
	Maguire_____	McGuire.
	Monaghan_____	Monahan, Moynihan.
	Murphy_____	
	O'Donnell_____	McDonnell, Donnelly, Donnellan, Donnell, McDaniel.
	Quinn_____	Quin, McQuin.
	Sweeney_____	Sweeny, McSweeney.
Leading names localized in Leinster.	Bolger_____	
	Brophy_____	
	Dempsey_____	
	Doran_____	
	Doyle_____	
	Farrell_____	O'Farrell, Farrelly.
	Flood_____	
	Hanlon_____	O'Hanlon.
	Hyland_____	
	Kavanagh_____	Kevane.
	Keegan_____	
	Keogh_____	Kehoe, McKeogh.
	Kiernan_____	McKiernan.
	Kinsella_____	
	Kirwan_____	
	Lawlor_____	Lalor, Lawler.
	McEvoy_____	
	Mooney_____	
	Nolan_____	
	Whelan_____	Whelehan, Phelan.
Munster (300 births or more registered).	Connor_____	Connors, O'Connor.
	McCarthy_____	McCarter, Carty, Carthy.
	Mahony_____	O'Mahony, McMahon, Mahon, Maughan.
	Ryan_____	
	Sullivan_____	O'Sullivan.

TABLE 31.—*Composition of classes of distinctively Irish names regarded as indicative of particular origins*—Continued

Character of class	Name designating the group	Related common and minor names and principal variants
Ulster	Boyle	Boylan.
	Cassidy	
	Coyle	
	Devlin	
	Doherty	Dogherty, O'Doherty.
	Gallagher	
	Greer	
	Hamill	
	Harkin	
	Heaney	
	Keenan	Keena.
	McArdle	
	McCabe	
	McCaffrey	McCafferty, McAfee, Cafferty, [Caffrey.
	McCann	
	McCloskey	McCluskey.
	McFadden	
	McGowan	Magowan, McGovern, Gowen,
	McGurk	McGuirk.
	McManus	
	McNally	McAnally.
	McNulty	
	McParland	McPartlan, McPartlin.
	McQuaid	McQuade.
	McVeigh	
	Magee	McGee.
	Morrow	McMorrow.
	Mulholland	
	Traynor	Treanor, Trainor.
Connaught (localized use)	Coyne	
	Durkan	
	Fallon	Falloon.
	Feeney	Feeny.
	Flaherty	O'Flaherty.
	Gannon	
	Geraghty	
	Glynn	McGlynn.
	Lydon	
	Malley	Mailey, O'Malley.
	Mannion	
(Somewhat broadly used).	Conlon	Conlan.
	Conroy	Conry.
	Costello	Costelloe.
	Dowd	O'Dowd.
	Egan	
	Flannery	
	Hannon	Hannan.
	Moran	Morrin, Morahan.
	Prendergast	

The completion of step 5 permitted a rating of Irish nomenclature according to distinctiveness which is important in disclosing the proportion of the stock not readily identified by name. Comparison of the distribution of bearers of common names with that of bearers of distinctive Irish names reveals the following percentages of the latter in the Provinces: Leinster 50.9, Munster 63.8, Ulster 30.0, Connaught 50.0, and in the country as a whole 47.6. These percentages indicate that the Irish in the several Provinces bore names originally used by other nationalities, or closely similar ones, in the proportions of half of the Leinster Irish, a third of the Munster, seven-tenths of the Ulster, and half of the Connaught.

Table 32 shows the number and distribution of births by the several classes of names, and the relative class importance by locality and frequency.

TABLE 32.—*Number and distribution of Irish accounted for by surnames in common use in Ireland, 1890*

[Numerals indicate births in that year]

Class of names	Total persons accounted for	Leinster	Munster	Ulster	Connaught
Names distinctively Irish: Usage, localized in— Leinster	3, 286	2, 208	479	359	240
Munster: Leading names in the Province (300 births or more registered)	3, 768	622	2, 621	249	276
Common names in the Province (50 to 299 births registered)	7, 157	1, 113	5, 247	319	478
Total, Munster	10, 925	1, 735	7, 868	568	754
Ulster	3, 904	575	150	2, 634	545
Connaught: Names with over half their usage in Connaught	900	144	70	64	622
Names peculiar to Connaught but somewhat broadly used	1, 145	311	241	83	510
Total, Connaught	2, 045	455	311	147	1, 132
Usage, general— Leading names of general Irish antecedents (200 births or more registered)	7, 935	2, 328	2, 254	1, 872	1, 481
Highly common names (100 to 199 births registered)	3, 006	1, 000	714	642	650
Common names (50 to 99 births registered)	1, 350	435	300	329	286
Total, general	12, 291	3, 763	3, 268	2, 843	2, 417
Total, distinctive	32, 451	8, 736	12, 076	6, 551	5, 088
Names not distinctively Irish	35, 664	8, 429	6, 845	15, 306	5, 084
Total abstract of surnames in common use	68, 115	17, 165	18, 921	21, 857	10, 172
Total number of persons (i. e., births) of all names	105, 254	26, 468	25, 681	37, 346	15, 759

AMERICAN USAGE OF IRISH NAMES

island's population were ordinarily more characteristic of other countries, it
island's population were ordinarily more characteristic of other countries, it

is immediately possible to measure Irish contributions to American population only to the extent of their reflection in the currency of distinctive Celtic names.

Step 6 forecast the number and variety of forms of Irish name roots which might be expected to occur in the American records of 1790. Matheson's record of variants appearing occasionally in Irish records, and the collections of similar names in Table 111, *CPG*, were the principal guides in developing a tentative codification of eighteenth century forms probable in American usage. Identification of name forms as proper to Irish surnouns rested on records of variants and variability in Irish nomenclature, and on the premise that forms apparently coined in America may usually be identified with similar immigrant names. Irish nomenclature may be likened to a stream which from time to time sent out branches to America, converging into a side current. This side stream passed through a gate or place of observation in 1790. The main stream was not subjected to observation until 1890. The proposed comparison, therefore, suggests a letter " Y," with a short arm in America reaching to 1790 and a longer main arm in Ireland reaching to 1890.

Step 7 distinguished more than 5,000 bearers of the selected Irish surnames or their variants in the 12 American indexes.

Some groups were readily distinguished; as *Sullivan*, for example. The record for North Carolina, where bearers of this name were most numerous, illustrates the variations: *Sulavan* 1, *Sulivan* 11, *Sullaven* 6, *Sullavent* 1, *Sullivan* 7, *Sullivant* 10, *Sullivent* 2, *Sylivant* 4. *Mulholland*, on which Matheson's study of variants was conclusive, was also readily identified. The records contained three authentic Irish forms—*Mahollum* 3, *Mulholland* 2, *Mulholm* 1; and six obviously affiliated—*Mahalan, Maholland, Molholam, Mulhollan, Mulhollen,* and *Mulhallen,* one each.

The composition of some other groups was only fairly clear. For example, *Ryan* had to be distinguished from German *Rhein,* and *Quinn* from English *Quinney* and Scotch *McQueen.*

Other groups were traced with difficulty and further inquiry may change their construction. The Leinster surname *Kirwan,* for example, shows but 1 listing for that spelling, but other spellings total 44: *Curwin* 19, *Curvin* 17, *Kirven* 3, *Carven* 2, *Carvins* 2, *Curwen* 1. The grouping here used is based on Irish usage of *Curwin,* and on Matheson's evidence of general variability and specific mention of *Carvin* as an Anglicization. This example illustrates codification by inference.

Branches of clans sometimes left the mother country in extraordinary numbers; for example, the *McGraws* came to America in such number as to leave few behind them, although the larger branch of the clan, the *McGraths,* with practically the same origin and grouped with them, found but scant representation in America.

The Middle and Southern States showed fair and sometimes large representation of the specific names; among the general names *Monaghan* was the only one failing representation in every State in this region. Provincial representation showed Leinster names with irregular occurrence, *Doyle,* the leader, having large numbers in Pennsylvania and Maryland: *Farrell* in North Carolina, and *Kirwan* in New York, had numerous entries. Munster names were rather uniformly represented in this district, except that *Ryan* was scant in South Carolina and *Mahony* in New York, and *Sullivan* was concentrated southward. Ulster names were irregular even in Pennsylvania where the class had 517 entries; the most uniform currency was developed south of

New England by *Doherty, McCann, Magee,* and *Morrow.* Connaught names had broken occurrence south of New England, heightened by a large *Dowd* colony in North Carolina, and another of *Moran* in Maryland.

In New England the selected names had only small and irregular members. The general class was best represented by *Kenny* (rather than by *Murphy*): *Carroll* outnumbered *Murphy* and was closely approached by *Burke.* Testing of provincial representation showed Leinster names with rather regular class totals, but erratic occurrence of individual names; the leaders were *Flood* and *Whelan,* the next most numerous *Mooney* and *Doyle.* Munster names recurred uniformly in this district, except for scantiness in Rhode Island, and commonness of *Connor* in New Hampshire. Ulster names were very irregularly represented, the principal numbers in this class accruing from *McGowan,* chiefly in Massachusetts and Maine, and from the bearers of a derivative of *Keenan* in Connecticut. In Massachusetts the leading Ulster groups were *McGowan, McFarland, Boyle, Magee,* and *Keenan;* in Maine, *Doherty, McGowan, McFadden,* and *McFarland* were particularly strong. Only about half of the Connaught names had any representation in New England, but *Dowd* had good numbers in four States, especially in Connecticut.

Step 8 scrutinized irregularities of names of doubtful derivation (and in some cases, considerable currency) in the American records. For example, *Kinsley,* which occurred mainly in Massachusetts and Pennsylvania, suggested derivation from the Leinster *Kinsella;* but Bardsley's Dictionary [3] shows *Kinsley* commonly used in Cheshire and Lancashire, and correspondence with a man of that name [4] revealed that some early settlers used it as a modification of the English *Kingsley.* Another example was *Keeney,* with 39 representatives in Connecticut, genealogy tracing this family from 1700 but giving no clue to European origin. It is identified in this study with *Keena* belonging to the Ulster group, headed by *Keenan;* alternative identification might assign it to the *Kenny* group, thus of general Irish rather than Ulster origin. But the genealogist, W. R. Cutter, reports English origin for certain *Kenneys* in Connecticut and this clouds the local interpretation of *Keena* and *Kenny.*

New England confronts one with its typical threefold problem of imputed English origin of persons with apparently non-English names, various derivatives of the names of early settlers, and the presence of substantial family groups known to have been represented in the early wave of settlement and on whose classification much depends. Some of the groupings under *Durkan, Glynn, Kavanagh, Doherty,* and *McGowan* are questionable, as are the local antecedents of *Dowd* and *Flood.* Over half of the names in some classes were not represented in some States, and median measurements are consequently zero. Arithmetic measures give the Irish the benefit of the doubt. The prevalent "all-one-family" hypothesis is to be guarded against in considering the clustered occurrences of certain names.

The irregularities of New England conditions are clearly brought out in Tables 33, 34, 35, 36, and 37, which show, by classes, the distribution of bearers of the selected Irish names.

---

[3] P. 453.
[4] Earle S. Kinsley, Rutland, Vt.

TABLE 33.—*Heads of families by Leinster names in New England, 1790*

	Maine	New Hampshire	Vermont	Massachusetts	Rhode Island	Connecticut	Total
Bolger							
Brophy							
Dempsey	1	1		1			3
Doran		1	2	1			4
Doyle	4			3	1	3	11
Farrell	2		3	2		1	8
Flood	5	11	1	11			28
Hanlon							
Hyland	1	3		4			8
Kavanagh	2	2		3			7
Keegan							
Keogh				1			1
Kiernan							
Kinsella							
Kirwan						1	1
Lawlor	1						1
McEvoy						1	1
Mooney		5	1	1	4	1	12
Nolan	1	1		3		1	6
Whelan	6	1	5	7			19
Total	23	25	12	37	5	8	110

HEADS OF FAMILIES BY LEINSTER NAMES IN THE REMAINING AREA OF RECORD, 1790

	New York	Pennsylvania	Maryland	Virginia	North Carolina	South Carolina	Total
Bolger		2	1	6		1	10
Brophy							
Dempsey	1	8	4	2	13	5	33
Doran	3	1	3	3	1	1	12
Doyle	2	25	11	3	4	3	48
Farrell	4	11	17	9	32	5	78
Flood		3	3	4	5		15
Hanlon		4					4
Hyland		8	5	2	1		16
Kavanagh	5	5		1	5	5	21
Keegan						1	1
Keogh		1	2				3
Kiernan			1	6			7
Kinsella		1		2		2	5
Kirwan	35	3	1		4	1	44
Lawlor	3						3
McEvoy	1		3		1	1	6
Mooney	16	17	10	6	15	1	65
Nolan	1	6	16	3	16	8	50
Whelan	7	10	14	2	2	1	36
Total	78	105	91	49	99	35	457

TABLE 34.—*Heads of families by Munster names in New England, 1790*

	Maine	New Hamp- shire	Vermont	Massa- chusetts	Rhode Island	Connec- ticut	Total
Connor	3	23		15		3	44
McCarthy	6	2	5	12	2	2	29
Mahony	8			7		2	17
Ryan	7	6	3	7		5	28
Sullivan	8	4	1	3		1	17
Total	32	35	9	44	2	13	135

HEADS OF FAMILIES BY MUNSTER NAMES IN THE REMAINING AREA OF RECORD, 1790

	New York	Pennsyl- vania	Maryland	Virginia	North Carolina	South Carolina	Total
Connor	32	46	32	30	40	27	207
McCarthy	28	36	20	33	10	19	146
Mahony	2	36	21	17	18	17	111
Ryan	15	34	23	10	12	6	100
Sullivan	10	16	26	34	42	14	142
Total	87	168	122	124	122	83	706

TABLE 35.—*Heads of families by Ulster names in New England, 1790*

	Maine	New Hamp- shire	Vermont	Massa- chusetts	Rhode Island	Connec- ticut	Total
Boyle			2	6		1	9
Cassidy				2			2
Coyle							
Devlin							
Doherty	9					1	10
Gallagher							
Greer			1			1	2
Hamill		1					1
Harkin			2	1		2	5
Heaney	1			1	1	1	4
Keenan				5		40	45
McArdle							
McCabe							
McCaffrey							
McCann		1		1		3	5
McCloskey							
McFadden	7			3		1	11
McGowan	8	2	1	16		1	28
McGurk							
McManus	2		2				4
McNally				1			1
McNulty							
McParland	7			8			15
McQuaid							
McVeigh						1	1
Magee	2		1	7	1	1	12
Morrow		3				1	4
Mulholland							
Traynor				1			1
Total	36	7	9	52	2	54	160

TABLE 35.—*Heads of families by Ulster names, 1790*—Continued

HEADS OF FAMILIES BY ULSTER NAMES IN THE REMAINING AREA OF RECORD, 1790

	New York	Pennsylvania	Maryland	Virginia	North Carolina	South Carolina	Total
Boyle	2	44	11	1	10	4	72
Cassidy	8	4	4	15	-----	3	34
Coyle	3	16	1	1	6	4	31
Devlin	-----	3	-----	-----	-----	1	4
Doherty	40	62	13	26	34	15	190
Gallagher	-----	35	3	2	2	-----	42
Greer	6	52	5	2	20	18	103
Hamill	6	15	-----	-----	-----	-----	21
Harkin	-----	9	1	-----	-----	4	14
Heaney	-----	30	5	52	11	11	109
Keenan	1	3	-----	8	4	2	18
McArdle	-----	3	4	-----	-----	-----	7
McCabe	4	5	3	6	5	2	25
McCaffrey	1	17	1	4	11	4	38
McCann	5	31	10	6	15	10	77
McCloskey	1	13	2	-----	2	7	25
McFadden	1	19	8	-----	4	11	43
McGowan	14	25	5	1	15	23	83
McGurk	4	-----	-----	-----	-----	-----	4
McManus	1	6	-----	-----	1	4	12
McNally	-----	4	13	5	3	1	26
McNulty	1	8	-----	-----	-----	-----	9
McParland	-----	-----	-----	-----	-----	-----	
McQuaid	1	5	1	-----	-----	-----	7
McVeigh	3	22	10	3	4	8	50
Magee	19	24	12	18	49	10	132
Morrow	7	54	4	11	22	31	129
Mulholland	1	7	1	1	-----	2	12
Traynor	1	1	3	-----	-----	-----	5
Total	130	517	120	162	218	175	1, 322

TABLE 36.—*Heads of families by Connaught names in New England, 1790*

	Maine	New Hampshire	Vermont	Massachusetts	Rhode Island	Connecticut	Total
Conlon	-----	-----	-----	-----	-----	1	1
Conroy	1	3	1	1	-----	-----	6
Costello	-----	1	-----	-----	-----	-----	1
Coyne	-----	-----	-----	-----	-----	-----	
Dowd	-----	-----	8	8	2	23	41
Durkan	6	8	-----	-----	-----	-----	14
Egan	-----	-----	-----	-----	-----	-----	
Fallon	-----	-----	-----	-----	-----	-----	
Feeney	-----	-----	-----	-----	-----	2	2
Flaherty	1	-----	1	-----	-----	-----	2
Flannery	-----	-----	-----	-----	-----	-----	
Gannon	-----	1	-----	-----	-----	1	2
Geraghty	-----	-----	-----	-----	-----	-----	
Glynn	-----	12	1	2	-----	-----	15
Hannon	-----	-----	-----	1	2	-----	3
Lydon	1	-----	-----	2	-----	-----	3
Malley	2	-----	-----	4	-----	-----	6
Mannion	-----	1	-----	-----	-----	1	2
Moran	1	-----	1	1	-----	2	5
Prendergast	-----	5	-----	3	-----	1	9
Total	12	31	12	22	4	31	112

TABLE 36.—*Heads of families by Connaught names, 1790*—Continued

HEADS OF FAMILIES BY CONNAUGHT NAMES IN REMAINING AREA OF RECORD, 1790

	New York	Pennsylvania	Maryland	Virginia	North Carolina	South Carolina	Total
Conlon			1				1
Conroy	4	3	1		1	2	11
Costello	2		2		6	4	14
Coyne	1	6	1	1	3		12
Dowd	2		1	4	35	3	46
Durkan		1	1	1	1	2	6
Egan	5	8	4	1	4	5	27
Fallon	1	2		10			13
Feeney							
Flaherty		2	5	1			8
Flannery					2		2
Gannon	1		3	1			5
Geraghty	2	2	1	1		1	7
Glynn	3	1	1			1	6
Hannon	4	7	3	1	5	4	24
Lydon			1				1
Malley	2	1	1		3		7
Mannion	1	8	2		14	1	26
Moran	5	1	17	4	7		34
Prendergast	2	3	1		10	1	17
Total	35	45	46	25	91	24	266

TABLE 37.—*Heads of families by general Irish names in New England, 1790*

	Maine	New Hampshire	Vermont	Massachusetts	Rhode Island	Connecticut	Total
Brady	1		1				2
Brennan	1			1			2
Burke	5	3	13	9	2	5	37
Carroll	1		6	30	3	7	47
Dolan	2	2	1	3		1	9
Fitzpatrick							
Flanagan							
Flynn	5	1	1	4		3	14
Kenny	39	18	16	30		21	124
Lynch		1		4			5
McDonagh	1		3		1		5
McGrath	3	1	1	1		1	7
Maguire	2				2	6	10
Monaghan		2					2
Murphy	12	15	1	8	6	1	43
O'Donnell	11	5	4	9		5	34
Quinn	3			4			7
Sweeney		1		2			3
Total	86	49	47	105	14	50	351

TABLE 37.—*Heads of families by general Irish names, 1790*—Continued

HEADS OF FAMILIES BY GENERAL IRISH NAMES IN REMAINING AREA OF RECORD, 1790

	New York	Pennsylvania	Maryland	Virginia	North Carolina	South Carolina	Total
Brady	9	27	9	5	27	8	85
Brennan	4	15	5	1	5	3	33
Burke	13	32	25	21	16	9	116
Carroll	6	31	47	26	48	19	177
Dolan	8	22	13	23	15	8	89
Fitzpatrick	2	8	4	12	6	6	38
Flanagan	3	12	10	8	5	3	41
Flynn	9	8	6	5	9	6	43
Kenny	34	51	13	20	28	16	162
Lynch	14	23	47	11	28	11	134
McDonagh	4	8	4	3	8	7	34
McGrath	9	25	7	7	7	12	67
Maguire	8	35	9	8	15	3	78
Monaghan	------	2	4	------	4	------	10
Murphy	24	65	48	35	65	45	282
O'Donnell	16	76	37	38	90	29	286
Quinn	1	20	12	10	16	7	66
Sweeney	5	21	10	20	6	4	66
Total	169	481	310	253	398	196	1,807

Step 9 compiled, for each class in each State, the numbers of entries of family heads identified as representatives of the distinctive Irish names, deriving from a total of 451,120 heads of families indexed in the 12 American records the following numbers: Leinster 567, Munster 841, Ulster 1,482, Connaught 378, general Irish 2,158; total, 5,426. The Rhode Island record invariably ranked lowest in number of entries per class, showing but 14 persons for the general list and only from 2 to 5 for any other list. Except for the Connaught list, Pennsylvania was at the other extreme, showing 481 for the general names, 105 for the Leinster, 168 for the Munster, and 571 for the Ulster. The Connaught list was best represented in North Carolina where it had 91 entries, or as many as in Maryland (46) and Pennsylvania (45) together.

Table 38 shows the representation of the classified names in each State and in the whole area of record.

TABLE 38.—*Heads of families in the 1790 records bearing names classified as distinctively Irish*

	Indicative of origins in—				The 4 Provinces	Ireland generally (control)
	Leinster	Munster	Ulster	Con-naught		
Area of record	567	841	1, 482	378	3, 268	2, 158
Maine	23	32	36	12	103	86
New Hampshire	25	35	7	31	98	49
Vermont	12	9	9	12	42	47
Massachusetts	37	44	52	22	155	105
Rhode Island	5	2	2	4	13	14
Connecticut	8	13	54	31	106	50
New York	78	87	130	35	330	169
Pennsylvania	105	168	517	45	835	481
Maryland	91	122	120	46	379	310
Virginia	49	124	162	25	360	253
North Carolina	99	122	218	91	530	398
South Carolina	35	83	175	24	317	196

INTERPRETATION OF AMERICAN OCCURRENCES

Step 10 interpreted the numbers of American bearers of distinctive Irish names by comparison with their numbers in Ireland. Bearers of the general Irish names constituted 75.39 and 4.78 per thousand of the population of Ireland and America, respectively. Since 4.78 is 6⅓ per cent of 75.39, the relative American occurrence of these names was 6⅓ per cent of that in Ireland, indicating 6⅓ per cent Irish heredity in 1790 American population. The fact that distribution of these names was not uniform in the Irish Provinces, together with considerations of factional migration and the limitation of this study to the Celtic, reduces this to an approximate estimate. It nevertheless indicates the measure of the whole stock which should derive from summation of provincial readings.

Ulster was the only Province rating above the general average. Indicators of Ulster origin constituted 37.1 and 3.3 per thousand of Ireland's and America's populations respectively, indicating slightly less than 9 per cent Irish representation in America had all Irish migration been at the Ulster rates. The other three Provinces had less than average share in Irish migration. Leinster indicators constituted 31.2 and 1.3 per thousand of Ireland's and America's populations repectively, denoting but 4 per cent Irish representation in America had all Irish migrated at the Leinster rate. Munster indicators constituted 35.8 and 1.9 per thousand of Ireland's and America's populations respectively, indicating 5.2 per cent Irish representation in America had all Irish moved at the Munster rate. Connaught indicators constituted 19.4 and 0.8 per thousand of Ireland's and America's populations respectively, denoting 4⅓ per cent Irish representation in America had all Irish migrated at the Connaught rate. Table 39 presents these calculations in detail.

TABLE 39.—*Percentages of Irish in the area of record, United States, 1790, as indicated by the relative occurrences of distinctive names*

Distinctively Irish surnames of origin	Bearers of specified names constituted (number per thousand of population)		Percentages of Irish if in accordance with relative American use of names of specified origin
	Ireland, 1890	Area of record, United States, 1790	
In Ireland, generally_____	75. 39	4. 78	6. 34
Principally in—			
Leinster_____	31. 22	1. 26	4. 04
Munster_____	35. 80	1. 86	5. 20
Ulster_____	37. 09	3. 29	8. 87
Connaught_____	19. 43	. 84	4. 32

The significance of percentages of Irish measured by relative American usage of provincial Irish names rests on the relative numbers available as emigrants from each Province. These can not be directly deduced from Matheson's record, as the distribution of Ireland's population was decidedly altered by heavy emigration in the middle of the nineteenth century, and provincial ratios must be calculated before that period; but the proportions indicated by the 1821 census probably fairly represent the relative significance of provincial rates of emigration of the time, and these are used in Table 40 to combine the provincial readings.

The weighting process gives measures of provincial contributions totaling 5.83 per cent Irish population in the American area of record. This is less than anticipated by the general reading of 6.34 per cent shown in Table 39 and gives a clue to regional and factional complications which will be considered later. This discrepancy between general and provincial readings is mainly occasioned by the fact that names popular throughout Ireland had bearers more representative of the island's population as a whole than had the collection of provincial names. Hence 5.83 per cent with the supporting details, approximates the proportion of American population which the Irish would have constituted had they been one homogeneous Celtic people.

This process does not show the extremes in provincial estimates, however, as the use of names having only majorities of their original bearers in the several Provinces tends to level provincial representation. The 2.61 per cent Ulster contribution should be read as somewhat more, even though it is recognized as derived from recurrences of peculiarly Celtic names. All the other ratings should be read as somewhat less than shown, particularly Connaught's, for its small population and lack of any considerable number of unique names necessitated liberality in selecting its distinctive names. Connaught readings are drawn upward toward a measure reflecting the composite rate of contributions to the American area of record as measured by recurrence of distinctive names of general background.

TABLE 40.—*Calculation of percentage contributions of provincial Irish to population of the area of record indicated by the recurrence of distinctive provincial names*

Province of origin	Percentages of Irish in American population indicated by recurrence of names originally localized in specified Provinces	Relative significance or weight of original numbers [1]	Derived percentage contribution of Irish of Province to population of American area
Leinster	4. 04	25. 8	1. 04
Munster	5. 20	28. 5	1. 48
Ulster	8. 87	29. 4	2. 61
Connaught	4. 32	16. 3	. 70
Total, Provinces		100. 0	5. 83

[1] Percentages of population of Ireland as shown by the census of 1821.

Attention was next directed to the distribution of the provincial stocks by States of record. Examination of the percentages of Irish indicated by classified name uses discloses possible inaccuracy in the estimates for some States. Occurrences of names of general origins suggest error in some provincial figures; but the general figures do not themselves constitute a perfect control, because of erratic readings. Imperfect relationships may be attributed therefore to the interpretation of either the general or the provincial names. On the whole, the estimates derived from the general names accord with the indicated averages of provincial representation.

In northern New England, however, lack of coordination between estimates is chiefly due to irregularity in the general estimate. General readings for Maine and Vermont are higher than those for any of the provincial lists, a reflection perhaps of accidental factors in small population. Combining these two States with New Hampshire to make a group of more substantial population results in coordination between the general and provincial ratings. The general control in Massachusetts is also relatively high in comparison with provincial figures, but lack of coordination is not striking.

In New York provincial figures are high in relation to the general approximation.

In Maryland the general control is much higher than any of the provincial figures, which show a markedly low Ulster rating compared with that of the adjoining States of Pennsylvania and Virginia; but the general figure for Maryland may have been increased by accidental inclusion in that record of a large number of heads of families with names of general origin, such as *Carroll*, characteristic of early settlement.

In Virginia the general figures are unexpectedly low in relation to corresponding figures for the adjoining States of Maryland and North Carolina; this drop of the general indicators being accompanied by decline in Leinster and Connaught measures, suggests defects in Celtic representation within the limits of Virginia's partial record.

Table 41 shows the percentage distribution of provincial stocks in the States of record had all been Irish of the origin specified, as calculated by relative American usage. These findings should be read both down and across, with special attention to relations in percentage of a given derivation from State to State, and to relations of State percentages derived from provincial and general names.

TABLE 41.—*Percentages of Irish in American population, 1790, if all of origin specified, as calculated from the relative uses of names*

| State of record | Percentages indicated by names of origin in— | | | | |
	Ireland generally	Leinster	Munster	Ulster	Connaught
Area of record	6. 34	4. 04	5. 20	8. 87	4. 32
Maine	6. 70	4. 32	5. 25	5. 72	3. 65
New Hampshire	2. 69	3. 33	4. 05	. 78	6. 64
Vermont	4. 17	2. 56	1. 68	1. 62	4. 12
Massachusetts	2. 14	1. 83	1. 87	2. 16	1. 75
Rhode Island	1. 67	1. 44	. 50	. 49	1. 85
Connecticut	1. 63	. 64	. 89	3. 59	3. 91
New York	4. 11	4. 58	4. 47	6. 42	3. 29
Pennsylvania	8. 57	4. 52	6. 28	18. 71	3. 09
Maryland	12. 57	8. 90	10. 42	9. 89	7. 26
Virginia [1]	8. 90	4. 16	9. 19	11. 59	3. 40
North Carolina	10. 04	6. 02	6. 48	11. 19	8. 90
South Carolina	10. 00	4. 32	8. 91	18. 17	4. 73

[1] Partial record only.

INTERPOLATION FOR STATES OF MISSING RECORDS

Step 11 established readings for New Jersey, Delaware, Kentucky, Tennessee, and Georgia on the basis of geographical distribution of provincial and total Irish stocks. In lieu of the missing records for these States, the trends of percentages in the adjoining States become determinative.

New Jersey may be confidently treated as intermediate between New York and Pennsylvania because of the definite relationships in the figures for those neighboring States.

Viewing Delaware as intermediate between Pennsylvania and Maryland, results in an approximate estimate, since it has been seen that Maryland figures are open to doubt; but as Delaware's population was small, inexactness in its estimate will not seriously change that of the Irish in the United States as a whole.

The estimate for Georgia rests on conditions obtaining in South Carolina, which are viewed as intermediate between those in North Carolina and Georgia.

Table 42 shows percentages of Irish contributions to population in New Jersey, Delaware, and Georgia, as estimated from trends in proportion of Irish per thousand.

TABLE 42.—*Percentages of Irish in population of certain States, if all of origin specified, as calculated from the trends in the relative uses of names locally*

| State | Percentages derived for origins in— | | | | |
	Ireland generally	Leinster	Munster	Ulster	Connaught
New Jersey	6. 10	4. 50	5. 30	11. 90	3. 20
Delaware	11. 20	7. 40	9. 00	13. 00	5. 80
Georgia	10. 00	3. 70	9. 60	20. 50	3. 20

Kentucky and Tennessee are construed as a unit drawing its population in equal amounts from Pennsylvania, Maryland, Virginia, and North Carolina, the simple averages of measures of Irish stock in these four adjoining States indicating the following percentages if all Irish had been of the specified origin: Leinster, 5.90; Munster, 8.10; Ulster, 12.80; Connaught, 5.70; general control, 10.00.

COORDINATION OF DATA ON PROVINCIAL ORIGINS

Step 12 was the weighting of percentages of Irish, indicated by the relative uses of names of provincial origin, to obtain measures of the contributions of Irish to population, in total and by Provinces. The process of weighting introduced in Step 10 gives consideration to the ratios of original population in the Provinces so that the shares of the several Provinces in a total may be evaluated. Provincial ratings can be adjusted to allow for the fact that Irish occurrences in 1890 had been influenced by changes in the distribution of Ireland's population during the eighteenth and nineteenth centuries, and a better measure of Irish emigration as a whole is obtained by combining provincial measurements than by relying on the indications of names in general use in Ireland in 1890.

Table 43 shows the changes in the total Irish population and its distribution by Provinces, as recorded at census periods from 1821 to 1911. According to the statement of the Irish authorities, the census of 1821 is the first that affords a means of comparison with those of subsequent decades. Although the census of 1821 was less accurate than that of 1831, it probably affords the best available basis for reckoning the original proportions of provincial stocks, their percentage distribution being as follows: Leinster, 25.8; Munster, 28.5; Ulster, 29.4; Connaught, 16.3.

TABLE 43.—*The total population of Ireland, by provinces, at each census period, 1821–1911* [1]

Census period	Ireland	Province of—			
		Leinster	Munster	Ulster	Connaught
1821	6, 801, 827	1, 757, 492	1, 935, 612	1, 998, 494	1, 110, 229
1831	7, 767, 401	1, 909, 713	2, 227, 152	2, 286, 622	1, 343, 914
1841	8, 175, 124	1, 973, 731	2, 396, 161	2, 386, 373	1, 418, 859
1851	6, 552, 385	1, 672, 738	1, 857, 736	2, 011, 880	1, 010, 031
1891	4, 704, 750	1, 187, 760	1, 172, 402	1, 619, 814	724, 774
1911	4, 390, 219	1, 162, 044	1, 035, 495	1, 581, 696	610, 984

[1] From Census of Ireland, 1911, General Report, page 62. The table cited showed each period.

CONTRIBUTIONS OF CELTIC IRISH TO AMERICAN POPULATION

Table 44 shows the percentage measures of Irish contributions to population based on the 1821 census percentages for measuring the relative significance of the provincial stocks. These figures show the classification of Irish stock by Provinces in the several States and in the United States as a whole. The principal qualification of their validity applies to the three Northern States in

New England for which the findings for Ulster and Connaught are inconclusive; further inquiry should reveal more regularly related percentages with distribution similar to that for Leinster and Munster stocks. Grouping of these three States to eliminate accidentals consequent on small population gives the measures: Leinster, 0.9; Munster, 1.1; Ulster, 0.7; Connaught, 0.9; total 3.6. In view of the activity of Ulsterites in settling this region, this low reading for a Celtic element from Ulster is striking.

TABLE 44.—*Apparent contributions of Irish to population, giving consideration to original proportions of provincial stocks and based on the recurrence of distinctive provincial names*

	Indicated percentages of population originating in—				
	Leinster (25.8) [1]	Munster (28.5) [1]	Ulster (29.4) [1]	Connaught (16.3) [1]	Ireland (100) [1]
United States	1. 10	1. 63	2. 80	0. 70	6. 23
Area of record	1. 04	1. 48	2. 61	. 70	5. 83
Maine	1. 1	1. 5	1. 7	. 6	4. 9
New Hampshire	. 9	1. 2	. 2	1. 1	3. 4
Vermont	. 7	. 5	. 5	. 7	2. 4
Massachusetts	. 5	. 5	. 6	. 3	1. 9
Rhode Island	. 4	. 1	. 1	. 3	. 9
Connecticut	. 2	. 3	1. 1	. 6	2. 2
New York	1. 2	1. 3	1. 9	. 5	4. 9
New Jersey [2]	1. 2	1. 5	3. 5	. 5	6. 7
Pennsylvania	1. 2	1. 8	5. 5	. 5	9. 0
Delaware [2]	1. 9	2. 6	3. 8	. 9	9. 2
Maryland	2. 3	3. 0	2. 9	1. 2	9. 4
Kentucky and Tennessee [2]	1. 5	2. 3	3. 8	. 9	8. 5
Virginia [3]	1. 1	2. 6	3. 4	. 6	7. 7
North Carolina	1. 6	1. 8	3. 3	1. 5	8. 2
South Carolina	1. 1	2. 5	5. 3	. 8	9. 7
Georgia [2]	1. 0	2. 7	6. 0	. 5	10. 2

[1] Original proportions used as weights in calculation.
[2] Not of specific record. Estimates derived from consideration of trends locally.
[3] Only partial record.

COMPARISON BETWEEN PROVINCIAL SUMMATION AND THE CONTROL

Summation of details for the Provinces, as shown in the foregoing calculations, gives 6.23 per cent Irish in the United States in 1790, while the control based on relative usage of general Irish names is 6.76 per cent. (On the basis of Table 41 and interpolations.)

Table 45 compares the percentage of Irish in the several States and in the United States as a whole, as derived by these two methods of estimating.

TABLE 45.—*Comparison of estimates of contributions of Irish to American population, 1790*

	From relative use of names of—			From relative use of names of—	
	Provincial anteced- ents	General anteced- ents		Provincial anteced- ents	General anteced- ents
United States	6. 23	6. 76	Pennsylvania	9. 0	8. 6
			Delaware	[1] 9. 2	[1] 11. 2
Maine	4. 9	6. 7	Maryland	9. 4	12. 6
New Hampshire	3. 4	2. 7	Kentucky and Ten-		
Vermont	2. 4	4. 2	nessee	[1] 8. 5	[1] 10. 0
Massachusetts	1. 9	2. 1	Virginia [2]	7. 7	8. 9
Rhode Island	. 9	1. 7	North Carolina	8. 2	10. 0
Connecticut	2. 2	1. 6	South Carolina	9. 7	10. 0
New York	4. 9	4. 1	Georgia	[1] 10. 2	[1] 10. 0
New Jersey	[1] 6. 7	[1] 6. 1			

[1] Based on regional rather than specific data.
[2] Only partial record.

The measures of apparent contributions of the Irish to American population, obtained from measuring the currency of distinctive names of provincial and general background, are so closely in agreement (see discussion under step 10) as to create a false confidence in their adequacy. Since, for the country as a whole, these measures show a relative difference of only 8.5 per cent (6.76 being 108.5 per cent of 6.23), it would seem that this stock has been adequately estimated.

An important thing to note in the findings for Irish based on occurrence of distinctive names is that the control estimates for most of the States and for the country as a whole are higher than the provincial totals, whereas if the Irish as a whole were satisfactorily accounted for they would be lower. The control figures are derived from the occurrences of leading names of general Irish antecedents, which, it happens (see Table 32) had less use in Ulster than they would have had if evenly distributed over the country. They had but 23.6 per cent of their bearers in a province responsible for 35.5 per cent of the births in 1890 and given a weight in this study of 29.4 per cent. Inasmuch as the Ulster list showed the highest measure of representation of any of the provincial lists, the weak bearing of Ulster antecedents on this general list should have caused it to show lower readings for Irish-American stock than did the provincial lists together. That the control list gains representation in the American records at a higher scale than expected provides a clue to the fact that the bearers of distinctive provincial names were not fully representative of the Irish.

It was shown in step 2 that the Irish made large use of names common to other parts of the United Kingdom. It was noted there, in testing the distinctiveness of common Irish names, that of 215 not surely distinctive, 112 were general British, 57 others shared with English, and 46 others shared with the Scots. The use of English names may be regarded as a result partly of compulsory conditions in early days and partly of growing English influence on Irish nomenclature. Generally speaking, however, the use of English and Scotch names in Ireland reveals the heterogeneous character of the population. Very largely the occurrence of non-Irish names is the result of the plantation of Ireland with settlements of English and Scots. Ireland contained important elements of population of English and Scotch origin not entirely assimilated. In my classification of common Irish names, a number are marked "not distinctive," to avoid confusion in reading the American records. Yet, as set forth in Table 32, possibly 36 per cent of the population of Munster was not of indigenous character, and this rating is the lowest for any of the four Provinces. In Ulster the proportion bearing names not distinctively Irish reached 70 per cent. The tendency of the control readings to move independently and to outrun the provincial Celtic summation indicates that Irish with names not definitely Celtic like those with names not narrowly provincial migrated at rates independent of those determined for the indigenous provincial stocks.

SUMMARY

All of the calculations of contributions of Irish to American population presented in this chapter have been subject to the condition of being valid only if the rate of migration of other Irish was the rate of those with peculiarly Irish names. Investigation of the recurrence of names shared by Scots and Irish will disclose that this was a condition contrary to fact. Hence, we must prepare to revise the estimates of Irish to allow for different measures of migration on the part of Scotch and English factions among them. It will be found that these factions had their principal numbers in Ulster and that it is not advisable to undertake revision of the estimated contributions of Irish from the three Southern Provinces. Inasmuch as the process of calculation employed in this chapter, effecting what is called a "smoothing" of the provincial percentages, tended to overstate somewhat the measures obtained for the three Southern Provinces having rates of migration lower than Ulster's, it is doubtful if upward revision is necessary for the three as a group, on account of non-Celtic factors.

So far as I am able to state at present, the contributions of Irish from the three southern Provinces were approximately as set forth in this chapter. When the details for these Provinces, drawn from Table 44, are reintroduced in Table 57, they are slightly modified to reflect the bearing of control figures on provincial totals. There the percentage contributions of these Provinces to 1790 population are stated as Leinster 1.2, Munster 1.7, Connaught 0.8 per cent. The estimate for Connaught is probably somewhat liberal because it is based on names not closely localized in that Province. That for Leinster, on the other hand, is probably a minimum measurement. It inadequately reflects migration of English-Irish, who were fairly numerous in this Province, at a greater rate than the Celtic element typified by those bearing distinctive names. My present finding is that Irish from the three southern Provinces constituted three and a fraction per cent of American population in 1790, apparently 3.7 per cent.

Chapter VI

THE IRISH CONTRIBUTION, PARTICULARLY THAT OF ULSTER

In the preceding chapter the Irish contribution to the population of 1790 was calculated on the basis of Celtic names. Such an appraisal is necessarily incomplete, because Irish-American nomenclature in 1790 was a mixed product; hence the need of further study of the Irish-American population. The present chapter continues the general study of the Irish, but inquires particularly into the numbers of Irish who bore names shared by the Scotch and the English; that is, of Ulster Irish. By this means the previous estimate of Irish is adjusted so as to allow for the very active migration of substocks.

It is a serious mistake to assume that the Irish population is adequately represented by the recognizable Celtic or Gaelic names, and yet this assumption has often been made, as when William Clemens, genealogist says: "Before 1699 only a handful of Celts or Scots made their appearance in the colonies, as is proven by a glance at the *Macs* and *Mcs* in the marriage list."[1]

Many of the Irish bore English names; Albert Cook Myers[2] points out that such was the case with most of the Irish Quakers. Irish Presbyterian settlements were largely formed of persons with English and Scotch names, yet appreciable numbers with English names were Episcopalians. Many Irish settlements, such, for example, as those of northern New England, were of almost purely Scotch nomenclature. The following list, showing the surnames of 25 men prominent in the Charitable Society for Irish, organized in Boston in 1737, is evidence of the mixed nature of this nomenclature: *Alderchurch, Bennett, Boyd, Clark* (2), *Drummond, Duncan, Egart, Freeland, Gibbs, Glen, Knox, Little, McFall, Maynes, Moor, Mortimer, Neal, Noble, Pelham, St. Lawrence, Stewart, Thomas, Walker, Walsh.*

The infusion of Irish before 1700 has been given insufficient attention. Very early in colonial history the Colonies assumed a somewhat cosmopolitan character to which scattered Irish contributed. Among the early records examined is a manuscript list preserved by the Maryland Historical Society, said to contain the names of 20,859 persons known to have lived in Maryland between 1633 and 1680. A test applied similar to that described in Chapter III showed not more than 93 per cent of these as English. Of the remaining 7 per cent a substantial proportion was Irish. There were Murphys and Kellys, a number of Celtic Mc's, and others of the stock there then. The Irish apparently increased slowly until the middle of the eighteenth century, but as early as 1720 were numerous in Massachusetts, for example. Clemens's comment led me to an examination of Boston marriage records to see what evidence was there of increase in Irish numbers. By a superficial test they proved as numerous in that State in the early part of the eighteenth century as in the latter part. Two volumes of Boston marriage records, for 1700–1751 and 1752–1809, show slightly more than 2 per cent *Mc* and *Mac* names. Accompanying names without the prefix indicate that the Irish were more numerous than the Scots, the two stocks together probably constituting at least a fifth of the city population

---

[1] *American Marriage Records before 1699*, p. 7.
[2] *Immigration of the Irish Quakers into Pennsylvania*, 1652–1675.

throughout the century.   (About 1 in 10 of these people inherits a name with the prefix.)

The total of Irish was never less than two or three times the number with peculiarly Irish names. Ulster immigrants in particular bore names other than those selected as distinctive in the preceding chapter wherein it was noted in Step 5 (especially Table 30) that the calculations of contributions of Ulster Irish rest on maintaining a ratio of 7 per cent for bearers of selected names peculiar to that province.   It is easily determined that men from Ulster were much more numerous than this ratio indicates. A single illustration is a list by Parker[3] of 319 heads of families planning to migrate to New England and including scarcely any persons of the names which I have specified as distinctive.   Ireland contained clusters of people from almost every country of western Europe.   These people, recalling ancestry in other lands, were particularly dissatisfied with the turbulent conditions in Ireland and inclined to seek better fortune in the New World.

William Douglass[4] in 1755 wrote quaintly, " Lately the long leases of the farmers in the north of Ireland being expired, the landlords raised their rents extravagantly.   This occasioned an emigration of many north of Ireland Scotch Presbyterians, with an intermixture of wild Irish Roman Catholicks; at first they chose New England, but being brought up to husbandry or raising of grain, called bread corn, New England did not answer so well as the colonies southward; therefore, at present they generally resort to Pennsylvania, a good grain colony."   A more modern view of the large measure of Scotch-Irish contributions is given by Henry Pratt Fairchild,[5] viz: " It is said that in 1718, forty-two hundred of the Scotch-Irish left for America, and that after the famine of 1740 there were 12,000 who departed annually.   In the half century preceding the American Revolution 150,000 or more came to America."   How nearly their contributions were approached by those of Irish with English names can not be said, but data are available on Irish with Scotch names, and I use these for adjusting the previous estimate of Irish so as to allow for the very active migration of substocks.

OUTLINE OF THE STUDY OF SCOTCH-IRISH

In the analysis of Scotch nomenclature, it was shown that most of the characteristic Scotch names were also borne by Irish. Those having substantial Irish usage (Table 21, ff.) were divided into two classes and the currency of one class is now used to measure the migration of Irish bearers.   Two of the 16 names known as Class III are eliminated for irregularities.   The 14 remaining names accounted for 3,843 families in the 1790 records, an average of about 270 apiece.   The numbers range from 780 for *Campbell* down to 79 for *Moffat*.   Significance of the numbers is ascertained from the original frequencies of the names in Scotland and Ireland.   Invariably when one subtracts from the actual number of bearers of a name the normal number of Scots due to bear it, as gaged by the measures of Scotch-American population previously obtained, a substantial proportion remains to be accounted for as Irish.

According to the established interpretation of Stark's data, the bearers of these names normally constitute 42 per thousand among Scots.   The ratio of 42 per thousand applied to the estimates of Scotch-American population indi-

---

[3] *The History of Londonderry, New Hampshire*, pp. 317–321.
[4] *British Settlements in North America*, vol. 1, pp. 367–368.
[5] *Immigration*, New York, 1925, p. 41.

cates the probable numbers of Scotch bearers of the names under consideration. Subtracting these numbers from the total numbers separates American usage into Scotch and Irish items. This separation is tested by name, but the estimate of Scotch-Irish in American population is based on separation of the collective number of bearers in the State lists. In the area of record as a whole it may be fairly estimated that 1,480 of the bearers of these names were of Scotch origin and the remaining 2,363 Irish.

Matheson's analysis of births in 1890 showed these names in a ratio of 17 per 1,000 among Irish, and their American occurrence indicates that had all Irish been represented in the same ratio as these Scotch-Irish they would have constituted 30 per cent of American population, mounting to 56 per cent in Pennsylvania, 46 per cent in South Carolina, and 48 per cent in Maine. Even on this hypothesis they would have shown but small numbers in New England, the lowest rating being 8.4 per cent in Connecticut. The relative occurrences of Scotch-Irish names clearly show a much higher migration rate of Scotch-Irish than of Celtic Irish, and not heretofore disclosed by American usage of distinctive Irish names.

These figures evidently represent the migratory rate of a minority in the original population, and the problem met at the close of this chapter is that of determining the influence of the migratory rate of this minority upon the stream of migration as a whole.

AMERICAN USAGE OF SCOTCH-IRISH NAMES

The 16 Scotch-Irish surnouns selected as indicators (below Table 21) were carefully defined, like the more purely Scotch groups, preliminary to searching the American records. Only special comment will be entered here.

Gordon is less liberally defined here than in *CPG*, because of possible mixed antecedents through common occurrence of *Gorton*, which is construed as Scotch-Irish with misgivings, and because of entries which suggest misspellings of French *Jourdon*. Study of this name brings to light an interesting book by J. M. Bulloch.[6] This book of 44 pages presents a considerable collection of changes of names. It is concerned entirely with usage in the Old World, but it might well be a model for other publications dealing with evolution of surname usage.

McDougall is here grouped with *McDowell* and its variants, on the authority of Johnston,[7] who speaks of the Scotch "*M'Dougal* with its Galloway form of *M'Dowall*." The name *McDowall*[8] is commonly referred to as Scotch-Irish. This group is a doubtful index of Scotch-Irish antecedents, because of coexistence of *Douglas* preventing ready identification of *McDougall* without the prefix. *Douglas* having had usage in several English counties is considered a separate name of mixed antecedents.

Table 46 shows the number of entries located in the 1790 records for the 16 Scotch-Irish surnames under investigation. Two totals are given, the second omitting *M'Innes* and *Paton* measures. Ordinarily *Paton* was written with double *t*. Baldwin[9] states that the origin of *Patten* is unknown, that its tradition is English, but that a survey of England for the period covering New England's settlement discloses few localities with extensive occurrence.

Table 46 shows the American occurrence of the Scotch-Irish surnouns.

[6] *The Name of Gordon; patronymics which it has replaced or reinforced.* Huntly, 1906.
[7] James B. Johnston, *The Scotish Macs,* Paisley, 1922, p. 6.
[8] John Hugh McDowell, *History of the McDowells and Connections,* Memphis, 1918.
[9] Thomas W. Baldwin, *Patten Genealogy: William Patten of Cambridge, 1635, and his Descendants,* Boston, 1908.

TABLE 46.—*Heads of families by Scotch-Irish names in New England, 1790*

Name [1]	Maine	New Hamp-shire	Ver-mont	Massa-chusetts	Rhode Island	Connec-ticut	Total
Black	22	4	8	35	3	1	73
Blair	5	5	5	35	1		51
Boyd	9	14	1	16	3	3	46
Campbell	22	32	21	47	1	20	143
Craig	13	14	4	9	1	2	43
Cumming	23	38	15	76	3	13	168
Cunningham	19	3	4	26		8	60
Ferguson	7	7	3	16	2	4	39
Findlay		2	2			6	10
Gordon	24	40	4	13	33	27	141
M'Dougall		3	1	2		2	8
M'Innes		1	1				2
Maxwell	19	2	3	9	4	3	40
Moffat	2	2	6	7	2	7	26
Orr	10	7	4	4			25
Paton	23	22		23	3	6	77
Total	198	196	82	318	56	102	952
Total omitting M'Innes and Paton	175	173	81	295	53	96	873

HEADS OF FAMILIES BY SCOTCH-IRISH NAMES IN REMAINING AREA OF RECORD, 1790

Name	New York	Penn-sylvania	Mary-land	Virginia	North Carolina	South Carolina	Total
Black	15	100	17	24	59	38	253
Blair	11	45	8	12	9	20	105
Boyd	29	102	29	35	61	44	300
Campbell	109	206	35	75	142	70	637
Craig	12	84	17	20	31	24	188
Cumming	47	52	27	12	30	10	178
Cunningham	28	71	17	48	28	25	217
Ferguson	71	56	28	56	51	28	290
Findlay	3	54	7	7	15	19	105
Gordon	28	64	28	34	48	50	252
M'Dougall	38	73	9	18	57	20	215
M'Innes	7	26	6	10	25	1	75
Maxwell	8	46	11	7	17	11	100
Moffat	16	13	9	2	7	6	53
Orr	12	27	7	8	17	6	77
Paton	13	74	10	10	35	16	158
Total	447	1,093	265	378	632	388	3,203
Total omitting M'Innes and Paton	427	993	249	358	572	371	2,970

[1] In alphabetic order.

SEPARATION OF AMERICAN CURRENCIES INTO SCOTCH AND IRISH ELEMENTS

Table 47 shows the separation of the American currency of each name, accomplished by subtracting from its total bearers the estimated number normal in the Scotch-American population as previously appraised. Column 1 shows the number of Scotch bearers per 100,000 in the motherland according to interpretation of Stark's report. Column 2 shows the estimated number of

Scotch bearers in the American area if the Old World ratio was maintained among the estimated 35,700 Scotch-American families covered by the American records. (See Table 25.) Column 3 shows the total American heads of families bearing these names, as disclosed in Table 46. Column 4 shows the estimated number of Irish bearers as deduced from these figures.

TABLE 47.—*Separation of the American currency of 16 Scotch-Irish names as Scotch and Irish*

Name [1]	Scots per 100,000 bearing the name in the motherland	Estimated number Scotch American heads of families of the name in area of record 1790	Total heads of families bearing the name in the American records	Indicated number of familes of Irish origin bearing the name in the area of record
Black	339	121	326	205
Blair	151	54	156	102
Boyd	186	66	346	280
Campbell	1, 079	385	780	395
Craig	271	97	231	134
Cumming	162	58	346	288
Cunningham	238	85	277	192
Ferguson	473	169	329	160
Findlay	241	86	115	29
Gordon	340	121	393	272
M'Dougall	252	90	223	133
M'Innes	150	54	77	23
Maxwell	133	47	140	93
Moffat	152	54	79	25
Orr	133	47	102	55
Paton	180	64	235	171
Total (16)	4, 480	1, 598	4, 155	2, 557
Total omitting M'Innes and Paton	4, 150	1, 480	3, 843	2, 363

[1] In alphabetic order.

Whether these numbers reflect Irish antecedents is determined by testing companionships. Hypothetical figures are obtained for the numbers of Irish families in the area of record, presuming all Irish represented in ratio to the estimated Irish usage of the selected surnouns. While hypothetical, the figures are determined by identical calculations, and consequently test similarities and dissimilarities in recurrence of these names viewed as Irish.

Table 48 shows calculations of significance of Irish usage of these Scotch-Irish names. Column 1 shows the numbers of Irish bearers per thousand of the population in Ireland as reported by Matheson from an analysis of the 1890 record of births which totaled 105,254; column 2 shows the estimated numbers of heads of families of Irish origin bearing these names, as calculated in Table 47. Dividing the latter figures by the former gives, in column 3, the indicated thousands of Irish families, presuming all Irish had American representation in their original proportions. The indicated numbers range from 300,000 measured by occurrence of the *Paton* group, to 18,900 measured by that of the *M'Innes* group.

Viewed collectively, the recurrence of the 16 names indicates 133,700 Irish families in the American area if all Irish were represented in ratio to the bearers of these Scotch-Irish names. The median measurement is somewhat lower, 132,400—a figure intermediate between the readings afforded by *Blair* and *Ferguson*. This test of companionship eliminates the names *Paton* and *M'Innes* from the class, and the remaining 14 names are hereinafter employed as Scotch-Irish appellations satisfactorily indicating by average occurrence the approximate representation of Scotch-Irish in the population. We shall later dispose of the hypothesis in the calculation of numbers of Irish families affecting Tables 48 and 49 which follow.

TABLE 48.—*Calculation of significance of Irish usage of specified Scotch-Irish names*

Name	Irish per thousand of the name in the motherland as per Matheson's report [1]	Estimated number of heads of families of Irish origin bearing the name area of record, 1790	Number of Irish families in population of area of record, 1790, if in ratio to estimated Irish usage of these names
Black	1. 10	205	186, 400
Blair	. 74	102	137, 800
Boyd	1. 47	280	190, 500
Campbell	3. 32	395	119, 000
Craig	1. 43	134	93, 700
Cumming	1. 24	288	232, 300
Cunningham	2. 04	192	94, 100
Ferguson	1. 26	160	127, 000
Findlay	. 72	29	40, 300
Gordon	1. 16	272	234, 500
M'Dougall	. 86	133	154, 700
M'Innes	1. 22	23	18, 900
Maxwell	. 65	93	143, 100
Moffat	. 65	25	38, 500
Orr	. 69	55	79, 700
Paton	. 57	171	300, 000
Collectively (16)	19. 12	2, 557	133, 700
Collectively, omitting M'Innes and Paton	17. 33	2, 363	136, 400

[1] See table 21 for number of entries in total of 105,254.

Table 49 recapitulates the 16 Scotch-Irish names in the order of recurrence viewed as Irish; and also shows the median measurement of 132,400, intermediate between readings of *Blair* and *Ferguson*.

TABLE 49.—*Scotch-Irish names arrayed in order of recurrence as Irish*

[Number of Irish families in population of area of record, 1790, if in ratio to estimated Irish usage of these names]

Paton	300, 000	Craig	93, 700
Gordon	234, 500	Orr	79, 700
Cumming	232, 300	Findlay	40, 300
Boyd	190, 500	Moffat	38, 500
Black	186, 400	M'Innes	18, 900
M'Dougall	154, 700		
Maxwell	143, 100	Collectively (16)	133, 700
Blair	137, 800	Collectively, omitting	
Ferguson	127, 000	M'Innes and Patton	136, 400
Campbell	119, 000	Median	132, 400
Cunningham	94, 100		

More fundamental than the separation of the currency of the individual names is the division of their collective currency, State by State, enabling estimating of Scotch-Irish contributions to each State, and observations of gradations along the seaboard.

Tables 50 and 51 present two phases of the data for each State that Table 47 showed for the whole area of record.

TABLE 50.—*Calculation of number of Scots with 14 specified Scotch-Irish names among heads of families by States, 1790*

Area	Estimated total number of Scotch families[1]	Number among these normally bearing the 14 selected names[2]	Area	Estimated total number of Scotch families[1]	Number among these normally bearing the 14 selected names[2]
Maine	760	32	Pennsylvania	6, 410	266
New Hampshire	1, 490	62	Maryland	2, 490	103
Vermont	760	32	Virginia	3, 840	159
Massachusetts	2, 890	120	North Carolina	7, 770	322
Rhode Island	640	27	South Carolina	3, 920	163
Connecticut	900	37			
New York	3, 820	159	Area of record	35, 690	[3] 1, 481

[1] From Table 25.
[2] Whose bearers constitute 41.50 per 1,000 among Scots.
[3] Corresponds to the total of 1,480 obtained in Table 47.

TABLE 51.—*Estimated numbers of heads of families of Irish origin with 14 specified Scotch-Irish names*

Area	Total bearers of the names	Estimated number Scotch	Derived number Irish[1]
Maine	175	32	143
New Hampshire	173	62	111
Vermont	81	32	49
Massachusetts	295	120	175
Rhode Island	53	27	26
Connecticut	96	37	59
New York	427	159	268
Pennsylvania	993	266	727
Maryland	249	103	146
Virginia	358	159	199
North Carolina	572	322	250
South Carolina	371	163	208
Area of record	3, 843	1, 481	[2] 2, 362

[1] By subtraction.
[2] Corresponds to 2,363 in Tables 47 and 48.

The calculations in Table 47 and 51 illustrate the dependability of the method of tracing origins on the basis of name currency. The number of bearers of individual names may be influenced by regional or factional emigration, time of arrival of particularly prolific colonies of immigrants, reproduction rates of certain families, and other factors. Estimates based on small numbers are particularly open to erratic findings. Yet in every instance the totals by surnoun and by State prove adequate for theoretical subclassification as Scotch and Irish. These studies of complex currency test the thesis of reflected frequency, and the orderly conditions uncovered support the estimated relative contributions of Scotch and Scotch-Irish.

RELATIVE AMERICAN CURRENCY OF SCOTCH-IRISH NAMES AS IRISH

When the currency of the individual Scotch-Irish names was tested (Table 49), it was observed that the estimated Irish usages of the 14 selected names point from 132,400 to 136,400 Irish families in the area of record if all Irish were represented in ratio to the bearers of these names. We now examine the situation in the several States to ascertain the distribution of the Irish. These calculations will be in percentages showing the variation in conditions in the several States. For the area of record as a whole, the percentage may be tested by the previous calculation. Table 52 shows by the Irish usage of the 14 selected names that if all Irish migrated at the rate of the bearers of these Scotch-Irish names, they would have constituted 30.24 per cent of the population of the area of record. The corresponding figure in terms of number of families is 136,400, which agrees with the arithmetic average previously obtained from the currencies of the individual names. (Table 49.)

The details of this determination of percentages are shown in Table 52. In column 1 are the totals for families of all origins covered by the indexes of 1790; and in column 2 the estimated numbers of heads of families bearing the 14 specified names as Irish. Comparison between these two sets of figures gives in column 3 the estimated number of Irish bearers of these names per thousand. Thus in the area of record as a whole the 2,362 bearers ascribed Irish origin constituted 5.24 per thousand of the total population. Table 48 showed that in Ireland, according to Matheson, the bearers of these names normally constituted 17.33 per thousand. Division of 5.24 by the number 17.33 representing Irish bearers per thousand among Irish gives the percentage of 30.24 Irish in the population by Old World ratios.[10]

---

[10] It is to be noted that the process of calculation is likely to exaggerate somewhat the degree of factional migration. The Scotch-Irish give evidence of factional migration of such marked character as partly to destroy the validity of Matheson's data on 1890 conditions as indicative of those in the eighteenth century. Ordinarily migration can show considerable irregularity of either regional or factional sort and still leave the relative frequency of names in the motherland after the migration in about the same coordination as before. Migration from certain corners of the land may be sufficient to give names peculiar ratios in the New World and yet not sufficient seriously to affect the residual ratios in the motherland. The exodus of most of the members of certain groups, however, gives their names more than the normal representation in the New World and leaves the population of the motherland with an unusually small proportion of bearers of these names. Consequently the comparison of the number of bearers in the New World with the number remaining in the old takes the form of a fraction which has a numerator of $a+$ and a denominator of $b-$, a and b being the numbers which would have been involved in the comparison had the special migration not reached unusual proportions. Hence the working statement of the migratory rate of the Scotch-Irish needs to be viewed in its full setting and coordinated with a conservative estimate of the numbers of Scotch-Irish available for migration.

TABLE 52.—*Calculation of apparent Irish contributions to population on the basis of Irish usage of Scotch-Irish names*

	Total heads of families indexed census of 1790	Estimated number of heads of families of Irish origin bearing 14 specified names [1]	Number of Irish bearers of these names per thousand [2]	Indicated percentage contribution of Irish to population if all migrated at the rate of Scotch-Irish [3]
Area of record_____	451, 120	2, 362	5. 24	30. 24
Maine_____	17, 020	143	8. 40	48. 47
New Hampshire_____	24, 090	111	4. 61	26. 60
Vermont_____	14, 970	49	3. 27	18. 87
Massachusetts_____	65, 230	175	2. 68	15. 46
Rhode Island_____	11, 140	26	2. 33	13. 44
Connecticut_____	40, 680	59	1. 45	8. 37
New York_____	54, 540	268	4. 91	28. 33
Pennsylvania_____	74, 510	727	9. 76	56. 32
Maryland_____	32, 690	146	4. 47	25. 79
Virginia_____	37, 710	199	5. 28	30. 47
North Carolina_____	52, 560	250	4. 76	27. 47
South Carolina_____	25, 980	208	8. 01	46. 22

[1] Numbers previously ascertained by eliminating normal Scotch usage from observed totals. (Table 51.)
[2] Entries in column 2 divided by those in column 1.
[3] Viewing the Irish of column 3 as normally constituting 17.33 per 1,000 among Irish.

PROPORTION OF SCOTCH-IRISH AMONG IRISH

Quite divergent views on the original proportion of Scotch-Irish among Irish are supported by the various data. The classification of names in Chapter V suggests about 25 per cent, half the population bearing names not distinctively Irish, these names divided almost equally between Scotch and English patterns; but a proportion of 10 per cent is derived from evidence that the Scotch-Irish centered chiefly in Ulster and constituted about a third of its population; and a still smaller proportion is inferred from the apparent accordance of estimates shown in Chapter V.

Step 2 in Chapter V established only about half the names in common use in Ireland as distinctive. The remainder were found identical with or similar to names of people of other nationalities, most of them borne by English *and* Scotch (British), some shared only with the English, others only with the Scotch, the last two classes being nearly equally important. On these grounds, half of Ireland's population was not indigenous and a quarter was Scotch-Irish. But this classification limited distinctive names to those not even similar to other British names, thus understating Celtic proportions and hence not affording a reliable basis for estimating the proportion of names of Scotch pattern. Many names characterized as similar to Scotch indicate no modern relationship of populations. Therefore it is considered that the Scotch-Irish were substantially less than a quarter of the Irish population originally available for migration.

The study previously made of contributions of Irish disclosed by the recurrence of distinctive names resulted in two sets of findings, both showing six and a fraction per cent as the measure of Irish among Americans. The similarity of these seems to indicate that the Irish were fairly accurately measured. However, names of general use in Ireland pointed toward a somewhat higher measure for the stock than was supported by the provincial detail. It may be thought that, since the estimate derived from the recurrence of these general names was but slightly more than that derived from the provincial names, very little modification of the provincial figures is necessary to obtain a satisfactory schedule for the population as a whole. It might be argued that even though the Scotch-Irish emigrated rapidly from the country, they must have had comparatively small numbers not to have carried with them many bearers of names that were popular among the Irish generally. This position has been shown as untenable. There were substantial migrations of Irish involving remarkably few bearers of names distinctive of Ireland generally or of Ulster in which these migrations usually originated. It is held in the preceding chapter that distinctively Irish names afford only hypothetical measurements of the stock, disclosing its proportions in America if all the Irish migrated at the rate of those most truly Celtic, consequently it must be held that the control measurements in that chapter are binding only on this hypothetical measurement of Celtic Irish and that a substantial migration of Scotch-Irish could have occurred without being fully reflected even in the currency of the names generally favored by the population as a whole.

While the Scotch-Irish had numbers substantially less than by a quarter of the original population, yet on the other hand they were by no means insignificant. One must take a moderate position as to their proportion in the population of the island available for migration. My position is that they may be reckoned as equivalent to about a third of the population of Ulster.

Table 53 (in the same general form as Table 28) shows the provincial Irish distribution of the 14 names selected from Matheson's record of a total of 105,254 births in 1890. Of their 1825 entries, more than two-thirds were found in Ulster, although at that time Ulster had but little more than a third of the population of the country, evidence that Scotch-Irish names were highly numerous in Ulster and uncommon if not rare in the other Provinces. Matheson's codification is here simplified, some of the names being grouped in Table 53 as in Tables 28 and 31. The two sets of side headings compare the Scotch and Irish forms of the 14 selected names; column 1 shows the numbers of entries which Matheson found for the specific names he used as group headings; column 2 shows total entries for each group, including all spellings; and columns 3, 4, 5, and 6 cover the provincial distribution of these totals.

TABLE 53.—*Distribution of Scotch-Irish names in Ireland*

Scotch caption	Irish caption	Sp.	Total	Leinster	Munster	Ulster	Connaught
Black	Same	116	116	15	1	96	4
Blair	Same	78	78	2	2	74	
Boyd	Same	154	155	10	1	141	3
Campbell	Same	349	349	39	8	279	23
Craig	Craig	120	120	7	1	111	1
	Creagh	17	17	6	8	1	2
	Cregg	13	13	1	1		11
Cumming	Cummins	77	77	37	25	11	4
	Cummings	10	20	4	2	12	2
	Commins	17	20	4	4	2	10
	Commons	13	14	7	1		6
Cunningham	Same	202	215	40	35	89	51
Ferguson	Same	130	133	11	1	107	14
Findlay	Finlay	69	76	17	1	54	4
Gordon	Same	118	122	22	3	82	15
M'Dougall	McDowell	89	91	9		80	2
Maxwell	Same	68	68	16	3	46	3
Moffat	Moffatt	11	68	7		45	16
Orr	Same	73	73	5	2	65	1
Total (14)		1,724	1,825	259	99	1,295	172

Classification of names in common use in Ireland (Table 32) noted that about 30 per cent of Ulster population had peculiarly Irish names, indicating, on the basis of the close definition of distinctiveness, up to 40 per cent with names indigenous to the island. Irish with Scotch and English names being approximately equal in number, the former being localized in Ulster, and the latter numerous there, it appears that the Scotch-Irish were equivalent to about a third of the population of Ulster, and the significance of the migration rate of Irish with Scotch names is developed on this basis.

<h2 style="text-align:center">THREE STREAMS OF ULSTER IRISH</h2>

It has been seen (Table 44) that Ulster Irish would have constituted 2.6 per cent of the population in the American area of record had they been represented in ratio to bearers of names distinctive in that Province; and as these indicators are practically limited to Celtic, this is interpreted as their proportion had all factions been represented in ratio to the Celtic.

Table 54 presents the corresponding figures for Ulster Irish representation if in ratio to Irish with Scotch-Irish names. This table uses the weighting of 29.4 per cent previously employed for determining the bearing of estimates for migration from the country as a whole on estimates of migration from that Province. Calculations from premises indicate 8.9 per cent Ulster Irish in contrast to the foregoing 2.6 per cent.

TABLE 54.—*Percentages of Irish in American population, 1790, if all Irish migrated at the rate of Scotch-Irish*

	Per cent Irish if all Irish migrated at rate of Scotch-Irish	Per cent Ulster Irish if they migrated at rate of Scotch-Irish [1]		Per cent Irish if all Irish migrated at rate of Scotch-Irish	Per cent Ulster Irish if they migrated at rate of Scotch-Irish [1]
Area of record_____	30. 24	8. 9	Connecticut_____	8. 37	2. 5
			New York_____	28. 33	8. 3
Maine_____	48. 47	14. 3	Pennsylvania_____	56. 32	16. 6
New Hampshire___	26. 60	7. 8	Maryland_____	25. 79	7. 6
Vermont_____	18. 67	5. 5	Virginia_____	30. 47	9. 0
Massachusetts_____	15. 40	4. 5	North Carolina____	27. 47	8. 1
Rhode Island_____	13. 44	4. 0	South Carolina____	46. 22	13. 6

[1] Weight of 29.4 per cent for Ulster applied to column 1.

The percentages of Ulster Irish on the Scotch-Irish basis decline southward and westward in New England to a low figure in Connecticut, rise through New York to a high measure in Pennsylvania, drop off in Maryland, Virginia, and North Carolina to measures fairly similar to the national average, and rise again in South Carolina.

There is sufficient coordination in these estimates to indicate approximate conditions in the States of missing records. Fair estimates are 9 per cent Ulster Irish in New Jersey (intermediate between New York and Pennsylvania) and 8 per cent in Delaware (intermediate between Pennsylvania and Maryland) under the ascribed conditions. These interpolations are based on the fact that the Scotch-Irish in Pennsylvania were largely in the western counties and on inference that their proportions showed little variation along the seaboard. In Georgia the Scotch-Irish are known to have been numerous, and the difference between estimates of their proportion in South Carolina and North Carolina indicates a marked rise in the southern part of the country; hence 17 per cent is considered a fair estimate of the Ulster Irish in the population of Georgia. A proportion of 10 per cent Scotch-Irish in Kentucky and Tennessee is obtained on the assumption that population in this area was drawn about equally from the four States to the east. These interpolations give a conditional total of 9 per cent Ulster Irish in the country as a whole.

But while the Scotch-Irish rate of migration would have given Ulster a representation of 9 per cent in American population, the Celtic rate would have given it only 3 per cent (on the basis of 2.6 per cent in the area of record). And these two figures present only two aspects of a 3-phase problem, for the part played by English-Irish in Ulster migration is yet to be investigated.

The English-Irish are appraised with some difficulty because they had no common characteristic other than the possession of English names, unless it was a lack of sympathy with Celtic ideals. Many were not of English ancestry and some were Celts renamed by choice or force. Their very heterogeneity suggests as the rate of their migratory activity, one between that of the Celts and that of the other unassimilated element, the Scotch-Irish.

Ulster Irish contributions to American population were therefore more than the 3 per cent indicated by the migration rate of the Celtic elements of that Province, and less than the 9 per cent indicated by the migration rate of the Scotch-Irish in that Province. If the migration rate of English-Irish approximated that of the Celtic, Ulster's contribution to American population was about 5 per cent; if like that of the Scotch-Irish, about 7 per cent. These two figures are not widely divergent. In the absence of specific evidence, the migration rate of the English-Irish is estimated as about the average of the rates of the Celtic and the Scotch-Irish originally in that Province, indicating 6 per cent contribution of all Ulster Irish to American population in 1790.

Table 55 shows, for the United States and for each State, percentage estimates of Ulster Irish based on the assumption that the migration rate of bearers of English names was intermediate between the rates of bearers of Celtic and bearers of Scotch-Irish names. Column 1 shows percentage contributions of Ulster Irish as indicated by recurrence of Celtic names, the figures drawn with some adjustment from Table 44. These adjustments result from observation (Chapter V) of some irregularities in representation of names from State to State, and of the fact that in northern New England and Maryland the provincial detail at first obtained was not in good coordination with estimates derived from currency of names of general Irish background. These adjustments improve gradations in State relationships and slightly increase the estimate of total contributions previously established. Column 2 reproduces the figures shown in column 3 of Table 54 and adds percentages as interpolated for the States of missing records. Column 3 gives the estimated percentages of Ulster Irish derived from the three streams of Ulster migration—Celtic, Scotch-Irish, and English-Irish.

TABLE 55.—*Estimated contributions of Ulster Irish to population, 1790, derived from calculations of Celtic and Scotch-Irish*

	Percentages of Ulster Irish in population indicated by the recurrence of—		Estimated percentages of Ulster Irish in population, 1790
	Celtic names from Ulster [1]	Scotch-Irish names from Ulster	
United States	3. 0	9. 0	6. 0
Maine	[2] 1. 8	14. 3	8. 0
New Hampshire	[2] 1. 4	7. 8	4. 5
Vermont	[2] 0. 9	5. 5	3. 2
Massachusetts	0. 6	4. 5	2. 6
Rhode Island	0. 1	4. 0	2. 0
Connecticut	1. 1	2. 5	1. 8
New York	1. 9	8. 3	5. 1
New Jersey	[3] 3. 5	[3] 9. 0	[3] 6. 3
Pennsylvania	5. 5	16. 6	11. 0
Delaware	[2] 4. 5	[3] 8. 0	[3] 6. 3
Maryland	[2] 4. 0	7. 6	5. 8
Kentucky and Tennessee	[2][3] 4. 1	[3] 10. 0	[3] 7. 0
Virginia	3. 4	9. 0	6. 2
North Carolina	3. 3	8. 1	5. 7
South Carolina	5. 3	13. 6	9. 4
Georgia	[3] 6. 0	[3] 17. 0	[3] 11. 5

[1] From table 44 with adjustments as noted.
[2] Estimates adjusted.
[3] Not of specific record.

BACKGROUND OF THE ENGLISH-IRISH

Occurrences of English names in Ireland reveal bearers particularly numerous in Ulster—though not so centered there as the Scotch-Irish—and also strong in Leinster.

Table 56 shows the distribution in Ireland of bearers of leading English names more than rarely used by Irish and not in common use in Scotland. Names rare in Ireland were the Anglican *Baker, Carter, Cooper, Harrison, Parker*; and the Cambrian *Edwards, Griffiths, James, Price, Roberts,* and *Thomas,* to which *Davies* may be added, having become a mere variant of *Davis.* Totals in this table apply to the specified names and their variants.

TABLE 56.—*Distribution of Irish bearers of leading English names more than rarely used by Irish* [1]

[Births, Ireland, 1890, in a total of 105,254, per Matheson]

Heading of Irish name group	Total, Ireland	By Provinces			
		Leinster	Munster	Ulster	Con-naught
Bennett	81	26	20	34	1
Davis [2]	104	41	17	34	12
Evans	55	22	11	19	3
Green	152	39	37	54	22
Hall	120	37	13	69	1
Harris	59	21	21	15	2

[1] Not including any also common in Scotland.
[2] With its "variant" Davies.

TABLE 56.—*Distribution of Irish bearers of leading English names more than rarely used by Irish*—Continued

Headings of Irish name group	Total, Ireland	By Provinces			
		Leinster	Munster	Ulster	Con-naught
Hughes	334	92	7	180	55
Jones	152	60	38	45	9
Lee	120	33	21	43	23
Lewis	51	16	16	18	1
Moore	396	135	52	185	24
Morgan	132	37	16	67	12
Morris	115	49	6	32	28
Phillips	77	27	8	21	21
Robinson	217	29	9	168	11
Turner	67	22	13	30	2
Ward	213	57	22	87	47
Williams	90	40	25	14	11
Total	2, 535	783	352	1, 115	285
Per cent distribution	100. 0	30. 9	13. 9	44. 0	11. 2
Compare per cent distribution of all births recorded	100. 0	25. 1	24. 4	35. 5	15. 0

ORIGINS IN THE SOUTH OF IRELAND

In the light of the investigation of factional migration, the studies of provincial Irish may now be coordinated for summation of southern Irish contributions.

The estimate of Leinster contributions based on provincial names now appears to be an understatement because of its disregard of the important English-Irish faction in that Province. Although it is employed with little specific adjustment in Table 57 at the close of this chapter, summing up the findings on the Irish, it is given a general qualification. It is founded on rather orderly recurrences of a fairly satisfactory class of distinctive names. The cryptic footnote, " or more," is added to denote the probability that the numerous English-Irish in Leinster migrated at a greater rate than the Celtic, and hence gave the Province a greater representation in American population than has so far been established. There is a specific change in the estimate for Virginia, dictated by observed irregularities in the series of Leinster findings for this region, this adjustment giving an estimate of 1.2 per cent Leinster contributions to American population.

The appraisal of contributions from Connaught based on the recurrence of provincial names tends toward overstatement because of the original spread of these names outside the Province. Connaught indicators were rather widely distributed abroad and gave readings intermediate between the true low ones for that Province and the general averages for Ireland as a whole; nevertheless, estimates for this provincial stock in three States are raised to improve coordination in findings for the States as a series, and Connaught is given a value of 0.8 per cent contributions to American population. To this figure is appended the footnote, " or less," as an expression of the author's opinion that origins in this Province are overstated.

The estimates for contributions from Leinster and Connaught are of more value as indicating approximate relative distribution of these stocks along the seaboard than as demonstrating their total contributions.

Since distinctive names for Munster are nearly ideal as provincial indicators and decidedly show regular recurrence in most of the country, only one adjustment is made, raising the estimate for this Province's contribution to North Carolina to 2.3 per cent in recognition of lack of coordination in the original findings for provincial detail in that State and of probable seried relationship in the proportions of Munster Irish in that region. This makes the total Munster rating 1.7 per cent.

AMERICAN IRISH BY PROVINCE OF ORIGIN

Table 57 shows percentage estimates of Irish contributions by Province of origin as follows: Leinster, 1.2 or more; Munster, 1.7; Connaught, 0.8 or less; Ulster, 6.0. Since the figures for Leinster and Connaught present compensatory errors, it is considered that the summation (column **4**) for the three southern Provinces—Leinster, Munster, Connaught—is a fair working statement of the total percentage of stock from southern Ireland and its seried distribution. The Ulster estimate of approximately 6.0 per cent is derived from its three migration streams. The Irish as a whole are estimated at approximately 9.7 per cent of American population in 1790, with distribution by States as here shown.

TABLE 57.—*Estimated percentages of white population of the United States constituted by Irish with details by Province of origin and by States, 1790*

State	Irish originating in—			Southern Provinces	Ulster	Total Irish
	Leinster	Munster	Connaught			
United States	[1] 1.2	1.7	[2] 0.8	3.7	6.0	9.7
Maine	1.1	1.5	[3] 1.1	3.7	8.0	11.7
New Hampshire	.9	1.2	[3] .8	2.9	4.6	7.5
Vermont	.7	.5	.7	1.9	3.2	5.1
Massachusetts	.5	.5	.3	1.3	2.6	3.9
Rhode Island	.4	.1	.3	.8	2.0	2.8
Connecticut	.2	.3	.6	1.1	1.8	2.9
New York	1.2	1.3	.5	3.0	5.1	8.1
New Jersey [4]	1.2	1.5	.5	3.2	6.3	9.5
Pennsylvania	1.2	1.8	.5	3.5	11.0	14.5
Delaware [4]	1.9	2.6	.9	5.4	6.3	11.7
Maryland	2.3	3.0	1.2	6.5	5.8	12.3
Kentucky and Tennessee [4]	1.7	2.4	1.1	5.2	7.0	12.2
Virginia	[3] 1.6	2.6	[3] 1.3	5.5	6.2	11.7
North Carolina	1.6	[3] 2.3	1.5	5.4	5.7	11.1
South Carolina	1.1	2.5	.8	4.4	9.4	13.8
Georgia [4]	.8	2.6	.4	3.8	11.5	15.3

[1] Or more.
[2] Or less.
[3] Estimates based on both regional and local occurrences of names.
[4] Not of specific record. Estimates derived from consideration of trends locally.

CHAPTER VII

GERMAN CONTRIBUTIONS TO 1790 AMERICA

The proportion of Germans in the American population has been more adequately recognized than that of the Scotch or Irish, since their language usually distinguished them even to the third and fourth generation. Seldom reckoned more than 10 per cent, the estimate in *CPG* is 5.6 per cent, and somewhere between these figures their true measure lies.

Germany in the eighteenth century was merely a geographical expression; therefore German stock is here defined as Teutonic other than Dutch or Scandinavian—equivalent to German-speaking people.

Germans are mentioned as accompanying John Smith's party to Virginia, and there were representatives of the stock in the early settlements of Dutch and Swedes. An important date in the history of migration is 1683, when the first shipload of Germans landed, coming in the *Concord*, commonly called the *Mayflower* of the Germans. Thereafter they began to appear in substantial numbers in several of the States.

The stock had its principal numbers in Pennsylvania, where Germans were so numerous that "Pennsylvania Dutch" (*Deutsch*) is an expression familiar to every American. Even before the middle of the eighteenth century Germans were estimated by certain well-informed observers to constitute a third of the population of the State. Beginning with 1710, New York also received settlements of Germans. New Jersey shortly had numbers of them in Hunterdon, Somerset, and Morris Counties. Delaware received but few. In Maryland the infiltration began in the seventeenth century, but the main current was from the Pennsylvania settlements and reached the State in its western counties. In Virginia there were Germans early in the eighteenth century, but the principal number came in the tide from Pennsylvania in the second quarter of the century. The Carolinas also received numerous descendants of the Pennsylvania Germans, mainly after 1750, and had substantial immigration direct to the coast. In general, the Germans in South Carolina came to the coast, while those in North Carolina were progeny of Pennsylvania settlers. These migrating sons ultimately became numerous on the Yadkin and the Catawba. Germans in Georgia became conspicuous after the settlement of the Austrian Salzburgers in 1734.

In New England the stock was not especially numerous, but there were settlements after 1741. The names of Frankfort, Dresden, and Bremen in Maine, and Adams, Bernardston, and Leyden in Massachusetts are some of the early locations in these States. In New England records it is difficult to detect the descendants of Germans by their names; but from New York southward the Germans regularly constituted substantial proportions of the population, and even though many names were changed, their contribution to the nomenclature is measureable.

SPECIAL PROBLEMS AND ADAPTATIONS OF PROCEDURE

Each of these studies involves special problems, and in none is it possible to make an ideal application of the system of distinctive names. The measurement of German stock in 1790 on the basis of its name uses also presents its own difficulties. One of these is lack of data on the frequencies of names in the European area. Another is evident variability of usage which makes it laborious to restore the picture of nomenclatural conditions among the immigrants. A third is the scant representation of the stock in New England. These are overcome by the correlation of data from many sources and the combination of other methods with the distinctive name system.

Because of the numerous modifications to which German nomenclature was subject when it played but a small part in the American mixture, the application of the study of distinctive names is limited to the States where the stock was well represented. And, because this inquiry is mainly concerned with refinement in rating a contribution of fairly well known degree, more than usual attention is given to criticism of the nomenclatural readings in the light of history and other synthesis.

The distinctive name system as developed here shows emphasis on steps 4, 7, and 8, which, as set forth in Chapter IV, are concerned, respectively, with determination of ultimate distinctiveness, interpretation of frequency ratios, and general coordination and criticism. The study of ultimate distinctiveness involves attention to the controls on changes of name and to the minute details of these changes. The lack of statistical information corresponding to that of the registrars on original frequencies prevents a direct study of recurrences, and frequency ratios are therefore interpreted from a basic estimate of absolute numbers in Pennsylvania. The American distribution of bearers of the names selected for study can be interpreted as well by comparison with conditions in the Keystone State, where the stock had its center, as it could by comparison with conditions in Europe, and perhaps better. This is because the usage of even the most distinctively German appellations dwindled under the influence of Americanization and because the regional and factional aspects of the migration were probably quite as complicated as those of the Irish. The study is favored by the facts that the stock largely entered through a Province which recorded the arrivals and that the great body remained in a limited area.

OUTLINE OF INQUIRY

From the Pennsylvania *Oath of Allegiance* record[1] a list of approximately 200 leading names, borne by "foreigners," was abstracted, and 63 distinctive German names selected by comparing the list with schedules of British, Dutch, and French usages, these indicators being regarded as key names for natural groupings of German nomenclature. Their definition proved exacting because German authorities discuss etymological connections rather than frequency distinctions, and because many original groups were disrupted by Americanization.

A search of the Pennsylvania census with the object of identifying American names properly assignable to the 63 groups disclosed that their bearers had very substantial numbers in that State and also that there was material diversity in the form or spelling employed. These 63 groups of names were found to account for about 3,400 entries among the 74,500 listings for heads of families in the Pennsylvania census, and to average 11 forms apiece. An illustration of the diversity which was encountered is provided by the *Schultz* group, which showed 71 entries, including the following: *Shultz*, 27; *Schultz*,

---

[1] Pennsylvania Archives, series 2, vol. 17.

5; *Shilt*, 2; *Shiltz*, 2; *Sholes*, 2; *Sholts*, 5; *Sholtz*, 4; *Shoults*, 4; *Shoultz*, 3; *Shults*, 3; *Shulz*, 3; and also single entries for 11 other forms.

After examining the occurrences of these 63 groups in Pennsylvania, I questioned the advisability of continuing the study with all of these names as indicators. It was seen that the occurrence of these names, as a class, was so great that the time available would scarcely permit tracing them in the other records. It also appeared that some of the groups had such diversity of content as to make their further identification unnecessarily laborious and that some were so little used as to interfere with their validity as indicators. In spite of the fact that these groups averaged over 50 entries, there were some among them which found but few bearers in Pennsylvania; for example, *Baum* 9 and *Spiess* 8. It was finally decided to rate the names on the basis of their number of entries and simplicity of content, and to continue the study with 32 of the groups thus specially selected. These accounted for about 2,300 heads of families in Pennsylvania, or an average of 72 apiece.

It appeared at the time that the effectiveness of the inquiry would be furthered by eliminating the names showing paucity of entries in the Pennsylvania census, but it later developed that scant use in Pennsylvania was caused mainly by the bearers of the names moving on to other localities. It was also found that some of the names which promised to be particularly good indicators because of their numbers in this one census were actually rather peculiar to the Pennsylvania stream of migration. Although further observations were confined to the 32 selected names, it was necessary later to subclassify them and make certain adjustments of preliminary findings based on the occurrences of those among them which were demonstrably in common use by all Germans whatever their port of arrival. The appraisals finally obtained make allowance for the special factors of secondary migration and Pennsylvania peculiarities which presented questions at this point of the procedure.

The next step was to determine the distribution of bearers of these 32 groups of names in the States of record where German influence on nomenclature was apparent. The entries noted for these names in the censuses of New York, Maryland, Virginia, North Carolina, and South Carolina were used to measure the numbers of Germans in these indexes relative to those in Pennsylvania. The readings immediately obtained from the average occurrences, expressed as medians, were that German elements in these indexes bore the following percentage relations to the German element in the Pennsylvania index: New York, 12.0; Maryland, 15.4; Virginia, 8.7; North Carolina, 5.4; South Carolina, 2.6.

Subclassification of the 32 names according to the degree of accuracy possible in definition of the surnouns disclosed that where the stock was several generations removed from immigration, some of the names showed weakness due to radical changes. Comparison of the characteristics of the several surnouns disclosed that those which might give way to other names in mixed populations averaged less use in Virginia and North Carolina than the full list of indicators. These names and their usual successors (when these extreme changes occur) are as follows: *Bachman, Bowman; Gerber, Carver,* and *Tanner; Jaeger, Hunter; Schaffer, Shepherd; Schneider, Taylor; Zimmerman, Carpenter.* Adjusting the readings of these names indicated that the rating of the German element in the Virginia index should be raised from 8.7 to 9.5 and the North Carolina rating from 5.4 to 6.5 per cent of the element indexed in Pennsylvania. These adjustments were anticipated by general study of change of name.

These percentages were converted into numbers by establishing a basic number in Pennsylvania. Examination of various data concerning the proportion of Germans in the Pennsylvania population—estimated at about a third in the latter part of the eighteenth century—revealed that the stock attained its highest measure there about 1760, constituting more than a third of the Province's population then and for some time afterward, but with a decline in ratio after this date caused partly by reduced immigration and partly by overflow to the south at a rate greater than other stocks in the Pennsylvania population. These circumstances are found to have reproduced the one-third ratio at about 1790. Computing the number of Germans in Pennsylvania on this basis gives the numerical equivalent of the stock as 140,983, and German heads of families in the State index as 24,837.

The percentages based on relative local occurrence of the 32 names, applied to this numerical base in Pennsylvania, gave the following percentages for German contributions: New York, 5.5; Maryland, 11.7; Virginia, 6.3; North Carolina, 3.1; South Carolina, 2.5. Combining these estimates with Nelson's 9.2 per cent for New Jersey,[2] and with estimates for the New England States and Delaware based on revision of those in *CPG*, gave a minimum measure of 8.1 per cent as German stock, or approximately 258,000 in a total white population of 3,172,444. Minimum, because much of the stock was derived independently of Pennsylvania, and some from different antecedents, and a possible understatement is occasioned by the use of some indicators peculiar to Pennsylvania. German settlers in Pennsylvania were of diverse origin, but in New York and the extreme south different balances of antecedents obtained. Comparison of details in the above estimate with findings of various historians summarized by Faust[3] confirmed the necessity of revision for areas which received immigration independently of Pennsylvania. This was accomplished by another subclassification of indicators followed by interpretation of occurrence measures of 12 names having most regular distribution, and hence, presumably, most nearly uniform usage by all groups of German immigrants.

Colonial German usage reveals the following 12 surnouns particularly characteristic and generally used: *Christ, Conrad, Ernst, Hoff, Huber, Keyser, Kolb, Kuhn* (with *Kuntz*), *Lentz, Schaffer, Schneider,* and *Zimmerman*. These names were important enough in Pennsylvania to account for more than 5 per cent of its estimated German population. Their relative occurrence in Maryland and Virginia, where German population was chiefly by migration from Pennsylvania, was practically the same as that of the other indicators, yet their prevalence in New York and the Carolinas was considerably higher. Although not important enough to constitute a base for a schedule of distribution of the stock, their ratios for New York and the extreme south are of such significance that they dictate adjustment of preliminary findings. This results in an estimate of 8.7 per cent for total German stock in the population.

EVIDENCE ON IMMIGRANT GERMAN NOMENCLATURE

German authorities usually refer to the relative importance of names of the period, thus revealing something of the structure of nomenclature when Germans began coming to America; but their emphasis on etymology gives the impression that German nomenclature consisted of a comparatively few great complex name groups. Heintze gave unusual attention to grouping, in his *Deutschen Familiennamen*, basing his codification on military rosters, but he did not show tables of the occurrences which guided him.

---

[2] *CPG*, pp. 119–121.

[3] Faust, Albert B. *The German Element in the United States.* 3d ed., New York, 1927.

Hence the first essential in measuring German contributions is to learn what name forms German emigrants favored and what supplementary forms supported them. The names of foreigners arriving in Pennsylvania, as recorded in the Pennsylvania *Oath of Allegiance* record,[4] were chosen as the basic source of information because of the activity of the port of Philadelphia during the eighteenth century and the lack of consistent records for other ports. This record establishes a list of important name forms with usage predominantly German, from which may be selected a list of definite outstanding groups practically limited to forms peculiar to German-speaking people.

While it is questioned whether the nomenclature of the mass of German arrivals in Pennsylvania was typical of the general German migration—and it could have been of normal pattern in general structure and use of leading names only if the Pennsylvania migration had practically the same background as that of the whole movement—yet the Pennsylvania record may be considered representative of immigrant non-British nomenclature in its first stage of Americanization. Previous investigators have pointed out repetitions and garbled entries, and Rupp [5] and Kuhns [6] note diverse spellings, but these do not detract from the value of the *Oath of Allegiance* as a schedule of leading names and name groups in the German migration. So many individuals are listed that duplication and irregularities in recording members of families other than the heads are of slight importance, and diversities in spelling help rather than hinder in the search for derivatives, since several spellings of the same surname indicate original variability leading to American variability and hence contribute to the study of surnouns.

PENETRATING THE DISGUISE OF MIXED LISTS

The selection of immediately distinctive German names was accomplished by eliminating those names in the *Oath of Allegiance* which were actually used by persons other than Germans. The schedule of names not immediately distinctive may be derived from the sets of eliminations later presented.

After establishing the originally distinctive groups, it remained to find which maintained their integrity in America. The answer came from a study of their reaction to social and linguistic influences in the New World, and a consideration of the general principles of modification of non-British names. The problem was to select names of such inherent German characteristics that American influence would not have obscured the root forms. To give the readers an illustration of the problem, a list of names of moderately common occurrence in the Pennsylvania *Oath of Allegiance* record—names a degree less common than those used in this study—is shown in Appendix II. Study of this list shows some names shared by English and some listed in their English forms. Their original forms and their companion names, brought into the new American nomenclature and under the dominance of British nomenclature, are to be studied. Some are badly spelled, and the difficulty of learning what these spellings disclose of their evolution and what original forms they symbolize may be gathered by perusing the parallel columns in the second part of Appendix I, giving Kuhns's illustration of the processes of Americanization of German names.

---

[4] Names of Foreigners Who Took the Oath of Allegiance to the Province and State of Pennsylvania, 1727–1775, with the Foreign Arrivals, 1786–1808. Pennsylvania Archives, series 2, vol. 17, Harrisburg, 1892. (Inclusion of arrivals to 1808 will not prove a defect in the present study unless there was marked change in the regional origins of the immigrants after 1790.)

[5] Rupp, I. D., *Collection of 30,000 Names*, etc., pp. 1–3.

[6] Kuhns, L. Oscar, *The German and Swiss Settlements of Colonial Pennsylvania*, New York, 1901.

The search for groups ultimately distinctive of German origin is guided by the question of what became of original German nomenclature as its structural units settled down into the complex American nomenclature. This involves three elementary considerations—the variety of forms in American nomenclature succeeding the original German clusters, the degree of similarity of German names to others possible without confounding them in the reconstruction of the mixed American nomenclature, and the content of German groups which remained independent after adjustment to American conditions.

FUNDAMENTALS IN NOMENCLATURAL EVOLUTION

Individuals hold appellations by the dictates of society. Specific families have particular names because these names are among the few available for them under the limitations of the surname system. Specific groups of people likewise find their nomenclature controlled by limitations rooted in their antecedents and their folkways. Thus different societies develop their own systems of nomenclature with characteristic features respecting forms employed, measures of use and relationships in forms and frequencies; and stocks among them, such as the colonial Germans among the other Americans, are carried in an evolutionary current. Only in a sense did the families of the eighteenth century direct the modification or stabilization of their own names. True, surnames are functions of families, for surnames are normally designations transmitted from fathers to sons. Yet this is only partially true, for the fathers did not obtain them by choice and the father-and-son relationship is soon complicated by the passage of generations involving uncles and cousins. It is more accurate to say that surname nomenclature is a function of society.

Fundamental social differences determine the structural arrangements of European nomenclature. Names are terms in which a society defines itself, and they arrange themselves in clusters which become the units in the nomenclatural structure and which vary in their conformation according to the definiteness of the concepts which they express. They also vary as folk-philosophy changes. Samples of the nomenclatures transmitted by migration to the New World are only weakly supported by old philosophies, for on arrival the immigrants' names begin to undergo modifications to bring them into alignment with characteristics of the new society. But these evolutionary changes are slow and many of the original characteristics are long apparent; hence names afford a sound basis of measurement for contributions of national stocks to America.

Where people of different origins mingle in a new environment, a new nomenclature gradually develops out of the composite of names, and its structure tends to be modeled on the lines of the dominant nomenclature in that composite. The pressure on original groupings results in stress, strain, and even disintegration, and a new structure is evolved, such as that in the United States in 1790; some of the name groups even then have nearly their original conformation, others but hint of it. Perspective on American changes in German name groups is afforded in the abstract from Kuhns's study. (Appendix I.)[7]

A foreign stock finding itself, as did the Germans, a minority in a new land maintains its nomenclature only to the degree that it enunciates new concepts. Namings not distinctive are drawn into a classification already developed in

---

[7] Kuhns usually shows only one American form for a German original, but there are variants in both columns: German names with variants succeeded by diverse American forms. His record of American forms for German names was drawn from current records and sometimes notes changes that occurred after 1790.

the new country, and the stable names are only those which show, with some regard for significance, a skeletal form which is favorably different.

Before standards for stability can be established, controls on the forces for change must be determined. Considered singly, these forces are almost incomprehensible, but coordination makes it possible to distinguish those which disrupt original groups. The principal coordinations of these forces for change are here designated controls, and there are two controls on evolution of nomenclature in the United States. One is social, relates to the use of names as such—tools for designating people—and produces imitative changes; the other is linguistic, relates to the use of names as terms in the language, and produces adaptive changes. These controls are characterized rather fully in Appendix III.

The social control on evolution until 1790 was almost entirely responsible for the development of new groupings. The linguistic control produced many new forms without radically affecting the structure of minority nomenclatures and may be almost disregarded in determining ultimate distinctiveness. In this work, the problem has been to determine which groups could withstand the forces for change operating under social control. This control functions through confusion of names.

Difficulty in differentiating names in the effort to classify them by origins but reflects the confusion among the people living where these names were prevalent in the American Colonies in 1790. Confusion causes minor differences to disappear. Similarities of form almost invariably lead to changes by analogy, commonly to blending of name groups and to reorganization of structure, whereas similarities of significance have limited influence; their relative importance in fostering association of names and resultant blending of groups is discussed in Appendix III. Dissimilarities fundamental to distinctiveness must have been sufficiently marked to have been recognized by eighteenth century Americans.

THE PENNSYLVANIA OATH OF ALLEGIANCE RECORD

Determination of distinctive German names was based on elimination of all German groups containing forms recognized by Americans of that period as closely similar to those already in use there by people of other origins. From the entries of foreign arrivals in Pennsylvania was compiled a list of names of substantial repetition. From this were eliminated all whose original or American usage is not readily distinguished from English, other British, Dutch, French, and French-Canadian.

Common names were specified as those having entries of more than two lines in the index to the Pennsylvania *Oath of Allegiance* record, the first line ordinarily containing eight page references and the second line nine. The abstract thus generally includes names having more than 18 references. Had it not been for irregularities in spelling and in the set-up of the index, these leading names would have been defined by a fixed minimum of entries; despite these drawbacks, however, this abstract is a good working schedule of leading names borne by foreigners.

The abstract distinguished diverse spellings accepted as "names"; and, if they stood the tests for distinctiveness, accepted as designations of surnouns. These spellings are neither original nor final Americanized forms, but ordinarily somewhat garbled versions of the European forms. But while some spellings are free interpretations of the originals, it is remarkable that there was such general consistency in the entries that even names most distorted are largely represented by some one spelling. These names were used as symbols to guide in tracing the important groups of names later discussed; they may be compared with those only moderately common, listed in Appendix II, in which will be seen variants of the outstanding forms, later reunited by grouping with the key forms.

This abstract established a list of 198 leading names among those in the Pennsylvania record of arrivals. Comparison with British, Dutch, and French usages eliminated, respectively, 98, 19, and 14 names, leaving 67 clearly German, four of which undergo combination as variants or resemblants of others, resulting in a schedule of 63 distinctive German name groups. The tests by comparison are detailed in the next section.

SPÉCIFICATION OF DISTINCTIVE GERMAN NAMES BY ELIMINATION

Comparison with British usage eliminated from the 198 names those with forms similar to British names of more than rare use, determining German names superficially different from those natural to British immigration. For example, the names *Arnold, Beck, Gunter, Horn, Jacob, Lang, May, Mayer, Nagle, Thomas, Walter,* and *Winter* can not be used as indicative of German origin, since they are also British. The *Oath of Allegiance* names were checked against Guppy's list of names native to one or more English countries, against Matheson's record of usages in Ireland, and against Giles's Directory of Scotland, and all names identical with or closely similar to English, Irish, or Scotch names, including all names given British spellings by the Philadelphia port recorders, were excluded.

Table 58 shows names excluded on account of apparent confusion with British-American usage; this is a working statement of bases of exclusion and not a complete survey of related British usages. Column 1 shows the spellings appearing in the Pennsylvania index. Column 2 contains notes on British usages which prevent retention of these names as distinctively German. Column 2 usually notes only English usage of names closely similar to English, since exclusion was made first on this basis without reference to other British usage; but the application of the designation British is not to be construed as implying that those designated English were not borne by other British; in a number of instances names are noted as not normally English, implying they are not characteristic of the English frequency pattern.

TABLE 58.—*List of names in common use by "foreigners" arriving in Pennsylvania which are not readily distinguished as non-British*

First exclusion to work toward determination of distinctively German names. Authorities for notes on British usage:
  (1) H. B. Guppy, *Homes of Family Names in Great Britain*, London, 1890.
  (2) Robert E. Matheson, *Report on Surnames in Ireland;* originally in the Twenty-ninth Annual Report of the Registrar General for Ireland, Dublin, 1893, reprinted, Dublin, 1909.
  (3) Arthur Giles, editor, *The County Directory of Scotland*, twelfth issue, Edinburgh, 1902.

Names of foreigners	Notes on British usage
Adam	British, Adams.
Andres	British, Andrews, Enders.
Arnold	An English name.
Bach	A rare English name; English, Brook, Brooke.
Bauman	English, Bowman.
Bauer	English, Bower, Bowers.
Beck	An English name.
Bender	Commonly became Painter, an English name.
Bernhart	Scotch, Irish, Bernard.

Names of foreigners	Notes on British usage
Beyer	English, Bowyer; Scotch, Byers, Byres.
Bischoff	English, Bishop.
Bowman	An English name; intended for Bauman, etc.
Brandt	English, Brand, Braund.
Brown	British name; intended for Braun, etc.
Buch	Book is not normally British; English, Buck.
Bucher	English, Booker.
Busch	English, Bush.
Christian	An Irish name; English, Christy; Scotch, Christie.
Eberhart	English, Everett, Everitt, Evered, Evershed; Scotch, Ewart; Irish, Everts; French, Evrard.
Eberle	English, Eveleigh, Evely.
Ebert	See Eberhart.
Fischer	English, Fisher.
Franck	English, Frank, Franks.
Frey	English, Fry.
Fuchs	English, Fox.
George	An English name.
Gerhard	English, Gerrard.
Graff	English, Graves, Greaves, Grove, Groves.
Grubb	English, Grove.
Gunter	An English name.
Guth	English, Goode; Irish, Good; Scotch, Guthrie. NOTE.— Commonly translated as Good. See distribution of Good, *CPG*, p. 242.
Haas	English, Hayes, Hays.
Hahn	English, Haine, Hayne.
Haller	English, Helleir, Heler.
Hammer	English, Hamar, Hamer.
Harte	English, Hart.
Heintz	English, Hind; Irish, Hynes, Hinds.
Henrick	British, Henderson; Scotch, Irish, Hendrick.
Hess	English, Hayes, Hays.
Heyl	British, Hill; English, Hale, Heal.
Hoch	English, Hodge, Houch, Hook.
Horn	An English name.
Jacob	English, Jacob, Jacobs.
Jung	British, Young.
Kern	Irish, Kearns.
Klein	Scotch, and Irish, Clyne.
Koch	British, Cook, Cox.
Königh	British, King.
Kohl	English, Cole.
Kohler	English, Collier, see *CPG* under Coller, Collier, Kayler, and Keeler.
Krauss	English, Cross, Creese, Craze.
Lang	British, Long; Scotch, Lang.
Leonardt	English, Leonard.
Lorentz	English, Lawrence.
Martin	Cosmopolitan.
May	An English name.
Mayer	}English, Mayer, Mayor; British, Myers.
Meyer	
Michael	British, Mitchell.
Miller	A British name; intended for Mueller and Moeller, etc.
Möller	British, Miller.
Mohr	British, Moore.
Müller	British, Miller.
Nagle	An Irish name.
Neuman	English, Newman.
Peters	An English name.
Petry	Scotch, Petrie.
Pfeiffer	English, Piper.
Reich	English, Rich.
Reichert	British, Richards.

Names of foreigners	Notes on British usage
Roth	English, Wroth, Roads, Rhoades, Rhodes, Rood, Root.
Schall	}Irish, Shiels, Sheils and Shelly; Scotch, Shiell.
Schell	
Schenck	Scotch, Shanks.
Scherer	Scotch and Irish, Shearer.
Schmidt	British, Smith.
Schnell	English, Snell.
Schreiber	English, Scrivener; Dutch, Schryver.
Simon	English, Simons, Simmons.
Smith	Intended for Schmidt, Schmitt, etc.
Sommer	English, Summers.
Stahl	English, Steel.
Stein	English, Stone, Stones, Staines.
Stephen	English, Stephens, Stevens.
Thomas	A Cambrian name.
Vogt	English, Vooght.
Volck	English, Foulke, Fowke.
Walter	English, Walter, Walters.
Waltz	Irish, Walsh.
Weber	English, Webber, Weaver.
Weil	English, Wiles; Scotch, Wylie.
Weiss	English, Wise, White, Vyse.
Werner	English, Warner.
Winter	An English name.
Wirth	English, Worth.
Weidman	English, Whiteman.
Wilhelm	English, Williams.
Wolff	Wolf is cosmopolitan, though seldom British; Irish, Woulfe.

Elimination of names shared with the Dutch was based on comparison with records of the principal colonies in New Netherland, which demonstrate standards of Dutch usage because there were scarcely any other Dutch in the country. These Dutch had a variable nomenclature [8] for about two generations, finally developing surnames peculiar to themselves. The most important of the New Netherland records is the marriage record of the Reformed Dutch Church of New York which shows the national origin of a large proportion of its entries.

Table 59 shows names, remaining after the British elimination, subject to confusion with variants of names used by the Dutch. Among the eliminations are those of *Mathias, Schott,* and *Schumaker; Mathias,* because of Dutch usage and because its Biblical root probably fostered confusion of its variants with diverse names of the same root: *Schott* and *Schumaker,* because of Dutch names similar in form though differently pronounced.

TABLE 59.—*List of names in common use by " foreigners " arriving in Pennsylvania providing no clear indication of German origin in distinction from Dutch.*

Second exclusion to work toward determination of distinctively German names.

Authorities for notes on Dutch usage:

(1) New York Genealogical and Biographical Society, Collections, Vol. I. Marriages from 1639 to 1801 in the Reformed Dutch Church, New York, N. Y., 1890.

(2) Pearson, Jonathan, Contributions for the Genealogies of the First Settlers of the Ancient County of Albany, from 1630 to 1800, Albany, 1872.

(3) Pearson and later A. J. F. van Laer, Early Records of the City and County of Albany, etc., 1656–1675, Albany, 1869, ff.

---

[8] Pearson, *Genealogies of . . . Albany,* introduction.

(4) Bergen, Teunis G., Register in alphabetical order of the Early Settlers of Kings County, Long Island, New York, N. Y., 1881.

(5) Hoes, R. R., Baptismal and Marriage Records of the Old Dutch Church of Kingston, N. Y., 1660–1810, New York, 1891.

Names of foreigners	Notes on Dutch usage
Becker	A Dutch name, as were also Bekker and Backer.
Berger	Burger, Bergen.
Bogert	Bogart, Bogaert.
Burghart	Burger.
Burger	A Dutch name.
Decker	A Dutch name, as were also Dekker and DeDecker.
Eckert	A Dutch name as were also Ekert, Ekkert, and Ecker.
Frantz	Frans, Fransse.
Friderich	Frederickse.
Hartman	A Dutch name.
Herman	A Dutch name, as was also Harman.
Hoffman	Usage probably Dutch, noted in Kings county; Swedish Hoppman took this form.
Mathias	Matthyse.
Merckel	Merkel.
Ritter	Ruyter, Ruiter, Ryder, Ridder.
Schott	Schut.
Schumaker	Schoenmaker.
Schwartz	Swart.
Wetzell	Wessel, Wessels.

Notes on usage other than Dutch:

Becker is a resemblant of the Anglican Baker.

Frederick is rarely British, but occasionally Scotch; Frederic was used by French Canadians.

Mathias also became confused with various other names with the root " Mathew."

Ritter may also be confused with the English Rider and Welsh Ryder.

Shoemaker, the usual translation for Schumacher, may have been a British name of rare use.

Eliminations for French usage were based on comparison with Dionne's list of French-Canadian names and with a 1914 roster of metropolitan troops in the French army. As Dionne does not give frequency measures, exclusions were based on his authority only when the French-Canadian names were very closely similar to those in the Pennsylvania record.

The French Army record of 1914 was used as evidence of the French usage, because the great number of names listed contribute to a better understanding of normal usage than would earlier records with few names. Fifteen listings in this roster were deemed indicative of French usage, lesser numbers betokening only the by-usage resulting from propinquity.[9]

Tests for French usage, like those for British (but not for Dutch), indicate only possible confusion in American usage; names with substantial French usage were not necessarily introduced into America through French migration.

TABLE 60.—*List of names in common use by " foreigners " arriving in Pennsylvania providing no clear evidence of German origins in distinction from French*

Third exclusion to work toward determination of distinctively German names.

Authorities for notes on French usage.

Dionne, Origine des Familles Canadiennes-Françaises, Quebec, 1914.

Annuaire Official de L'Armée Française, 1914.

---

[9] Kremers, Josef, *Beiträge zur Erforschung der französischen Familiennamen*, Bonn, 1910.

Names of foreigners.	Notes on French usage
Engel	Not uncommon French (A. L'A.).
Fries	Fraise, Freese (Dionne).
Götz	Gets, Goetze (Dionne).
Gross	Gros (Dionne).
Hauser	Hausser (Dionne).
Keller	Not uncommon French (A. L'A.).
Kieffer	Not uncommon French (A. L'A.).
Lauer	Laurier, Laur, Laure (Dionne).
Lehman	Lemaine (Dionne), Lehmann (A. L'A.).
Maurer	Maury (Dionne).
Metz	Motz (Dionne), Metz (A. L'A.).
Reinhardt	Renard (Dionne).
Sauer	Saure (Dionne).
Wagner	Not uncommon French (A. L'A.).

It will be seen from the above that Engel, Keller, Kieffer, Lehman, Metz, and Wagner must be considered French names as well as German.

Notes on usage other than French:

Angel, a common translation for Engel, is not normally British.

Fries means "the Frisian" and had a variety of forms. The Dutch used DeVries and Vries and later Fries.

Goetz may be confused with English Geach and Gedge.

Gross gained some English use probably for Grose, a Cornish name.

Keller is also confused with the Scotch Kellar and Irish Kelleher.

Lauer was often respelled Lower. This is not normally a British name.

With Wagner, the Dutch Wagenaar needs to be noted. Waggoner is not normally British.

Table 61 shows the 67 distinctive German names compiled through the foregoing processes of elimination.

TABLE 61.—*The 67 prominent names in the Oath of Allegiance record of arrivals for " foreigners " in Pennsylvania selected by process of elimination as distinctively German*

Albrecht.	Gerber.	Lentz.	Schweitzer.
Bachman.	Grim.	Ludwig.	Seiberth.
Baum.	Hoff.	Lutz.	Seitz.
Baumgardner.	Huber.	Metzger.	Seyfert.
Brunner.	Hummel.	Moser.	Seyler.
Christ.	Jäger.	Ott.	Snyder.
Conrad.	Jost.	Rauch.	Spengler.
Diedrich.	Kauffman.	Rudolph.	Spiess.
Diehl.	Kesler.	Schaffer.	Stauffer.
Dietz.	Keyser.	Schaub.	Stumpf.
Doll.	Kolb.	Schneider.	Styner.
Ernst.	Krämer.	Senreiner.	Ulrich.
Finck.	Krafft.	Schütz.	Vogel.
Fritz.	Kreps.	Schultz.	Weygandt.
Funck.	Kuhn.	Schuman.	Ziegler.
Gebhert.	Kuntz.	Schuster.	Zimmerman.
Geiger.	Kurtz.	Schwaab.	

NOTE.—" Doll " is probably mainly for *Thal.* " Schaffer " for *Schaefer*, etc. *Snyder* is a variant of *Schneider. Seiberth* and *Seyfert* are closely related. " Styner " is for *Steiner*, etc.

Table 62 is a commentary on some of the selected 67 names whose usages sometimes confuse recognition of their original forms or seem to refute their German origin.

TABLE 62.—*Notes on usages which may, on occasion, interfere with the recognition of forms of selected names or deny the imputation of German origin*

Names of foreigners	Notes
Bachman	English, Bowman (Bachman may "arrive" at this form via the naïve Boughman).
Conrad	Occasionally French.
Diedrich	Was a Dutch given name but not a surname in any of the principal Dutch settlements.
Diehl	English Dale, Deeley.
Doll	Possibly some Dutch use (Kingston); French-Canadian, Dolle.
Finck	English, Finch.
Fritz	English, Frith; French-Canadian, Friche.
Gebhert	Scotch, Gebbie.
Gerber	French-Canadian, Gerbert.
Hoff	English, Hough.[1]
Huber	English, Hooper, Hopper; French-Canadian, Hubert.
Hummel	English, Humble.
Jäger	English, Jagger; Irish, Jagoe.
Jost	Dutch, Joosten, occasionally Joost.
Kauffman	Occasionally French.
Kolb	English, Cobb.
Krämer	French-Canadian, Cremer.
Kreps	English, Crisp.
Kuhn	Irish, Cooney.
Kuntz	Occasionally French.
Kurtz	English, Curtis.
Lentz	Dutch, Lent, van Lent.
Metzger	Dutch, Metselaer.
Moser	French, Mossé.
Ott	Dutch, Otten, Otte.
Rauch	Irish, French, Roche; French-Canadian, Rauque; English, Rook.
Rudolph	English, Randolph.
Schaffer	Shaver is not normally British; French-Canadian, Schappert.
Schneider	Occasionally French, and Snider and Snyder, occasionally Dutch.
Schütz	Dutch, Schaets.
Schultz	Occasionally French. Also has Swedish use abroad.
Schweitzer	Irish, Switzer (rare).
Stauffer	Stover is not normally British.
Zimmerman	Dutch, Timmerman; Zimmerman occasionally French.

[1] The confluence of Hoff and Hough is discussed in Chapter II. Hoff is advisedly retained here as ordinarily German from New York south.

DEFINITION OF DISTINCTIVE GROUPS

After the list of distinctive names was established, consideration was given to its significance as a specimen of German nomenclature becoming German-American.

Each name is representative of a group yet to be defined, and the first task is to define these groups in original German nomenclature. This has to be by compilation of sundry data, for information is incomplete. While there are numerous publications on the etymology of German names, there is none on relative measures of use nor on natural groupings on which to frame a codification of forms supplementary to outstanding names.

The main problem in defining name groups whose key forms are known is that of limiting groupings to specific forms and deciding which of the uncommon forms to include. Definition of German groups is a question of how little to include rather than how much, since etymologists stress ancient relations of many names only slightly similar. The present classification is based on the principle that with nomenclatural structure continually evolving, groupings can be described only as of a given time. The German groups here considered are defined as of the time of German emigration, and etymological considerations are accepted only when they favor the grouping of names whose similarity was recognized by Germans of the eighteenth century.

Definition of German name groups was begun in the process of noting specific forms of independent importance, for high frequency is a guide to clear-cut groups, as it tends to prove discontinuity. If no significant usage of intermediate forms is found, separate groups are recognized, even though etymology discloses ancient connections; for example, the derivation of *Albert* and *Albrecht* from the same root does not prevent recognition of separate groups under these headings (one of which is distinctive) because intermediate forms do not appear in the usage of immigrants.

Among the 67 selected names there are three pairs—*Kuhn* and *Kuntz, Diehl* and *Doll, Seiberth* and *Seyfert*—rather distinct in original usage, tending to coalesce under American conditions. These must be combined before groups can be defined. Another combination is *Schneider* and *Snyder*, an instance of a large number of entries for practically identical names recorded partly under their German and partly under their Americanized form. Combining reduces the number of groups to be defined from 67 to 63.

Defining these 63 groups by determining the limits of variation entitled to recognition proceeds fairly readily when based on conditions of time and place. For example, *Schuster* and *Suter* illustrate the test of time. *Schuster* comes from *schuh-suter*, which may be translated "*shoe-tailer*," acknowledging the ancient debt of *Schuster* to *Suter*. But *Schuster* evolved as an independent name several centuries before the German migration to America;[10] in this study, therefore, the two are considered independent and the distinctive *Schuster* group does not include forms of *Suter*.

Other questions inspired by the concern of German authorities with the continuity of all nomenclature become insignificant in the light of nonoccurrence of confusing names. The *Fritz* group affords an example; there might be a theoretical question as to the lines of demarcation between forms properly associated with *Fritz* and those of *Frisch*, for *Fritsch* is an intermediate form; but since few, if any, bearers of *Frisch* seem to have migrated, the question is automatically disposed of. Again, it might be questioned how the variants of *Huber* can be differentiated from those of *Ober* and *Hafer*. Both *u* and *a* often become *o*, and *b* becomes *v*, *v* becomes *f*, and names beginning with vowels occasionally acquire initial *H*. But again the difficulty is not met, these latter names having almost complete nonoccurrence.

Old World variability has important bearing on the definition of German surnouns, for while German nomenclature of the eighteenth century had a fairly modern form, it had dialectical features, and it reflected some of the uncertainty arising from emphasis on oral rather than on written usages. These antecedent conditions are illustrated by Faust and Brumbaugh [11] concerning the record of eighteenth century migration from Basel:

The spelling of the names varies greatly, not only between different sources, but also in the same source. . . . In the first place variations arise from doubling or not doubling of consonants . . . also changes between *ck* and *k, tz* and *z* . . . ; then the interchanges between *b* and *p*, especially *sb* and *sp, d* and *t* or *dt, ff* and *ph* or *pf, f* and *v, ä* and *e* or *ö* and *e;* furthermore, the omission or nonommission of *n* after *i* in diminutives or otherwise, e. g., *Kuntzli, Kuntzlin (Kuntzlein)* ; *Tschudi, Tschudy, Tschudin.*

---

[10] Heintze, *Die Deutschen Familien namen.*
[11] Faust and Brumbaugh. *List of Swiss Emigrants*, p. 84.

The original variability of German nomenclature is hardly stressed enough by Kuhns, and in this respect Heintze is a better guide.

Some of the distinctive German groups are more easily defined than others; for example, *Fink, Funk,* and *Rudolph* show little variability and promise no confusion. But two of the groups formed by combining pairs of indicators— *Seibert-Seyfert,* and *Diehl-Doll*—prove difficult despite combination.

The *Seiberth-Seyfert* group shows 38 different forms in Pennsylvania alone, ranging alphabetically from *Cybert* to *Syvert,* and including more than one entry for each of the following: *Seibert, Seifert, Seivert, Seybert, Seyfert, Seyfried, Siegried, Siffort, Sigfried, Sypher.*

The *Diehl-Doll* group, representing the collection of derivatives of such fairly-like German names as *Diehl, Thal,* and *Thiel,* shows interplay also with some-what similar British names, hence is not considered satisfactorily indicative of German origins. It illustrates original variability tending to stimulate American variability, which scarcely needed stimulation.

Other instances of diversity having apparently sprung not from various German forms, but from only one or two, suggest that Americanization until 1790 tended toward diversity even where there was no particular impetus from original variability.

That there was considerable regularity in the evolution of the name groups is shown in Kuhns's discussion, partly quoted in Appendix I. Nevertheless, linguistic developments were sometimes diverted and sometimes delayed, and changes by analogy were often more important than norms of phonetic evolution. Kuhns's pairs of German and German-American names are instructive of evolutionary trends, but they are not pure couplets recording automatic supplanting of one form by another. The main lines of evolution for most of the groups were broken by side lines, accelerations and retardations, and inevitable exceptions. Again factors of time and place enter; distribution of stock, length of time in the new world, association with non-Germans, localization of American settlements, dialectic backgrounds—all these color the readings.

DIVERSITY OF AMERICAN FORMS

German settlements in Pennsylvania were of many local origins, and hence displayed differences in name forms and frequencies. Learned [12] summarizes the outstanding features of these communities whose settlers came mainly from an area having roughly the shape of a capital "L" with its angle in the Rhenish Palatinate, its stem along the Rhine and its lower bar crossing Bavaria, with additions from the lower Rhine, Switzerland, northern Austria, and Silesia. Communities of such diverse origin naturally showed inherent differences in emphasis on the selected groups and in preferences for particular forms within them. Descendants of these people were amalgamated through German expansion in America, and the tracing of their name usages would follow many lines of migration radiating from these communities and showing not only differences consequent on the character of the original name uses but individuality in their changes.

The main movement of German stock southward suggests progressive relationships in Pennsylvania, Maryland, Virginia, and the Carolinas which might show fairly regular evolution of names, the modifications of the original forms and groupings beginning on the immigrants' arrival and undergoing successive changes as the stock spread. But the records by States do not show such progressive differences. Pennsylvania's area in colonial times was relatively

---

[12] Learned, *Pennsylvania German Dialect,* Baltimore, 1889, Pr. I, pp. 8, 9.

so extensive that many of the name evolutions ran their course within its boundaries, a number of diverse forms usually developing side by side with the original forms in Pennsylvania, but not elsewhere. The development southward shows main lines and supplementary lines of evolution, but with few new forms and without agreement on Americanized forms.

The evolutionary trends are illustrated in the *Huber* group which as here defined showed 11 forms in the 162 entries in the Pennsylvania record, among them being *Huber*, 71; *Hoover*, 59; *Hover*, 11; *Hoober*, 8. The original *Huber* was the outstanding form in Pennsylvania, but southward gained only two more entries, suggesting that its maintenance in Pennsylvania depended on close grouping of Germans there. The principal Americanization, *Hoover*, developed in Pennsylvania and was the key form of its group southward; only one of its important supplements, *Hover*, is shown in all southern records, indicating it a secondary Americanized form. *Hoober* shared importance with *Hover* in Pennsylvania, but gained only one additional entry in Virginia. Of the 11 Pennsylvania forms, 6 did not appear in the records of States southward. Hence the group showed in Pennsylvania both considerable use of the original form and also a diversity not matched southward. The Maryland census showed entries for 3 of the Pennsylvania forms and single entries for 3 other forms not in Pennsylvania nor elsewhere; the Virginia record showed entries for 4 of the Pennsylvania forms and introduced 1 new form; the North Carolina record merely showed entries for 3 of the Pennsylvania forms; and the South Carolina record but 2. Analysis of this group therefore suggests that much of the diversity of content of the name groups was confined to Pennsylvania and that a number of lines of evolution began and ended in that State.

Some highly important lines of evolution were not carried southward. For example, the *Lentz* group showed a normal tendency to replace *e* with *a*, but decided variability of the original termination *tz* or *z*, the Americanized forms ending in *ce*, *ch*, *des*, *dice*, *dis*, *tis*, etc. In Pennsylvania *Landis* emerged as the principal form with 24 entries, supplemented by *Landes* with 21 entries—a division of emphasis occasioned partly by original diversity and partly by Americanization—while *Lentz* showed 10, and *Lantz* 3. Southward the emphasis on *Lan-* persisted, but *Lance*, with only six entries in Pennsylvania, became the principal Americanized form with 16 entries in the records of States to the south.

The *Kuhn-Kuntz* group was remarkable for its diversity both in Pennsylvania, where it showed 21 forms with emphasis on *Coon*, *Coons*, *Kuhn*, and *Kuntz;* and in the Southern States where the Maryland census showed 3 more forms, the Virginia record another 5, and the North Carolina record an additional 4.

The spellings in the census records add to the difficulties of codification and disguise the evidences of original variability and American evolution. The orthography of the marshals of the Pennsylvania census was so bad that it proves their unfamiliarity with German names. (Only 5 of the 34 assistant marshals for Pennsylvania had names suggesting German ancestry.) Names terminating in -*man* and -*mann*, were sometimes rendered -*mon*, reflecting the Pennsylvania broad *a*. From *Zimmermann* came *Zimmermon* and also *Cimermin*, *Semerman*, *Simberman*, and *Zemerman*. Other entries interpreted as misspellings are *Lunch* for *Lantz; Stiffy* for *Stauffer; Hoof*, *Have*, and *Off* for *Hoff; Kicker* (with *Gicker*) for *Geiger; Ghost* for *Jost; Dates* and *Deeds* for *Dietz*. The *Schaub* group showed 18 varieties, including *Shupe*, the natural Americanization, with five entries, and *Soop* with six. The spelling of *Soop* follows the logic that if initial *S* is commonly pronounced as *Sh*, the sound *Sh* is to be transcribed as *S*. Misspellings would have weakened the authenticity of the census forms even had the names been written by the people who bore them, but undoubtedly the marshals' interpretation added incongruities.

Despite the factors for diversity, there were also factors for uniformity in the development of German names, the main one being that German name groups inclined to center about one or two Americanized forms. Another was the influence of the Irish, companions of the Germans on the frontier. From them the Germans learned English colored by Irish characteristics, and whether or not Irish dialect played a part in linguistic control in the evolution of German names, it is plain that Irish names influenced the social control developing new names for the Germans. One of the most regular adaptations in the German names was the substitution of *gh* for *ch*—*ach* became *augh*, *ech* became *igh*. Thus *Bach* became *Baugh; Achenbach, Aughenbaugh; Herbach, Harbaugh; Brechbühl, Brightbill;* changes that had their inspiration apparently in Irish *gh* as a guttural with pronunciation similar to the German *ch*, as in *Dougherty, McCullough, McLaughlin,* and *McNaughton.* In this respect and others Irish names offered what seemed to be a good English rendering of little understood German elements.

USAGE OF 63 SURNOUNS IN PENNSYLVANIA

The 63 distinctive German surnouns accounted for about 3,400 of the 74,500 entries in the Pennsylvania census, indicating the importance of the Germans in that State, but suggesting by their number that the distribution of the stock might be adequately measured without using all of them.

Table 63 compares, in columns 1 and 2, the outstanding forms of these names in the Pennsylvania *Oath of Allegiance* record with their Americanized forms in the Pennsylvania census. When two forms represent equal numbers, both appear in column 2. Note the convergence of *Diehl* and *Doll* on *Deal*, the divergence under *Hoff* allowing *Huff* equal standing, and the evolution of the *Seyler-Zeller* and the *Vogel-Fegely* (*Voegeli*) groups. The *Weygandt* group includes forms indicating that *g* was converted into *y*, which became silent and was dropped. Since the list of indicators was reduced on the basis of the Pennsylvania record, and only half of the surnouns were traced to the other State records, slight changes in count may be noted for those fully searched.

TABLE 63.—*Occurrences of selected German name groups in Pennsylvania, 1790*

[Defined without reference to conditions in other States]

Outstanding form		Number of—	
Oath of allegiance	Pennsylvania census, 1790	Forms	Entries
Albrecht	Albright	7	50
Bachman	{Bachman, Baughman}	12	54
Baum	Bawm †	5	9
Baumgardner	Bumgarner †	7	11
Brunner	Bruner	3	43
Christ	Christ	9	38
Conrad	Conrad	7	73
Diehl, Doll	}Deal †	20	101
Diedrich	Dietrich †	8	17
Dietz	Dietz †	16	42
Ernst	Earnest	4	21
Finck	Fink	2	26
Fritz	Fritz	10	54

† Eliminated from further study on account of diversity of forms and/or paucity of entries.

TABLE 63.—*Occurrences of selected German name groups in Pennsylvania, 1790—*
Continued

Outstanding form		Number of—	
Oath of allegiance	Pennsylvania census, 1790	Forms	Entries
Funck	Funk	3	43
Gebhert	Gebhart †	14	30
Geiger	Geiger †	18	58
Gerber	Gerber	5	25
Grim	Grim †	10	35
Hoff	{ Hoff / Huff }	9	50
Hummel	Hummel	6	26
Huber	Huber	11	162
Jaeger	Yeager	8	51
Jost	Yost †	9	37
Kauffman	Kauffman	14	97
Kesler	Kesler	13	31
Keyser	Keyser	13	81
Kolb	Culp	10	52
Kraemer	Kremer †	16	64
Krafft	Craft †	8	27
Kreps	Krebs †	10	20
Kuhn } Kuntz	} Coons	19	103
Kurtz	Kurtz †	9	34
Lentz	Landis	15	86
Ludwig	Ludwig †	7	24
Lutz	Lutz	8	66
Metzger	Metzger †	7	22
Moser	Moser	7	87
Ott (including Otto)	Ott	7	40
Rauch	{ Rock † / Rugh }	14	27
Rudolph	Rudolph	2	17
Schaffer	Shafer	18	233
Schaub	Soop †	18	46
Schneider } Snyder	} Snyder	19	327
Schreiner	Shreiner †	5	19
Schütz	Sheets †	15	56
Schultz	Shultz †	22	71
Schuman	Shuman †	6	20
Schuster	Shuster	2	16
Schwaab	Swope †	8	21
Schweitzer	Switzer	7	39
Seiberth } Seyfert	} Seibert †	38	65
Seyler	Zeller †	18	66
Seitz	Seitz †	11	29
Spengler	Spangler	4	40
Spiess	Spies †	6	8
Stauffer	Stover	19	128
Stumpf	Stump	2	21
Styner	Stoner	9	75
Ulrich	Ulrich †	11	25
Vogel	Fegely †	12	30
Weygandt	Weand †	15	27
Ziegler	Ziegler †	16	64
Zimmerman	Zimmerman	11	62
Total, 63 groups		674	ª 3, 422
Average per group		11	54
Average per form			5

† Eliminated from further study on account of diversity of forms and/or paucity of entries.
ª There is a total of 74,510 entries in the Pennsylvania census.

On account of the extensive use of the 63 groups and the variations in number of entries and number of forms, it was decided to cut the list in half, retaining the groups which combined frequency with uniformity. A process of scoring in terms of frequency versus scarcity and of uniformity versus diversity led to the selection of 32 surnouns as prime indicators.

Scarcity combined with diversity appeared, with reason, to merit disqualification, but scarcity itself is not the defect which it seemed at an earlier stage of the investigation.

Complications in the relation of numbers in the records of arrivals and of Pennsylvania population are disclosed by the range in numbers of Pennsylvania census entries for groups selected on the basis of frequency in arrivals. Scarcity in the Pennsylvania census may indicate late arrival lacking opportunity for reproduction, but it may indicate also removal to other States; frequency may indicate early arrival, favorable reproduction, satisfied settlement or peculiarity to the Pennsylvania stream of migration. This last factor, detected late in the investigation, required scrutiny of the merits of the 32 indicators.

DISTRIBUTION OF 32 SELECTED SURNOUNS

Search for bearers of these 32 name groups was centered in State records from New York southward, occurrences in New England being insufficient to afford a measure of the German stock.

Table 64 shows the entries in six States for these 32 names, listed in the order of occurrences in Pennsylvania.

TABLE 64.—*Thirty-two German name-groups and the number of entries assignable to them in specified State indexes of heads of families, 1790*

[Cited in order of currency in Pennsylvania]

Group [1]	New York	Pennsyl-vania	Mary-land	Virginia	North Carolina	South Carolina
Schneider	120	327	40	17	15	10
Schaffer	72	233	44	29	13	6
Huber	5	162	29	17	19	10
Stauffer	17	128	10	18	-------	2
Kuhn	91	105	37	17	16	16
Kauffman	1	97	4	29	-------	4
Moser	1	90	8	6	11	-------
Lentz	2	86	9	4	10	7
Keyser	22	81	4	10	3	3
Styner	4	75	19	2	7	-------
Conrad	16	73	10	10	10	2
Lutz	2	66	6	4	3	-------
Zimmerman	4	62	14	5	5	10
Bachman	11	55	3	4	-------	4
Fritz	22	54	3	-------	2	4
Kolb	2	52	5	3	3	11
Jaeger	8	51	-------	3	-------	1
Albrecht	2	50	4	1	21	-------
Hoff	24	50	8	13	13	14
Brunner	-------	43	27	4	4	3
Funck	5	43	12	12	-------	-------
Ott	9	42	17	4	-------	12
Spengler	-------	40	2	2	-------	-------
Schweitzer	2	39	6	7	-------	2
Christ	17	38	14	3	2	1

[1] Designated by the principal spelling in the *Oath of Allegiance* record.

TABLE 64.—*Thirty-two German name-groups and the number of entries assignable to them in specified indexes of heads of families, 1790*—Continued

Group	New York	Pennsylvania	Maryland	Virginia	North Carolina	South Carolina
Finck	17	26	4	1	2	
Hummel	5	26		4	4	
Gerber		25	6	2		
Ernst	3	21	6	2	5	8
Stumpf	1	21	9	10		
Rudolph		17	4	2	2	
Schuster	2	16	3			

In the absence of information about the ratios of original usage, the distribution of German stock was measured from the occurrence of the 32 selected name groups relative to their numbers in Pennsylvania. This comparison avoids the question whether individuals properly belonging to these groups can be counted in full strength. Most of these names probably lost usage through translation, transliteration, and supersedure by English names; but as changes were very active in Pennsylvania, losses were as great there, presumably, as elsewhere, and comparability is maintained. Allowance is to be made, however, for certain exceptional losses in North Carolina and Virginia and, finally, for scarcity of some of these names in New York and the Carolinas suggesting peculiarity to the Pennsylvania stream of migration.

Distribution of Germans in the States from New York southward was studied by converting the numbers of bearers of these names in the other State Indexes into percentages of their number in Pennsylvania. These percentages are derived from Table 64 and shown in Table 65. For example, the *Schneider* group showed entries as follows: Pennsylvania, 327; New York, 120; Maryland, 40; Virginia, 17; North Carolina, 15; South Carolina, 10; or percentages relative to Pennsylvania as follows: New York, 36.7; Maryland, 12.2; Virginia, 5.2; North Carolina, 4.6; South Carolina, 3.1.

State averages were obtained as the medians of these percentages, lack of conformity causing arithmetic means to be biased by exceptional percentages. Medians are gained from arrays of State percentages in order of magnitude, being intermediate between the readings of the sixteenth and seventeenth of the 32 names. For example, New York percentages range from zero to 86.7; the nearest the middle are 11.6 (*Funck*) and 12.5 (*Schuster*), and the median is 12.0 per cent.

Medians are slightly influenced by special problems in the definitions of the surnouns; hence the inclusion of a few New York Dutch in the *Schneider* group introduces no bias. *Ernst* affords an extreme example of the advantage of medians: In Virginia the question arises as to whether the *Ernst* group, whose principal American form is *Earnest*, should include people recorded as *Harness*, whose given names disclose them to be Germans. *Ernst* had the forms *Arnst* and *Arnis*—one each in Maryland and South Carolina; and *Earness*—one in New York; moreover, German names beginning with a vowel sometimes assumed an initial *H* in Americanization, as *Herkimer* for *Ergheimer*. *Harness* may be an odd version of *Ernst*, or a transliteration of *Harnisch*, or even an abbreviated translation of *Riemenschneider;* but whether these Virginians are included in the *Earnest* group or not the *Ernst* percentage in Virginia is higher than the median, and the latter remains unaffected.

Table 65 shows percentages of the 32 groups in the other State indexes relative to their percentages in the Pennsylvania index, and gives the median for each of the five specified States, as follows: New York, 12.0; Maryland, 15.4; Virginia, 8.7; North Carolina, 5.4; South Carolina, 2.6. (It should be recalled that the Virginia tax list covered a population only about half that in 1790.) It is noted that names important in the Pennsylvania record of arrivals occurred with the greatest consistency in Maryland and Virginia.

TABLE 65.—*Percentages which the entries for thirty-two German name-groups in other indexes constitute of the number in Pennsylvania index.*

Group	New York	Maryland	Virginia	North Carolina	South Carolina
Schneider	36. 7	12. 2	5. 2	4. 6	3. 1
Schaffer	30. 9	18. 9	12. 4	5. 6	2. 6
Huber	3. 1	17. 9	10. 5	11. 7	6. 2
Stauffer	13. 3	7. 8	14. 1	--------	1. 6
Kuhn	86. 7	35. 2	16. 2	15. 2	15. 2
Kauffman	1. 0	4. 1	29. 9	--------	4. 1
Moser	1. 1	8. 9	6. 7	12. 2	--------
Lentz	2. 3	10. 5	4. 7	11. 6	8. 1
Keyser	27. 2	4. 9	12. 3	3. 7	3. 7
Styner	5. 3	25. 3	2. 7	9. 3	--------
Conrad	21. 9	13. 7	13. 7	13. 7	2. 7
Lutz	3. 0	9. 1	6. 1	4. 5	--------
Zimmerman	6. 5	22. 6	8. 1	8. 1	16. 1
Bachman	20. 0	5. 5	7. 3	--------	7. 3
Fritz	40. 7	5. 6	--------	3. 7	7. 4
Kolb	3. 8	9. 6	5. 8	5. 8	21. 2
Jaeger	15. 7	--------	5. 9	--------	2. 0
Albrecht	4. 0	8. 0	2. 0	42. 0	--------
Hoff	48. 0	16. 0	26. 0	26. 0	28. 0
Brunner	--------	62. 8	9. 3	9. 3	7. 0
Funck	11. 6	27. 9	27. 9	--------	--------
Ott	2. 4	40. 5	9. 5	--------	28. 6
Spengler		5. 0	5. 0		
Schweitzer	5. 1	15. 4	17. 9	--------	5. 1
Christ	44. 7	36. 8	7. 9	5. 3	2. 6
Finck	65. 4	15. 4	3. 8	7. 7	--------
Hummel	19. 2	--------	15. 4	15. 4	--------
Gerber	--------	24. 0	8. 0	--------	--------
Ernst	14. 3	28. 6	9. 5	23. 8	38. 1
Stumpf	4. 8	42. 9	47. 6	--------	--------
Rudolph		23. 5	11. 8	11. 8	--------
Schuster	12. 5	18. 8	--------	--------	--------
Medians	12. 0	15. 4	8. 7	5. 4	2. 6

PROPORTION OF GERMANS IN PENNSYLVANIA

Pennsylvania was the center of German colonization; hence the proportion of the stock there, on which authorities agree fairly, affords a basis for calculating numbers in the several States where distinctive name uses were significant.

Observations and studies of this proportion are summarized by Faust,[13] Kuhns,[14] and Diffenderffer.[15] Faust said: " It is difficult to estimate the number of Germans in Pennsylvania before the Revolution, but an approximation can be made far more satisfactorily than for the other Colonies." He estimated

[13] Faust, *The German Element in the United States*, p. 128.
[14] Kuhns, *German and Swiss Settlements of Colonial Pennsylvania*, pp. 58, 59.
[15] Diffenderffer, *The German Immigration into Pennsylvania Through the Port of Philadelphia, 1700–1775*, Chap. IX, pp. 99–108.

about 110,000 Germans in Pennsylvania in 1775, slightly less than one-third of the Continental Congress estimate of 341,000 persons in Pennsylvania in a total of 2,243,000 in the whole country. Faust followed Kuhn's general reasoning and agreed in the estimate, although he added an investigation of emigration from the State. Diffenderffer's study was more detailed; he estimated one-third Germans in Pennsylvania in 1790, and stressed the point that computations should include considerable numbers not in the so-called German settlements, Germans among Swedes, and infiltration before the settlement of Germantown in 1683; he said that while Germans did not arrive in large numbers after the Revolutionary War, the stock was augmented by 5,000 Hessian deserters from the British forces. These comments are important, since colonial national stocks are too commonly appraised on the basis of known groups without allowing for more obscure numbers.

Comparison of these recent studies with contemporary observations reveals general agreement in rating the Germans in the latter part of the eighteenth century at about one-third of the population of Pennsylvania. Diffenderffer noted this:

There is, however, considerable unanimity in one particular among most of the authorities, and that is that the Germans at any and every period between 1730 and 1790 constituted about one-third of the total population. This statement is unquestionably correct as we approach the years nearest the Revolutionary period.

This ratio was given by Michael Schlatter for 1751, Proud [16] (who estimated "a third at least") for 1770, Benjamin Franklin and Doctor Rush for 1776, and Ebeling [17] for 1790.

There are estimates of two types, those based on contemporary observation and those based on subsequent reasoning. The former, even when they agree closely, only roughly approximate the measure of Germans; the latter can be analyzed. Since in the first quarter of the century Germans were not numerous, criticism of these estimates is concerned with examining the ratio's change including questioning whether it rose to a fixed value or not. The concept of a constant ratio is waived; there must have been an impossible nicety of balance between numbers of arrivals, rate of reproduction, and rate of Pennsylvanian emigration to maintain a ratio of one-third Germans in the population of Pennsylvania over three-quarters of a century.

Calculations of absolute and relative numbers in these estimates do not show the accord they first promised. The estimate of 110,000 Germans commonly construed as one-third of the Pennsylvania population in 1775 really indicates a ratio of 36 per cent, since comparison of the Continental Congress estimate for 1775 with the 1790 census shows that the Congress overestimated the Province's population by about 10 per cent. Faust and Kuhns, therefore, support a ratio of more than one-third Germans in the Pennsylvania population at the time of the Revolution.

A summary appraisal by reasoning is to be divided into three parts, with dividing points at 1727 and 1775. Official records of arrivals were not systematically kept until 1727, when a number of authorities agree that Germans in Pennsylvania numbered 15,000; Kuhns said German settlers numbered 15,000, and with descendents 20,000; Diffenderffer estimated more than 15,000. Based on 15,000 for 1727, the German element of early arrival may be calculated at 60,000 for 1775, since at that time population is observed to have doubled by reproduction in less than 25 years, and to have redoubled in less than 50 years.

[16] Proud. *History of Pennsylvania*, Vol. II, pp. 273–275.
[17] Ebeling, *Beschreibung der Erde: Abtheilung, Pennsylvania.*

Between 1727 and 1775, tabulations by Kuhns [18] and Rupp [19] indicate that 69,000 foreigners, mostly German speaking, arrived. A conservative estimate is 50,000 German arrivals and settlers during this period. The peak years being 1749–1754, and the mean date of arrival, 1750, they would have constituted a population of about 100,000 in 1775.

These two elements of the stock therefore totaled about 160,000 at the beginning of the Revolution. But though based on arrivals in Pennsylvania, this figure does not represent Pennsylvania population, since many immigrants merely passed through that State on migration southward into the valley of Virginia, and the numbers remaining in Pennsylvania are determined by deducting for this migration. Faust deducted one-third for German removals prior to 1775, but relative occurrences of names do not confirm this ratio even by 1790; a conservative deduction of one-fourth determines 120,000 Germans remaining in Pennsylvania in 1775, constituting an element of 40 per cent.

From 1775 to 1790 the ratio was moving downward. Completion of an estimate for 1790 is accomplished by changing viewpoint and establishing a curve reflecting the reaction of the ratio to cessation of immigration.

The highest ratio was attained some time between 1740 and 1760. Contemporary estimates for the decade 1740–1750 show a high average: For 1740 Stille [20] said a half; for 1747 Governor Thomas said three-fifths; for 1751 Schlatter held for a third; for 1752 Seidensticker [21] estimated nine-nineteenths; average 48 per cent. As immigration reached its peak in the years 1749 to 1754, it was about 1760 when the ratio began to decline definitely. After 1773 the only augmenting of the stock was from the settlement of the 5,000 " Hessians "; and emigration outweighing reproduction carried the ratio downward. Hence immigration increased the ratio continuously until about the middle of the century, and reproduction sustained it until about 1760; then immigration began to favor other stocks, particularly the British who arrived much more steadily, and decline in German proportions was accentuated by their emigration southward at a greater rate than that of the general population.

This exodus went particularly from the back countries where Germans were numerous; they and the Irish were the chief contributors to the migration from Pennsylvania into western Maryland and Virginia. The present nomenclatural studies indicate one-fourth German migration from Pennsylvania by 1775, and two-sevenths by 1790. Occurrences of Pennsylvania-German names show that Germans listed in the indexes of States south of Pennsylvania bore the following ratios to those in the Pennsylvania index: Maryland, 15.5, Virginia, 8.7, North Carolina, 5.4, South Carolina 2.6. As the Virginia tax list covered a population equivalent to only half that in 1790, its figure can be doubled. Occurrences of names therefore indicate that the German stock south of Pennsylvania in 1790 was at least 40.8 per cent as numerous as in Pennsylvania, or four-fourteenths that of the original German stock in the whole area. These figures are about correct for Germans removed from Pennsylvania as an upward adjustment yet to be made in nomenclatural readings will take care of independent immigration at southern ports; and they show clearly that increasing emigration occasioned a decline in the German proportion in Pennsylvania after 1760 down to 1790. The total population of Pennsylvania having been commonly overestimated, as by the Continental Congress in 1775, and not accurately known until

[18] Kuhns, *German and Swiss Settlements,* pp. 54–58.
[19] Rupp, I. D., *Thirty Thousand Names* (general introduction).
[20] Stille, *Life and Times of John Dickinson,* pp. 46–47.
[21] Seidensticker, *Geschichte der deutschen Gesellschaft von Pennsylvania,* p. 18.

the 1790 census, this decline can not be accurately gaged, but evidence points toward restoration of the one-third ratio at the time of the 1790 census.

Computing the number of Germans in Pennsylvania on the basis of one-third gives 24,837 German heads of families in the State index.

PROPORTIONS OF GERMANS FROM NEW YORK SOUTH

Before the calculation of numbers by relation to those in Pennsylvania was completed the derivation of median percentages was reviewed and the preliminary readings carefully tested. The chief test concerns differences in geographical distribution, since some names spread from New York to South Carolina, while others were almost restricted to the Pennsylvania-Virginia area. This test becomes part of a final study of the Pennsylvania stream of migration. The many irregularities in relative occurrences of the 32 distinctive German names are indicated in Table 65.

Another test concerned extreme changes of names, particularly those effected through translation. In the selection of distinctive German names eliminations were based on similarities in form rather than in meaning, the latter being considered only when supported by analogies of forms. (See Appendix III.) Hence occurrences of those distinctive German names which have obvious meanings were tested to determine whether changes traceable to analogies of meaning unsupported by analogies of form had marked influence on their occurrence, and whether such changes were uniform in the specified States. For example, there was need to determine whether the similar meaning of German *Gerber* and English *Tanner* and *Currier* disguised the *Gerber* lineage, and what losses *Gerber* sustained through transliteration from *Garver*—a natural Anglicization—to *Carver* which is apparently distinct.

Among the 32 German indicators there are five names besides *Gerber* which were subject locally to noticeable loss through Anglicization: *Bachman* (*Bachmann*) commonly became *Baughman* and occasionally *Boughman*, and if mispronounced (no longer analagous to Irish *Dougherty* and *McCullough*), the new spelling was *Bowman*, an English name; *Jaeger* was translated *Hunter;* *Schaffer* (*Schaefer*) became *Shepherd*, with various English spellings, this one favored because a literal translation of German *Schafhirt;* *Schneider* became *Taylor;* *Zimmerman* (*Zimmermann*) became *Carpenter* and sometimes *Joiner* (like *Schreiner*). Such changes are noted by Faust, Haldeman, Kuhns, Rupp, and others, as occasional in colonial times.

Since these marked changes occurred in varying measure in the specified States, the geographical distribution of the 32 indicators had to be verified. Differences were looked for particularly in Virginia and North Carolina, because the German population in the western valley was made up largely of descendants of Pennsylvania settlers, several generations removed from immigration. With each generation showing increased Anglicization, there were communities in which the original German names became extremely Anglicized or literally translated. The occurrences of these six names provided a basis for gaging the extreme changes. Though frequently used, these six names hardly picture adequately the occurrence of names practically distinctive but subject to special losses; yet they give a basis for a test by which to measure the degree of Anglicization in this area where German population was completely severed from its original influences.

The median percentage occurrence of these six names in the specified States relative to their occurrences in Pennsylvania is as follows: Maryland, 15.6, as against 15.4 for the full list of indicators, hence showing slight Anglicization; Virginia, 7.7, in contrast to 8.7 for the full list; North Carolina, 2.3, in contrast with 5.4; South Carolina, again little influenced by Anglicization, 2.5, practically identical with that (2.6) for the full list of indicators. Hence the evidence of these six names confirmed the impression that even distinctive German names suffered loss of usage in Virginia and North Carolina.

The weight to be attached to this evidence is difficult to determine. The reading for these six names in Virginia is about an eighth less than that of the full list of indicators, and in North Carolina about six-tenths less. Adjustment must be arbitrary. In the author's tentative opinion the readings of the full list of indicators were suitably revised if the estimated percentage of Germans in the Virginia index relative to those in the Pennsylvania index was moved from 8.7 to 9.5 and the North Carolina figures moved from 5.4 to 6.5 per cent.

With the completion of this adjustment of the occurrence rates, preliminary estimates were prepared of German contributions to specified States in 1790. The form of calculation will be illustrated by that for New York. Heads of families originally with German names indexed in the Pennsylvania census have been determined as 24,837, or one-third of the total entries in that index. The indicative names having an occurrence in the New York index, 12 per cent of that in the Pennsylvania index, it appears that 2,980 German heads of families were covered by the New York index, for 2,980 is 12 per cent of 24,837, As the New York index contains 54,540 heads of families, German contribution to its population was 5.5 per cent, the ratio of 2,980 to 54,540.

Table 66 shows the numbers of German families in specified States as estimated in a similar manner by relative occurrences of the 32 indicators.

Table 67 shows the percentages these constitute of the total number of families in the specified State indexes.

TABLE 66.—*Preliminary estimate of numbers of German families in specified State indexes determined by comparison with Pennsylvania on the basis of relative occurrences of distinctive German names, 1790* [1]

	Percentages of Germans indexed relative to those in the Pennsylvania index [2]	Indicated number of German families in specified index [3]
New York	12. 0	2, 980
Maryland	15. 4	3, 825
Virginia	9. 5	2, 360
North Carolina	6. 5	1, 614
South Carolina	2. 6	646

[1] 32 names important in Pennsylvania immigration and settlement.
[2] Indicated by the relative occurrences of the 32 distinctively German names, with adjustments as noted for Virginia and North Carolina.
[3] By application of the percentages to 24,837, which has been established as the numerical equivalent of German families in the Pennsylvania index.

TABLE 67.—*Preliminary estimates of contributions of Germans to population of specified States on the basis of numbers of German families indexed, 1790*[1]

	Estimated number of German families in specified index[2]	Total number of families covered by index	Indicated percentage contribution of Germans to population
New York	2, 980	54, 540	5. 5
Maryland	3, 825	32, 690	11. 7
Virginia	2, 360	37, 710	6. 3
North Carolina	1, 614	52, 560	3. 1
South Carolina	646	25, 980	2. 5

[1] Indicated by the relative occurrences of 32 distinctively German names important in Pennsylvania immigration and settlement.
[2] From Table 66.

PRELIMINARY ESTIMATE OF GERMAN STOCK

Inquiry thus far showed German percentages in the specified States in 1790 as follows: New York, 5.5; Pennsylvania, 33.3; Maryland, 11.7; Virginia, 6.3; North Carolina, 3.1; South Carolina, 2.5.

To complete a preliminary estimate of Germans in the whole country, information was drawn from *CPG* on the proportions of bearers of recognizably German names in the other States of record; and conditions in Kentucky, Tennessee, and Georgia were determined as heretofore by appraisal of regional trends.

In New Jersey, Nelson has estimated 9.2 per cent Germans. This was accepted as adequate for conditions intermediate between those in Pennsylvania and New York, though New Jersey conditions were more like those in the latter State, as Germans in Pennsylvania focused in the central (then western) part of the State and were not numerous in the eastern part.

In Kentucky and Tennessee the German population, like the other stocks, is assumed to have been drawn about equally from the four States to the east, but the resultant estimate of 13.6 per cent Germans is an understatement because Germans were concentrated in the western parts of the older districts.

For Georgia German proportions were rated temporarily at 3.9 per cent, or approximately 2,000, a somewhat arbitrary estimate to complete this tentative schedule. Historical evidence does not support the downward trend in German proportions in the extreme South, as shown in Table 67, but points to a higher proportion of Germans in Georgia than in either of the Carolinas.

For Delaware and the six New England States, estimates were based on criticism and adjustment of the *CPG* survey of recognizably German names.[22] As already noted, the proportions of bearers of recognizably non-English names invariably understate non-English numbers, and review of the *CPG* findings, with study of local histories, warrants radical adjustments. Germans in Delaware were estimated at 1.1 per cent instead of the 0.4 per cent derived by the *CPG* analysis; and Germans in New England were rated at 0.4 per cent, as in this area the *CPG* analysts failed to note many obviously German names.

Briefly recapitulating, the bases for these estimates are as follows: For Pennsylvania and New Jersey, historians' estimates; for New York, Maryland, Virginia, North Carolina, and South Carolina, relative occurrence of leading Pennsylvania-German names; for Kentucky and Tennessee and for Georgia, regional trends; for Delaware and New England, criticism and adjustment of *CPG* estimates.

[22] *CPG*, p. 121, and Table 112.

Table 68 shows that the foregoing percentages of Germans in the specified States account for 8.1 per cent of the white population of the country, equivalent to 257,775 persons.

TABLE 68.—*Preliminary schedule of estimated contributions of Germans to the population of 1790 expressed in absolute numbers obtained from percentages derived mainly from relative occurrences of distinctively German names*

	White population 1790	Estimated percentages of Germans[1]	Estimated numerical equivalents of German stock
United States	3,172,444	8.1	257,775
New England	992,384	.4.	3,969
New York	314,366	5.5	17,290
New Jersey	169,954	9.2	15,636
Pennsylvania	423,373	33.3	140,983
Delaware	46,310	1.1	509
Maryland	208,649	11.7	24,412
Kentucky and Tennessee	93,046	13.6	12,654
Virginia	442,117	6.3	27,853
North Carolina	289,181	3.1	8,965
South Carolina	140,178	2.5	3,504
Georgia	52,886	[2] 3.9	[2] 2,000

[1] The bases of this estimate are detailed in the text. For Pennsylvania and New Jersey, it rests on historians' estimates; for New York, Maryland, Virginia, North and South Carolina, on the relative occurrences of leading Pennsylvania-German names; for Kentucky and Tennessee and Georgia, on secondary relationships in the above estimates; and for New England and Delaware on revision of estimates in *CPG*.
[2] Estimated as 2,000 persons.

COMPARISON WITH FAUST'S ESTIMATES

Table 69 reproduces Faust's[23] estimates of Germans in the whole country and in the specified areas in 1775. His numbers are related to the estimates of population made by the Continental Congress and are derived by various calculations for the several parts of the country.

TABLE 69.—*Faust's estimates of Germans in the United States and specified areas, 1775*

	Estimated German stock[a]		Estimated German stock[a]
United States	225,000	Maryland	20,000
New England except Vermont	1,500	Virginia and Kentucky	25,000
New York and Vermont	25,000	North Carolina and Tennessee	8,000
New Jersey	15,000		
Pennsylvania	110,000	South Carolina	15,000
Delaware	500	Georgia	5,000

Tables 68 and 69 are best compared by converting Faust's schedule for 1775 to a 1790 basis, since the 1790 population is accurately known, while that of 1775 is not. The conversion involves an interesting problem because of the coördination of Faust's estimate with the inaccurate Congressional schedule involving decided overestimate of the population of Pennsylvania. Using the ratio of Pennsylvania population at the two dates as a guide in recasting Faust's estimate on a 1790 basis gives quite different results from

[a] In a population of 2,243,000—the estimate of the Continental Congress.
[23] Faust, *The German Element,* Vol. I, pp. 263–285.

those derived by using the ratio of national population at the two dates. Both of these conversions must be qualified to allow for a shifting of the German stock between 1775 and 1790.

Table 70 shows Faust's schedule recast by these two different calculations. Column 1 shows Faust's numbers increased by 41.4 per cent, the percentage by which the total white population of 1790 America exceeded that estimated by the Continental Congress in 1775. Column 2 shows an increase of 24.2 per cent, the percentage by which Pennsylvania population in 1790 exceeded that estimated for 1775. While two conversions are shown the second is deemed more nearly correct because of the importance of the Pennsylvania element and Faust's reliance on the oft-reported one-third ratio in that province. Both of the converted estimates may be compared with the author's tentative estimates for Germans in these areas.

TABLE 70.—*Comparison of estimates of German contributions to population of the United States, 1790*

	Faust's estimate for 1775 recast for 1790 by two methods—		Tentative estimate based mainly on relative occurrence of distinctive German names [3]
	Method A [1]	Method B [2]	
United States_____	318, 150	279, 340	257, 775
New England except Vermont_____	2, 120	1, 860	_____
New England_____	_____	_____	3, 969
New York and Vermont_____	35, 350	31, 040	_____
New York_____	_____	_____	17, 290
New Jersey_____	21, 210	18, 620	15, 636
Pennsylvania_____	155, 540	136, 570	140, 983
Delaware_____	710	620	509
Maryland_____	28, 280	24, 830	24, 412
Virginia and Kentucky_____	35, 350	31, 040	_____
Virginia_____	_____	_____	27, 853
Kentucky and Tennessee_____	_____	_____	12, 654
North Carolina and Tennessee_____	11, 310	9, 930	_____
North Carolina_____	_____	_____	8, 965
South Carolina_____	21, 210	18, 620	3, 504
Georgia_____	7, 070	6, 210	2, 000

[1] In this schedule all items are increased 41.4 per cent, which is the excess of the white population of 1790 (3,172,444) over the estimate used by Doctor Faust for 1775 (2, 243, 000).
[2] In this schedule all items are increased 24.2 per cent, which is the excess of the white population of Pennsylvania in 1790 (423,373) over the estimated figure (341,000) used for 1775.
[3] From Table 68.

Comparison of the author's figures with Faust's on the second basis shows that the two estimates of Germans in Pennsylvania are in close accord; in one instance, one-third; in the other, slightly less. It also shows that the figures for Maryland are nearly alike. The 20 per cent more Germans in Virginia, North Carolina, and Kentucky and Tennessee, shown by the author, is probably accounted for by the fact that the population of the Kentucky and Tennessee area increased during those 15 years at a much greater rate than is allowed for in adjusting the estimates from 1775 to 1790. The author's estimate for New Jersey, borrowed from Nelson, is somewhat lower than Faust's and probably more accurate, as Nelson worked more in detail, surveying all stocks by counties.

Sharper contrasts appear in the estimates for the extreme northern and southern parts of the area of principal German settlement. Faust's estimate for New York and Vermont is over a half more than the tentative estimate, and for South Carolina more than four times as much. His appraisal for South Carolina was based on church attendance measured in average congregations by guidance of records of German congregations in Pennsylvania; but it is questioned whether church adherents in South Carolina were as numerous as in Pennsylvania and whether congregations were as homogeneous. Church records show that rites were administered to many non-Germans, even many who did not understand the language; marriage and baptismal records list many entries for people who availed themselves of these sacraments in the church most readily accessible. Figures for Georgia are also markedly different, the tentative estimate being arbitrary.

This comparison of estimates leads to the more fundamental inquiry as to why the tentative estimates run below Faust's in the areas populated largely by immigration independent of that from Pennsylvania. It raises the questions whether name frequencies among arrivals in Pennsylvania fully portray the nomenclature of German immigration to the whole American area, or whether German immigration to New York and to the extreme south involved local origins in different ratios from those based on immigration to Pennsylvania.

As Faust's estimate summarizes and coördinates the best historical evidence of the period, inquiry in the next section centers on determining whether the author's tentative estimates adequately appraise the German stock in the regions for which the two sets of findings differ widely.

PENNSYLVANIA NOMENCLATURE AS A TYPE

Difference in nomenclature may be rooted in the local origins of Germans mmigrating to New York and to the extreme South, in distinction to those arriving in Pennsylvania.

The German-speaking population of Pennsylvania reflected a variety of local origins, not by any means restricted, as is sometimes thought, to the upper Rhine and the German cantons of Switzerland, but including stock from Crefeld, Bern, Gnadenhut, and other districts apart from that area. This suggests that the Pennsylvania-German population was more diversified than at first appears.

Kuhn's study of local origins of names has contributed to specification of original homes of emigrants, and Heintze's chapter on distribution of forms suggests effective study of local origins based on types of forms rather than on specific forms. Names derived from designations of Provinces and principalities—as *Beyer*, *Boyer* (Bavarian), *Fries* (Frisian), *Schweizer* (Swiss), *Westfall* (Westphalian)—do not necessarily indicate direct origins, but disclose ancestral backgrounds and probably owe their existence as names to the removal of forbears to other localities in Germany before migration to the New World.

German arrivals in New York without doubt differed in geographical background from those in Pennsylvania; a number of the 32 selected groups were not represented in New York at all. Kocherthal's company were forerunners of actual Pennsylvania migration, but before Kocherthal there were Germans in fair numbers among the Dutch in New York; east Frisians were probably common among New Netherland settlers, and Pomeranians may have moved in from an early colony among the Swedes on the Delaware River. Historical analysis of early settlements in New York might show numbers of Germans from all of the Provinces bordering the North Sea and the Baltic, but probably there were few Swiss since Swiss names are rare in the New York records. Hence it is assumed that the geographical center of origin for New York Germans was north and east of that of Pennsylvania Germans.

Germans in the south undoubtedly included many of different locale from those represented in the Pennsylvania arrivals. A large proportion of Germans in South Carolina like most of those in Georgia came direct from the coast; many of them were Swiss, and if the strength of the Moravian Church in the Carolinas is indicative, Austrian origins in this southern region were especially important. Hence it is surmised that the European center of origin of German stock in the extreme South was somewhat south and east of that of the Pennsylvania Germans.

These geographical differences support the inference that the nomenclature of Germans arriving in New York and the Carolinas differed from that of those arriving in Pennsylvania, and therefore imply differences in the proportions of bearers of names selected as indicative.

German names common in Pennsylvania were dependably represented in Maryland, where only *Jaeger* and *Hummel* are not recorded, and in Virginia, where only *Fritz* and *Schuster* are not recorded. But outside of this area gaps in representation were more marked. *Brunner, Spengler, Gerber*, and *Rudolph* were not represented in New York, nor were the last three names in South Carolina; hence they may be considered rather peculiar to the Pennsylvania stock. German nomenclature in the extreme south was in striking contrast to that in Pennsylvania, certain names showing common use, while others are quite unrepresented. In neither of the Carolinas do the records show entries for *Funck, Spengler, Gerber, Stumpf*, or *Schuster*. In North Carolina there were no listings for *Stauffer, Kauffman, Bachman, Jaeger, Ott*, or *Schweitzer*. In South Carolina, *Moser, Steiner, Lutz, Finck, Hummel, Rudolph* and *Albrecht* were not listed, though the last name was highly common in North Carolina.

These differences demonstrate that the preliminary appraisal of German stock in 1790 America is biased by reliance on occurrences of names, some of which were peculiar to the Pennsylvania stream of migration, and suggest a further study of the distribution of distinctive names before the German contributions are finally appraised.

REAPPRAISAL RECOGNIZING GEOGRAPHICAL FACTORS

The problem of allowing for Germans who differed in geographical background, and in nomenclature, from those in Pennsylvania has some aspects like those presented by the Irish stock, several branches of which also showed little use of the names selected as indicators. The data immediately available do not permit special classification of indicators on the basis of antecedents, such as was effective in treatment of the Irish. Nor can the difficulty be overcome by measuring German stock in each State through calculation from usage of names actually occurring in that State, for lack of usage is itself indicative. If in any State only those names showing more than zero occurrence were selected as indicators, rating of the stock would be based unfairly on superior representation. This defect does not apply, however, to general freedom from nonusage. Hence reappraisal is directed by a testing of indicators for regularity of usage.

In all of the States of record from New York southward a number of the 32 selected names had usage so regular as to denote commonness among all Germans of whatever port of arrival, as is indicated by their failure to decline to zero occurrence in any State, and this level of representation does not seriously exaggerate relative distribution of the stock, since superior occurrence in other States but reflects that in Pennsylvania, on which comparison is to be based.

Hence the following names—*Christ, Conrad, Ernst, Hoff, Huber, Keyser, Kolb, Kuhn* (with *Kuntz*), *Lentz, Schaffer, Schneider, Zimmerman*—are abstracted from the whole list of indicators in recognition of regular occurrence in the Middle and Southern States, denoting general occurrence in German-speaking usage.

These 12 German name groups had 1,290 entries in the Pennsylvania index, their bearers constituting 1.7 per cent of the total population in Pennsylvania, and 5.2 per cent of its German element.

The significance of the frequencies of these 12 names is qualitative rather that quantitative. Their strength was of two kinds, (1) general and (2) specific, in New York and the Carolinas where German population differed in geographic background from that in Pennsylvania. Their general strength can be roughly measured by comparing their occurrences in Maryland and Virginia with ratings for the full list of indicators in the same areas.

Table 71 shows the median measures of the relative numbers of bearers of these 12 names, compared with similar measures of the full list of indicators, and shows that their occurrences in Maryland and Virginia were on nearly the same scale as that of the whole list of indicators, but that in New York and the Carolinas they were considerably higher. Column 1 gives the ratings of the German element in specified State indexes relative to those in the Pennsylvania index, as indicated by the 12 names of particularly regular geographic distribution. Column 2 gives these ratings discounted 8 per cent to allow for overstatement caused by the general strength of these indicators, as indicated by comparison with column 3 which shows readings obtained from the full list of indicators. This indicates that percentages of German relatives to those in the Pennsylvania index may have been as follows: New York, 22.6 instead of 12.0; North Carolina, 9.0 instead of 6.5; South Carolina, 6.6 instead of 2.6. Further study of distinctive usages of more names not peculiar to the Pennsylvania migration might more effectively disclose conditions in New York and the extreme South, but with the limited information available this tabulation indicates that the preliminary estimates of German stock should be increased by the following percentages: New York, 50; North Carolina, 50; South Carolina, 100. The final estimate will show these adjustments.

TABLE 71.—*Percentage ratings of the German elements in specified indexes relative to that in the Pennsylvania index by two bases of calculation*

	Indicated by relative occurrence of 12 important name groups of regular American occurrence—		Indicated by relative occurrence of 32 important name groups [1]
	Without adjustment	Adjusted for overstatement [2]	
New York	24.6	22.6	12.0
Maryland	17.0 } 27.0	15.6 } 24.8	15.4 } 24.9
Virginia	10.0	9.2	9.5
North Carolina	9.8	9.0	6.5
South Carolina	7.2	6.6	2.6

[1] From Table 66.
[2] Reduced 8 per cent.

Estimates of German proportions in New England are not based on the distinctive name system, because German settlers there were not numerous enough to justify the selection of a list of surnouns by which to test their contributions, nor are characteristic German names frequent in the New England State records; hence few tests of companionships can be made.

But the scarcity of characteristic German names does not imply insignificant proportions of the stock. Measurement of name distribution shows the slight continuity between New England nomenclatures and Old World patterns, and this discontinuity necessitates genealogical investigation in New England. Details concerning names probably German and allowance for the disguises of Anglicization support the preliminary estimate (Table 68) of approximately 4,000 Germans in New England. At least 1,200 of these were in Maine, many of them listed under Nobleborough [24] in the census, but really belonging to Waldoborough, a strong German settlement. The State index contains enough other German names to justify rating the stock in the whole State as equivalent to these 1,200 persons in Waldoborough, scattered Germans in Maine being estimated as having been equal in number to such persons in Waldoborough as were not of that stock.

The other New England States show names of German character but not in the numbers or with the geographic concentration of those in Maine. Their numbers warrant the present estimates, even though these estimates identify German stock in only one of three nomenclatural classes which take limits from historical evidence and study of the census. These classes are in order: Population descended from the early wave of immigration, that descended from infiltration or desultory immigration from the middle of the seventeenth century to the middle of the eighteenth, and that made up of late arrivals and their descendants. Only the latter favors the recognition of non-English names.

As already noted, some irregularities in New England nomenclature, considered from the angle of its European origins, lie in early changes, and examination of developments period by period will indicate the problem of fully identifying Germans.

Early immigration apparently drawn from specific areas of the Old World may explain the comparatively limited occurrences of some potentially common names, particularly leading English names. In the succeeding period immigration was supposedly so scant as scarcely to constitute infiltration, but it may be postulated that desultory immigration during this time accounts for erratic representation of names. Hence there may have been two groups of progenitors with peculiar nomenclature susceptible of interpretation only by elaborate tests. Furthermore, settlers of the first period, and probably the subsequent arrivals of the doubtful periods, followed a name-as-you-please method, as is shown in Savage's Dictionary (which records marked variability), and in two other records of "those who came before 1692" and later. Result: The two classes of progenitors largely responsible for 1790 population present a nomenclature peculiar to New England's evolution and tending to disguise minor contributions.

Although the nomenclature of descendants of the earlier settlers showed diversity, New England usage as a whole showed a high average of families per name; perhaps this is because of the decline of name experimentation in

---

[24] Through error in the printed transcript of the Maine census, a population of 1,206 is listed under Nobleborough, which should be credited, with the names on pages 41–42 of the census, to Waldoborough. The correct readings are: For Bristol town (census, pp. 9, 35) read Nobleborough; for Nobleborough (census, pp. 9, 41, 42) read Waldoborough; for Waldoborough (census, pp. 9, 48, 49) read Bristol.

later years, but it is more surely because the State records of this area show a very small proportion of names borne by single families. This indicates the slight importance of immediate immigrants relative to the descendants of earlier settlers.

Estimates of Germans in New England therefore rest on names not otherwise readily accounted for. The *CPG* classification is not closely followed here, since that publication shows less than one-tenth of 1 per cent of the 1790 population in most of the New England States as recognizably German. In Connecticut only four persons, probably one family, are recognized as German; yet among entries under " H " and " S " in the Connecticut census the following names—borne by single families unless otherwise stated—suggest German origin: *Haun, Haws, Hoffman, Horcheild, Sangar* (7), *Sanger* (3), *Seger* (4), *Seib, Shrinner, Sizer* (5). Bearers of some of these names may not have been German, but those that were must have had companions whose names were less obviously Teutonic, for interpretation based on evidence of names ordinarily appraises the stock in States where Germans were numerous at about twice the proportions directly disclosed by recognizably German names. Hence, even after adjustment of the *CPG* classification—or complete substitution for its findings for this area—further allowances for Anglicization are warranted.

Usage in the 1790 lists of New England shows a special type of nomenclature which *CPG* analysts considered chiefly English, but which the present analysis on the basis of leading English surnames finds weak in content of leading English names. Whether Germans contributed to usage much more than now known can be determined only by investigation of genealogical data, but meantime the present estimate of 0.4 per cent German contributions to New England is a conservative rating.

GENERAL CHARACTER OF NEW ENGLAND POPULATION

CPG too readily assumes homeogeneous population in New England. Witness the statement:[25]

It is a significant fact suggested (by Tables 43 and 44) that Massachusetts, the population of which was almost exclusively of British extraction, closely followed by most of the New England States, reports the highest proportion of families per name and consequently of persons per name. Table 44 reflects, in general, the tendency of homeogeneous population to show a smaller proportion of surnames to population than does a mixed population, such as that of Pennsylvania and South Carolina.

This explanation of lack of variety is only a partial truth. Variety in names depends on original sources, degree and time of mixture, and phases of evolution. Among the countries whose emigrants came to America, Wales had the least diversified nomenclature, with Scotland, Ireland, England, and the continental countries following in approximate order. These nomenclatures were not wholly distinct; hence they reacted on each other, and variety in America was affected both by national sources and by environmental influences which developed combined structures in the New World. Ordinarily the greater the mixture of stocks, the greater the variety of names. The proportion of non-British is also important because their names were particularly subject to change. Hence variety depends on a number of factors.

Concentration and diversity are the two extremes between which variety of nomenclature moves, reflecting the derivation of the population, or resulting from unifying or diversifying tendencies in name evolution. In the United States, diversification beyond a certain point ordinarily reflects mixture of

[25] *CPG*, Chap. X, p. 114.

stocks, particularly recent mixture, and results especially from the infusion of non-British stocks whose names undergo many experimental changes before they settle into permanent forms. Continuous immigration contributes to diversity by keeping experimentation active and by adding new forms. Concentration may disclose homogeneity of population; it certainly reveals a high degree of amalgamation, for usage in populations which receive little new immigration and are well beyond the adaptive stage shows a tendency toward concentration irrespective of origins.

The States shown in Table 44, *CPG*, in order of their average number of white families per name are: Massachusetts 14.6, Connecticut 11.9, New Hampshire 9.3, Rhode Island 7.8, New York 7.3, Virginia 7.1, North Carolina 7.1, Maine 6.4, Vermont 6.1, Pennsylvania 5.5, Maryland 4.9, South Carolina 4.7.

These ratings are merely averages and sometimes they hide important differences in the proportions of names of high, low, and medium degree of frequency. New York's high rating is significant because that State records a large proportion of names borne by single families; hence, concentration on certain names produced a high average degree of usage per name, in spite of much rare usage.

The proportion of names borne by single families constitutes the most significant difference between conditions in New England and those in the rest of the country. New England State records, other than that of Maine, show only about a third of the names borne by single families, whereas in the rest of the country this ratio was more nearly a half, in New York more than a half.[26] This reveals the slight importance of recent immigration, and also recent experimental usage in New England.

The high degree of usage of names of moderate frequency in New England is not presented clearly in *CPG*. Table 42, *CPG*, sets forth gradations in name frequency in the States, by applying the same statistical intervals to all; but obviously names borne by 25 to 49 families—to cite one interval—have a different significance in a population of 16,000 families, as in Maine, from that in a population of 65,000 families, as in Massachusetts. New England's concentration on names of moderate frequency would be more apparent if the intervals were based on hundredths of a per cent of population. What one finds there was a fairly settled nomenclatural condition and a relative deficiency of forms of recent introduction or coinage. This peculiarity in New England nomenclature supports the inference that while its population may have been well fused it was nevertheless heterogeneous in origin, its considerable mixture including at least the proportion of Germans here estimated.

FINAL ESTIMATE OF THE GERMAN CONTRIBUTION

Table 72 shows the final estimate of the German contribution to 1790 America, with detail for New England and with adjustment of the preliminary estimate (Table 68) particularly by allowing for German arrivals in New York and the extreme south whose nomenclatural characteristics were different from those in Pennsylvania. These adjusted percentage estimates are as follows: New York 8.2, instead of 5.5, North Carolina 4.7 instead of 3.1, South Carolina 5.0 instead of 2.5. Estimates for German proportions in Georgia, Kentucky, and Tennessee, are correspondingly increased to conform with these new findings in adjoining territory. This makes the final estimate of the German contribution to the American population in 1790, 8.7 per cent. Findings are based largely on relative measures of American usage of distinctive Ger-

---

[26] CPG Table 42

man names; but since German names were subject to marked changes through Americanization, their occurrence does not reveal evidence of origin which can be employed automatically, and a consideration of variables is implicit in estimating the German proportion in every State.

TABLE 72.—*Estimated numbers and proportions of Germans in the white population of the United States, 1790*

	White population	German	
		Per cent	Number
United States	3, 172, 444	8. 7	276, 960
Maine	96, 107	1. 3	1, 250
New Hampshire	141, 112	. 4	560
Vermont	85, 072	. 2	170
Massachusetts	373, 187	. 3	1, 120
Rhode Island	64, 670	. 5	320
Connecticut	232, 236	. 3	700
New York	314, 366	8. 2	25, 800
New Jersey	169, 954	9. 2	15, 640
Pennsylvania	423, 373	33. 3	140, 980
Delaware	46, 310	1. 1	510
Maryland	208, 649	11. 7	24, 410
Kentucky and Tennessee	93, 046	14. 0	13, 030
Virginia	442, 117	6. 3	27, 850
North Carolina	289, 181	4. 7	13, 590
South Carolina	140, 178	5. 0	7, 010
Georgia	52, 886	7. 6	4, 020

APPENDICES

Three appendices supplement this chapter on German contributions. The first quotes Kuhns on entries in the Pennsylvania *Oath of Allegiance* record and shows his illustrative material on Americanization of German names. The second consists of a schedule of names a degree less common in the usage of foreigners arriving in Pennsylvania than those considered in this appraisal. It is based on entries in the *Oath of Allegiance* record, and discloses the character of immigrant nomenclature, illustrating the changes through which German nomenclature established itself as German-American. The third discusses the forms of German names and the controls on American changes.

118640—32——20

Chapter VIII

SUMMARY OF CONTRIBUTIONS OF NATIONAL STOCKS TO 1790 AMERICA

As this study of names distinctive of English, Scotch, Ulster Irish, southern Irish, and of German-speaking peoples (including Swiss and Austrians) is now complete, estimates of the contributions of these stocks to the 1790 population of America may be based on the results.

These findings are now combined with the preliminary figures for Dutch, French and Swedish contributions estimated by my associate Doctor Hansen.[1] His final ratings may show some changes, but it is not anticipated that they will materially modify the statement here presented coordinating the two inquiries.

The estimates of the several stocks when brought together for an examination of the population as a whole reveal a contrast which divides the country into two distinct areas one covering the seaboard from New York southward, where the origin of the population seems to be satisfactorily accounted for, the other covering New England, where the origin of 17 per cent of the population remains to be determined.

Records of States south of New England contain certain miscellaneous entries not clearly representative of any of the principal national stocks with frequencies indicating a miscellaneous origin for from 1½ to 4 per cent of the population. Adding these estimates to those of Scotch, Irish, German, Dutch, French, and Swedish stocks, and subtracting the total from 100 per cent, gives new ratings of English contributions for each State in this area, showing that the English proportion was about four-fifths of that indicated by the occurence measures of leading English names. In other words, figures derived as maxima for English contributions require a discount of approximately 20 per cent to allow for supplemental use of English names.

This coordination of estimates gives a definite outline to the composition of the population in each State from New York south. But for the New England area it is only possible to set down the measures of the several stocks as ascertained and to designate the remaining percentage of population as of unassignable origin on the basis of evidence now available.

Table 73 shows the approximate percentages of national stocks, as revealed by the present inquiry, as follows: English, 60; Scotch, 8; Ulster Irish, 6; southern Irish, 4; German, 9; Dutch, French, and Swedish, 6; unassignable, 7.

---

[1] Hansen's estimates are conformable with those presented in this study except in the findings for New Jersey. As the trends in nomenclatural ratings shown in this study conform so well with Nelson's estimates for English, Scotch, and Germans in New Jersey (*CPG*), without marked discrepancy for the Irish, the author is unable to accept Hansen's wide departure in his estimate of 20.6 per cent Dutch contributions, but gives equal weight to Nelson's 12.7 per cent estimate, and computes 16.6 per cent Dutch contributions to New Jersey.

TABLE 73.—*Per cent distribution of white population of the United States according to nationality mainly as indicated by the usage of family names, 1790*

Area	English	Scotch	Ulster Irish	South Irish	German	Dutch, French, Swedish	Unassignable and miscellaneous
United States_	60. 9	8. 3	6. 0	3. 7	8. 7	5. 4	7. 0
Maine_____	60. 0	4. 5	8. 0	3. 7	1. 3	1. 3	21. 2
New Hampshire_____	61. 0	6. 2	4. 6	2. 9	. 4	. 8	24. 1
Vermont_____	76. 0	5. 1	3. 2	1. 9	. 2	1. 0	12. 6
Massachusetts_____	82. 0	4. 4	2. 6	1. 3	. 3	1. 0	8. 4
Rhode Island_____	71. 0	5. 8	2. 0	. 8	. 5	1. 2	18. 7
Connecticut_____	67. 0	2. 2	1. 8	1. 1	. 3	1. 2	26. 4
New York_____	52. 0	7. 0	5. 1	3. 0	8. 2	21. 5	3. 2
New Jersey_____	47. 0	7. 7	6. 3	3. 2	9. 2	23. 1	3. 5
Pennsylvania_____	35. 3	8. 6	11. 0	3. 5	33. 3	4. 3	4. 0
Delaware_____	60. 0	8. 0	6. 3	5. 4	1. 1	14. 8	4. 4
Maryland_____	64. 5	7. 6	5. 8	6. 5	11. 7	1. 9	2. 0
Kentucky and Tennessee_____	57. 9	10. 0	7. 0	5. 2	14. 0	3. 6	2. 3
Virginia_____	68. 5	10. 2	6. 2	5. 5	6. 3	1. 9	1. 4
North Carolina_____	66. 0	14. 8	5. 7	5. 4	4. 7	2. 2	1. 2
South Carolina_____	60. 2	15. 1	9. 4	4. 4	5. 0	4. 5	1. 4
Georgia_____	57. 4	15. 5	11. 5	3. 8	7. 6	2. 8	1. 4

As the figures for maxima of English contribution based on occurrence measures of leading English names are not used in these computations for the States from New York southward, the present ratings show a seried arrangement somewhat different from that indicated in the preliminary study. It is now found that the high point for English in the South was in Virginia, rather than in North Carolina, where the leading English names had such remarkable occurrence. The percentages of English rose from 60 in Maine to 82 in Massachusetts, declined to 35 in Pennsylvania, rose to 68.5 in Virginia, and declined again to the South. The conformation of this curve accords with historical evidence, but the percentages of English in the New England States remain as derived in the chapter on English stock and present a new departure in findings.

Scotch proportions at a high level, 15 per cent, in Georgia and the Carolinas, dropped to 10 per cent in Virginia and to less than 8 in Maryland, rose to over 8 in Pennsylvania, declined northward to 2.2 in Connecticut, rose north and east to 6.2 in New Hampshire, the high point for New England, and declined to 4.5 in Maine.

Ulster Irish contributions resulting from fairly distinct streams of Scotch-Irish, English-Irish, and native Irish from Ulster show a percentage curve roughly inverse to that of the English, with three high points—11.5 in Georgia, 11.0 in Pennsylvania, and 8.0 in Maine. From 11.5 per cent in Georgia, the Ulster Irish declined to about 6 in North Carolina, Virginia, and Maryland, rose abruptly to 11 in Pennsylvania, dropped sharply northward to 5.1 in New York, and to 1.8 in Connecticut (their lowest rating), and rose north and east to 8.0 in Maine. There is fair similarity between the Ulster Irish and the Scotch measures, though the latter is in general about a third higher and provides a more even curve, except that in Connecticut both show strikingly low figures.

Southern Irish contributions were at their highest, 6.5 per cent, in Maryland, declined steadily southward to 3.8 in Georgia, and northward to 1.1 in Connecticut, faltered at about 1 per cent in central New England and rose to 3 per cent and more in New Hampshire and Maine.

The proportions of Germans (including Swiss and Austrians) ranged from 33 per cent in Pennsylvania, through 12 per cent in Maryland to less than 5 in North Carolina, and rose to 8 in Georgia, while northward they dropped to 9 per cent in New Jersey and 8 in New York, and to a low level of a fraction of a per cent in New England, with the exception of Maine (1.3 per cent).

Dutch, French, and Swedish contributions collectively, according to the author's adjustment of Hansen's preliminary figures, reached their high point of 23 per cent in New Jersey, with 21.5 in New York and 15 in Delaware. From there southward they dropped to 4 per cent in Pennsylvania and to a level of about 2 per cent from Maryland to North Carolina, then shifted to 4.5 in South Carolina and 3 per cent in Georgia. In the New England area they were consistently about 1.1 per cent.

The distribution of population unassigned by origin is not quite so readily summarized as that of the definite stocks.

Southward from New York these people reached their highest proportions, 4.4 per cent, in Delaware, but this State had a comparatively small population, and its 1790 record is missing; therefore the author considers that this figure shows some lack of coordination in the estimates, and that this element constituted 3 to 4 per cent in the combined area of New York, New Jersey, Pennsylvania, and Delaware, 2 per cent in Maryland, and slightly less than 1.5 per cent from Virginia southward. Readings for the unassignable element in New England are quite different; from 8 per cent in Massachusetts they increased in all directions, ranging from 13 in Vermont to 26 in Connecticut, the next highest proportions being in New Hampshire and Maine.

The contrast between the proportion of unassigned in New York and Connecticut is marked. New York with 3.2 per cent is fairly characteristic of conditions in the Middle and Southern States, while Connecticut's 26.4 per cent focuses the uncertainty applying to the New England area.

Occurrences of leading English names indicate maxima of 57 per cent English in New York and 67 per cent in Connecticut, these figures forming part of the percentage sequence running from a low rating in Pennsylvania to a high rating in Massachusetts, indicating graduated English proportions along this stretch of seaboard. But non-English ratings, on the contrary, indicate a definite break east of the Hudson. Tables 12 and 13, showing the relative occurrences of English indicators, give no clue to a striking difference in the significance of English names as indicators for New York and Connecticut, nor does Table 7, showing the ratio of Cambrians to Anglicans, disclose a break in English proportions between New York and New England. In New York, as all through the Middle and Southern States, the liberal English estimates based on nomenclatural ratios must be reduced by allowing for established proportions of non-English, and subtraction of known non-English reduces to 52 per cent the preliminary estimate of 57 per cent English in the State. In Connecticut, on the contrary, allowance for known non-English stocks still leaves one-fourth of the population not accounted for either as English or as known non-English.

The conditions which result in New York showing a small proportion of unassignable population, in sharp contrast to the large proportion in Connecticut, require further examination.

From New York southward, estimates for this unclassified population are based on occurrences of various names not obviously natural to the principal national stocks. Certain names known to have designated southern Europeans, Slavs, Scandinavians other than Swedes, and other immigrants distinguish what Franklin called "miscellaneous and recalcitrant elements" and what Schoepf and St. John styled the "promiscuous crowd." But it is possible that better known names had roots quite as strange or obscure. Illustrative of names which probably indicate origins in countries other than those contributing substantial proportions to American population are: *Antissel, Antonides, Bockius, Burtis* (Italian), *Banta* (Hungarian), *Bestpitch, Blazo, Bonawitz, Copenhaver* (Danish ?), *Formicola, Gergainus, Gornto, Hutto, Holvah, Jeter, Khuince, Kral, Lemgotha, Lyda, Lumber* and *Lumbard* (from Lombardy?), *Mozingo, Mygatt, Messuskey, Ostean, Pappoo, Purviance, Robinsky, Sistarre, Sitkup, Spiva, Srum.* While most of these names had only sporadic occurrence, the aggregate ratings of such names are so considerable as to necessitate making allowances for miscellaneous and practically unassignable contributions to population from New York southward.

In New England, however, the crux of the problem of unassignable population is the shortage of bearers of potentially common names, particularly those of familiar English names. Antecedents of about one-sixth of the population are not disclosed by the occurrence measures of common European names. The scant measures of leading English names in a population heretofore supposed to have been well over 90 per cent English are striking and perplexing. If a large proportion of the English came from localities of the motherland where variety of nomenclature was the rule, it would be held that the unassignable element consisted of English with rather uncommon names. Examination reveals close relationship between occurrence measures of leading English names in the several New England States and decline of their ratios in all directions from Massachusetts. If this difficulty of classification on a nomenclatural basis is occasioned by the presence of English with rare and uncommon names, it remains to be learned how it came about that they were mainly settled in the northern and western parts of the New England area and not particularly in Massachusetts which was the center of early settlements.[2]

Judged by evidence in over two-thirds of the 1790 population, it was normal for leading English names to have substantial numbers of non-English bearers. For this reason, the ratios of leading English names may need to be discounted in estimating English contributions to population in New England, as in the other areas. Even the rather scant number of bearers of common English names in New England must have included people of non-English origins. But a study of non-English usage indicates that English ratings in New England probably need not be discounted on this account.

Non-English use of leading English names centered in the South, voluntary usage and by-usage being less evident northward. Contrasting the maxima for English obtained from the ratios of Farr's names with the measures now obtained by subtracting known non-English from the total population shows that the bearers of leading English names among Americans of all origins exceeded those among English-Americans by the following percentages: South Carolina, 25; North Carolina, 48; Virginia, 23; Maryland, 12; Pennsylvania, 13; New York, 10. North Carolina proves to have had only about two-thirds as many English as were indicated by occurrences of leading English names,

---

[2] This shows that the later settlements of New England involved a considerable mixture of other peoples with the descendants of the early colonists and emphasizes the need of further study of the second stage of migration into New England. Chapter VII, p. 302, and also Chapter III, p. 178, ff.

the proportion being 100 in 148. And from North Carolina northward, voluntary and incidental usage of English names declined steadily, until in New York the nomenclatural measurement of English stock is an overestimate of only 10 per cent. On the evidence of this decline northward in non-English use of common English names, the English in New England appear to have been about as numerous as is indicated by the ratios there of Farr's names.

Summarizing the New England situation, the author considers that the New Englanders of 1790 were much more largely derived from infiltration than has heretofore been appreciated; that their origins were commonly disguised by modification of their names [3]; and that special nomenclatural features of eastern and southern England, from whence many of them came, may hide the true proportions of English.

A survey of name usages in 1790, as indicative of antecedents, discloses a seried relationship in the state populations that reveals considerable fusion of stocks and suggests that the seaboard population had by that time lost most of the characteristics of separate settlements. American measures of names important in the principal countries of origin reveal an orderly condition that shows that the occurrence measures of distinctive names afford a clear picture of antecedents of the general American population, aside from that proportion of New England population which must be left unassigned for the present.

For the country as a whole, the author estimates that the population of America in 1790 was certainly less than two-thirds English, about 10 per cent Irish, 9 per cent German (including fair numbers of Swiss and Austrians), 8 per cent Scotch, and 6 per cent Dutch, French, and Swedish; and that in addition at least 3 per cent of the people were of various antecedents at present unassignable on the basis of the available data.

---

[3] French names constitute the chief probability.

EXCERPTS FROM STUDIES IN PENNSYLVANIA GERMAN FAMILY NAMES [1]

By Oscar Kuhns, Americana Germanica, 1902

PART A. TYPES OF CHANGES OF NAME (PAGES 319–321)

An interesting illustration of the way in which many names received an English form is seen in the "Pennsylvania Archives," second series, Vol. XVII, which contains a list of the German and Swiss settlers in Pennsylvania during the eighteenth century, the names of the vessels in which they came, and the dates of their naturalization. Often there are two lists given, one called the "original list," which apparently was made by an English-speaking person, who took down the names as they were given to him orally, and who spelled them phonetically. These duplicate lists throw a great deal of light on the pronunciation of the name by the immigrants themselves. We find the same person's name spelled *Kuntz* and *Cooncs*, *Kuhle* and *Keeley*, *Huber* and *Hoover*, *Gaul* and *Kool*, *Vogelin* and *Fagley*, *Grauce* and *Krautz*, *Froehlich* and *Frailick*. Often there are some marvelous examples of phonetic spelling. Thus, Albrecht Graff is written Albrake Grove, George Heinrich Mertz is called Jurig Henrich March, and George Born is metamorphosed into Yerrick Burry. Thus even before the immigrant landed the impulse toward a change of name was given.

Again when the Germans came to be naturalized many of them could not write their names, and the clerk of the court had to take them down according to his own phonetic methods. Of course the spelling in such cases differed with the accuracy of hearing of the writer.

Sometimes the change was gradual, and we may trace many intermediate steps between the original name and its present form. Thus for *Krehbiel* we have *Krebill*, *Grebill*, *Grabill*, and finally *Graybill*. So *Krumbein* gives us *Krumbine*, *Grumbein*, and *Grumbine*. Often members of the same family spelled their names differently. In Lancaster there once lived two brothers, one named *Carpenter* and the other *Zimmermann*.

In some cases the changes were slight, owing to the similarity between the English and the German, as in *Baker* (*Becker*), *Miller* (*Mueller*), *Brown* (*Braun*), *Weaver* (*Weber*), *Beaver* (*Bieber*), *Pepper* (*Pfeffer*); of course *Schmidt* became almost at once Smith. In other cases the differences are so great that it is difficult to discover the original German form, and it is only by searching public documents and church records that the truth is found. Who, for instance, could see any connection between *Seldomridge* and *Seltenreich*, or between *Rhoades* and *Roth?* Yet nothing is surer than that in many cases these names are one and the same. It is undoubtedly true that most Pennsylvania Germans of modern times have no conception of the changes that have taken place.

In the present discussion we must bear in mind that we are speaking of the names of those Germans who came to America before the Revolution, and who

---

[1] See comment pp. 275, 276, 285, 332.

were subject to an entirely different set of influences from the Germans of recent times, who changes his name consciously and bodily into English. The names of the early Pennsylvania Germans were changed unconsciously and according to forces with which they had little to do. The difference between the two is like that between *mots savants* and the *mots populaires* of French philology.

The number of different ways of spelling even the simplest names is often surprisingly large: Thus, for the original *Graaf* we find to-day *Graf, Graff, Groff, Groft, Graft,* and *Grove.* So *Baer* gives us *Bear, Bare, Bair.* Of course, the vagaries of English orthography are largely responsible for this ` * * *.

There were three ways in which the change of names took place: First, by translation; second, by spelling German sounds according to English methods; and third, by analogy. The former is the most natural in cases where English equivalents exist for the German: Hence for *Zimmermann* we have *Carpenter;* for *Steinbrenner, Stoneburner;* for *Schumacher, Shoemaker;* for *Seidensticker, Silkknitter;* for *Lebengut, Livingood;* for *Fuchs, Fox;* for *Hoch, High;* for *Klein,* both *Little* and *Small,* and so forth. Often only half the name is translated, while the other half is changed phonetically, as in *Slaymaker* (for *Schleiermacher*), *Wanamaker* (for *Wannemacher*), *Lineaweaver* (for *Leineweber*).

PART B. ALPHABETIC LIST OF CURRENT PENNSYLVANIA GERMAN NAMES WITH BOTH THEIR GERMAN AND THEIR ANGLICIZED FORMS

[From Studies in Pennsylvania German Family Names, Oscar Kuhns, 1902]

Anglicized	German	Anglicized	German
Albright	Albrecht	Bear	Baer
Algaier	Algäuer	Beaver	Bieber
Altic	Altag	Beckley	Bickeli
Althouse	Althaus	Beckler	Boeckler
Ansorge	Ohnesorge	Beidler	Beutler
Armpriester	Armbrüster	Beltzhoover	Beltzhuber
Aughey	Ache	Berkheiser	Berghäuser
Aughenbaugh	Achenbach	Berkey	Bürki
Ault	Alt	Bettikoffer	Büttikoffer
Aument	Amend	Betts	Betz
Amwake	Amweg	Bewighouse	Bibighaus
		Beyerly	Bäuerle
Baggenstose	Bachenstoss	Bickley	Bickeli
Bair	Baer	Billmeyer	Bühlmeyer
Baker	Becker	Bichsler	Büchsler
Baketell	Bechtel	Bishop	Bischof
Balsbaugh	Pfaltzbach	Bitner	Büttner
Balsgrove	Pfaltzgraf	Bixler	Büchsler
Bare	Baer	Book	Buch
Barger	Berger	Booker	Bucher
Barnhart	Bernhard	Bookwalter	Buchwalder
Barringer	Behringer	Boose	Buss
Barshinger	Bertschinger	Bordlemay	Bartlemé
Bartsch	Bertsch	Bordner	Portner
Bashore	Le Baiseur	Bossler	Bassler
Baugh	Bach	Bowers	Bauer
Baugher	Bacher	Bowman	Baumann
Baughman	Bachman	Boyer	Beyer
Baustian	Bastian	Brackbill	Brackbühl
Baxstresser	Bergstresser	Brenizer	Brenneiser
Baylor	Beiler	Brenneman	Brünneman
Beam	Boehm	Bricker	Brücker
Bean	Behn	Brickner	Bruckner

PART B. ALPHABETIC LIST OF CURRENT PENNSYLVANIA GERMAN NAMES WITH BOTH
THEIR GERMAN AND THEIR ANGLICIZED FORMS—continued

Anglicized	German	Anglicized	German
Bridenbaugh	Breitenbach	Diffenderfer	Tiefendörfer
Bright	Brecht	Dotts	Datz
Brightbill	Brechbühl	Drawbaugh	Drawbach
Brimmer	Brümmer		
Brobst	Probst	Eaby	Ebi
Brown	Braun	Earhart	Ehrhard
Brownback	Brumbach	Earley	Ehrle
Brua	Bröe	Earp	Erb
Brubaker	Brupbacher	Ebaugh	Ibach
Brumbaugh	Brumbach	Eberly	Eberli
Buckwalt	Buchwald	Eby	Ebi
Buckwalter	Buchwalder	Egle	Egli
Bumgardner	Baumgärtner	Eichly	Eicheli
Burkey	Burki	Elick	Illig
Burkheiser	Burghäuser	Ellmaker	Ellmacher
Bushong	Beauchamp or	Ensminger	Eisenmenger
	Bossongs	Eppley	Epple
Butts	Butz	Ermentraut	Irmintraut
		Erney	Erni
Capehart	Gebhard	Esbenshade	Espenscheid
Carpenter	Zimmermann	Eshbaugh	Eschenbach
Carver	Gerber	Eshelman	Eschlimann
Casselberry	Kasselberg	Everhart	Eberhard
Caylor	Koehler	Exley	Oechsli
Charles	Karl		
Cline	Klein	Fair	Fehr
Clinedinst	Kleindienst	Fate	Veit
Clouse	Klause	Fease	Füss
Clouser	Klauser	Fegley	Voegli
Coar	Kohr	Felker	Völcker
Cockel	Kachel	Ferree	Fuehre or Fery
Coffman	Kaufman	Fetter	Vetter
Coler	Kohler	Finnefrock	Fünfrock
Coogler	Kugler	Flickiger	Flückiger
Coon	Kuhn	Flinchbaugh	Flentsbach
Coons	Kuntz	Focht	Vogt
Cooper	Böttcher	Fogel	Vogel
Coover	Kober	Foltz	Voltz
Copenhaver	Kopenhöfer	Fon der Smith	Von der Schmiede
Coppersmith	Kupferschmidt	Fooks	Fuchs
Cramer	Kraemer	Foose	Fuss
Crater	Kräuter	Forney	Fortuné
Creider	Kraüter	Fortinbaugh	Fortinbach
Cripps	Krebs	Fosnot	Fasnacht
Croll	Krall	Foust	Faust
Crook	Krug	Foutz	Pfautz
Crouse	Krause	Fow	Pfau
Crum	Krum	Frailey	Fröhlich
Culp	Kalb	Freas	Fries
		Frederick	Friedrich
Dabler	Döbler	Free	Fuehre or Fery
Deal	Diehl	Fridy	Freytag
Deardorf	Dürrendorf	Fritchey	Fritschi
Dearing	Düring	Fry	Frey
Dearwechter	Thürwächter	Fryhafer	Freyhöfer
Deatrick	Dietrich	Fulmer	Volmar
Deem	Diem		
Delliker	De la Cour?	Gairing	Gehring
Denlinger	Dehnlinger	Garber	Gerber
Derr	Dürr	Gardner	Gaertner
Diffenbaugh	Tiefenbach	Garman	Germann

Anglicized	German	Anglicized	German
Garret	Gehret	Hines	Heintz
Garver	Gerber	Hivner	Hübner
Gearhart	Gerhard	Hoak	Hoch
Geer	Gehr	Hoffmaster	Hofmeister
Getty	Götti	Hoober	Huber
Getz	Göetz	Hoover	Huber
Ginter	Günther	Hostetter	Hofstetter
Gipe	Geib	Hougentougler	Hagantobler
Gise	Geiss	Hower	Hauer
Givler	Kübler	Howry	Hauri
Glossbrenner	Glasbrenner	Hubley	Hubeli
Glossmoyer	Glasmeyer	Hunter	Jäger
Gobin	Gabin		
Gobright	Gabrecht	Johns	Tschantz
Good	Gut		
Goodchild	Gottschalk	Kale	Kehl
Graft	Graf	Kaler	Koehler
Graybill	Krähenbühl	Kayley	Kühle
Graver	Gräber	Kaylor	Koehler
Greenawalt	Grünewald	Keagey	Kagi
Groff	Graf	Keely	Kühle
Groft	Graf	Keen	Kühn
Grove	Graf	Keeny	Kühne
Grumbine	Krummbein	Keeportz	Kynport
Gruver	Gruber	Kelker	Kollicker
		Kemmerer	Kämmerer
Hafer	Höfer	Kendig	Kündig
Hager	Häger	Kendrick	Kündig
Hagy	Hägi	Keneagy	Knägi
Hailman	Heilmann	Kephart	Gebhard
Hain	Höhn	Kester	Küster
Haines	Haintz	Keyser	Kaiser
Hake	Höck	Kimmel	Kümmel
Hamacher	Heumacher	Kindig	Kündig
Hambright	Hambrecht	King	König
Harbaugh	Herbach	Kinnard	Kühnert
Harman	Hermann	Kinsel	Kunzel
Harter	Herter	Kinser	Künzer
Hartsock—sough	Hertzog	Kinsey	Künzi
Hartwick	Hertwig	Kinsler	Künzler
Hartwig	Hertwig	Kleckner	Glöckner
Hartz	Hertz	Kline	Klein
Hartzell	Hirtzel	Knerr	Knörr
Hartzler	Hirtzler	Knipe	Kneib
Haverstick	Haberstick	Knisely	Kneissli
Hawn	Hahn	Knouse	Knauss
Heebner	Hübner	Kolb	Kalb
Heidelbaugh	Heidelbach	Koogel	Kugel
Heikes	Heiges	Koogler	Kugler
Hemperley	Hemberle	Koon	Kuhn
Hench	Hentsch	Koonce	Kuntz
Henry	Heinrich	Koons	Kuntz
Hershey	Hirschi	Koots	Kutz
Hetrick	Hädrich	Kouns	Kuntz
Heverling	Heberling	Krehbiel	Krähenbühl
Heydrick	Heidrick	Kreider	Kräuter
Hibsman	Hübschmann	Kripps	Krebs
Hiester	Heister	Kuhns	Kuntz
High	Hoch	Kuhnsman	Kuntzmann
Hillegass	Hilleges	Kulp	Kalb
Himmelwright	Himmelreich	Kunsman	Kuntzmann
Hine	Hein	Kynet	Keinath

PART B. ALPHABETIC LIST OF CURRENT PENNSYLVANIA GERMAN NAMES WITH BOTH
THEIR GERMAN AND THEIR ANGLICIZED FORMS—continued

Anglicized	German	Anglicized	German
Lance	Lantz	Pifer	Pfeiffer
Lape	Leib	Piper	Pfeiffer
Leader	Lüder	Price	Preiss
Lear	Lühr	Prince	Printz
Lease	Liess		
Leffler	Loeffler	Rawn	Rahn
Lehr	Lühr	Ream	Rehm
Leiby	Leibig	Redsecker	Ruegsegger
Leidy	Leidig	Reeser	Riese
Leinbaugh	Leinbach	Rehrig	Röhrig
Lichliter	Lichtleitner	Reifsnyder	Reifschneider
Light	Licht	Reinhold	Reinoehl
Lightner	Leitner	Reynolds	Reinoehl
Lineaweaver	Leinaweber	Rhine	Rhein
Lipe	Leib	Rhoads	Roth
Livingood	Lebengut	Rhule	Ruhl
Long	Lang	Rice	Reiss
Lower	Lauer	Richards	Reichert
		Ricksecker	Ruegsegger
Markel	Merkel	Rieger	Rüger
Markley	Märkli	Riemensnyder	Riemenschneider
Mayer	Meyer	Righter	Richter
Mease	Miess	Rightmeyer	Rechtmeyer
Mercer	Musser	Rinehart	Reinhard
Messersmith	Messerschmidt	Risser	Rüsser
Mickley	Micheli	Rittenhouse	Rittenhuysen
Miley	Meili	Rhode	Roth
Miller	Müller	Rodenbaugh	Rodenbach
Minich	Münch	Rodermel	Rothaermel
Minnick	Münch	Rood	Roth
Mish	Müsch	Rorbaugh	Rohrbach
Mishler	Mischler	Rowe	Rau
Mitchler	Mischler	Rubley	Rubli
Moore	Mohr	Ruby	Rubi
Mosser	Moser	Rudy	Rudi
Mowrer	Maurer	Rudisill	Rüdisühli
Musselman	Mosliman	Rurapaw	Rohrbach
Musser	Mosser	Russel	Rössel
Myers	Meyer	Rymer	Reimer
Mylin	Meili		
		Saylor	Seiler
Neagley	Nägeli	Schelly	Schillig
New	Neu	Seldomridge	Seltenreich
Newman	Neumann	Sensenig	Sensenich
Newschwanger	Neuenschwander	Shaner	Shöner
Ney	Neu	Shaub	Schaub
Nissler	Nüssler	Schearer	Scherer
Nissley	Nüssli	Sheeleigh	Schillig
Nyce	Neuss	Sheets	Schütz
		Sherrick	Scherck
Oak	Eich	Shertz	Schertz
Oaks	Ochs	Shimer	Schäumer
Oakley	Eichli	Shipe	Scheib
Omwake	Amweg	Shively	Scheibli
Overholt	Oberholtzer	Shnavely	Schnaebeli
		Shoffroth	Schaffrath
Paff	Pfaff	Shools	Schultz
Palsgrove	Pfaltzgraf	Shora	Jury
Parthemore	Porthuma or Par-	Shriner	Schreiner
	themer	Shriver	Schreiber
Pennypacker	Pannebecker	Shunk	Schunck or Jean
Petry	Petri	Sides	Seitz

PART B. ALPHABETIC LIST OF CURRENT PENNSYLVANIA GERMAN NAMES WITH BOTH
THEIR GERMAN AND THEIR ANGLICIZED FORMS—continued

Anglicized	German	Anglicized	German
Sigafoos	Sigafuss	Waidley	Weidli
Sipe	Seip	Wanamaker	Wannemacher
Sites	Seitz	Wambaugh	Wambach
Slagel	Schlegel	Wanger	Wenger
Slaughter	Schlachter	Warfel	Würfel
Slayback	Schlabach	Waughtel	Wachtel
Slaymaker	Schleiermacher	Weaver	Weber
Slosser	Schlosser	Weidly	Weidli
Smith	Schmidt	Weighley	Weigli
Smyser	Schmeisser	Welty	Wälti
Snader	Schneider	Werts	Wirtz
Snaveley	Schnaebeli	Westheffer	Westhöfer
Snell	Schnell	Whitescarver	Weissgerber
Souders	Sauter	Whitman	Widmann
Sourbier	Sauerbier	Wiant	Weiand
Sourwine	Sauerwein	Widener	Weidner
Sowers	Sauer	Wike	Weik
Spangler	Spengler	Witman	Widman
Stahr	Staar	Witmer	Widmer
Staley	Stäheli	Wittenmeyer	Widmeyer
Staver	Stöber	Wollenweaver	Wollenweber
Stehlig	Stäheli		
Steyerwald	Steigerwald	Yackley	Jäckli
Stine	Stein	Yeager	Jäger
Stone	Stein	Yeagy	Jäggi
Stehman	Steinmann	Yeakley	Jäckli
Stoneburner	Steinbrenner	Yeisser	Geisser
Stonecypher	Steinschleifer	Yeissler	Geissler
Stoner	Steiner	Yentzer	Gentzer
Stoneseifer	Steinschleifer	Yergens	Jürgens
Stover	Stöber	Yerger	Jörger
Strasbaugh	Strasbach	Yerkes	Jörges
Strine	Strein	Yerrick	Jörg
Swarr	Schwehr	Yertz	Goertz
Swegler	Schwegler	Yetter	Götter
Sweigert	Schweiger	Yillis	Gillis
Switzer	Schweitzer	Yingst	Jüngst
Swope	Schwab	Yoder	Goder
		Yohn	John
Tice	Theiss	Yost	Jost
Trexler	Trechsler	Young	Jung
Trout	Traut		
Troxell	Trachsel	Zarcher	Zürcher
Tyson	Theissen	Zercher	Zürcher
		Ziegenfoos	Sigafuss
Updegrave	Op de Graf	Zook	Zug

APPENDIX II

NAMES OF MODERATELY COMMON USE BY FOREIGNERS TAKING THE OATH OF ALLEGIANCE TO THE PROVINCE OR STATE OF PHILADELPHIA, 1727–1808 [1]

These names have entries sufficient (ordinarily 9 to 17, inclusive) to make two lines in the index of the publication, Pennsylvania Archives, second series, vol. 17.

This index covers (a) Names of foreigners who took the oath of allegiance, 1727–1775, and (b) immigration into Pennsylvania, 1786–1808

[The spellings and order are those of the index]

Acker	Cuntz	Geyer	Holtz
Ackerman		Gilbert	Hörner
Albert	Dammer	Giessler	Huss
Alleman	Detweiler	Glasser	Huntsecker
Anspach	Dewald	Glass	Hubner
Antonie	Diterichs	Gobell	Huth
Appel	Dill	Gottschalk	
Arent	Dick	Gramlich	Janson
	Diem	Gruber	Jordan
Bär	Dobler	Grün	
Bastian	Dörr	Grünwaldt	Kampff
Bader	Dreissbach	Guttman	Kärcher
Barth	Dürr		Kautz
Batholomus		Hamon	Katz
Bast	Eckel	Haus	Kaiser
Basler	Edelman	Haupt	Kappes
Backer	Eller	Haag	Keppler
Bald	Emmert	Haussman	Keil
Baker	Emrich	Häfener	Kirschner
Bentz	Engelhardt	Hann	Kircher
Beyerle	Ensminger	Hamm	Kleim
Benner	Endres	Hasler	Klockner
Berkman	Erb	Hauch	Klyne
Betz	Erhard	Heckman	Klapper
Bertsch	Eschelmann	Heinrich	Knabe
Berg	Essig	Heyer	Köhler
Beringer	Eschbacher	Herts	Köster
Bieber	Esch	Hein	Kopp
Blank		Henssel	Kriebiel
Blum	Faust	Heller	Kratz
Böhmer	Farnie	Hecker	Kreider
Bossert	Fetter	Heim	Krum
Bock	Feler	Henderich	Kunstman
Bott	Fegely	Heck	Kunkel
Bonet,	Fischbach	Henninger	Kuhlemann
Born	Foltz	Heylmann	
Boos	Förster	Herr	Lautermilch
Bower	Freund	Hetrich	Lambert
Böhm	Freitag	Hetzel	Lantz
Brechbuhll	Frederick	Henckels	Lautenschläger
Bruch	Friedle	Heger	Leher
Brucker	Frick	Heyser	Linder
Brobeck	Fuhrmann	Helt	Linck
Bremer		Heiss	Licht
Brenner	Gass	Henn	Lintz
Burkhalter	Gärtner	Hertzog	Lindeman
Buhler	Gabele	Hildebrand	Löhr
Buchman	Gantz	Hinkell	Long
	German	Hirsch	Lotz
Carl	Gerlach	Hofner	
Carle	Gesell	Holl	Mack
Christman	Gerster	Hostetter	Maul
Claus	Geiss	Hoffer	Mauss

[1] See comment pp. 275, 278.

NAMES OF MODERATELY COMMON USE BY FOREIGNERS, ETC.—Con.

Maag	Riegel	Selster	Vollmer
Mann	Riehl	Seybolt	Voltz
Marx	Richter	Seeger	
Mertz	Riess	Seidel	Wachter
Messerschmidt	Roodt	Sower	Walder
Moll	Rohrbacher	Sontag	Warner
Mumma	Rorer	Solomon	Waller
	Rorich	Speck	Wannamacher
Naas	Ruhl	Strome	Wall
Naffe	Russ	Stoll	Welde
Neidig	Ruppert	Stock	Weigell
Neff	Rudi	Strubel	Wendel
Nichols	Ruff	Steinmetz	Wertz
Nickel	Rupp	Stocker	Wentz
Nieman	Ruth	Steger	Weymer
Noll	Runckel	Steinbach	Wenger
		Steinmann	Werlie
Oberdorff	Sasamandshouse	Strauss	Wenssel
Opp	Sautter	Staudt	Welsch
Orth	Schnäble	Straub	Weibel
Orendorff	Schroter	Stamm	Weychell
Oswald	Schlachter	Stöhr	Weller
Otto	Scheibe	Stauch	Weidner
	Schenkel	Stark	Weyman
Paul	Schellenberger	Stoltz	Will
Paulus	Schaad	Staube	Wittmer
Peck	Schmeltzer	Summer	Wise
Petersohn	Schlosser	Süss	Witman
Peterman	Schaffner	Swartz	Wilt
Pfister	Schermann		Winkler
Pfeill	Schuller	Teich	Wild
Philip	Schuber	Theil	Wolfart
Potts	Schwenck	Theiss	Wurtz
	Schantz	Trump	Wunderlich
Rabe	Schram	Trautman	
Rau	Schweikharth		Zeyler
Reütter	Schoch	Unger	Zimmer
Reiter	Schatz	Uhl	Zoller
Reynold	Schaff	Ulmer	Zacharias
Reisinger	Schneck		Zorn
Reiss	Scheid	Vetter	
Rieger	Schilling	Vogler	

APPENDIX III

GERMAN NAME FORMS, ORIGINAL AND AMERICAN

Determining German contributions to 1790 America on a nomenclatural basis is complicated by remarkable variability in original usage, changes through misapprehension by neighbors and by the marshals of the census, and disguise through Anglicization.

Since statistical units in this inquiry are names in the generic sense, it is essential to generalize on changes in individual and family nomenclature in order to have guides to influences on alignment of names and hence on nomenclatural structure. Selection of names as indicators necessitates knowing the types of changes which entirely recast names and those which only slightly modified originals without obscuring them, and recognizing the conditions under which German name groups maintained or lost their identity in American usage.

Most studies of name changes of the Germans have given little attention to effects on nomenclatural structure. Such authorities as Rupp, Haldeman, and Kuhns (whose discussion is partly quoted in Appendix I) give attention to trends but do not measure results.

This study, particularly in its selection of indicative surnouns, must reckon with the forces which moved the individual in his name changes. An individual may have thought he was changing his name voluntarily, but actually he could do little but choose a new name from the few alternatives rated by his neighbors as suitable for names in the locality in which he lived and the society in which he moved. The terms open to him as a name were only those appropriate to the language spoken or appropriate to family nomenclature, in his locality. This distinction is important. As an agent affecting names, nomenclature is practically distinct from the language of general communication.

Name changes are directed by two forces: One, the social control, governing use as names, and evolving changes toward names of recognized similarity; the other, the linguistic control, governing use as terms in the language, but not ordinarily finding nomenclatural pattern and hence tending to produce obvious alterations.

The social control tended, in the 1790's as now, to force names into forms like other names, and was a reaction from the use of names as identifiers and classifiers of people. For example, the German name *Schmidt* was converted into *Smith* because associated with this more common name and drawn into the same classification. A German name *Schmidt* may soon have found that his neighbors in America referred to him as " a German with a name almost like *Smith*," or "a German with the name *Smith* spelled in German," and presently allowed himself to be known as *Smith* because it was more convenient to accept this classification than to resist it.

The linguistic control, in distinction, first modified the pronunciations of German names slightly, then developed new spellings to convey these new pronunciations. Sometimes the vagaries of English orthography let it to promote several sets of changes as each new spelling initiated a new pronunciation; in this manner, for example, *Albrecht* became *Albright*, which on misinterpretation became *Albrite*. The linguistic control, therefore, produced new forms of names considered to represent current pronunciations to better advantage in English orthography. Further illustrations are the changes from *Schwab* to *Swope*, *Alt* to *Ault*, *Rahn* to *Rawn*, *Amweg* to *Omwake*, these particular changes witnessing interpretation of broad *a* as *au*, *aw*, or *o*.

Although the social control functions through comparison of names, it is not dependent on requirements of speech. While family nomenclature is a department of language, it is always a distinct and peculiar category because of its high proportion of loan words or borrowed terms. Names of eighteenth century American usage included many old forms long since abandoned as common nouns in the English language, many borrowed by the English for use as names without otherwise influencing speech, and many which were introduced into American usage by bearers not of English origin. The social control therefore did not necessarily produce names on the English pattern, but on the order of other common names whatever their origin. For example, in localities where the Irish were numerous the names of German settlers tended toward Irish forms of names not even commonly used by the English. Hence, control of name changes effected through popular comparison of names is fairly distinct from control through general speech.

The linguistic control is commonly called Anglicization, but is perhaps better termed Americanization since it is the general control of speech, irrespective of whether it is English, or, if so, of the type of English. American speech was not always English in the localities where the Germans settled, but sometimes

Dutch, or possibly Swedish. American-English differed from the speech of England, neither attaining the standard of elegant English nor, on the other hand, following all the dialects of the motherland. It was also more Irish and Scotch than the native English, because infused with Irish and Scotch terms. In England, there were, of course, some English-speaking Irish and Scotch among the native English, but in America there was a mixture of these stocks such as to produce a modified language common to all the people.

Practically all name changes which destroyed the identity of original German groups were developed through the social control, blending names of recognized similarity. Resultant changes led directly to reconstruction of nomenclature. Names different in origin but enough alike in sound to be confused in localities where both were current inclined to develop various intermediate forms while their original groupings tended to disappear.

Name changes resulting from confusion are best observed in the instances where they did not effect complete fusion of name groups; as changes to simulate *Taylor*, where the Germans used *Baylor* for *Beiler*, *Caylor* for *Koehler*, *Saylor* for *Seiler*—names which show imitation of *Taylor* without submerging the modified names in that group. Also, a number of German names changed final *li* or *lich* to *ley* without losing their identity; *Eberli* becomes *Everley*; *Ehrli*, *Earley*; *Markli*, *Markley*; *Wörlich*, *Worley*; examples of evolutionary imitation of names like *Bailey*, *Bradley*, *Buckley*, *Findley*, and *McKinley* (mainly Irish). These terminal changes caused the disappearance of but few German names, though *Stehli* changing to *Staley* (British) wrought a structural modification in the mixed nomenclature.

These changes based on recognized analogy with other names resulted very generally in the blending of name groups beyond the possibility of distinguishing the contributions of different nationalities in the resultant new group. For instance, it is practically impossible to determine German contributions to the *Roads* groups of American names because derivatives of German *Roth* are so inextricably confused with variants of the British name *Rhodes*. Nor is it possible to distinguish between German *Scherer* and Scotch *Shearer*, and these two distinct names are to be held jointly responsible for an American aggregate of names. The extraordinary complexities developed through structural evolution in American nomenclature are illustrated in the fusion of German *Koehler* and British *Collier;* this aggregate was partitioned by *CPG* analysts under the headings *Coller*, *Collier*, *Kayler*, and *Keeler*,[1] but the lines of national origin are not distinguishable.

Change by analogy is not dependent so much on the fact of analogy as on its assumption and hence results from both ease of comparison and from force of comparison. Consequently, interaction among name groups is controlled both by the absolute similarities in names, and by their frequencies. In instances of change such as from *Muldor* to *Miller* and from *Mertden* to *Martin*, it was the high frequencies of the established names (*Miller* and *Martin*) which forced comparison. For this reason, names selected as ultimately distinctive of German origin can be but slightly similar to names commonly used by other Americans. As German name groups subject to confusion with names of other origins in the eighteenth century had little chance of retaining their original groupings in American usage, from the tentative list of distinctive German names there must be eliminated those similar to names introduced by people of other origins on a test of similarity grounded in the reactions of the eighteenth century. Name groups ultimately distinctive of German

---

[1] *CPG*, table 111.

origin can be only those which contain forms dissimilar to names introduced by other people.

Whether meaning prompted the association of names, is a very important point in the study of name evolution through social control. The author believes that changes of name based on similarity in meaning unsupported by analogy of form are not extensive, but more exact knowledge might show that translation occasioned the disappearance of considerable numbers of people from the ranks of those bearing German names. A question arises, for example, whether *Zimmerman* was likely to be closely associated with *Carpenter*, an independent British name of the same meaning. Only comparison of the American occurrences of the two names would reveal whether a shortage in the measures of *Zimmerman* was balanced by an excess in the measures of *Carpenter*. This would require extended comparison of British-American and German nomenclatures, but such tests would indicate the extent to which analogy of meaning, considered alone, is effective in producing changes. Inasmuch as German stock is to be determined by reference to Pennsylvania as a base of comparison, bias arising from this type of translation may be prevented by examination of the occurrence of *Zimmerman* among German names in other States relative to its occurrence in Pennsylvania. Secondary features of translation will be discussed later.

In contrast to the use of names as identifiers and classifiers of persons, their use as terms in the language is influenced by more abstract considerations. Linguistic control of changes may be defined as the evolution of names by the general influence of the American dialect of the English language, directing cultural changes in names, in contrast to the practical changes directed by social control. Linguistic modifications included mainly adaptations in pronunciation, and a great variety of changes in spelling with the intent to represent in English orthography either original or modified pronunciations. As changes of pronunciation may be recognized only by spellings employed in the records, study of spellings is paramount in the appraisal of linguistic control.

American spellings of German names were subject to phonetic laws but not strictly controlled by them. Despite considerable regularity, the laws were not uniformly operative. Kuhns[2] summarizes normal phonetic changes. As a mere example, German *u* was generally represented by *oo*, as *Hoon* for *Huhn*, *Fooks* for *Fuchs*, *Hoober* for *Huber*. German vowels were more subject to change than their consonants. Changes from *i* to *y*, *k* to *c*, and *b* to *v* were frequent; interchange of *f* and *v*, *b* and *p*, *d* and *t*, common. One of the most regular changes through American spelling was the simplification of *sch* to *sh* or to *s*.

Irregularity in phonetic changes of names is probably accounted for by three factors—the bearer's idiosyncrasy, local geographical conditions, and permissible variability based on original variability. Bearers of the same original foreign name were not all influenced in the same way by the forces for change, and those who were did not react identically. Alternatives in nomenclature were always available and phonetic laws controlled only the alternatives and were not absolutely determinative. Local conditions probably were the chief influence for variations in degree and character of modifications. Presumably in some localities the original name was well understood, while in others one or more elementary forces for change were effective.

Name spelling is not controlled by fixed standards as is word spelling, and in colonial times even the latter was not rigidly controlled.

---

[2] Kuhns, *Studies in Pennsylvania German Family Names.*

As this discussion is concerned particularly with the evolution of German name groups in American usage, it suffices to point out that much of the variety in name usage by early German-Americans was based on variety in antecedent usage. For example, a name spelled variously with *f*, *ff*, *v*, or occasionally *ph*, does not necessarily indicate its evolution toward a convenient English spelling, but may merely betoken its original variability. The units under consideration here are groups originally containing some supplementary forms, and American variability is partly carried over from original diversity. For example, forms of *Schultz* in Pennsylvania do not demonstrate extraordinary irregularity in American spelling of the name, for Heintze notes 13 genuine German variants of the root. German usage comprises forms ranging from *Schultheiss* to *Scholzen* and also sets a precedent for *ts* instead of *tz* or *z*. The only definite Americanization in the American *Shultz* group is the common elimination of *c*, the forms beginning with *sh* instead of *sch*. Important entries of this surnoun in Pennsylvania include *Schultz* 5, *Shilt* 2, *Shiltz* 2, *Sholes* 2, *Sholts* 5, *Sholtz* 4, *Shoults* 3, *Shults* 3, *Shultz* 27, *Shulz* 3.

Entries in the 1790 census usually show, among a number belonging to the same German group, some with the original name little changed, if at all, and others with new forms derived through various processes. For example, of the 162 entries, in the Pennsylvania census, assigned to *Huber*, the original leading form, *Huber*, has 71, indicating perhaps that its bearers lived in localities very solidly settled by Germans. *Hoover*, the ultimate Americanization, has 59 entries; *Hover*, the secondary Americanization, 11, changing *b* to *v* without changing *u* to *oo*. A number changed the original *u* to *oo* without changing *b* to *v*, as *Hoober* 8; others show *f* instead of *b* or *v*, a use of *f* which may have been carried over from original German conditions, or may indicate a phase in evolution later than the change from *b* to *v*, for *f* is interchangeable with *v*. Forces for Americanization were not completely operative in Pennsylvania and the original form *Huber* was the one most widely used, but the State census shows 11 different forms which may be assigned with fair certainty to the *Huber* group. Outside of Pennsylvania only two instances are found of the spelling originally dominant. Records of States further south show four more forms, forces for Americanization tending to bring *Hoover* to the fore, with *Hover* as its principal supplement.

Generally a German group shows 10 or 12 forms for Pennsylvania alone, and derivatives in the South show nearly as many more. But diversity in content of German name groups in the 1790 census is not without limit. For some surnouns, apparently only a few of the possible spellings were acceptable; *Fink*, *Funk* and *Rudolph*, for example, show little diversity.

What changes through linguistic control produced new groupings of names is debatable, but observation indicates that this development is rare. The natural grouping of Americanized German names generally followed the lines of the original grouping if changes through social control did not evolve blended groups. Americanization usually affected only the content of the groups and was not a force for change strong enough to destroy original relationships. Nevertheless linguistic evolution includes some changes disruptive of original groupings and very difficult to trace, some of them responsible for separation of name groups and some for revival of old names.

Divergent group elements, when identified, are here returned to their fold; but there may be some whose origin is not suspected. In *CPG*, connection is not shown between *Albrecht* and *Albright*, *Ehrlich* and *Early*, *Eberli* and *Everly*, *Steiner* and *Stoner*, *Schweizer* and *Switzer*, instances of apparent break with old world standards.

The almost unconscious reproduction of old names is illustrated in the use of *Good* and *Goode*. *Good* was a rare British name, and *Goode* local to Northamptonshire; but most bearers of these names listed in the 1790 census were Germans who converted *Guth* to *Good* or *Goode* probably without even knowing of the existence of these last two forms as names. Cases like these emphasize the distinction between the changes through linguistic control and those through social control.

The only Americanization which may be seriously destructive to original name groups is translation on the basis of meaning. Consideration of the extent to which translation disrupted the original structure of German nomenclature is consequently important for determining whether and when translatable names may be included in the list of selected indicators of German origin.

Translation proceeded under both the social and the linguistic control and the relationships of the two phases warrant a joint consideration. Analysis of the processes of name translation indicates four types: (1) Translation of German names into English equivalents, favored by analogy of form; (2) translation likewise of names but unfavored by similarities in form; (3) translation into words of approximately the same meaning and form; (4) translation into words of the same meaning but dissimilar in form. That neither these classifications nor a grouping of the first two as social and the last two as linguistic are entirely distinct is indicated by the conversion of *Guth* to *Good*, which was of the third type but could readily have been of the first type.

The first two types of translation are without the artificiality of the other two and are not only more active but more detrimental to nomenclatural determination of origins. The third and fourth complicate the inquiry but do not destroy evidences of origins. The first and third gain impetus from naturalness, whereas the second and fourth can only be intentional. For these reasons investigation of origins on the basis of names must guard most against confusion of evidence through type one; guard least against type four. That translation occurred under most unfavorable circumstances in indicated by finding *Fidler* with *Geiger*, *Joiner* with *Schreiner*, and even *Turnipseed* with *Ruebsamen*—changes of the fourth type.

The first type of translation doubtless became very effective in nomenclatural changes. Hence all names subject to such changes are eliminated from the tentative list of distinctive German names, thus disposing, for example, of *Becker*, *Scherer*, and *Koenig;* common changes from *Becker* to *Baker*, from *Scherer* to *Shearer*, and from *Koenig* to *King* being apparent.

It is questioned whether Pennsylvania Germans knew the meaning of their names well enough to recognize English equivalents in meaning when analogies in form did not suggest them. Translation based on meaning unaided by similarity of form, while not to be disregarded, lacks evidence of sufficient effectiveness to preclude using as definite indicators of German origin those names whose meanings were also represented by names of other origins. For example, *Jaeger*, *Schaffer*, and *Zimmerman* are retained as distinctive German names despite their translation to *Hunter*, *Shepherd*, and *Carpenter*, respectively. Inasmuch as calculations of absolute numbers of the stock are not based on the ratio of original bearers of these names to the total number of Germans, it is tentatively assumed that this type of translation was practiced fairly equally in different parts of the country, and does not interfere with calculations of relative numbers of Germans in the several States. This is mathematically tested in the study of German contributions, Chapter VII.

There are three reasons for disregarding translation other than that of the first type. First, people generally did not know the meaning of their own names. Kuhns[3] and Rupp[4] point out some changes based on pure meaning and some effort to educate people to these changes; but other evidence indicates that colonial Germans as a class were little aware of the significance of names. Second, the meanings of names, even if understood, were often so far disregarded that name changes were frequently merely empty transliteration, such as *Stonecypher* for *Steinschleifer* (stone polisher), *Balsgrove* for *Pfaltzgraf*, and many less extreme modifications quite disregarded original significance, indicating that meaning was not a vital factor in the evolution of new name forms. Third, had the colonial Germans made any studied effort to translate their names they might have disposed of a great mass of usage whose persistence despite opportunity for translation argues against the practice. Hence it appears that translation of German names, except when favored by other names of similar meaning and form in American nomenclature, was not a factor in disrupting the original structure of German nomenclature.

Summarizing the forces for name changes, with particular emphasis on changes affecting groupings, analysis uncovers such a measure of change of name applying to German nomenclature that many of the most important original German groups must be eliminated from the list of indicators of German origin, but reveals that the original German name groups maintained their integrity in the development of American nomenclature when they were not subject to general confusion with names of other origins already in use. German-American nomenclature in the eighteenth century developed through two controls: The social control, effective through comparison of names, tending to disrupt original groups and produce new nomenclatural alignments; and the linguistic control, concerned with the more general adaptation of names to American speech, tending to produce new forms still revealing original affiliations, and constituting with the unchanged German names, a recognizable German-American addition to American nomenclature. Evolution through the social control produced many radical changes; that through the linguistic control, mostly superficial modifications. Between these two millstones hardly half of the name uses of the German-speaking immigrants and their descendants were left " recognizably " German.

It is with due recognition of these circumstances that names are chosen as indicators of the stock.

---

[3] Kuhns, Studies, p. 321.
[4] Rupp, Interpretation of Names (appendix pp. 8, 9).

BIBLIOGRAPHY

The following bibliography varies in its content from part to part. On some topics the literature is copious and there is no need for an exhaustive list here. On other topics there is literature of a sort, and the list covers all references known. Again, on other topics there is little closely to the point, and the record is almost entirely one of suggestive reading.

The captions employed here recognize the division of the text into studies of particular stocks, but the matter of correlation, which is represented in the text by the one chapter on interpretation of names, has five subdivisions here.   H. F. B.

THE POPULATION OF 1790, ITS COMPOSITION AND GENERAL HISTORY

ABBOTT, WILBUR CORTEZ. *The expansion of Europe; a social and political history of the modern world, 1415–1789.* 2 v. in 1. New York, 1924.

ADAMS, JAMES TRUSLOW. *Provincial society, 1690–1763.* New York, 1927. *History of American Life* series, Vol. III.

> A survey of the population by origin, p. 1–10.

BELCHER, ERNEST A. C., and WILLIAMSON, JAMES A. *Migration within the Empire.* London, 1924.

> The first six chapters provide an excellent survey of expansion from Britain and settlement in the colonies to the end of the eighteenth century.

BELKNAP, JEREMY. *The history of New Hampshire.* 3 v. Boston, 1813.

> 1st ed.: Vol. I, Philadelphia, 1784; Vol. II, Boston, 1791; Vol. III, Boston, 1792. Other editions: Dover, 1812, 1831, 1862.
> One of the State histories written at the end of the eighteenth century. See also Proud, Ramsay, Trumbull, and Williamson, for histories of other States.

BLODGET, SAMUEL. *Economica; a statistical manual for the United States of America* . . . Washington, 1806.

—————— —————— *Thoughts on the increasing wealth and national economy of the United States of America.* Washington, 1801.

BOLTON, HERBERT E., and MARSHALL, THOMAS M. *The colonization of North America, 1492–1783.* New York, 1920, 1927.

> Particularly Chapters XII, XVII, XVIII.

BROMWELL, WILLIAM J. *History of immigration into the United States . . . 1819 to . . . 1855 . . . with an introductory review of the progress and extent of immigration . . . prior to 1819 . . .* New York, 1856.

> P. 13–16, pertinent part of the introduction.

CHALMERS, GEORGE. *An introduction to the history of the revolt of the American colonies . . .* 2 v. Boston, 1845.

> Vol. I appeared in 1782 and was suppressed. The present edition reprints that volume, and gives the remaining contents of the original manuscript.

CHICKERING, JESSE. *A statistical view of the population of Massachusetts, from 1765 to 1840.* Boston, 1846.

———— ———— *Immigration into the United States.* Boston, 1848.

COMMONS, JOHN R. *Races and immigrants in America.* New York, 1907, 1920.

> Colonial race elements: Chap. II. Stresses the Scotch-Irish.
> References cited in footnotes; p. vii–xiii. .

COXE, TENCH. *A view of the United States of America . . .* Philadelphia, 1794.

CRÈVECOEUR, MICHEL GUILLAUME ST. JEAN DE. *Letters from an American farmer . . .* London, 1782.

———— ———— *Sketches of eighteenth century America; more Letters from an American farmer.* New Haven 1925.

DEXTER, FRANKLIN BOWDITCH. *A selection from the miscellaneous historical papers of 50 years.* New Haven, 1918.

> Estimates of population in the American colonies, p. 153–178. Reprinted from the proceedings of the *American Antiquarian Society* for October, 1887.

DOYLE, JOHN ANDREW. *The American colonies previous to the Declaration of Independence.* London, 1869.

EBELING, CHRISTOPH DANIEL. . . . *Erdbeschreibung und geschichte von Amerika. Die Vereinten Staaten von Nord-amerika . . .* 7 v. Hamburg, 1793–1916.

EGLE, WILLIAM H., *ed. Names of foreigners who took the Oath of Allegiance to the Province and State of Pennsylvania, 1727–1808, with the foreign arrivals, 1786–1808.* Harrisburg, 1892.

> Added title-page: Pennsylvania Archives, series 2, Vol. XVII.

FAIRCHILD, HENRY PRATT. *Immigration, a world movement and its American significance.* Rev. ed. New York, 1925.

FARRAND, MAX. *The development of the United States from colonies to a world power.* Boston and New York, 1918.

FAUST, ALBERT BERNHARDT. *The German element in the United States* . . . 3d. ed. 2 v. in 1. New York, 1927.

> A comprehensive work; full outline, numerous citations, and extensive bibliography.

FELT, JOSEPH B., comp. *Collections of the American Statistical Association.* Boston, 1847.

> Statistics of population in Massachusetts: Vol. I, Pt. II, p. 212–214. For material concerning strangers in 1777, see p. 165.

FLICK, ALEXANDER C. *Modern world history, 1776–1926; a survey of the origins and development of contemporary civilization.* New York, 1926.

> The first four chapters present the picture for eighteenth century America.

HARLOW, RALPH V. *The growth of the United States.* New York, 1925.

HIGBY, CHESTER PENN. *History of Europe (1492–1815).* New York, 1927.

HUGUENOT SOCIETY OF AMERICA. *Tercentenary celebration of the promulgation of the Edict of Nantes* . . . *1598.* New York, 1900.

> A collection of papers.

JAMESON, JOHN FRANKLIN. *American blood in 1775.*

> Manuscript.

—— —— *The American revolution considered as a social movement.* Princeton, 1926.

JOHNSON, STANLEY CURRIE. *A history of emigration from the United Kingdom to North America, 1763–1912* London, 1913.

> Ch. I treats 1763–1815.

KINGDOM, WILLIAM, Jr. *America and the British colonies.* London, 1820.

KUHNS, L. OSCAR. *The German and Swiss settlements of colonial Pennsylvania* . . . New York, 1901.

LEARNED, MARION DEXTER. *The Pennsylvania German dialect.* Pt. I. Baltimore, 1889.

LIPPINCOTT, ISAAC. *Economic development of the United States.* 2d ed. New York, 1927. New York and London, 1929.

> Exploration and settlement: Ch. III. Growth of population and extension of national domain, Ch. VII.
> Population in 1790, p. 144–146.

LODGE, HENRY CABOT. *A short history of the English colonies in America.* Rev. ed. New York and London, 1909.

MILLS, WILLIAM STOWELL. *Foundations of genealogy* . . . New York, 1899.

> History and genealogy, colonial history and stocks, Ch. II.
> Bibliography, p. 114.
> The first American book on systematic genealogical research.

NEW YORK GENEALOGICAL AND BIOGRAPHICAL SOCIETY. *Collections.* New York, 1890.
Marriages from 1639 to 1801 in the Reformed Dutch church, New York, Vol. I.

> This volume is remarkable for detail on origins of the persons listed, and illustrative of diversity in a so-called " racial " settlement.

OLDMIXON, JOHN. *The British Empire in America* . . . London, 1708, 1741.

OSGOOD, HERBERT L. *The American colonies in the seventeenth century.* 3 v. New York and London, 1904–1907.

——— ——— *The American colonies in the eighteenth century.* 4 v. New York, 1924.

PARKER, EDWARD L. *The history of Londonderry, comprising the towns of Derry and Londonderry, N. H.* Boston, 1851.

PHILLIMORE, WILLIAM P. W. *Pedigree work; a handbook for the genealogist* . . . 2d ed., rev. by T. M. Blagg. London, 1914.

> 1st ed. Chicago, 1881.

PROPER, EMBERSON E. *Colonial immigration laws; a study of the regulation of immigration by the English colonies in America.* New York, 1900.

PROUD, ROBERT. *The history of Pennsylvania* . . . *till after the year 1742* . . . Philadelphia, 1797–1798.

RAMSAY, DAVID. *The history of South Carolina, from* . . . *1670 to* . . . *1888.* 2 v. Charleston, S. C., 1809.

> Chapter I concerns population.

RHODE ISLAND HISTORICAL TRACTS. *Memoir concerning the French settlements in the colony of Rhode Island. Rhode Island historical tracts,* 1st series, No. 5, by Elisha R. Potter. Providence, 1879.

RUPP, ISRAEL DANIEL. *General remarks on the origin of surnames; interpretation of baptismal names, which occur in the Collection of thirty thousand names of German, Swiss, and other immigrants; to which are added other baptismal names, both males and females.* Harrisburg, 1856.

SCHOULER, JAMES. *Americans of 1776.* New York, 1906.

A study of the life and manners, social, industrial, and political, of the revolutionary period.

SEIDENSTICKER, OSWALD. *Geschichte der deutschen Gesellschaft von Pennsylvania. Von der Zeit der Gründung, 1764, bis zum Jahre 1876* . . . Philadelphia, 1876.

SEYBERT, ADAM. *Statistical annals; embracing views of the population [etc.] of the United States of America; founded on official documents* . . . *1789–1818.* Philadelphia, 1818.

STEPHENSON, GEORGE MALCOLM. *A history of American immigration, 1820–1924.* Boston, New York, [etc.], 1926.

STILLÉ, CHARLES JANEWAY. *Life and times of John Dickinson. 1732–1808* . . . Philadelphia, 1891.

SÜSSMILCH, JH. PT. *Gottliche Ordnung in d. Veränder. des menschl. Geschlechts.* Berlin, 1761. 3 v.

TRUMBULL, BENJAMIN. *A complete history of Connecticut* . . . *from* . . . *1630 to* . . . *1764.* 2 v. New Haven, 1818.

TUCKER, GEORGE. *Progress of the United States in population and wealth in fifty years* . . . New York, 1843.

In Chapter I the census of 1790 is discussed and compared with others to the sixth.

UNITED STATES, BUREAU OF THE CENSUS. *A century of population growth from the First census of the United States to the Twelfth. 1790–1900.* Washington, 1909.

Table 111, p. 227–270, gives a codification of some 3,600 names represented by at least 100 white persons, by States and territories, at the First Census, 1790.

———— ———— *Heads of families at the first census of the United States, taken in the year 1790.* 12 v. Washington, 1907 and 1908.

Covering the following States: Maine, New Hampshire, Vermont, Massachusetts, Rhode Island, Connecticut, New York, Pennsylvania, Maryland, North Carolina, South Carolina; and a record of the State enumerations (1782–1785) for Virginia.

UNITED STATES, SENATE DOCUMENTS. *National origin provision of the Immigration Act of 1924. Message from the President of the United States transmitting* . . . *a copy of the joint report of the Secretary of State, the Secretary of Commerce, and the Secretary of Labor, made to the President, in pursuance of section 11(E) of the Immigration Act of 1924.* United States 69th Congress, 2d sess., S. Doc. No. 190. Washington, 1927.

UNITED STATES, SENATE DOCUMENTS. *Immigration quotas on the basis of national origin. Message from the President of the United States transmitting . . . a copy of the joint report . . . relative to the provision of the Immigration Act of 1924.* United States 70th Congress, 1st sess., S. Doc. No. 65. Washington, 1928.

WILLIAMSON, HUGH. *The history of North Carolina.* 2 v. Philadelphia, 1812.

NOMENCLATURE OF AMERICA AND NORTHERN EUROPE

BARBER, HENRY. *British family names; their origin and meaning, with lists of Scandinavian, Frisian, Anglo-Saxon and Norman names.* London, 1894, 1903.

BARDSLEY, CHARLES W. E. *A dictionary of English and Welsh surnames, with special American instances* . . . London and New York, 1901.

————— ————— *English surnames; their sources and significations.* London, 1874, 1875.

BARKER, HOWARD F. Our leading surnames. *American Speech*, Vol. I, No. 9, June, 1926.

————— ————— Hall, Parker & Co., surnames. *American Speech*, Vol. I, No. 11, August 1926.

————— ————— Surnames in *-is*. *American Speech*, Vol. II, No. 7, April, 1927.

————— ————— How we got our surnames. *American Speech*, Vol. IV, No. 1, October, 1928.

BOWDITCH, N. I. *Suffolk surnames.* 3d ed. London and Boston, 1861.

> Concerns the Boston area particularly. The book is mainly a commentary on the analogies of names and words. In the preface to the 3d edition reference is made to a number of records dated 1789–1805. Index, p. 497–757.

COGSWELL, WILLIAM. Individual and family names. *New England Historical and Genealogical Register*, Vol. II (1848), p. 162–165.

CORNHILL MAGAZINE (LONDON). Surnames in England and Wales. *Cornhill Magazine*, Vol. XVII (1868), p. 405–420.

> Comment apparently by some member of the registrar's staff on frequencies shown by the registrar's files.

DIXON, BENJAMIN HOMER. *Surnames.* Boston, 1855. With supplement, Boston, 1857–1858.

> Gives particular attention to discrimination of national origins of of American names.

DUNLAP, FAYETTE. A tragedy of surnames. *Dialect Notes.* New Haven, 1913.

> Vol. IV, Pt. I, p. 7–8. Degeneration of Dutch, French, and Flemish names in Kentucky.

FARR, WILLIAM. Family nomenclature in England and Wales. *Sixteenth annual report of the Registrar-General of Births, Deaths, and Marriages in England* (London, 1856), p. xvii–xxiv.

> Published in the name of George Graham, Registrar-General.
> Transcribed in Lower's *Patronymica Britannica.*

FERGUSON, ROBERT. *Surnames as a science.* London and New York, 1883.

> See other works by this author. Not commonly considered trustworthy on derivations, but instructive on diverse origins of identical forms.

FOLKARD, ARTHUR. The multiplication of surnames. *The Antiquary.* (London), Vol. XIV, No. 81 (September 1886), p. 89–96.

FOX-DAVIES, ARTHUR C. *A treatise on the law concerning names and changes of names.* London, 1906.

> Excellent discussion of origins of names and customary usages in the several parts of the United Kingdom, p. 13–42.

GATES, SUSA YOUNG, ed. *Surname book and racial history* . . . Salt Lake City, 1918.

> Covers more names than any other American compilation.

GENTRY, THOMAS G. *Family names from the Irish, Anglo-Saxon, Anglo-Norman, and Scotch . . . with brief remarks on the history and languages of the peoples to whom we are indebted for their origin.* Philadelphia, 1892.

GILES, ARTHUR, comp. *The county directory of Scotland.* Edinburgh, 1912.

GUPPY, HENRY B. *Homes of family names in Great Britain.* London, 1890.

HARRISON, HENRY. *Surnames of the United Kingdom; a concise etymological dictionary.* 2 v. London, 1912–1918.

HEINTZE, ALBERT. *Die deutschen Familiennamen, geschichtlich, geographisch, sprachlich.* Halle, 1822, 1903, 1925.

> An etymological study giving consideration to ratios shown in enlistment records of 1870–71. The preface to the 1st edition reviews studies in the field from Foerstemann on.

HOLMES, FRANK R., *comp.* *Directory of the ancestral heads of New England families, 1620–1700.* New York, 1923.

> Includes discussion of names. Notes variations in spelling. Overly interested in medieval antecedents of names.

HOWELL, GEORGE ROGERS. *The origin and meaning of English and Dutch surnames of New York State families.* Albany (?), 1894 (?).

> A pamphlet of some value for Dutch names.

INGRAHAM, EDWARD D. *Singular surnames collected by late Edward D. Ingraham, Esq.* Edited by William Duane. Philadelphia, 1873.

> This is a really good treatment of curious names. It is valuable, too, as demonstrating the influence of ridicule on the desire to change a name.

KEIPER, PHILLIPP. *Französische Familiennamen in der Pfalz. (Neue urkindliche beiträge zur geschichte d. gelehrten Schulwesens im früheren Herzogt.)* Zweibrücken, 1891.

KRAPP, GEORGE PHILIP. *The English language in America.* 2 v. New York, 1925.

> Discussion on proper names, Chapter I, p. 169–224, with discussion on personal names, p. 200, 212, *ff.*, etc.

KREMERS, JOSEF. *Beiträge zur Erforschung der französischen Familiennamen.* Bonn, 1910.

> Excellent short history of names in France. Good on manifold origins, and on folk etymology. Good bibliography.

KUHNS, L. OSCAR. *Studies in Pennsylvania German family names.* New York, 1902.

> Reprinted from *Americana Germanica* (1902), p. 299–341.

LORDAN, C. L. *Of certain English surnames and their occasional odd phases when seen in groups.* London, 1874, 1879.

LOWER, MARK A. *Patronymica Britannica. A dictionary of the family names of the United Kingdom.* London, 1860.

> The preface includes notes on American, English, Welsh, Scottish, and Irish names; and reprints Graham's report.

————— ————— *English surnames. An essay on family nomenclature, historical, etymological, and humorous . . .* 3d ed., London, 1849.

MASSACHUSETTS, SECRETARY OF THE COMMONWEALTH. *List of persons whose names have been changed in Massachusetts, 1780–1892.* Boston, 1893.

> Index of original names, p. 313–417.
> Index of adopted names, p. 418–522.
> Illustrative of legalized changes; a class neither so numerous nor so varied as that comprising changes of less formal character.

MATHESON, *Sir* ROBERT E. *Special report on surnames in Ireland, wtih notes as to numerical strength, derivation, ethnology, and distribution based on information extracted from the indexes of the general register office.* Reprinted, with Terry's list of names of Irish septs, Dublin, 1909.

> Originally issued as an appendix to the *29th detailed annual report of the Registrar-General* . . . Dublin, 1894.

——— ——— *Varieties and synonyms of surnames and Christian names in Ireland* . . . Dublin, 1890.

> Compare Woulfe's work listed, p. 354.

McKENNA, LLEWELLYN B. *Surnames; their origin and nationality* . . . Quincy, Ill., 1913.

> Very superficial.

NATION, THE (NEW YORK). Transformation of surnames. *The Nation* (N. Y.) Vod. XLIV (1887) p. 230, 250, 272, 318, 342–343, 404.

> Letters to the editor, from various correspondents, concerning changes made by foreigners especially.

NOTES AND QUERIES (London). Variation of surnames. *Notes and Queries* (London) series 4, Vol. I (1868) p. 603; and Vol. II (1868) p. 91, 139, 167, 231–232.

> Letters to the editor, from various correspondents.

O'BRIEN, MICHAEL JOSEPH. *The McCarthys in early American history.* New York, 1921.

> Excellent pattern for a study of the bearers of a name, without undue emphasis on certain families.

SALVERTE, EUSÈBE. *Essai historique et philosophique sur les noms d'hommes, de peuples, et de lieux* . . . 2 v. Paris and Boston, 1824. Translated by L. H. Mordacque. 2 v. London, 1862–1864.

STARK, JAMES. Nomenclature in Scotland. *Sixth detailed annual report of the Registrar-General of Scotland* (1864) p. liv–lx.

——— ——— Nomenclature in Scotland. *Twelfth detailed annual report of the Registrar-General of Scotland* (1869) p. xlviii–li.

UNITED STATES, BUREAU OF THE CENSUS. *A century of population growth from the first census of the United States to the twelfth. 1790–1900.* Washington, 1909.

> Table 111, p. 227–270, gives a codification of some 3,600 names represented by at least 100 white persons, by States and territories, at the first census, 1790.

NOMENCLATURE AS A PART OF LANGUAGE

ANDRESEN, KARL G. *Konkurrenzen in der Erklärung der deutschen Geschlechtsnamen.* Heilbronn, 1883.

ARMITAGE, LIONEL. *An introduction to the study of Old High German.* Oxford, 1911.

BRADLEY, HENRY. *The making of English.* New York and London, 1904.

GESELLSCHAFT FÜR DEUTSCHE PHILOLOGIE IN BERLIN. *Jahresbericht über die Erscheinungen auf dem Gebiete der germanischen Philologie.* 49 v. Berlin and Leipzig, 1879–1930.

JESPERSON, JENS OTTO HARRY. *Growth and structure of the English language.* 4th ed., New York and Oxford, 1923.

———— ———— *Language; its nature, development and origin.* London, 1922.

———— ———— *The philosophy of grammar.* London and New York, 1924.

> Bibliography, p. 11–13.

KENNEDY, ARTHUR G. *A bibliography of writings on the English language from the beginning of printing to the end of 1922.* Cambridge, Mass., and New Haven, 1927.

> See index under proper and personal names.

KRAPP, GEORGE PHILIP. *The English language in America.* 2 v. New York, 1925.

KREMERS, JOSEF. *Beiträge zur Erforschung der französischen Familiennamen.* Bonn, 1910.

LANG, ANDREW. *The origin of terms of human relationship. Proceedings of the British Academy,* Vol. III (1908?).

> A few suggestive points about the identification and classification of humans.

MENCKEN, HENRY LOUIS. *The American language; an inquiry into the development of English in the United States.* 3d ed., rev. and enlarged. New York, 1923.

MÜLLER, FRIEDRICH MAX. *Lectures on the science of language* . . . 2 v. London, 1861–1864.

ORBECK, ANDERS. *Early New England pronunciation* . . . Ann Arbor, 1927.

> Many illustrations of modifications of names, especially naïve forms. Includes an investigation of county origins of English.

PALMER, ABRAM SMYTHE. *Folk-etymology* . . . London, 1882.

PROKOSCH, EDUARD. *The sounds and history of the German language.* New York, 1916.

SAPIR, EDWARD. *Language, an introduction to the study of speech.* New York, 1921.

SKEAT, WALTER WILLIAM. *Principles of English etymology.* 2 v. Oxford, 1891.

> 1st series; the native element.
> 2d series: the foreign element.

SWEET, HENRY. *A new English grammar, logical and historical.* 2 v. Oxford, 1900–1903.

VENDRYES, JOSEPH. *Language; a linguistic introduction to history.* Tr. by P. Radin. London and New York, 1925, 1931.

WEISE, OSKAR. Zur charakteristik der Volksetymologie. *Zeitschrift f. Völkerpsychologie u. Sprachwissenschaft*, 12 b. (Berlin, 1880), p. 203–223.

WRIGHT, JOSEPH. *Historical German grammar* . . . *Vol. I, phonology, word-formation and accidence.* Oxford, London, New York, and Toronto, 1907.

WYLD, HENRY C. K. *A history of modern colloquial English.* 2d ed. London, 1921.

INDEXES AND LISTS, PARTICULARLY LISTS SUITABLE FOR STUDY OF CURRENCY OF SURNAMES

There are many types of lists available, tax lists, calendars of wills, military rosters, etc., but really extensive lists are not numerous.

BELL, LANDON C. *The Old Free State; a contribution to the history of Lunenberg County and Southside Virginia.* 2 v. Richmond, 1927.

> This county originally embraced what are now six or seven counties. The book contains a great quantity of genealogical data.

BERGEN, TEUNIS G. *Register in alphabetical order, of the early settlers of Kings County, Long Island, N. Y., from its first settlement by Europeans to 1700; with contributions to their biographies and genealogies* . . . New York, 1881.

BOSTON REGISTRY DEPT. . . . *Records relating to the early history of Boston* . . . *Boston marriages, 1700–1751;* Vol. XXVIII (1899). *Boston marriages, 1752–1809;* Vol. XXX (1902).

BRADFORD, SAMUEL, *comp.* Names of the inhabitants of the town of Boston in 1790. *Twenty-second report of the record commissioners of the city of Boston* (1890), p. 443–511.

> Printed from the original manuscript in the library of the New England Historical and Genealogical Society.

CASEY, JOSEPH J., *comp.* *Personal names in Hening's statutes at large of Virginia (13 vols. to 1792) and Shepherd's continuation (3 vols.).* New York, 1896.

CLEMENS, WILLIAM MONTGOMERY, *ed.* AND *comp.* *American marriage records before 1699.* Pompton Lakes, N. J., 1926.

> Mainly from the records of New England, New York, and New Jersey.

DAUGHTERS OF THE AMERICAN REVOLUTION. *Index of the Rolls of Honor (Ancestor's Index) in the Lineage Books of the National Society of the Daughters of the American Revolution.* Vols. I–XL. Pittsburgh, 1916.

DRAKE, SAMUEL GARDNER. *Result of some researches among the British archives for information relative to the founders of New England; made in the years 1858, 1859, and 1860. Originally collected for and published in the New England Historical and Genealogical Register, and now corrected and enlarged.* Boston, 1860.

EGLE, WILLIAM HENRY. *Pennsylvania genealogies; Scotch-Irish and German.* Harrisburg, 1886, 1896.

FARMER, JOHN. *A genealogical register of the first settlers of New England* . . . Lancaster, Mass., 1829.

> Forms the basis of Savage's genealogical dictionary.

FORCE, PETER, *ed.* *Tracts and other papers relating principally to the origin, settlement, and progress of the colonies in North America* . . . *to* . . . *1776.* Washington, 1836–1846.

> Letter to the trustees for establishing the colony of Georgia . . . signed by settlers, freeholders, and inhabitants of Georgia: Vol. I, Ch. IV, p. 37–42.
> List of signers, p. 41–42.
> Letter similar to that above, Vol. I, appendix, No. 8, p. 51–56.
> List of signers, p. 54–56.

GENEALOGICAL SOCIETY OF PENNSYLVANIA. *Publications.* Lancaster, 1895–1920.

GREER, GEORGE CABELL. . . . *Early Virginia immigrants.* (*1623– 1666.*) Richmond, 1912.

This contains nearly 25,000 names in alphabetic order, but no notes on antecedents.

HOTTEN, JOHN CAMDEN, *ed. The original lists of persons . . . who went from Great Britain to the American plantations, 1600–1700 . . .* From MSS. in the public record office, England. London, 1874.

Various lists and fragments of records. Note particularly the lists of persons sent to the Barbadoes, p. 315–344. And those sent from the Barbadoes to New England, Carolina, Virginia, and New York, p. 347–418.

MACKENZIE, GEORGE N., AND RHOADES, NELSON O., *editors. Colonial families of the United States of America . . . 1607 to . . . 1775.* 7 v. New York and Boston, 1907–1920.

MYERS, ALBERT COOK. *Quaker arrivals at Philadelphia, 1682–1750; being a list of certificates of removal received at Philadelphia monthly meeting of Friends.* Philadelphia, 1902.

Small volume, indexed. Gives the original home of most of the persons listed.

NEAD, DANIEL W., *comp.* Index to the proper names mentioned in the proceedings and addresses of the Pennsylvania-German society, Vol. I–VI. *Proceedings and addresses of the Pennsylvania-German society,* Vol. VIII (Lancaster, 1898), p. 1–100.

Covers about 15,000 entries under some 4,700 surnames.

NEW ENGLAND HISTORICAL AND GENEALOGICAL REGISTER. *Index to genealogies and pedigrees in the New England historical and genealogical register for 50 years . . . 1847 (Vol. I) to . . . 1896 (Vol. L).* Compiled by William W. Wight . . . Boston. Reprinted from the *New England Historical and Genealogical Register* for 1896.

Index to genealogies and pedigrees. Boston, 1896.
Index of persons. Boston, 1905–1907.

NEW JERSEY, ADJUTANT GENERAL'S OFFICE. *Official register of officers and men of New Jersey in the revolutionary war.* Compiled . . . by Wm. Scudder Stryker, adjutant general, Trenton, 1872.

Two good lists of privates; continental troops, p. 140–318; State troops, p. 484–831. No index of all officers and men. Illustrative of many other military records.

118640—32——22

NEW YORK GENEALOGICAL AND BIOGRAPHICAL SOCIETY. *Collections.* New York, 1890+. *Marriages from 1639 to 1801 in the Reformed Dutch church, New York,* Vol. I.

This volume is remarkable for detail on origins of the persons listed, and illustrative of diversity in a so-called " racial " settlement.

NEW YORK (CITY) ORPHANMASTERS. *The minutes of the orphanmasters of New Amsterdam, 1655–1663.* Tr. and edited by Berthold Fernow. 2 v. New York, 1902–1907.

Good index, though short.

PENNSYLVANIA ARCHIVES. *Names of persons for whom marriage licenses were issued in the Province of Pennsylvania previous to 1790.* Series 2, Vol. II. Harrisburg, 1874–1875.

—— —— *Record of Pennsylvania marriages prior to 1810.* Series 2, Vol. VIII, Harrisburg, 1878.

Listed under the names of the various churches.

—— —— *Names of foreigners who took the oath of allegiance to the Province and State of Pennsylvania, 1727–1775; with the foreign arrivals, 1786–1808.* Series 2, Vol. XVII, Harrisburg, 1892.

—— —— *Tax lists, about 1767 to 1786, arranged by townships.* Series 3, Vols. XI—XXII, Harrisburg, 1897.

RUPP, ISRAEL DANIEL, ed. *A collection of thirty thousand names of German, Swiss, Dutch, French, Portuguese, and other immigrants in Pennsylvania; chronologically arranged from 1727 to 1776 . . .* Harrisburg, 1856.

Compare with the Oath of Allegiance lists, mentioned above.

SAVAGE, JAMES. *A genealogical dictionary of the first settlers of New England.* 4 v. Boston, 1860–1862.

UNITED STATES, BUREAU OF THE CENSUS. *Heads of families at the first census of the United States, taken in the year 1790.* 12 v. Washington, 1907 and 1908.

Covering the following States: Maine, New Hampshire, Vermont, Massachusetts, Rhode Island, Connecticut, New York, Pennsylvania, Maryland, North Carolina, South Carolina; and a record of the State enumerations (1782–1785) for Virginia.

VIRKUS, FREDERICK A., ed. *The abridged compendium of American genealogy.* 4 v. Chicago, 1925–1930.

Vol. I contains 5,000 records and 7,000 lineages.
Vol. II contains 1,600 records and 5,000 lineages.
Both volumes are indexed, and there is a tabulation of principal immigrant ancestors.

ECONOMIC AND SOCIAL ASPECTS: INTERCONNECTIONS OF STATES, INTER-
RELATIONS OF POPULATION GROUPS, FUSION OF STOCKS, DISPERSION OF
DECENDANTS OF FIRST SETTLERS

BEARD, CHARLES ADAMS. *Economic origins of Jeffersonian democ-
racy.* New York, 1915.

BOGART, ERNEST LUDLOW. *An economic history of the United States.*
4th ed., New York, 1925. Reprinted, New York, 1929.

BRUCE, PHILIP ALEXANDER. *Social life of Virginia in the seventeenth century.* Richmond, 1907.

DIFFENDERFFER, FRANK RIED. *The German immigration into Pennsylvania through the port of Philadelphia from 1700 to 1775.*
Lancaster, 1900.

> The redemptioners, Pt. II.

DOUGLASS, WILLIAM. *A summary, historical and political, of the
first planting, progressive improvements, and present state of the
British settlements in North-America* . . . Boston, 1747 [etc.];
London, 1760.

FAULKNER, HAROLD UNDERWOOD. *American economic history.* New
York and London, 1924, 1928, 1931.

> The westward movement before the revolution: Ch. VI.
> Bibliography: p. 138–139.
> Treats areas rather than stocks.

HART, ALBERT BUSHNELL, *ed. The American nation; a history from
original sources by associated scholars.* 28 v. New York and
London, 1904–1918.

> Particularly the first 10 volumes.

HERRICK, CHEESMAN A. *White servitude in Pennsylvania* . . .
Philadelphia, 1926.

HULBERT, ARCHER BUTLER. *Historic highways of America* . . . 16
v. Cleveland, 1902–1905.

————— ————— *The paths of inland commerce; a chronicle of trail,
road, and waterway.* New Haven, 1920.
> *Chronicles of America* series, Vol. XXI.

JOHNSON, ALLEN, *ed. The Chronicles of America.* Series, 49 v.
New Haven, 1918–1921.
> Particularly the first 16 volumes.

JONES, HOWARD MUMFORD. *America and French culture, 1750–1848.*
Chapel Hill, N. C., and London, 1927.

> The chapters on "the rise of conflicting forces" are highly instructive
> of the social and psychological developments bearing on the formation of a
> modified nomenclature on an English pattern. Nomenclature is not specifi-
> cally considered.

KERCHEVAL, SAMUEL. *A history of the valley of Virginia.* 3d ed., Woodstock, Va., 1902. Rev. ed. Strasburg, Va., 1925.

KRAUS, MICHAEL. *Intercolonial aspects of American culture on the eve of the revolution, with special reference to the northern towns.* New York and London, 1928.

LALOR, JOHN J., *ed. Cyclopaedia of political science, political economy, and of the political history of the United States* . . . 3 v. New York, 1904.

First published, Chicago, 1881.

PARRINGTON, VERNON LOUIS. *Main currents in American thought; an interpretation of American literature from the beginnings to 1920.* 3 v. New York, 1927–1930.

Vol. I, the colonial mind, 1620–1800.

PAXSON, FREDERIC LOGAN. *History of the American frontier, 1763–1893.* Boston, 1924.

SCHLESINGER, ARTHUR MEIER. *New viewpoints in American history.* New York, 1926.

SCHOULER, JAMES. *Americans of 1776.* New York, 1906.

A study of the life and manners, social, industrial, and political, of the revolutionary period.

SEMPLE, ELLEN CHURCHILL. *American history and its geographic conditions.* Boston and New York, 1903.

SIMONS, ALGIE MARTIN. *Social forces in American history.* New York, 1911. Reprinted, New York, 1912.

TURNER, FREDERICK JACKSON. *The frontier in American history.* New York, 1920, [etc.], 1926.

UNITED STATES, LIBRARY OF CONGRESS. *American and English genealogies.* 2d ed. Washington, 1919.

WEEDEN, WILLIAM BABCOCK, *Economic and social history of New England, 1620–1789.* 2 v. Boston and New York, 1891.

STOCKS GIVEN ONLY PASSING CONSIDERATION IN THIS REPORT: DUTCH, FRENCH, JEWS, SWEDES, AND OTHERS

ACRELIUS, ISRAEL. *A history of New Sweden; or, the settlements on the River Delaware.* Tr. from the Swedish by William M. Reynolds. Publications of the historical society of Pennsylvania, *Memoirs,* Vol. XI, Philadelphia, 1874. First published in Stockholm, 1759.

An exact list and roll of all the men, women, and children which are found and still live [1693] in New Sweden, now called Pennsylvania, on the Delaware River, p. 190.

BAIRD, CHARLES, WASHINGTON. *History of the Huguenot emigration to America.* 2 v. New York, 1885.

Many names of colonists are given. Index at end of Vol. II.

BERGEN, TEUNIS G. *Register in alphabetical order, of the early settlers of Kings County, Long Island, N. Y., from its first settlement by Europeans to 1700: with contributions to their biographies and genealogies . . .* New York, 1881.

BRODHEAD, JOHN ROMEYN. *History of the State of New York.* 2 v. New York, 1853–1871.

Vol. I covers the period from 1609 to 1664.

COMPANIUS HOLM, THOMAS. *A short description of the Province of New Sweden, now called, by the English, Pennsylvania, in America . . .* Tr. from the Swedish . . . by Peter S. Du Ponceau. Philadelphia, 1834.

The original was first published in Stockholm in 1702.
Comment on names, p. x.
Families in New Sweden in 1693, p. 164.

CHINARD, GILBERT. *Les réfugiés Huguenots en Amérique . . .* Paris, 1925.

DIONNE, NARCISSE EUTROPE. *Les Canadiens-Français. Origine des familles émigrées de France, d'Espagne, de Suisse, etc. . . . et Signification de leurs noms.* Quebec, 1914.

Recognizes Swiss and Spanish in this stock.

EVJEN, JOHN OLUF. *Scandinavian immigrants in New York, 1630–1647. . . .* Minneapolis, 1916.

Distribution of Scandinavians before 1674, p. xii. German immigrants in New York, 1630–1674, Appendix IV, p. 390–436.

FERNOW, BERTHOLD. *New Amsterdam family names and their origin.* New York and London, 1898.

Instructive pamphlet.

FLOM, GEORGE TOBIAS. *A history of Norwegian immigration to the United States from the earliest beginning down to the year 1848.* Iowa City, Iowa, 1909.

The earliest immigrants from Norway, 1620 to 1825, Ch. III.

FRANCE. MINISTÈRE DE LA GUERRE. *Annuaire officiel de l'armée française pour 1914.*

Contains extensive lists for determining the currency of names.

GOODWIN, MAUD WILDER. *Dutch and English on the Hudson; a chronicle of colonial New York.* New Haven, 1919, 1921.

Chronicles of America series, vol. VII.

HIRSCH, ARTHUR HENRY. *The Huguenots of colonial South Carolina.* Duke Univ. publication, Durham, N. C., 1928.

HOES, ROSWELL RANDALL, ed. *Baptismal and marriage registers of the old Dutch church of Kingston, Ulster County, New York. . . . for one hundred and fifty years from their commencement in 1660.* New York, 1891.

    Not an exclusively Dutch congregation.

INNES, JOHN H. *New Amsterdam and its people; studies, social and topographical, of the town under Dutch and early English rule.* New York, 1902.

JAMESON, JOHN FRANKLIN, ed. *Narratives of New Netherland, 1609–1664.* New York, 1909.

    Published in the *Original narratives of early American History* series.

JOHNSON, AMANDUS. *The Swedish settlements on the Delaware; their history and relation to the Indians, Dutch and English, 1638–1664 . . .* 2. v. Philadelphia and New York, 1911.

    List of officers, soldiers, servants and settlers in New Sweden, 1638–1656, Vol. II, appendix B, p. 699–726.
    Bibliography, specific and general, p. 767–812.

JONES, HOWARD MUMFORD. *America and French culture, 1750–1848.* Chapel Hill, N. C., and London, 1927.

MARGOLIS, MAX L., AND MARX, ALEXANDER. *A history of the Jewish people.* Philadelphia, 1927.

    Jews in America in colonial and revolutionary times (1654–1790), Ch. LXXIX, p. 603–607.

NEW YORK GENEALOGICAL AND BIOGRAPHICAL SOCIETY. *Collections.* New York, 1890.
    Marriages from 1639 to 1801 in the Reformed Dutch church, New York, Vol. I.

    This volume is remarkable for detail on origins of the persons listed, and illustrative of diversity in a so-called "racial" settlement.

PEARSON, JONATHAN. *Contributions for the genealogies of the first settlers of the ancient county of Albany, from 1630 to 1800.* Albany, 1872.

———— ———— *Contributions for the genealogies of the descendants of the first settlers of . . . Schenectady, from 1662 to 1800.* Albany, 1873.

PEARSON, JONATHAN, *tr.* *Early records of the city and county of Albany, and colony of Rensselaerswyck (1656–1675).* Tr. from the original Dutch . . . by Jonathan Pearson, Albany, 1869. (See also van Laer, below.)

> Index of names, p. 511.
> It was not until after 1675 that the nomenclature of New Netherland lost its patronymic features.

SCHOONMAKER, MARIUS. *The history of Kingston, New York.* From its early settlement to the year 1820. New York, 1888.

THWAITES, REUBEN GOLD. *France in America, 1497–1763.* New York and London, 1905.

> *American Nation* series, Vol. VII.

VAN LAER, ARNOLD JOHAN F., *tr.* AND *ed.* *Van Rensselaer Bowier manuscript.* Tr. and ed. by Arnold Johan F. van Laer. Albany, 1908.

> New York State Library history bulletin, no. 7. Well indexed.

—— —— *ed.* *Early records of the city and county of Albany, and colony of Rensselaerswyck* . . . Albany, 1869+.

> Vol. II, *ff*; succeeding Pearson.

WEISS, CHARLES. *History of the French protestant refugees* . . . Tr. from the French by Henry William Herbert. With an American appendix . . . 2 v. New York, 1854.

> The refugees of America, Vol. I, p. 327–382. American Huguenots, Vol. II, p. 283–333. Huguenot names found in the register of baptism [Manikin Town, in Virginia, see p. 320], p. 322.

WINKLER, JOHAN. De Nederlandsche Geslachtsnamen . . . 2 v. Haarlem, 1885.

—— —— Studiën in Nederlandsche Namenkunde. Haarlem, 1900.

ENGLISH STOCK, AND ENGLISH INFLUENCE ON NOMENCLATURE

BRADSLEY, CHARLES W. E. *Curiosities of Puritan nomenclature.* New York and London, 1880. 2d ed. London, 1897.

—— —— *English surnames, their sources and significations.* London, 1874, 1875.

—— —— *A dictionary of English and Welsh surnames, with special American instances* . . . London and New York, 1901.

BARING-GOULD, SABINE. *Family names and their story*. London, 1910.

BARKER, HOWARD F. Hall, Parker & Co., surnames. *American Speech*, Vol. I, No. 11, August, 1926.

BROWNING, CHARLES HENRY. *Welsh settlement of Pennsylvania*. Philadelphia, 1912.

CARY, D. M. How we got our surnames. *Word Lore*, Vol. I, No. 6, 6. p. 268–270. London, 1926.

CORNHILL MAGAZINE. Surnames in England and Wales. *Cornhill Magazine*, Vol. XVII (London, 1868), p. 405–420.

> Comment on the currency of names as shown by the registrar's files.

COX, JOHN CHARLES. *The parish registers of England*. London, 1910.

> List of printed parish registers, Appendix IV.

DOYLE, JOHN ANDREW. *English colonies in America*. 5 v. New York, 1882–1907.

FARR, WILLIAM. Family nomenclature in England and Wales. *Sixteenth annual report of the Registrar General of Births, Deaths, and Marriages in England* (London, 1856), p. xvii–xxiv.

> Published in the name of George Graham, Registrar-General.
> Transcribed in Lower's *Patronymica Britannica*.

FINLAYSON, JAMES. *Surnames and sirenames. The origin and history of certain family and historical names; with remarks on the ancient right of the crown to sanction and veto the assumption of names. And an historical account of the names Buggey and Bugg*. London, 1863.

GREAT BRITAIN, CENSUS OFFICE. Estimated population of England and Wales, 1570–1750, with table compiled by John Rickman. *Census 1841. Enumeration abstract* (London, 1843), Pt. I, p. 34–37. Based on parish records of baptisms, burials, and marriages.

GUPPY, HENRY B. *Homes of family names in Great Britain*. London, 1890.

HITCHING, F. K., AND S. *References to English surnames in 1601; an index giving about 19,650 references to surnames contained in the printed registers of 778 English parishes during the first year of the seventeenth century*. Walton-on-Thames, 1910.

> *References to English surnames in 1602; an index giving about 20,500 references to surnames contained in the printed registers of 964 English parishes during the second year of the seventeenth*

century. With an appendix indexing the surnames contained in 186 printed registers during 1601 (omitted from the volume for that year). London, 1911.

These two books together cover more than 40,000 references to the English parish registers of the early seventeenth century. •

LOWER, MARK A. *English surnames. An essay on family nomenclature, historical, etymological, and humorous* . . . 3d ed., London, 1849.

————— ————— *Patronymica Britannica. A dictionary of the family names of the United Kingdom.* London, 1860.

ORBECK, ANDERS. *Early New England pronunciation* . . . Ann Arbor, 1927.

Many illustrations of modifications of names, especially naïve forms. Includes an investigation of county origins of English.

TYLER, LYON GARDINER. *England in America, 1580–1652* New York and London, 1904.

American Nation series, Vol. IV.

WATERS, HENRY FITZ-GILBERT. *Genealogical gleanings in England.* 2 v. Boston, 1901. New series, ed. and arranged by Lothrop Withington, Salem, 1907.

WEEKLEY, ERNEST. *The romance of names.* London, 1914.
————— ————— *Surnames.* London, 1916, 1917. New York, 1927.

THE SCOTCH, THEIR NOMENCLATURE, AND THEIR PART IN COLONIAL HISTORY

ANDERSON, WILLIAM. *Genealogy and surnames* . . . Edinburgh, 1865.

BUCANAN, WILLIAM. *An inquiry into the genealogy and present state of ancient Scottish surnames; with the origin and descent of the Highland clans, and family of Buchanan.* 2 v. in 1. Edinburgh, 1723, 1775; Glasgow, 1820.

CRAIGHEAD, JAMES GEDDES. *Scotch and Irish seeds in American soil; the early history of the Scotch and Irish churches, and their relations to the Presbyterian Church of America.* Philadelphia, 1878.

DRAKE, SAMUEL GARDNER. *Result of some researches among the British archives for information relative to the founders of New England; made in the years 1858, 1859, and 1860. Originally collected for and published in the New England historical and genealogical register, and now corrected and enlarged.* Boston, 1860.

Scotch prisoners sent to Massachusetts in 1652, p. 72.
. . . these prisoners . . . may have been among those taken at Dunbar. 272 persons embarked on the "John and Sara" of London.

FRASER, G. M. Gaelic surnames. *Word Lore*, Vol. II, no. 6 (December, 1927), p. 192–195. London.

GIBBON, JOHN MURRAY. *Scots in Canada* . . . London, 1911.

GUPPY, HENRY B. *Homes of family names in Great Britain.* London, 1890.

HANNA, CHARLES AUGUSTUS. *The Scotch-Irish; or, the Scot in North Britain, North Ireland, and North America.* 2 v. New York and London, 1902.

> Map of settlements, Vol. II, frontispiece. Bibliography, Vol. II, p. 531–551.

INNES, COSMO NELSON. *Concerning some Scotch surnames.* Edinburgh, 1860.

JOHNSTON, JAMES B. *The Scottish Macs, their derivation and origin.* Paisley, 1922.

> Arranged in tabular form, with the following headings: Surname; Found to-day in; Root and meaning; Place of origin and early instances.

MACBAIN, ALEXANDER. *Etymology of the principal Gaelic national names, personal names and surnames* . . . Stirling, 1911. Reprinted from Macbain's *Etymological dictionary of the Gaelic language*, Inverness, 1896; Stirling, 1911.

———— ———— *Personal names and surnames of the town of Inverness.* Inverness, 1895.

> Summary and conclusion, p. 79–82. This summarizes the currency of these names by types.

MACLEAN, JOHN PATTERSON. *An historical account of the settlements of Scotch Highlanders in America prior to the peace of 1783* . . . Cleveland, 1900.

PERRY, ARTHUR. *Scotch-Irish in New England.* Boston, 1891. Reprinted from the *Proceedings of the Scotch-Irish Society of America*, 2d congress at Pittsburgh, Pa. (Cincinnati, 1890), p. 107–144.

> The length of residence in Ireland of a few of these families is given on p. 7–8.

REID, WHITELAW. *The Scot in America, and the Ulster Scot.* London, 1911, 1912.

ROSS, PETER. *The Scot in America.* New York, 1896.

SIMS, CLIFFORD S. *The origin and signification of Scottish surnames* . . . Albany, N. Y., 1862.

STARK, JAMES. Nomenclature in Scotland. *Sixth detailed annual report of the Registrar-General of Scotland* (Edinburgh, 1864), p. liv–lx.

———— ———— Nomenclature in Scotland. *Twelfth detailed annual report of the Registrar-General of Scotland* (Edinburgh, 1869), p. xlviii–li.

GENEALOGICAL MATERIALS ON BEARERS OF SCOTTISH SURNAMES UNDER STUDY

Special attention is given to family histories of the Scotch and Scotch-Irish because the clan spirit favors the compilation of records. In addition to what is found in works of the type below, material on American branches of the clans is to be looked for in genealogical periodicals and in local histories. The detail available on some names is much greater than on others. The clan and family name is listed in the first column below.

BLACK————— Clemens, Wm. M., *ed.* . . . *Early marriage records of the Black family in the United States . . . from 1628 to 1865.* New York, 1916.

BLAIR————— Blair, John Chalmers. *Scotch and Irish Blairs. Biographical sketches.* Huntingdon, Pa., 1894. Reprinted from several sources.

Buchanan, Roberdeau. *Blair family.* Washington, 1906.

Horner, Frederick. *The history of the Blair, Banister, and Braxton families* . . . Philadelphia, 1898.

Leavitt, Emily W. *The Blair family of New England.* Boston, 1900.

BOYD————— Boyd Association. *Proceedings of the first [seventh] Boyd reunion . . . 1881–1892.* Youngstown, Ohio, 1882–1894.

Boyd, Wm. P. *History of the Boyd family and descendants, with historical sketches of the ancient family of Boyd's in Scotland from the year 1200, and those of Ireland from the year 1680, with records of their descendants* . . . 1st ed., Conensus, N. Y., 1884, Rochester, N. Y., 1912.

Boyds in New York, Massachusetts, Pennsylvania, and Southern and Western States.

BOYD_____ Ayrshire and Galloway, Archaeological Association. *Archaeological and historical collections relating to Ayrshire and Galloway.* 10 v. Edinburgh, 1878–1899.

> The Boyd papers; Vol. III (1882), p. 110–111.

BRUCE_____ Weeks, Lyman H. *Book of Bruce* . . . New York, 1907.

> Special reference to the Bruces of Clackmannan, Cultmalindie, Caithness, and the Shetland Islands, and their American descendants.

BUCHANAN_____ Clemens, Wm. H. *Buchanan family records. An account of the first American settlers and colonial families of the name* . . . New York, 1914.

CAMERON_____ Mackenzie, Alexander. *History of the Camerons* . . . Inverness, 1884.

CAMPBELL_____ Numerous genealogies have been consulted for this name.

CUMMINGS_____ Cummins, Albert O. *Cummings genealogy* . . . Montpelier, Vt., 1904.

> Descendants of Isaac Cummings of Massachusetts, 1638.

Cummings, Coroden. *A record of the Cummings family* . . . Nashua (?), N. H., 1916.

CUNNINGHAM___ Several genealogies have been consulted for this name.

FERGUSON_____ Ferguson, James, and R. M. *Records of the clan and name of Fergusson, Ferguson and Fergus.* Edinburgh, 1895.

Ferguson, Martin L. *The Ferguson family in Scotland and America.* Canandaigua, N. Y., 1905.

> Settlement in Maryland particularly.

FLEMING_____ Hunter, Wm. *Biggar and the house of Fleming* . . . 2d ed., Edinburgh, 1867.

MAGRATH, JOHN R., ed. *The Flemings in Oxford, being documents selected from the Rydal papers, in illustration of the lives and ways of Oxford men, 1650–1700* . . . *Oxford historical society publications,* Vols. XLIV, LXII, LXXIX, Oxford, 1904–1924

> From the collection of manuscripts of S. H. le Fleming of Rydall Hall.

FORBES_____ Forbes, Wm., ed. *Genealogy of the family of Forbes.
From the account of Mathew Lumsden of Tul-
liekerne. Written in 1580 . . .* Inverness,
1819, 1883.
Ferguson, James. *Two Scottish soldiers . . .*
Aberdeen, 1888.
Pierce, F. C. *Forbes and Forbush genealogy. The
descendants of Daniel Forbush, who came from
Scotland about the year 1655 and settled in Marl-
borough, Mass., in 1675.* Chicago, 1892.

FRASER_____ _____ Several genealogies have been consulted
on this name.
Frazer, Persifor. *Persifor Frazer's descendants.*
2 v. Philadelphia, 1906–1907.

> Pennsylvanians of Irish descent.

GORDON_____ Bulloch, John Malcolm. *The name of Gordon;
Patronymics which it has replaced or reinforced.*
Huntly, 1906.
Gordon, Armistead C. *Gordons in Virginia, with
notes on Gordons of Scotland and Ireland.* Hack-
ensack, N. J., 1918.

> Numerous other genealogies have been consulted
> on this name, especially concerning bearers in Scotland.

HAMILTON_____ Phelps, James Andrew. *The Hamilton family in
America . . .* New York, 1913.

Hamilton, S. K. *The Hamiltons of Waterborough
(York County, Maine), their ancestors and descendants.* Boston, 1912.

LINDSAY_____ Linzee, John Wm. *The Lindeseie and Limesi families of Great Britain . . .* 2 v. Boston, 1917.

McDOWELL_____ McDowell, John Hugh. *History of the McDowells
and connections . . .* Memphis, 1918.

McGREGOR_____ Macleay, Kenneth. *Historical memoirs of Rob Roy
and the clan Macgregor . . . With an introductory
sketch illustrative of the condition of the Highlands,
prior to the year 1745.* Glasgow, 1818.

> Several genealogies have been consulted on this name;
> also publications of the Clan Gregor Society.

McLACHLAN_____ Brown, John Patrick. *The MacLaughlins of clan
Owen. A study in Irish history.* Boston, 1879.

McLeod_____ Macleod, Roderick C. *The Macleods; a short sketch of their clan, history, folk-lore, tales, and biographical notices of some eminent clansmen.* Edinburgh, 1906.

Matheson_____ Mackenzie, Alexander. *History of the Mathesons* . . . Edited, largely rewritten, and added to, by Alexander Macbain. 2d ed., Stirling and London, 1900.

Maxwell_____ Houston, F. A. (Wilson). *Maxwell history and genealogy* . . . Indianapolis, 1916.

Maxwell, Henry D. *The Maxwell family* . . . Easton, Pa., 1895.

Munro_____ Munroe, James Phinney. *A sketch of the Munro clan, also of William Munro who, deported from Scotland, settled in Lexington, Mass., and some of his posterity* . . . Boston, 1900.

Paton_____ Baldwin, Thomas W. *Patten genealogy. William Patten of Cambridge, 1635, and his descendants.* Boston, 1908.

Ritchie_____ ———— No genealogies have been found in book form.

Robertson_____ Osborne, Kate (H.), *ed. An historical and genealogical of Andrew Robeson, of Scotland, New Jersey, and Pennsylvania, and of his descendants from 1653 to 1916, begun by Susan Stroud Robeson, assisted by Caroline Franciscus Stroud, compiled, edited, and published by Kate Hamilton Osborne.* Philadelphia, 1916.

Ross_____ Read, Harmon P. *Rossiana; papers and documents relating to the* . . . *house of Ross* . . . *and* . . . *family of Read.* Albany, N. Y., 1908.
Wright, Anne J. (Mims), *comp. A record of the descendants of Isaac Ross and Jean Brown* . . . Jackson, Miss., 1911.

Sinclair_____ Sinclair, Thomas. *The Sinclairs of England.* London, 1887.
Morrison, Leonard A. *The history of the Sinclair family in Europe and America* . . . Boston, 1896.

STRACHAN_____ Rogers, Charles. *Memorials of the Scottish families of Strachan and Wise.* Edinburgh, 1877.

Austen-Leigh, Richard A. *The story of a printing house; being a short account of the Strahans and Spottiswoodes.* 2d ed., London, 1912.

Roberts, Ellwood. *Old Richland families . . .* Norristown, Pa., 1898.

SUTHERLAND___ Merritt, Douglas, *comp. Sutherland records.* New York, 1918.

THE IRISH, THEIR BACKGROUND, THEIR NOMENCLATURE, AND THEIR PART IN THE COLONIZATION OF AMERICA

AMERICAN-IRISH HISTORICAL SOCIETY. *The Journal of the American-Irish historical society.* New York, 1898–1927.

AUGUSTA COUNTY, VIRGINIA. *Chronicles of the Scotch-Irish settlements in Virginia extracted from the original court records of Augusta County, 1745–1800, by Lyman Chalkley.* Rosslyn, Va., 1912–13.

BAGENAL, PHILIP H. *The American Irish . . .* London, 1882.

BARNES, ISAAC O. *An address, delivered at Bedford, N. H., on the one hundredth anniversary of the incorporation of the town, May 19, 1850.* Boston, 1850.

BOLTON, CHARLES KNOWLES. *Scotch-Irish pioneers in Ulster and America.* Boston, 1910.

 Home towns of Ulster families, 1691–1718; Appendix VI, p. 339–377. Lists about 1,200 Irish surnames in New England and gives their home towns in Ireland. Mainly concerned with New England. Compare with the earlier works of Green, Hanna, and Perry.

BOLTON, HERBERT E., AND MARSHALL, THOMAS M. *The colonization of North America, 1492–1783.* New York, 1920, 1927.

 Particularly p. 322–326.

CHRISTIAN, BOLIVAR. *The Scotch-Irish settlers in the valley of Virginia.* Richmond, 1860.

CLEMENS, WILLIAM M., *ed.* AND *comp. American marriage records before 1699.* Pompton Lakes, N. J., 1926.

 Marriages of known date only, and mainly from the records of New England, New York, and New Jersey.

COMMONS, JOHN ROGERS. *Races and immigrants in America.* New York, 1807, 1920.

 Colonial race elements: Ch. II, stresses the Scotch-Irish.

CRAIGHEAD, JAMES GEDDES. *Scotch and Irish seeds in American soil; the early history of the Scotch and Irish churches, and their relations to the Presbyterian Church of America.* Philadelphia, 1878.

DE GOESBRIAND, LOUIS. *Catholic memoirs of Vermont and New Hampshire* . . . Burlington, 1886.

DINSMORE, JOHN WALKER. *The Scotch-Irish in America* . . . Chicago, 1906.

DUBLIN, N. H. *The history of Dublin, N. H.* . . . Boston, 1855. Reprinted and augmented, Dublin, N. H., 1920.

EGLE, WILLIAM HENRY. *Pennsylvania genealogies; Scotch-Irish and German.* Harrisburg, 1886, 1896.

ENO, JOEL N. Verified origin of Irish Gaelic clan names and family names abundant in America. *Americana* (American Historical Society), Vol. XXI (1927), p. 415–435.

FORD, HENRY JONES. *The Scotch-Irish in America.* Princeton, 1915.

FROUDE, JAMES ANTHONY. *The English in Ireland in the eighteenth century.* 3 v. New York, 1873–1874.

> Review of the history of Ireland during the sixteenth and seventeenth centuries: Vol. I, p. 1–270.

GARLAND, ROBERT. *The Scotch-Irish in western Pennsylvania.* Pittsburgh. 1923.

> Some specific names.

GREEN, SAMUEL SWETT. *The Scotch-Irish in America.* Worcester, 1895.

HALTIGAN, JAMES. *The Irish in the American revolution, and their early influence in the colonies.* Washington, 1908.

HANNA, CHARLES AUGUSTUS. *Ohio Valley genealogies, relating chiefly to families in* . . . *Ohio and* . . . *Pennsylvania.* New York, 1900.

———— ———— *The Scotch-Irish; or, the Scot in north Britain, north Ireland, and North America.* 2 v. New York and London, 1902.

> Map of settlements, Vol. II, frontispiece.
> Bibliography, Vol. II, p. 531–551.

HARRIS, JOSEPH SMITH. *Record of the Smith family descended from John Smith, born 1655, in County Monaghan, Ireland.* Philadelphia, 1906.

> Illustrative of intermarriages in Pennsylvania.

LECKY, WILLIAM EDWARD H. *A history of Ireland in the eighteenth century.* 5 v. New York, 1893.

LINEHAN, JOHN C. *The Irish Scots and the Scotch-Irish.* Concord, N. H., 1902.

McCORMICK, ANDREW P. *Scotch-Irish in Ireland and in America* ... New Orleans, 1897.

> Especially in North Carolina, Kentucky, Missouri, and Texas.

McGEE, THOMAS D'ARCY. *A history of the Irish settlers in North America, from the earliest period to the census of 1850.* Boston, 1851, 1852.

> The first 11 chapters deal with the period before 1790.
> The first Irish immigrants in New York, Pennsylvania, and the South, Ch. II.
> The Irish in New England, Ch. III.

MATHESON, *Sir* ROBERT E. *Varieties and synonymes of surnames and Christian names in Ireland* ... Dublin, 1890.

> Compare Woulfe's work below.

―――― ―――― *Special report on surnames in Ireland, with notes as to numerical strength, derivation, ethnology, and distribution, based on information extracted from the indexes of the General Register Office.* Reprinted, with Terry's list of names of Irish septs, Dublin, 1909.

> Originally issued as an appendix to the *29th detailed annual report of the Registrar-General* ... Dublin, 1894.

MYERS, ALBERT COOK. *Immigration of the Irish Quakers into Pennsylvania, 1682–1750, with their early history in Ireland.* Swarthmore, Pa., 1902.

> Racial origin of the Friends in Ireland, Ch. IV.
> Bibliography, p. 434–444.

O'BRIEN, MICHAEL JOSEPH. *A hidden phase of American History. Ireland's part in America's struggle for liberty.* New York, 1919.

―――― ―――― *The McCarthys in early American history.* New York, 1921.

O'HANLON, JOHN. *Irish-American history of the United States.* Dublin, 1903.

PENNSYLVANIA SCOTCH-IRISH SOCIETY. *Annual meeting and banquet* ... Philadelphia, 1890+.

PERRY, ARTHUR LATHAM. *Scotch-Irish in New England.* Boston, 1891. Reprinted from the *Proceedings of the Scotch-Irish Society of America*, 2d congress at Pittsburgh, Pa. (Cincinnati, 1890), p. 107–144.

PLOWDEN, FRANCIS P. *An historical review of the state of Ireland . . . to its union with Great Britain . . .* 2 v. in 3. London, 1803.

QUIGLEY, HUGH. *The Irish race in California . . . with . . . a vocabulary of ancient and modern Irish family names.* San Francisco, 1878.

> The vocabulary is short but of some value; not nearly so good as Eno's.

READE, COMPTON. *The Smith family . . .* London, 1902, 1904.

REID, WHITELAW. *The Scot in America, and the Ulster Scot.* London, 1911, 1912.

SCOTCH-IRISH SOCIETY OF AMERICA. *Proceedings and addresses . . .* 10 v. Cincinnati, 1889–1902.

WAKEFIELD, EDWARD. *An account of Ireland, statistical and political.* 2 v. London, 1812.

WILLIS, WILLIAM. *Genealogy of the McKinstry family, with a preliminary essay on the Scotch-Irish immigrations to America.* Boston, 1858.

WOULFE, PATRICK, *ed. Irish names and surnames . . .* Dublin, 1923.

> Treats of the evolution of Irish nomenclature, and particularly of English and Irish equivalents.
> English-Irish surnames, p. 55–161.
> Irish-English surnames, p. 219–682.
> Bibliography, p. xxxiv–xli.

YOUNG, ARTHUR. *A tour in Ireland . . . made in the years 1776, 1777, and 1778 . . .* 2 v. Dublin and London, 1780. New edition, selected and edited by Constance Maxwell, Cambridge, England, 1925.

GERMANS IN COLONIAL AMERICA

BEIDELMAN, WILLIAM. *The story of the Pennsylvania Germans . . . their origin, their history, and their dialect.* Easton, 1898.

BERNHEIM, GOTTHARDT DELLMANN. *History of the German settlements and of the Lutheran church in North and South Carolina . . .* Philadelphia, 1872.

BITTINGER, LUCY FORNEY. *The Germans in colonial times.* Philadelphia and London, 1901.

> Concerned mainly with the early leaders.

CHAMBERS, THEODORE F. *The early Germans of New Jersey; their history, churches, and genealogies.* Dover, N. J., 1895.

COBB, SANFORD HOADLEY. *The story of the Palatines . . .* New York and London, 1897.

Deals with Germans in New York.

DIFFENDERFFER, FRANK RIED. *The German immigration into Pennsylvania through the port of Philadelphia from 1700 to 1775.* Lancaster, 1900.

ESHLEMAN, H. F. *Historic background and annuals of the Swiss and German pioneer settlers of southeastern Pennsylvania . . . to . . . the revolutionary war. Lancaster,* 1917.

FAUST, ALBERT BERNHARDT. *The German element in the United States . . .* 3d ed. 2 v. in 1. New York, 1927.

This is a comprehensive work. Full outline. Numerous citations, and extensive bibliography.

———————— and BRUMBAUGH, G. M. *comp.* and *ed. Lists of Swiss emigrants in the eighteenth century to the American Colonies.* 2 v. Washington, 1920–1925.

Vol. I: Zurich, 1734–1774, from the archives of Switzerland.

Vol. II: From the State archives of Bern (1706–1795) and Basel, Switzerland (1734–1794).

FRIES, ADELAIDE L., *ed. Records of the Moravians in North Carolina.* 4 v. Raleigh, 1922–1930.

GERBER, ADOLF. *Beiträge zur Auswanderung nach Amerika in 18. Jahrhundert, aus Altwürttemburgischen Kirchenbüchern.* Stuttgart, 192-(?), 1928.

Short discussion of the exodus.
List of authenticated names of emigrants.
Index.

GIBBONS, PHEBE H. (EARLE). *Pennsylvania Dutch and other essays.* 3d ed., revised and enlarged. Philadelphia, 1882.

GRUMBINE, LEE L. Provincialisms of the "Dutch" Districts of Pennsylvania. *Proceedings American Phil. Assn.,* 17: xii–xiii, 1886.

HALDEMAN, S. S. *Pennsylvania Dutch: A dialect of South German with an infusion of English,* Philadelphia, 1892.

Section on names, pp. 60–63.

HEYDRICK, B. A. Pennsylvania (dialect words). *Dialect Notes,* 4: 337–9, 1916.

HOFFMAN, W. J. "Grammatic notes and vocabulary of Pennsylvania German dialect." *Proceedings of the American Philosophical Society*, 26 : 187–285, 1889.

HORNE, ABRAHAM R. *Pennsylvania German Manual, for pronouncing, speaking and writing English.* Kutztown, Pennsylvania.
3d edition, 1895; last reprint, 1910.

JACOBS, HENRY EYSTER. The German emigration to America, 1709–1740. *Proceedings and addresses of the Pennsylvania German Society*, Vol. VIII (Lancaster, 1898), p. 29–150.

KRIEBEL, HOWARD WIEGNER. *The Schwenkfelders in Pennsylvania*, Lancaster, 1904.

KUHNS, L. OSCAR. *Studies in Pennsylvania German Family Names.* N. Y. 1902. Reprinted from the *Americana Germanica*, 1902, pp. 299–341.

———— ———— *The German and Swiss settlements of colonial Pennsylvania* . . . New York, 1901.

LEARNED, MARION DEXTER. *The Pennsylvania German Dialect.* Pt. I. Baltimore, 1899, 114 pp.

———— ———— "Application of the phonetic system of the American Dialect Society to Pennsylvania German," *Modern Language Notes*, 5 : 237–241, 1890.

LINNS, JAMES C. *Common Sense Pennsylvania German Dictionary.* Kempton, Pa., 1887, 1895.

MORAVIAN HISTORICAL SOCIETY. *Transactions*, Nazareth, Pa. 1876, 1900.

PENNSYLVANIA ARCHIVES. *Names of persons for whom marriage licenses were issued in the Province of Pennsylvania previous to 1790.* Series 2, Vol. II. Harrisburg, 1874–1875.
———— ———— *Record of Pennsylvania marriages prior to 1810.* Series 2, Vol. VIII, Harrisburg, 1878.
Listed under the names of the various churches.
———— ———— *Names of foreigners who took the oath of allegiance to the Province and State of Pennsylvania, 1727–1775; with the foreign arrivals, 1786–1808.* Series 2, Vol. XVII, Harrisburg, 1892.
———— ———— *Tax lists, about 1767 to 1786, arranged by townships.* Series 3, Vols. XI–XXII, Harrisburg, 1897.

PENNSYLVANIA GERMAN SOCIETY. *Proceedings and Addresses*, Vols. 1–28, Lancaster, Pennsylvania, 1891–1917.

RAUCH, E. H. *Pennsylvania Dutch Handbook*, Mauch Chunk, Pa., 1879.

RICHARDS, HENRY, M. M. The Pennsylvania German in the Revolutionary War. In vol. 17 of the Proc. and Addr. of the Pa. Ger. Soc., 542 pp., Lancaster, 1908.
 Index pp. 515–537 finds its base in lists of soldiers.

RICHARDS, M. H. *German Emigration from New York Province into Pennsylvania*, Pa. Ger. Soc. Proc. Vol. VII, Lancaster, 1899.

RUPP, ISRAEL DANIEL, ed. *A collection of thirty thousand names of German, Swiss, Dutch, French, Portuguese, and other immigrants in Pennsylvania; chronologically arranged from 1727 to 1776* . . . Harrisburg, 1856.
 Compare with the Oath of Allegiance lists, mentioned above.

SCHEFFER, J. G. DE HOOP. *Mennonite Emigration to Pennsylvania.* Translated from the Dutch by S. W. Pennypacker, *Pa. Mag. Hist. and Biog.*, 2:117 ff, 1878.

SCHULTZ, EDWARD T. *First Settlements of Germans in Maryland.* Frederick, Maryland, 1896.

SCHULTZE, AUGUSTUS. *Guide to the Old Moravian Cemetery of Bethlehem, Pennsylvania, 1742–1510.* Lancaster, 1912. Published in Vol. XXI of *Proceedings and Addresses of the Pa. Ger. Society.* List of the graves and often considerable detail on the people. All indexed, pp. 190–218.
 This record refers to a community somewhat mixed in origin but mainly German and from a few limited areas. The list is not long enough to prevent blood connections having considerable bearing on the relative uses of names. The forms are but slightly affected by Anglicization. The record contains some detail on specific changes of names and also discloses instances of Scandinavians and Austrians with apparently German names.

SCHURICHT, HERRMANN. *History of the German Element in Virginia.* 2 v. in 1. Baltimore, 1900.

SEIDENSTICKER, OSWALD. *Geschichte der deutschen Gesellschaft von Pennsylvania. Von de Zeit der Gründung, 1764, bis zum Jahre 1876* . . . Philadelphia, 1876.

EARLIER WORKS ON GERMAN NOMENCLATURE

BECKER, FRIEDRICH. *Die deutschen Geschlechtsnamen, ihre entstehung und Bildung.* Basel, 1864.

CARSTENS, KARL. *Beitraege zur Geschichte der bremischen Familiennamen.* Marburg, 1906.

DÄNDLIKER, JAKOB. *In Winterthur vorkommende deutsche Personen und Familiennamen nach Entstehung und Bedeutung.* Winterthur, 1867.

HEINTZE, A. Cascorbi's revision is cited below.

HESSEL, C. *Die deutschen Familiennamen und ihr Zusammenhang mit der deutschen Cultur.* (*Erläutert an den in Kreuznach vorkommenden Namen.*) Kreuznach, 1869.

JOACHIM, CARL. *Landshuter Geschlechtsnamen*, Landshut, 1893. Pamphlet of 38 pages based on lectures delivered, 1891–92.

KAPFF, REINOLD. *Deutsche Vornamen mit den von ihnen abstammenden Geschlechtsnamen.* Ulm, 1889.

KREMERS, JOSEF. *Beiträge sur Erforschung der französischen Familiennamen.* Bonn, 1910.

MANKE, PAUL. *Die Familiennamen der Stadt Anklam.* Two sections, Anklam, 1887, 1889.

REICHERT, HERMANN. *Die deutschen Familiennamen nach breslauer Quellen.* Breslau, 1908.

STEUB, LUDWIG. *Die oberdeutschen Familiennamen.* Munich, 1870.

TOBLER-MEYER, WILHELM. *Deutsche Familiennamen nach ihrer Entstehung und Bedeutung mit besonderer Rücksichtnahme auf Zürich und die Ostschweiz.* Zurich, 1894.

Good on localization but perhaps follows Steub too closely.

BOOKS ON FAMILY NOMENCLATURE PUBLISHED IN GERMAN SINCE 1917

FRIEDRICH, LUDWIG. *Die Geographie der ältesten deutschen Personen-Namen.* Giessen, 1922.

GÖTZE, A. A. W. *Familiennamen in badischen Oberland.* Heidelberg, 1918.

HEINTZE, ALBERT AND CASCORBI, PAUL. *Die deutschen Familiennamen, geschichtlich, geographisch, sprachlich.* Sixth enlarged edition revised by Heintze's former associate, Paul Cascorbi, Halle, 1925.

KAPFF, RUDOLF. *Schwaebische Geschlechtsnamen.* Stuttgart, 1927.

KLARMANN, J. L. *Zur Geschichte der deutschen Familiennamen.* Lichtenfels, 1927.

KLUGE, FREIDRICH. *Deutsche Namenskunde.* Leipzig, 1926.

König, Emil. *Alte Eschweger Familiennamen.* Eschwege, 1927.

Kull, Ferdinand. *Deutsche Stammbüchlein.* 1924.

Nied, E. *Familiennamen-Buch für Freiburg, Karlsruhe und Mannheim.* Freiburg, 1924.

Schaeffler, Julius. *Wie heisst du?   Ein Büchlein uber Ursprung, Entwicklung u. Bedeutung unserer Familiennamen.* Berlin, 1924.

Steubler, H. *Über Lausitzer Familiennamen.* 1917.

ANNEX B.—THE MINOR STOCKS IN THE AMERICAN POPULATION OF 1790

By MARCUS L. HANSEN

CHAPTER I

INTRODUCTION

The American population of 1790, considered with respect to origins, divides naturally into three clearly defined groups. Colonists and emigrants from Great Britain and Germany were so numerous that even a superficial examination indicates that English, Scotch, Irish, and Germans were the major stocks composing that population. The motley collection of representatives from almost all races and nations who had been brought to American soil by chance or adventure is conveniently classified as "all other." But between these two groups is a third, whose presence can not be accounted for by chance or adventure, but whose numbers do not entitle them to be ranked with the first. These are the minor stocks—the Dutch, Swedes, and French.

Of these three, two are the products of colonial empires. When New Sweden and New Netherland dissolved, they left a residue of population, and it is from these nuclei rather than from any later influx that the Dutch and Swedes of 1790 sprang. The French, like the Germans, were the product of immigration, coming in moderate-sized groups of religious refugees or filtering in as individuals.

The determination of the numbers of these minor stocks involves peculiar difficulties. The historian of one of the "all other" groups is obliged to identify individuals, but after a study of the sources of local history he can make a reasonable estimate of the scores or hundreds to be assigned to the group. The materials dealing with the major stocks are so abundant that the use of quantitative methods is encouraged. But the number of any particular minor stock is too great to make individual identification possible and too small to warrant reliance upon mechanical computations. Wherefore the result must be an estimate, but an estmate made in the light of positive historical knowledge regarding the settlement, growth, and distribution of that stock in America.

The historian, like the statistician, must place his main reliance upon the lists of "heads of families" of the 1790 census. These lists, when read as they appear in the township and county rolls, are an unworked mine of history. Individually they reveal the influence of environment upon non-English nomenclature; collectively they show groupings which are unmistakably family, religious, or racial in their nature. When studied with a contemporary map or plot in hand it is possible to follow the actual route traversed by the enumerator and to see the local units of an expanding society advancing along the valleys, invading the forests, and pushing up the hillsides and down into the swamps. The farms of sons and grandsons bear a logical geographical relationship to what is evidently the ancestral estate.

It is this grouping, evidenced by the repetition of a comparatively limited number of family names, that gives the safest assurance that it is possible

360

to estimate the number of any national stock in that community. The clue may be given by genealogy, church records, local traditions, or the position of the community with respect to the normal course of expansion from older regions whose history is known and with which there are distinct nomenclatural ties. By the combination of these local figures a total for the Nation may be obtained; and while the result is frankly an estimate, it is an estimate based not upon one judgment but upon a multitude of judgments, and it may be confidently believed that errors in one locality will be balanced by opposite errors in another.

Such a task would be almost endless were it not for the concentration of stocks not only in certain Colonies but in distinct areas in those Colonies as well. Colonial population was not fluid. There was movement, but it was the movement of groups rather than of individuals. Considered as a whole the inhabitants of any Colony might include a fair representation of many nations or races, but considered geographically it was not a mixture of individuals. It was a mosaic, local groups being distinctly marked off one from the other by walls of forests, swamps, and mountains. Looking down upon a county as a map, says the author of an unusually careful pioneer history, "there may be seen patches of various workmanship and color widely dispersed, indicating to an experienced eye their respective national manufacture . . . " the whole bearing the appearance of a "bedquilt constructed of many pieces, a few of which are large, but the residue quite small and irregularly placed upon the groundwork." [1]

This concentration was the natural result of the conditions of settlement. In colonial times as at present the family was the social instrument that guided migration. In the shipping lists certain names are usually repeated several times, indicating the presence of brothers, uncles, or cousins among the passengers. These persons located in proximity to one another and added to their settlement by drawing to them relatives and friends from Europe. In this manner it received a characteristic stamp which was intensified as native population grew and accessions from the outside ceased. It is enlightening to observe how large a percentage of the bearers of a certain name within a State in 1790 were found in one county or in a township of that county. Even the distribution of the Smiths bears little relationship to general population distribution.

When the second or third generation of an original settlement was ready to swarm the movement was not individual. Young men or newly established families banded together for the advance into the wilderness. Almost every frontier community in the Colonies was the offshoot of some distinct region nearer the coast, and this process was continued in naturally modified forms across the continent. The historian of a prolific family which spread from the Atlantic to the Pacific notes in the marriage records of succeeding generations the constant reappearance of the same family names. Neighbors were migrating in company or responding to common economic and geographical forces that determined the route.[2]

The operation of this principle reduces to sizable proportions the task of estimating the minor stocks. Because Dutch and Swedes colonized the valleys of the Hudson and Delaware their descendants of 1790 were not necessarily spread from Maine to Georgia and Tennessee. Scattered individuals, of course,

---

[1] Samuel W. Eager, *An outline of history of Orange County* . . . (Newburgh, 1846–47), 48.

[2] George B. Kuykendall, *History of the Kuykendall family* . . . Portland, Oreg., 1919), 190.

there were. But the bulk of the nationality was found in the area of original settlement and in the remoter territories that were populated from this base. A liberal judgment in apportioning the peoples in these communities compensates for the leakage caused by irregular individuals.

This judgment can be expressed numerically only by the use of the family names appearing in the First Census. The validity of such use rests upon the assumptions that the original names imported by the stock may be discovered and that in their migrations the transfomations were not so extensive as completely to obliterate all trace of their origin. The first of these assumptions may be readily agreed to. Tax lists, church records, land books, and census reports are sources from which satisfactory and complete catalogues of names may be constructed. The second appears more doubtful. Every nationality provides its quota of amusing and bewildering corruptions. But a close study of genealogy and local history discounts their numerical importance and leaves a clear impression of the tenacity with which succeeding generations clung to the original names or recognizable variations even amid surroundings most conducive to change.

It is not the purpose of the sketches that follow to narrate the history of the minor stocks. Their social and economic development is still an unwritten story. Here it is intended merely to describe the conditions under which they settled in America and to explain the factors that influenced their growth and distribution. Most of the labor has been expended in making the estimates which appear in the tables. The text is only a commentary upon those estimates.

CHAPTER II

THE DUTCH

The Dutch stock in the United States in 1790 was the product of the seventeenth century colonization of New Netherland. There is no evidence of any increase from outside sources during the eighteenth century. That individuals, professional and business men, and an occasional adventurer did take up residence in the New World would be only natural in view of the close commercial relations existing between American ports and those of the Netherlands. It is also possible that the tide of German emigration flowing down the Rhine and perhaps remaining a while in the ports should draw in its wake a sprinkling of Hollanders. But the movement, in any case, was not large enough to be characterized as an " immigration," and the internal history of the Dutch communities in America during the eighteenth century shows a complete intellectual and social break with the life of Holland. About 1760–1763 the question whether henceforth the services in the Reformed churches in New York City should be conducted in the English or Dutch languages was hotly disputed. But those who favored retention of the Dutch never made use of the argument that newcomers needed the gospel preached in their own tongue. The absence of this, which would have been their most effective argument, is a striking testimony to the fact that there was no Dutch immigration.[1] The rural regions also lived a life apart, those in northern New York speaking and writing a " Mohawk Dutch " which was a combination of their original tongue with the Indian language and a medley which defied all dictionaries, being intelligible in its last years only to the " very old men."[2]

This isolation is not surprising to any student of eighteenth century history. None of the recognized motives for emigration were operating in Holland. There was no religious or intellectual restraint, no political unrest, no social discontent. A growing population was absorbed by the development of commerce, and those who were inclined to emigrate had no desire to become expatriates in America, where an uncertain lot awaited them, when free passage, farms, cattle, and implements were offered them in the Dutch possessions in South Africa. In spite of these inducements, there was in South Africa a constant call for labor which could not be satisfied by emigration from Holland; and many of the present-day Boers are descendants not of Dutchmen but of the hundreds of German and Huguenot families which were imported to colonize the Cape.[3]

For fifty years the valley of the Hudson was in Dutch hands. An energetic policy of settlement continued during this period would have given the region, in fact all the middle colonies, an ethnic stamp which would have profoundly changed all social development. But the policy was neither energetic nor

---

[1] Hugh Hastings (Ed.), *Ecclesiastical records, State of New York* (7 vols., Albany, 1901–1916), VI, 3819, 3826–3827.

[2] Jonathan Pearson, *A history of the Schenectady patent* . . . (Albany, 1883), 388.

[3] George M. Theal, *History and ethnography of Africa south of the Zambesi, from* . . . *September, 1505, to* . . . *September, 1795* (3 vols., London, 1907–1910), II, 186, 190, 313, 330–349,

consistent. The first inhabitants were servants of the Dutch West India Company, but of them many returned home "carrying with them nothing except a trifle in their purse and, for the country, the bad reputation of great hunger."[4] The system of patroonships was devised to enlist the cooperation of men of means but the rewards of the Indian trade were so alluring that their attention was turned to this source of profit and even their agriculturists introduced at great expense found it possible to desert to the woods and engage in the barter for furs.[5] The records of the company abound in recommendations looking toward a furthering of settlement, but few of the plans materialized, and some observations on the state of the colony, written about 1649, declare "It has been so long proclaimed, in New Netherland, that more people were coming, that the Indians laugh at it, and say: 'The Dutch do nothing but lie.'"[6]

But even precise information as to the number of colonists actually introduced would provide an unreliable basis for estimating the later population. New Netherland was visited by Indian wars and massacres that destroyed hundreds, retarded the natural growth, and caused others to desert. Several statements have come down to us regarding its population.[7] One only gives direct information regarding the Hollanders, a report from the Dutch authorities in 1673 stating that they numbered between six and seven thousand.[8] It is not entirely safe, however, to use this figure as a base because the succeeding quarter of a century was filled with more wars, Indian massacres, and the disturbing revolt of Leisler. Therefore an attempt has been made to estimate the size of the Dutch element included in the census of 1698, which gives the population by counties and for several of which the original lists have been preserved.[9]

According to this census there were in the city and county of Albany 1,453 white inhabitants. In Munsell's *Annals of Albany*[10] is a list of these inhabitants with a statement of their nationality. The non-Dutch numbered 105, which leaves about 1,350 Dutch. The combined population of Ulster and Dutchess Counties was 1,228. A list of the male inhabitants of Ulster county in 1689 totals 223, of whom 160, or 72 per cent, are Dutch.[11] At this time the population of Dutchess County was so small that it was attached to Ulster County for administrative purposes. A list of the inhabitants in 1714 shows about the same percentages as in Ulster in 1689.[12] As the one was settled from the other, it is safe to apply the 72 per cent to the above total, which results in 800 Dutch.

Orange County had a population of only 200. Before 1700 four settlements had been made, of which one was French, one Scotch, and two Dutch.[13] But as the French and Scotch settlements were weak and their early careers checkered, it is advisable to ascribe 150 to the Dutch. New York City and county numbered 4,237. There is extant a list of the inhabitants in 1703; of the 818

---

[4] E. B. O'Callaghan (ed.), *Documents relative to the colonial history of the State of New York* . . . (15 vols., Albany, 1853–1887), I, 296.

[5] *Ibid.*, 246; E. B. O'Callaghan, *The documentary history of the State of New York* (4 vols., Albany, 1849–1851), IV, 4.

[6] O'Callaghan, *Docs. col. hist. N. Y.*, I, 263.

[7] O'Callaghan, *Doc. hist. N. Y.*, I, 689–697.

[8] O'Callaghan, *Docs. col. hist. N. Y.*, II, 526.

[9] *Id.*, IV, 420.

[10] Joel Munsell, *Annals of Albany* (10 vols., Albany, 1850–1859), IX, 81–89.

[11] Nathaniel B. Sylvester, *History of Ulster County, New York* . . . (Phila., 1880), Part I, 69–70.

[12] Philip H. Smith, *General history of Dutchess County* . . . (Pawling, N. Y., 1877), 60.

[13] Edward M. Ruttenber (Comp.), *History of Orange County, New York* . . . (Phila., 1881), 12, 13.

heads of families there recorded, less than 50 per cent are Dutch, so that 2,000 will be a generous apportionment.[14]

Staten Island formed the county of Richmond. The inhabitants were 654 in number. Dutch, English, and French partook in its colonization, but the only definite information as to proportions is contained in the *Journal of Jasper Danckaerts*,[15] a statement that "the English constitute the least proportion and the Dutch and French divide between them about equally the greater portion." A liberal estimate based on this rather cryptic division would assign to the Dutch 300. This agrees fairly well with the statement of an English traveler in 1695 that the Dutch families on the island numbered 44." [16]

The early settlers of Westchester County were also drawn from various sources. Some were Dutch from the city of New York, others English from Long Island and New England, and New Rochelle was the site of the well-known Huguenot colony.[17] Of the seven churches founded in the county before 1700 only one was Dutch Reformed.[18] Therefore to ascribe to the Dutch one-third of the 917 inhabitants would be the maximum. Dutch, 300.

The easternmost of the three counties on Long Island was Suffolk. It was populated entirely by Englishmen and Huguenots and there is no trace of Dutch at this time. In Queens County the towns of Jamaica and Oyster Bay were entirely English, but in Newton, Flushing, and Hampstead there were some Dutch, who from a study of name lists may be estimated at 250 out of a total of 3,366.[19] Kings County composed the Dutch part of the island. Only Gravesend, among its towns, was settled by English people, but even among them may be found Dutch names. Therefore of the 1,721 inhabitants undoubtedly 1,500 were Dutch.[20]

Summary of New York, 1698

	White population	Dutch population
Albany	1, 453	1, 350
Ulster and Dutchess	1, 228	800
Orange	200	150
New York	4, 237	2, 000
Richmond	654	300
West Chester	917	300
Suffolk	2, 121	---------
Kings	1, 721	1, 500
Queens	3, 366	250
Total	15, 897	6, 650

[14] O'Callaghan, *Doc. hist. N. Y.*, I, 395–405.

[15] Bartlett B. James and J. Franklin Jameson (eds.), *Original narratives of early American history* (N. Y., 1913), XIV, 70.

[16] John Miller, *New York considered and improved, 1695* (Victor H. Paltsits, ed., Cleveland, 1903), 54.

[17] Jacques W. Redway, "Some side lights on the passing of New Netherlands viewed from Westchester County," *Proceedings of the New York State historical association*, IX, 152–159.

[18] John T. Scharf (ed.), *History of Westchester County*, New York . . . (2 vols., Phila., 1886), 28, 29, 173.

[19] Benjamin F. Thompson, *History of Long Island* . . . (N. Y., 1839), 320, 349, 362, 370, 382, 410; O'Callaghan, *Doc. hist. N. Y.*, I, 432.

[20] Thompson, *Hist. L. I.*, 431, 437, 450, 456, 462.

This total of 6,650 for 1698, derived entirely from local sources, is in reasonable accord with the generalization made in 1695 by John Miller that "The number of the Inhabitants in this Province are about 3,000 families, whereof almost one halfe are naturally dutch."[21]

Unfortunately New Jersey was not included in this census, but in 1700 a reliable authority gave the population of East Jersey at 8,000 living in eight settlements. Of these eight, only two, Bergen and Aqueckenock, were of Dutch origin. The Dutch migration to New Jersey did not being in full force until after 1700.[22] Therefore it is difficult to judge the number of Dutch in these two regions, but from a study of the contemporary church records there would seem to have been less than 200 families, which would account for a thousand souls.[23] West Jersey, with the exception of a few Swedes on Raccoon Creek, was entirely English.[24]

New York and New Jersey are the only two Colonies for which information in any way satisfactory is available. There were Dutch settlements planted on the Delaware, but they were hardly more than temporary. As early as 1630 a trading post with 10 or 12 servants was maintained and after the conquest of New Sweden an attempt to plant settlers was made. In 1658 the number of souls was reported at 600. But "unhealthiness, sickness, desease. violent and pestilential fevers, and other tedious disorders," such as are common to all pioneer settlements, took an annual toll of death, and in a list of "responsible householders" on the Delaware about 1680, only 15 out of 195 are Dutch.[25]

Many had undoubtedly been lost by migration. Maryland and Virginia were convenient places of refuge for runaways, fugitives, and those dissatisfied with political conditions on the Delaware. The governor reported in 1659 "everyone is trying to remove and escape" and "My own opinion is that almost all the people will leave that place."[26] An agent was sent to the Governor of Maryland to demand the return of these persons, but he met with no success.[27] Later, upon the capitulation to the English in 1664, there followed a second dispersion, many, the Dutch claimed, being sold as slaves to Virginia.[28]

Any estimate of the size of this diaspora must be of the most general character. Runaways and fugitives have no desire to emphasize their origin. Therefore the estimate must be based upon the number from which they had sprung. The few hundreds living upon the Delaware in 1658 could not have multiplied at the rate usually ascribed to the colonial population. In 1700 a thousand would be the extreme limit.

This gives us a total of 8,650 as the maximum of Dutch in America in 1700, and it is the maximum rather than the actual numbers that we are interested in at present. For, assuming that this stock doubles every 25 years, their

---

[21] Miller, N. Y. . . . 1695, 40.

[22] Proceedings of the New Jersey historical society, 4th series, IV; Franklin Ellis, History of Monmouth County, N. J. . . . (Phila., 1885), 82.

[23] Abraham Messler, First things in old Somerset . . . (Somerville, N. J., 1899), 161; Reformed Church of America, A history of the classis of Paramus of the Reformed Church in America (N. Y., 1902), 39; Records of the Reformed Dutch churches of Hackensack and Schraalenburgh, New Jersey . . . (2 vols., N. Y., 1891), I, 1–3; Hastings. Eccl. rec. N. Y., II, 795: Charles H. Winfield, History of the county of Hudson, New Jersey . . . (N. Y., 1874), 129; Edwin F. Hatfield, History of Elizabeth, New Jersey . . . (N. Y., 1868), 159.

[24] Edwin P. Tanner, The province of New Jersey . . . (N. Y., 1908), 28.

[25] O'Callaghan, Doc. hist. N. Y., III, 31; Docs. col. hist. N. Y., II, 51, 68, 113.

[26] O'Callaghan, Docs. col. hist. N. Y., II, 115.

[27] Ibid., 82, 89.

[28] Ibid., 369.

number in 1790 would be about 120,000. Such a rate of increase, however, is most unlikely, as in the year 1702 smallpox and fever carried off several hundred in New York alone.[29] In any case analysis of the 1790 population should produce a figure which bears some reasonable correspondence to this derived maximum estimate.

There were in the history of the colonial Dutch certain regions which may be considered areas of original settlement. These were the hives from which later migrating groups swarmed, and from them radiate the lines of Dutch expansion. A study of this expansion in relation to colonial immigration and dispersion in general, to changing crops and markets, to land tenure and population growth, to politics and Indians is a fertile field for historical investigation. Here we are concerned with numbers and the discussion is limited to a consideration of these general features of Dutch settlement which help to explain the results embodied in the tables.

In presenting the estimates, first the three States of original settlement (New York, New Jersey, and Delaware) will be considered; thereafter the relation of the Dutch to New England; then the States which received the first waves of distinct migration (Pennsylvania, Maryland, and Virginia); and finally the Southern and Southwestern States.

NEW YORK

The first Dutch occupation of New Netherland, being of a commercial and military nature, seized upon the two sites which strategically were of the greatest importance. New Amsterdam was located at the juncture of the Hudson River, Long Island Sound, the Atlantic Ocean, and the overland route to the Delaware. Fort Orange was placed near the confluence of the Hudson and Mohawk Rivers. A large proportion of the Dutch residents of these posts were soldiers who returned to Holland upon the surrender to the English. Therefore it was the agricultural regions tributary to these centers rather than the centers themselves which produced the Dutch stock of 1790.

New Amsterdam was at first fed by the farms on Manhattan and Long Island, and the flour which they produced was a leading article in the trade of the growing city.[30] But the English had already established themselves upon Long Island; and although they were not able to force the Dutch from their homes, they did prevent any eastward expansion on the island, and above Manhattan they were so early settling along the banks of the Hudson that they presented an effective barrier against a Dutch advance to the north. When these original Dutch farming communities could no longer provide for their natural increase a distinct migration was necessary and their descendants are in 1790 to be found in northern New Jersey and in remoter settlements of the West.

Fort Orange, later Albany, was surrounded by rich farming lands, but although the growth of the population seems to have been normal, the territorial dispersion of the stock was more limited than the geographical possibilities suggest as likely. Perhaps the system of patroonships did not foster the development of those qualities which are essential to pioneering. Necessity may not have impelled a movement toward the frontier; and as the Dutch farmer was thrifty and industrious and the Dutch laws and customs sanctioned the equal division of property among heirs, the tendency was to multiply holdings within

---

[29] *Calendar of state papers, Colonial series* . . . *America and West Indies, 1702–1703* (London, 1860–1919), 27.

[30] O'Callaghan, *Doc. hist. N. Y.*, I, 267.

the general area of original occupation.[31] Advance was slow, first along the banks of the Hudson and then upward into the hills along the tributaries. It was later comers from Europe and New England who located in the back country away from the natural communications.[32]

Other factors contributed to this localization of the Dutch stock. The political voice of Albany was strong, and it was the mouthpiece of the trading elements whose prosperity depended upon the continued existence of the neighboring Indian frontier. Therefore it was their policy to hinder all extension of settlement.[33] Popular experience also discouraged such ventures. Those farmers who had dared to establish themselves beyond the protection of Albany met disaster during the wars that immediately preceded and followed 1700. Many were scalped and murdered and their families taken into captivity. Those who escaped did so only by the prudent desertion of their homes.[34] This terror continued until after the peace of Utrecht in 1713, and even as late as 1743 fear of the Indians prevented the success of the official attempts which were made to secure settlers for the vicinity of Ticonderoga.[35] In the meantime other elements had started to come in. The Germans had occupied the flats along the Mohawk and New Englanders had started that movement which attained such great proportions in the years between the close of the Revolution and 1790. Both of these elements were affected by the presence of the Dutch. Care must be used in separating them from the Hollanders, a task which in the case of the Germans is the more difficult because of the Teutonic nature of the names. Even the British stocks were influenced appreciably. In the records Thomas Smits becomes Tam Smit, Yates changes into Yets and Yetz, Arnold appears as Arnoud, Brooks as Broecks, Michael Basset as Mynkill Bessidt; and among the Scotchmen Alexander Lindsay loses his nationality when his name is written Leendertse and an unknown personage from Inverness passes on to his family the name of Van Ness.[36] A traveler from these regions where the New England tongue was spoken in all its original purity was astonished to note how the " articulation even of New-England people is injured by their being intermingled with the Dutch, Irish, and Scotch." [37] Only by detailed study is it possible to disentangle the non-Dutch from the nationality that established the language and social customs of northern New York, and although no estimate is here ventured, it is suggested that many who have hitherto been considered of Holland descent should actually be assigned to the German total.

But the original habitat to which the greatest number of the now widely spread descendants of colonial Dutch trace their ancestry lies midway between New York and Albany, the region then known as " the Esopus," now Ulster County, or more generally the hinterland of Kingston and Newburgh. Sound strategy and agricultural possibilities combined to encourage the settlement of this area. Three tributaries flowed into the Hudson, forming three routes by which enemies might approach and control the Hudson, the artery of New Netherland. But the reason for its persistent occupation, in spite of two bloody Indian wars, is found in its economic riches. The metropolis had

[31] Ibid., 102; Pearson, Hist. Schenectady pat., 82. By article 11 of the terms of capitulation in 1664 the Dutch were allowed to continue their own customs concerning inheritances. O'Callaghan, Docs. col. hist. N. Y., II, 251.

[32] George R. Howell and Jonathan Tenney (eds.), Bi-centennial history of Albany. History of the county of Albany, N. Y. . . . (N. Y., 1886), 777, 801.

[33] Cal. st. p. col., 1701, 236.

[34] Cal. st. p. col., 1702, 606; O'Callaghan, Docs. col. hist. N. Y., III, 159, 245, IV, 752.

[35] O'Callaghan, Docs. col. hist. N. Y., VI, 207, 225.

[36] Pearson, Hist. Schenectady pat., XI, 113; Joel Munsell (ed.), Collections on the history of Albany (4 vols., N. Y., 1865–1871), IV, 94, 95, 105.

[37] O'Callaghan, Doc. hist. N. Y., III, C85.

to be fed and the lowland meadows which here border the river had long been the garden of the river Indians. The Indian fields were seized and the natural meadows and later clearings became not only the granary of New York but developed an export trade to the West Indies which brought continued prosperity to the settlers. One visible result of this prosperity was a multitude of children, and these children, soon householders themselves, cleared the hillsides, and when no more hill farms could be profitably operated in the Highlands they pushed up the valleys that led in a southwestwardly direction to the banks of the Delaware.[38]

Esopus and the Catskills are the classic ground of Dutch-American romance. But Washington Irving and local tradition have colored the pages of history, and this region was far from being a hundred per cent Dutch. In social customs, religion, and language it was more Dutch than in blood. As in the valley of the Mohawk, many nationalities contributed to the population, but lost their characteristics in the predominant atmosphere. There were English among the first settlers, the progenitor of a prolific Masten family being a certain Marston, whose descendants were among the leaders of the Dutch.[39] Before the close of the seventeeth century a Huguenot settlement was made at New Paltz. For the first 50 years the church records were kept in the French language, but thereafter for the next 75 years the influence of the prevailing nationality was so strong that the records of the "French Church" appear in Dutch.[40] Early in the eighteenth century the "Palatines" arrived, and in their history there is also a case of a congregation which in a generation or two gave up the use of the German, substituting therefor not English but Dutch.[41] The result of this "Dutchification" has been an overestimation of the numerical strength of the stock, this county being one of the few in the country for which the *Century of Population Growth* exaggerates the numbers of a non-English stock.

The main current of Ulster County expansion was to the southwest into New Jersey and Pennsylvania. Some moved up the river to meet the growth southward from Albany and a few crossed the river to become the pioneers of Dutchess County. But east of the Hudson, except on the patroonships to the north, the Dutch always remained a minority. Poughkeepsie and Kinderhook, it is true, were villages as Dutch as any in Ulster County, but they were islands among the British and Germans, the former coming "in shoals" from Connecticut and Long Island and the latter being the descendants of the Palatines. Without an appreciation of the extent of this German colonization any estimate of the Dutch is liable to err. Investigators have the tendency to put every non-English looking name into the Dutch column. The Palatines, however, did not provide all the German blood. One result of the uncertain policy adopted by the authorities towards these foreigners was their spread, and families and groups of families, after drifting about, settled wherever opportunity offered, becoming the nuclei about which a constant infiltration of

---

[38] *Olde Ulster, an historical and genealogical magazine* . . . (Kingston, N. Y.), I, 97, III, 361, V, 274; Ralph LeFevre, *History of New Paltz, New York* . . . (Albany, 1909), 191; Sylvester, *Hist. Ulster Co.*, 222.

[39] "The Esopus settlers and the Indians," *Olde Ulster*, I, 97; Gerrit H. Van Wagenen, "The early settlers of Ulster Co., N. Y. The Masten family," *New York Genealogical and biographical record*, XX, 171–174.

[40] LeFevre, *Hist. New Paltz*, 3, 60.

[41] Eager, *Hist. Orange Co.*, 312.

Germans gathered.[42] After the battle of Princeton, we are informed, Hessian prisoners found their way to German communities on the Hudson.[43]

It was in the regions noted above that the New York Dutch were concentrated. They were also concentrated genealogically. Genealogically speaking, concentration means the emphasis of a comparatively limited number of family groups and the inclusion of the bulk of a stock within those family groups. The development of this characteristic on the part of the Dutch was fostered by their linguistic, religious, and geographical clannishness and was so highly developed by the earliest generations that when dispersion did begin the family imprint was not obliterated.

Therefore the first step has been the determination of these families, not merely the families that were socially or politically prominent, but all Dutch families existent in the last quarter of the eighteenth century. It meant extracting all Dutch families referred to in the 57 volumes of the *New York Genealogical and Biographical Register*, in the 47 volumes of the *Yearbook* of the Holland Society, in the 12 volumes of the series of New York genealogical dictionaries edited by W. R. Cutter and approximately 150 volumes of local New York and New Jersey history. The result of this research was the isolation of about 400 Dutch family names other than those prefixed with a "van." But this did not provide a measuring rod which could be applied mechanically. Cole, for instance, in Ulster County was Dutch, but in the other counties of New York, English. Bloom on Manhattan was Danish; on Long Island, Dutch. Snider in Ulster County was Dutch; in Dutchess County, German. For every county an independent decision had to be made, in which the appearance of these names on the 1790 census or other lists, naturally constituted the weightlest factor. But allowance had to be given to anglicization and discretion used in the interpretation of the cosmopolitan Smiths, Millers, Petersons and Paulsons, the criterion being the complexion of their immediate neighbors. The results are estimates, and estimates which are open to revision upon the discovery of new and pertinent information.

The estimate for the state is 55,000 out of a total white population of 314,366. To make the figures in the table more informative the settlement of each county should be recounted in detail. That would constitute a history of colonial New York. The above remarks are presented as a commentary upon the comparatively small number of Dutch in the State; that is, a figure which is small when compared with one's expectations. Two explanations of this circumstance are emphasized: First, that two of the three principal Dutch settlements were so placed that in its expansion the stock was directed into New Jersey and Pennsylvania to swell the estimates there; and, second, that the State was more Dutch in society and language than in blood, many nationalities who had no contemporary historians having participated in the process of peopling.

NEW JERSEY

The site of the only original Dutch settlement in New Jersey was the vicinity of Bergen. But by 1790 the northern part of the State was as completely Dutch as any region in New York. With a few noteworthy exceptions the Hollanders in America participated little in commercial activities. They were agriculturists and the plains of New Jersey offered the richest fields. As we have seen, settlers came from Ulster County. The farms of western Long Island, unable to expand, sent a continual stream of sons to the other side of the metropolis, and from New York City there was a constant outflow, a movement to the land

---

[42] Edward M. Smith, *Documentary history of Rhinebeck, in Dutchess county, N. Y. . . .* (Rhinebeck, 1881), 86; Isaac Huntting, *History of Little Nine Partners . . . of Duchess county* (Amenia, N. Y., 1897), 133.

[43] Eager, *Hist. Orange Co.*, 253.

as the city gradually lost its rural character.[44] The 2,000 Dutch whom we found in New York County in 1700 had increased to only 5,000 in 1790, and the 1,500 in Kings County (western Long Island) were 1,500 in 1790. To describe this migration and settlement would be an enlightening chapter in colonial history. In the struggle for possession the Dutch were victorious over English, Scotch, and Germans, and the impress of their society is noticeable to-day in the counties which they occupied.[45]

Many phases of American development during the nineteenth century can be interpreted in the light of those periodic waves of immigration and dispersion that carried American population to the Pacific and transformed the character of economic life and many aspects of national administration. Such periodicity was also a factor in colonial growth. The older treatment of this era traced the founding and governmental evolution of each of 13 Colonies until their political activities were merged into a concerted movement. The more recent school of historians has made the empire the unit and fitted American events into a frame which includes all quarters of the globe. But "colonial history" may, and perhaps ought, to be written in the terms of its growing population, marking off the stages in the occupation of the land and emphasizing those advances which provided the supplies for larger markets, forced a readjustment of Indian relations, and in general demanded a continual modification of the imperial system until modification became unsatisfactory and the whole structure was overthrown.

It was one of these periods of change that determined the direction of Dutch expansion. Toward the close of the seventeenth century the third generation was getting ready to establish itself, but there were few prospects within the Colony of New York. During the administration of Governor Fletcher land grants had been distributed with a lavish hand, and these, together with the old patroonships, created a practical monopoly of land which caused prospective homemakers to look elsewhere. The Earl of Bellomont reported the explanation of this movement, as given to him by one of the inhabitants:

"What man will be such a fool," he said, "to become a base tenant to Mr. Dellius, Colonel Schuyler, Mr. Livingston (and so he ran through the whole rôle of our mighty landgraves), when, for crossing Hudson's River, that man can for a song purchase a good freehold in the Jersies?"[46]

Other conditions tended to set in motion even those who were or could be established. There were Indian wars upon the northern frontiers. The youth of New York were compelled to serve in protecting parties. To avoid this obligation they settled in New Jersey, which had no frontier, or in Pennsylvania, which refused to sanction such expeditions.[47] Fear of the French and their Indian allies impelled the less venturesome on the exposed districts to remove themselves to more quiet regions.[48]

But the most general cause was an economic crisis induced by the conditions of the war. Spain was involved, and the market for flour in the Spanish West Indies, which was so indispensable a factor in the agricultural expansion of New York and other Provinces was lost. Farmers were impover-

---

[44] O'Callaghan, *Doc. hist. N. Y.*, I, 103; Minor Swick, "A Dutch migration from the Raritan valley to New York State in 1785 and later," *Somerset County historical quarterly*, IV, 21–25.

[45] John D. Prince, "Netherland settlers in New Jersey," N. J. hist. soc. *Proceedings*, 3d ser., IX, 1–7.

[46] O'Callaghan, *Doc. hist. N. Y.*, I, 253; *Docs. col. hist. N. Y.*, IV, 334. The quotation is in *Cal. st. p. col., 1700*, 678.

[47] O'Callaghan, *Docs. col. hist. N. Y.*, IV, 53; *Cal. st. p. col., 1704–05*, 141.

[48] "I have latlie seen with a heavie hart, fourscore fine farms all deserted about Albany, after the great expence of the owners in building and Improving." Letter of Governor Benjamin Fletcher, May, 1694. *Minutes of the provincial council of Pennsylvania . . .* (10 vols., Phila., 1852), I, 459.

ished, and employers of labor were forced to release their servants. These classes, obliged to shift for themselves, saw prospects for the future only in beginning anew in the wilderness. During the first decade of the eighteenth century there was a pronounced movement from the older regions into Pennsylvania, and in the South into the Carolinas.[49]

To the Dutch in New York the plains of northern New Jersey were inviting. The terms on which land could be secured were attractive. The growing city of Philadelphia, which at the end of 20 years rivaled its neighbor on the Hudson, offered a promising market. Access was convenient. So the movement from Long Island and Manhattan, which had started about 1690, gathered force. After 1700 Dutch names become increasingly common upon the local records, and the banks of the Raritan and Passaic were occupied principally by that stock.[50] The hold of the Dutch upon northern New Jersey was strengthened by a contemporary movement southward from Ulster County, and later there was a further addition of families from the vicinity of Albany. Until 1800 the use of the Holland tongue was general.[51] But here again caution must be used in the interpretation of Teutonic-looking names. For spread among the Dutch and the English were also colonies of Germans, the products of an eastward migration from the larger German communities in Pennsylvania.[52]

Unfortunately, the threads of family migration (always important as indicators of the larger movements) can not be traced carefully, as the early New Jersey census schedules are missing. The Dutch estimates of 1790 suffer from the same loss, and it has been necessary to depend upon less comprehenive data. For some counties it has been possible to find the Revolutionary muster rolls, and these lists have been the basis for establishing the ratios to be applied to the 1790 population. In some cases, the assumption here involved, that the nationalities in a county were represented in the Army in the same proportion as they existed in the population at large, suggests the possibility of error. But in agricultural communities such as those in New Jersey the danger is less, and in lieu of better sources these rolls may be used with comparative confidence. There are three counties for which even such rolls are not available, and for them dependence must be placed upon the varied materials indicated below. The analysis of the population by counties results in a total of 35,000 Dutch in a population of 169,954.[53]

---

[49] Cal. st. p. col., 1704–05, 167, 1706–08, 759.

[50] Ellis, Hist. Mon. Co., 82; James P. Snell, History of Hunterdon and Somerset counties, N. J. . . . (Phila., 1881), 299; Edmund D. Halsey, History of Morris County, N. J. (N. Y., 1882), 268.

[51] James P. Snell (Comp.), History of Sussex and Warren counties N. J. . . . (Phila., 1881), 24; Halsey, Hist. Morris Co., 284.

[52] Snell, Hist. Sussex & Warren cos., 32.

[53] Muster rolls: Bergen County in W. Woodford Clayton (Comp.) History of Bergen and Passaic counties, New Jersey . . . (Phila., 1882), 71, 72; Burlington County in Evan M. Woodward and John F. Hageman, History of Burlington and Mercer counties, New Jersey . . . (Phila., 1883), 31 ff.; Cumberland County in Thomas Cushing and Charles E. Sheppard, History of the counties of Gloucester, Salem, and Cumberland . . . (Phila., 1883), 49 ff.; Essex County in William H. Shaw, History of Essex and Hudson counties, New Jersey (2 vols., Phila., 1884), I, 31 ff.; Gloucester County in Cushing and Sheppard, History, 41 ff.; Middlesex County in W. Woodford Clayton (ed.), History of Union and Middlesex counties, New Jersey . . . (Phila., 1882), 492 ff.; Monmouth County in Ellis, Hist. Mon. Co., 229 c.; Morris County in Halsey, Hist. Morris Co., 27 ff.; Salem County in Cushing and Sheppard, History, 46 ff.; Sussex County in Snell, Hist. Sussex & Warren cos., 68 ff. For the counties whose rolls have not been preserved, use has been made, in the case of Cape May County, of the list of eighteenth century names found in the State of New Jersey Index of wills, inventories, etc. . . . (3 vols., Trenton, 1912–13), I, 249–271; for Hunterdon County, id., II, 679–772; for Somerset County, a general estimate of the ratio of the Dutch element can be secured from the list of residents published in the Somerset Co. hist. quart., I, 281–286.

DELAWARE

The history of the Dutch in Delaware is much the same as that of the Swedes. The feeble colony clustered about the military post at New Castle gained a firm foothold in the surrounding territory, but the inrush of immigrants from Great Britain was so great that by 1790 the Dutch element, though noticeable because of national characteristics, was numerically small. As in the case of the Swedes, they possessed strength only in the northernmost county, New Castle. The two southern counties, Kent and Sussex, were occupied largely by the expansion of the British settlements from the Maryland Eastern Shore. Census schedules of 1790 are not available, but using the almost contemporary lists of taxables, it appears that approximately 2,000 out of 46,310 were Dutch.[54]

EXPANSION INTO NEW ENGLAND

A casual look at the map would suggest that the Dutch contributed a not unappreciable element to the population of colonial New England. New York was settled by Dutch, would run the argument; it was adjacent to Connecticut, Massachusetts, and Vermont; and as the English were found in New York, so the Dutch would be found in New England, the nationalities shading off one into the other. But as already emphasized, colonial population was not fluid, and even as late as 1790 settlements were islands in a comparative wilderness and the population of each island was usually characterized by a common origin.

The location and extent of these islands were determined by perhaps a score of factors, among them the most important being geography, markets, prejudice, and land tenure. In an earlier paragraph emphasis is placed on the fact that the largest Dutch settlement on the middle Hudson, starting on the west bank, pushed its way inland. West of the river there are tributaries which could convey products of the remoter farms to market; east there are none. The territory that later became Dutchess County was more heavily timbered and pioneering was, at its best, hard enough. Therefore, the more open lands to the west were first occupied.[55] The east bank had a reputation for unhealthiness, and the river itself was a barrier, if only a psychological barrier. To those on the west as well as on the east, its crossing, says James D. Pinckney in his *Reminiscences of Catskill* (p. 17), was deemed "a perilous and foolhardy undertaking, and the friends of those who ventured to 'go over' were as hopeless of their return as though they had made the Stygian passage."

But pioneers will endure much for land; and though the immediate east bank was not so fertile, beyond the hills lay inviting valleys. Connecticut had had its Dutch period, the trading post of the West India Co. at Hartford antedating the arrival of the emigrants from Massachusetts. But this handful of traders and soldiers, after a brief period of contention with the English settlers, departed, and there is no trace of any Connecticut family springing from this source. Along the shore of the Sound the occupation was more permanent; and although there was a general political emigration of Hollanders when the English title was belligerently asserted, a few families remained.[56] Dutch

[54] John T. Scharf, *History of Delaware, 1609–1888* (2 vols., Phila., 1888), II, *passim*.
[55] Smith, *Hist. Dutchess Co.*, 98.
[56] Duane H. Hurd (Comp.), *History of Fairfield County, Conn*. . . . (Phila., 1881), 266, 313, 368, 683.

servants, fleeing from the harsh rule of New Netherland, found refuge in these English towns.[57] This accounts for the Dutch trace apparent along the coast in the census of 1790.

It was early in the eighteenth century that the wilderness of the New York-New England back country was approached—northward from the Sound, westward from the Connecticut, and eastward from the Hudson. An investigation of local history reveals among the early settlers of almost every community some one who is designated "the Dutchman." But this group was always under a disadvantage in the one feature of pioneer life that meant the most. The pioneer could live without roads or spacious buildings, he could live without markets, but he was not willing to endure the privations of such life without an unclouded title to the land that he improved—the assurance that the results of his labors would lighten his old age and descend to his children. In this respect the Dutch lost. The borderland between New England and New York was debatable ground. In Massachusetts and Connecticut there were legal conflicts between rival titles and in Vermont the struggle over the New York grants almost reached the proportions of a frontier war. In these conflicts the New Englanders were usually successful, as the Dutch could not maintain their possessions against the armed bands that opposed them.[58] But by persistence and marriage a noticeable number of Dutch struck root. Again, it must be remarked that among those who were popularly designated as "Dutch" were a large proportion of Hudson River "Dutchified" Germans. An investigation of the German element in New England in 1790 will probably produce a figure for Germans considerably larger than now suspected.[59]

Dutch blood was infused into New England by one other factor—commerce. As has been suggested, the American Dutch were not primarily traders, but they did evolve in New York an aristocracy, and the constant coastal trade between Boston, Providence, Newport, and the cities on the Sound brought this New England commercial aristocracy in touch with their social equals in New York. So marriages and trading connections prompted minor migrations which are recorded only in family histories and recognized by the rare occurrence of names on the city census rolls. Our analysis finds in Connecticut 600, in Massachusetts 600, in Vermont 500, and in Rhode Island 250.

Maine and New Hampshire seem to be outside the sphere of both this agricultural and commercial expansion of the Dutch, and on the census lists of 1790 there are no familiar names. A generation later there is a marked sprinkling, but their origin is curious. Among the loyalists who settled in the Canadian Maritime Provinces were several families of New York Dutch. The drift southward along the coast in the early years of the nineteenth century brought these names into New England. But the drift had not commenced in 1790 and the apportionment of 100 to each of these States is a matter of courtesy and the recognition of a strong probability.[60]

[57] O'Callaghan, *Docs. col. hist. N. Y.*, I, 342.

[58] O'Callaghan, *Doc. hist. N. Y.*, III, 479.

[59] It is also enlightening to note that as Burgoyne's army crossed Massachusetts as prisoners, many Hessians managed or were allowed to escape and settle wherever they happened to find an opportunity. Lucius R. Paige, *History of Hardwick, Mass.* (Boston, N. Y., 1883), 386; Daniel W. Wells, *A history of Hatfield, Massachusetts, in three parts* . . . (Springfield, Mass., c. 1910), 247; Adin Ballou, *History of the town of Milford, Worcester County, Massachusetts* . . . (Boston, 1882), 1141; Hiram Barrus, *History of the town of Goshen, Hampshire County, Massachusetts* . . . (Boston, 1881), 210.

[60] George T. Little (ed.), *Genealogical and family history of the State of Maine* (4 vols., N. Y., 1909), IV, 2211–12.

FIRST EXPANSION TO THE SOUTHWEST: PENNSYLVANIA

Leading westward from the Esopus is a thoroughfare known as "The Old Mine Road." Its terminus is Port Jervis on the Delaware. Tradition assigns to the road a romantic past. In the middle of the seventeenth century (the story recounts) the Dutch opened up rich mines in the mountains about the Delaware Water Gap, and it was to facilitate the transportation of ore that the road was built.[61] More recent history places the settlement of the Delaware Flats, also known as Minisink region, early in the eighteenth century. Minisink was at first merely a place of Indian trade, but in 1730, when Pennsylvania surveyors reached the locality, they found the flats on both sides of the river fully occupied by the Dutch, who were so completely associated with the Dutch on the Hudson that they had no idea where the river ran, and who were obliged to converse with the English through the medium of the Indian tongue.[62]

This part of Pennsylvania (in 1790 in Northampton County, now in Monroe County), being principally mountain and swamp, offered little opportunity for the extension of agricultural settlement, and the generations that succeeded the first pioneers had to disperse among the British and Germans in the neighboring counties. Bucks County, though its population was not as large as that of Northampton, drew from other sources. Some were evidently descended from the old Delaware region colonists and others came down from the upper settlements.[63] But the largest contingent was drawn from New Jersey. The trail from New York to Philadelphia reached the Delaware at the falls (Trenton) and made the region accessible.[64] New York also was sending forth its contingent of sons. The large estates were still undivided; their possessors looked upon them as investments for their children, and New York remained, during most of the colonial period, "a nursery of people" for the neighboring Provinces.[65] It would seem that at two periods, however, the movement was especially strong, one in the late thirties, when the development of Pennsylvania was especially marked, and again following the peace of 1763, when dangers of frontier settlement appeared less threatening.

The number of Dutch in other Pennsylvania counties might easily be related to their geography and history. There were two other centers of concentration—York County and the western parts of the State. The York County colony was the result of an influx of emigrants from northern New Jersey in the decade 1760–1770, a mixed group of Huguenots and Hollanders who planned to erect a new county in which their influence would be dominant.[66] Most of the pre-Revolutionary settlers in the western parts of Pennsylvania came from Virginia and Maryland, and among them was a liberal sprinkling of Dutch,

---

[61] Samuel Hazard (ed), *Hazard's register of Pennsylvania* . . . (16 vols., Phila., 1828–1835), I, 437–438.

[62] Israel D. Rupp, *History of Northampton, Lehigh, Monroe, Carbon, and Schuylkill counties* . . . (Harrisburg, 1845), 146, 160; Charles G. Hine, *History and legend, fact, fancy, and romance of the Old Mine Road* . . . (N. Y., 1908), 5–12; Kuykendall, *Hist. Kuykendall fam.*, 41.

[63] W. W. H. Davis, "Early settlers in Bucks County," *A collection of papers read before the Bucks County historical society*, II, 192.

[64] Warren E. Ely, "Dutch settlement in Bucks County," *Bucks Co. hist soc. Collections*, V, 1–11; William J. Hinke (ed.), "Church record of Neshaminy and Bensalem, Bucks County, 1710–1738," *Journal of the Presbyterian historical society*, I, 111–134.

[65] See Colden's report on lands in the province of New York in O'Callaghan, *Doc. hist. N. Y.*, I, 249–255.

[66] George R. Prowell, *History of York County, Pennsylvania* (2 vols., Chicago, 1907), I, 139–43.

descendants of an earlier emigration from the original American homes.[67]   Of the total Pennsylvania population of 423,373 in 1790, approximately 7,000 were Dutch.

MARYLAND

Although there were no Dutch posts in Maryland, the Hollanders appeared so early that the northeastern counties may practically be considered an area of original colonization.   As early as 1659 the records show the Dutch on the Delaware asking the assistance of the Maryland authorities in securing the return of soldiers who had deserted and fled to the growing settlements on Chesapeake Bay, and the constant fear of attack by the English led to the removal of Dutch families from the vicinity of Newcastle to Maryland and Virginia.   In 1683 the Labadists settled at Bohemia Manor, and among the hundred souls comprising this colony were a few Dutch families that left a numerous progeny.[68]   The results of this Dutch pioneering are seen in the geographical distribution of 1790 stock, the counties about the head of Chesapeake Bay being the regions of Dutch concentration.   In the lower counties there are no traces of their presence, and in the table the zeros following the county names are to be taken almost literally.

The history of western Maryland is a different story.   A few of the pioneers, but more especially the landowners and speculators, came from the east; the majority of the actual settlers originated in Pennsylvania.[69]   From the Susquehanna River to the Monocacy River in Maryland there led an Indian trail, and as early as 1710 Pennsylvania Germans, following this trail which later became the famous Monocacy Road, founded the first permanent settlement of Germans in western Maryland.[70]   A few Hollanders were drawn in by this southward movement from Pennsylvania, but most of the Dutch found in these western counties came from New York and New Jersey, introduced about 1726 by John Van Metre, whose later land speculations in Virginia were to have a pronounced influence on the distribution of the Dutch stock.[71]   The census schedules for three Maryland counties are missing, but in only one of them (Allegheny) is it likely that Hollanders were present.   The analysis of the lists which are extant indicates that about 1,000 Dutch were to be found in the total population of 208,649.

VIRGINIA

Passing over the infiltration of Hollanders into tidewater Virginia, a movement to which we have reference but unsatisfactory methods of measuring, the two names associated with Dutch immigration into Virginia are John Van Metre and Joist Hite.   The Monocacy region of Maryland was but one of Van Metre's land speculations, and it was merely a resting place for many of his colonists.   In 1730 he and his brother secured a grant in the valley of Virginia which they peopled in part with these temporary Marylanders, in part with emigrants from New Jersey.   The residue they disposed of to a person of

[67] James N. Fullerton, " Squatters and titles to land in early western Pennsylvania . . .," *Western Pennsylvania historical magazine*, VI, 172; Kuykendall, *Hist. Kuykendall fam.*, 321.

[68] George Johnston, *History of Cecil County, Maryland* . . . (Elkton, 1881), 28, 31; Bartlett B. James, *The Labadist colony in Maryland* (Baltimore, 1899), 38, 39.

[69] John T. Scharf, *History of western Maryland* . . . (2 vols., Phila., 1882), II, 981.

[70] Daniel W. Nead, *The Pennsylvania-German in the settlement of Maryland* (Lancaster, 1914), 45, 46.

[71] Samuel G. Smith, *Origin and descent of an American Van Metre family* . . . (Lancaster, 1923), 30, 31.

uncertain nationality, Hite, who thereafter became the active agent.[72] Whatever his nationality, Hite had married in Ulster County, New York, and by
this act attained a relationship with the entire Hudson River Dutch community. This acquaintance he extended by a residence in Pennsylvania.
Therefore when he began colonizing among the families that he introduced were
a number of New York, New Jersey, and Pennsylvania Hollanders, who have
until this day left their nomenclature upon the region—now Hampshire and
Hardy Counties, W. Va.[73]

As the Shenandoah Valley was the route through which so many of the lines
of migration to the South and West passed, it is doubly unfortunate that the
census schedules of 1790 are not extant. This loss is offset in part by the
publication of Virginia State census lists of 1782, 1783, and 1785; but even these
are incomplete, and the years immediately preceding 1790 were an era of considerable shifting of population. But using these lists it is possible to identify
about a thousand people of Dutch descent in Virginia. These schedules include Hampshire County, but they do not include Berkeley and Hardy Counties,
which were also areas of Dutch colonization. Therefore an estimate of 1,500
Dutch in Virginia's total population of 442,117 seems a reasonable judgment.

THE SOUTH

The presence of Dutch in central Pennsylvania and the valley of Virginia
insures their presence in the Carolinas. The southward tide of population,
sweeping through the German and Scotch-Irish counties of the middle colonies,
could not but draw with it some Hollanders. They came for the most part in
small groups, the uniform distribution in most of the frontier districts suggesting their complete identification by this time with the Pennsylvania Dutch,
and except for the natural grouping of certain family names there is no place
that can be considered a Dutch settlement. There was on the Yadkin River
in Watauga County a "Jersey settlement," and it is likely that in this district
there were some directly from the areas of original Dutch colonization.[74]

In general, South Carolina received its contingent a little later than North
Carolina. Judging by the grants of land to persons of Dutch name as recorded in the North Carolina colonial records, it was about 1750–1760 that
the Dutch were entering the State, this being the generation following the one
that had pioneered in Virginia. Their children, in turn, became the colonizers
of South Carolina. Dutchmen from other colonies who had fought with Greene's
troops in the South, immediately after the Revolution came back as settlers
in these States.[75] Among the Dutch, especially in Charleston, there was also
a small element that traced its descendant back to a group of Hollanders who in
1671 deserted New York to try their fortunes in the South.[76] Many of these,
however, died; and it is probable that the names of some have been com-

[72] *Ibid.*, 31–34; Samuel G. Smyth, *A genealogy of the Duke-Shepherd-Van Metre family* . . . (Lancaster, 1909), 28, 58; S. Gordon Smyth, "Records relating to the Van
Metre, Dubois, Shepherd, Hite, and allied families," *The West Virginia historical magazine*, III, 45–55.

[73] Samuel G. Smyth, "Jost Hite, pioneer of Shenandoah valley, 1732," *W. Va. hist.
mag.*, III, 99–127; S. Gordon Smyth, "Bucks County pioneers in the valley of Virginia,"
Bucks Co. hist. soc. *Collections*, IV, 447–466.

[74] John P. Arthur, *A history of Watauga County, North Carolina* . . . (Richmond,
1915), 87–90.

[75] Kuykendall, *Hist. Kuykendall fam.*, 192–196.

[76] Edward McCrady, *The history of South Carolina under the proprietary government, 1670–1719* (N. Y., London, 1897), 144, 145.

pletely anglicized, the well-known A. B. Longstreet, for instance, being a descendant of one of these Dutchmen, Dirck Langestraet.[77] An analysis reveals 800 Dutch among the 289,181 whites in North Carolina and 500 among the 140,178 in South Carolina.

There are no census lists for Georgia, and in the indices to the voluminous published colonial records there appear only one or two entries of names that may be considered Dutch. Therefore only 100 are assigned the State.

THE WEST

A possible method of determining the number of Dutch in the West (Kentucky and Tennessee) would be applying to the population the same percentage that they bore in the rest of the country on the theory that the inhabitants of those States were drawn rather evenly from all sections and classes of the longer-settled areas. This would mean that about 3 per cent were Dutch. But 3 per cent of the total population of Kentucky and Tennessee would amount to almost 3,000, and of that number there is no trace. The Dutch stock in America was concentrated in the valley of the Hudson and in New Jersey, and from those parts the emigration was directed more to the lands north of the Ohio River. Our estimate must be based upon the scanty data available.

In the *Register of the Kentucky State Historical Society* (Vol. XXI), is reprinted the Certificate Book of the Virginia Land Commission, a book which contains the names of all landholders (practically equivalent to "heads of families") in the State before 1779–1780. Of the 2,250 recorded only 15 are Dutch—less than 1 per cent. But in the following decade when peace was established, there was a large immigration. One prominent colony of Hollanders came from York County, Pa., in 1784, and it is likely that because of the close family connections existing between all the Dutch communities in America this organized movement drew in others.[78] The Kentucky Historical Society has recently been publishing tax lists of various counties, most of them for the year 1795.[79] In these the percentage of Dutch is usually between one and two. Accordingly, it will not be far amiss to say that about 1.5 per cent of the Kentucky population in 1790 was Dutch, or, roughly, a thousand.

In Tennessee the ratio is clearly not so large. Its inhabitants of 1790 were more than pioneers; they were the advanced frontiersmen drawn from the back regions of the Carolinas at the time that the Dutch were coming into those Colonies from the north. The historian who has made the closest investigation of Tennessee origins emphasizes the fact that among the early pioneers of the State, one seldom finds names of Teutonic origin.[80] Nor does this situation seem to have changed before 1800. From 1790 to 1796 Tennessee was known as "The Territory of the United States south of the River Ohio." The journal of Governor Blount is published,[81] and among the hundreds of names mentioned—justices of the peace, militia officers, sheriffs, and the like—there are only two that can be recognized as Dutch. Of the people married in Knox County, only one has a Dutch name.[82] Certainly much less than 1 per cent were

---

[77] John D. Wade, *Augustus Baldwin Longstreet* . . . (N. Y., 1924), 2.

[78] "Low Dutch colony," *Register of the Kentucky state historical society*, XX, 301–303.

[79] Ky. st. hist. soc. *Register*, XIX, No. 57, 67–78; XXII, 220–243; XXIII, 5–17, 116–141, 209–229; XXIV, 5–23, 95–104.

[80] Albert C. Holt, *The economic and social beginnings of Tennessee* (Nashville, 1923), 43.

[81] "Governor Blount's journal," *The American historical magazine*, II, 213–277.

[82] Kate White, "Marriage record of Knox County, Tennessee," *Tennessee historical magazine*, VI, 10-14.

Dutch. A fair estimate will be 200. Therefore of the 93,046 whites in the West about 1,200 were of Holland descent.

The total derived from the State estimates is 106,750. This is about 10 per cent less than the maximum of 120,000 which might have been derived from the Dutch stock present in the Colonies about 1700. But there is no assurance that colonial population grew—apart from immigration—at a rate which doubled itself in 25 years. War and disease checked the growth and in the loyalist exodus after 1783 were probably several hundreds of families of Dutch descent. Therefore the derived figure is not unreasonable. That 90,000 of them should be concentrated in a region included in the original area of Dutch colonization indicates that the Hollanders were less mobile than the majority of their colonial neighbors.

Chapter III

THE FRENCH

The well-known failure of France to participate in that great westward movement of peoples which was the outstanding population phenomenon of the
nineteenth century Europe has stamped the French as a nonmigratory race.
Upon this circumstance the generalization has been built that the French birth
rate or the French love of country or the wars of French imperalism have
kept the Gaul at home, so that to-day, though the French flag flies over territory in America, Asia, and Africa, the people beneath that flag are brown,
black, and yellow and the civil or military administrator, when his term of
service is ended, returns to pass his last years in his beloved France.

Perhaps a century from now when the Canadian conquest of New England is
complete and the French-Canadian tongue, church, and mill worker are the
dominant features in New England society, historians will center their studies
upon that compact group of Quebec *habitants* from whom millions of Americans
have sprung. Proceeding a step farther into the Old World origin of these
pioneers they will reach seventeenth century France and a nation, not only
active in politics and war but seething with religious ferment, industrial
development, and world-wide commercial expansion. They will read of religious refugees in Holland, England, and Germany; of adventures in Guiana
and Surinam; of traders on the coast of Africa and in the wilds of Mada-
gascar; and they will also learn that these energetic spirits were not obliv-
ious to the opportunities offered by the growing Colonies directly across the
Atlantic, but that in a population in which British, Germans, Dutch, and
Swedes are clearly recognized there were also French whose very energy so
mingled them with the mass that their national characteristics were soon
obliterated.

It must be emphasized at the outset that they were a minor stock. They
can not compare in numbers with the varieties of British or the Germans.
But they deserve a recognized position along with the Dutch and the Swedes,
and the history of colonial culture will probably ascribe to them as great an
influence as that exerted by some of the more numerous groups. Nor will
it be difficult to explain why their identity was lost. Concentration and isolation are the great preservers of individual national traits. Prejudice is
effective for only one generation. The Dutchman whom chance placed in a
Puritan community may have built his Dutch barn, have continued to smoke
his Dutch pipe, have been proud of his Dutch accent, and have deliberately
refused to make his habits conform to those of this neighbors. His son,
however, who has always been sensitive to these peculiarities, deliberately
throws them off. He becomes as his neighbors and he is reckoned one of them.
But for half a century the Dutch on the Hudson were residents of New Netherland and for a generation the Swedes on the Delaware lived in New Sweden.
Those inhabitants who were not Dutch or Swedes were the peculiar individuals
whose children tried to conform. Local standards and customs perpetuated the
national traits and their great-grandchildren remained Dutch and Swedes long
after English sovereignty was asserted. Likewise the bulk of the Germans in

the middle Colonies lived in German communities that were separated from adjacent Scotch-Irish and Quaker communities by boundaries as sharp as any ethnological lines in central Europe.

The history of the colonial French is a story of dispersion. They came in various streams. Even that group which naturally possesses the most cohesion was forced to divide. The English Puritans appropriated New England; the German sectarians followed an established route to Pennsylvania; but the religious refugees of France were obliged to leave their native country in comparative haste and they began their exile in various lands—some in Switzerland, some in Germany, some in Holland, and others crossed the channel to Great Britain. Those who made these countries merely temporary resting places and sought America, then naturally continued their journey along those lines of communictation which tied each country to the New World. The religious groups were distributed from Massachusetts to South Carolina. Moreover, many of their original settlements were located in regions which geographically were the channels through which the currents of American colonial expansion were flowing. These two factors will be illustrated below.

There was a third factor the significance of which can only be hinted at until the movements of colonial population have been the subject of systematic research. That there have been periods in American development characterized by marked expansion of population has been suggested in the paper dealing with the colonial Dutch. It was there stated that one of these periods of expansion occurred shortly before and after 1700. In the last third of the seventeenth century many of the existing communities were experiencing what may be described as relative overpopulation. Indian hostility made pioneering almost suicidal and the political uncertainty threw doubt upon the validity of the titles to many frontier land grants. But it happened that during these years the influx of French was at its height; their original settlements were of necessity rather temporary; and before they struck root the defeat of the Indians and the clearer political atmosphere made possible a wave of frontier advance that was urged on by the economic depression which was greatly accentuated by the economic disorders resulting from the war. The French, settled in groups, now broke into smaller groups and following the geographic tendencies prevalent in each particular community were scattered from Maine to the Carolinas. The Dutch and the Swedes, who by all the circumstances of their existence were more firmly attached territorially, were influenced but not so universally affected by this upheaval. The era of distinct German immigration had not begun.

The majority of these French settlers were Huguenots. The process of denationalization had commenced before their arrival on American shores. Residence in the low countries, in England, and on the Rhine had already caused a readjustment of French manners and ideas and subordination of the French language. Necessity had forced adaptation upon them, and in America they conformed to the prevailing American environment. Being rebels in religion at a time when state and church were closely allied, they had no patriotic motives for retaining the characteristics of their nationality, and it has been suggested that they entered the more readily into the new life because they deliberately sought to forget the language and the customs associated with the land from which they felt they had been unjustly driven.[1]

It is impossible to obtain any satisfaction from the estimates hitherto made regarding the number of Huguenot emigrants from France to America. The

---

[1] Arthur H. Hirsch, *The Huguenots of colonial South Carolina* . . . (Durham, N. C., 1928), 77.

figures run from "a few thousands" to 50,000 "before 1750." [2] Even with respect to a limited area such as New England there are great variations. The historian Palfrey suggests 150 families numbering perhaps a thousand souls, while Fosdick considers it not possible that they amounted to less than four and five thousand. [3] But these variations are accounted for in part by differing judgments as to what is or is not a Huguenot. How, for instance, should these families be classified that had lived two or more generations in England before departing across the Atlantic?

The situation may be somewhat clarified by considering the principal Huguenot settlements. In New England the pioneer group in 1686 attempted a colony at the present-day Oxford, Mass., but the Indian hostilities soon broke it up. [4] This led to a general scattering. Some went to Boston, where a few Huguenots were already living, and among their descendants were the Bowdoin, Faneuil, Sigourney, and Brimmer families. [5] Others went to Rhode Island. The climate and the soil of the Narragansett country were considered proper for vineyards, and the French hoped that this industry might be developed and serve as an inducement to draw in many of their compatriots skilled in such matters. But the project failed. A contemporary explains that they were "most barbarously persecuted and driven away by the people of Rhode Island." [6] Those who remained, after a generation or two, partook in the general dispersion which spread the Rhode Islanders through New York and the middle Colonies. Some migrated to the South, the well-known Dabneys being descendants of an Oxford d'Aubigne; and at various places in New England traces of these Massachusetts and Rhode Island Huguenots may be found. [7]

There were French among the founders of New Amsterdam, and it is claimed that in 1685 they composed one-fourth of the population. [8] This immigration continued in 1688, the classes of Amsterdam being informed that the number of French was increasing "by daily arrivals" from Carolina, the Caribbean Islands, and Europe. [9] But many of these were merely passing through. The stay may have been of a few months' duration only; and when they did settle, farm lands in the vicinity of the city were so high in value that they were obliged to locate their homes in the more remote and newer communities. [10] Many became residents of Staten Island, whence they spread into New Jersey.

There were, however, two distinct Huguenot colonies in New York (founded about 1685–1690) which on account of their geographical position participated

---

[2] Herbert L. Osgood, *The American colonies in the eighteenth century* . . . (4 vols., N. Y., 1924), II, 489; Henry H. Ranck, "The Huguenots and American life," *The Reformed Church review*, 5th series, III, 327–346.

[3] John G. Palfrey, *History of New England* (5 vols., Boston, 1858–1890), I, viii; Lucian J. Fosdick, *The French blood in America* . . . (N. Y., 1911), 209.

[4] George F. Daniels, *The Huguenots in the Nipmuck country* . . . (Boston, 1880), 66–87.

[5] Justin Winsor (ed.), *The memorial history of Boston* . . . *1630–1880* (4 vols., Boston, 1880–1881), II, 553; Worthington C. Ford, "Ezekiel Carré and the French church in Boston," *Proceedings of the Massachusetts historical society*, LII, 121–132; Matthew C. Julien, "The Huguenots of old Boston," *Huguenot society of America, Proceedings*, III, Part I, 52–70.

[6] *Cal. st. p. col.*, *1700*, 674.

[7] E. R. Potter, "Memoir concerning the French settlements . . . in . . . Rhode Island," *Rhode Island historical tracts*, No. 5; William H. Dabney, *Sketch of the Dabneys of Virginia* . . . (Chicago, 1888); Sherman W. Adams, *The history of ancient Wethersfield, Connecticut* . . . (2 vols., N. Y., 1904), II, 42–44.

[8] James G. Wilson (ed.), *The memorial history of the city of New York* . . . (4 vols., N. Y., 1892–93), IV, 371–379.

[9] Hastings, *Eccl. rec. N. Y.*, II, 956, 959.

[10] James Riker, *Harlem* . . . (N. Y., 1881), 418.

in two of the main currents of colonial expansion; New Rochelle in Westchester County, which lay in the path of the English emigrants from Long Island who were moving up to occupy the east bank of the Hudson, and New Paltz in Ulster County, the inhabitants of which were caught in the westward stream of Dutch migration.[11] Both of these centers were prolific in descendants and many of the most honored of Huguenot names of to-day are survivals, transformations, or translations of the French names introduced by the colonists.

Into New Jersey the Huguenots came as a product of secondary migration. David Des Marest, who had already lived on Staten Island and in Harlem, received in 1677 a grant known as the " French patent "; and settling with the seven adult members of his family, he formed the nucleus of a French community which soon lost its identity in the larger Dutch element that controlled church and society.[12] But the French blood was there and it was distributed widely over the frontier by the emigrants originating in New Jersey.

From southern New York and northern New Jersey the Huguenot blood was carried over to Pennsylvania. But Pennsylvania received two more contributions—original Huguenot settlement and admixture with the Germans. By far the greater part of them came along with groups of other nationalities, but there were some direct refugees in Philadelphia, and the nearest approach to a distinct colony was the settlement in the Pequea Valley of Lancaster County.[13] This early mingling has obscured the importance of the stock in the development of Pennsylvania, and the subject is worthy of a thorough and prolonged investigation.[14] The same generalization may be made with respect to Maryland and Delaware, although in the former the prominence of certain families emphasizes the presence of the stock.[15]

Early Virginia was not a location which fostered the maintenance of compact national colonies. A Huguenot settlement was planted at Manakin town as early as 1700. At first it was the intention of the authorities to keep this group together, and farmers in the neighboring colonies were warned not to receive " into their houses as retainers " any who were destined for this settlement.[16] But within a few months the entire policy was changed. Only with difficulty could the Huguenots maintain themselves on the frontier. The charity of their neighbors was their principal support, and in October, 1700, families were allowed to disperse that they might more readily support themselves.[17] This dispersion, occurring in an established society, hastened the process of denationalization, and it is only due to the faithful work of Virginia genealogists that their original names may be recognized in present-day

[11] Robert Bolton, *The history of the several towns, manors, and patents of the county of Westchester* (2 vols., N. Y., 1881), I, 581–596; Scharf, *Hist. Westchester Co.*, I, 685–698, 709–713; LeFevre, *Hist. New Paltz*.

[12] David D. Demarest, *The Huguenots on the Hackensack* . . . (New Brunswick, N. J., 1886).

[13] James B. Laux, " The Huguenot element in Pennsylvania," Hug. soc. Amer. *Proceedings*, III, Part I, 96–116; Amon Stapleton, " The Huguenot element in the settlement of Berks County," *Transactions of the historical society of Berks County*, II, 386–401; Charles I. Landis, " Madame Mary Ferree and the Huguenots of Lancaster County," *Papers read before the Lancaster County historical society*, XXI, 101–124.

[14] A. C. Bachert, " Huguenot absorption in America," *The Pennsylvania-German* . . . (Lebanon, Pa., 1900–1911), XI, 21–28.

[15] M. R. Duvall, " Huguenots in Maryland," *The Patriotic Marylander* (Balto., 1914–1917), I, No. 4, 36–39; Mary R. Duvall, " The Duvalls of Maryland," Hug. soc. Amer., *Proceedings*, III, Part II, 137–148.

[16] H. R. McIlwaine (ed.), *Executive journals of the council of colonial Virginia* . . . (Richmond, 1925–), II, 107.

[17] McIlwaine, *Ex. jour. col. Va.*, II, 107, 113; *Cal. st. p. col., 1700*, 762.

forms.[18] In the valley of Virginia, progenitors are to be sought in Pennsylvania rather than in the tidewater counties, the opinion having been recently expressed that nine-tenths of the early settlers along the Shenandoah were emigrants from that State.[19]

In dealing with the South it is necessary to shift the base. The several Huguenot centers in South Carolina were the parent colonies from which most of the French in Georgia, North Carolina, and Tennessee were descended. It is unnecessary to enter into the history of these colonies as the subject has been exhaustively treated in a recent monograph.[20]

At the opening of the eighteenth century there was every indication that the French would be among the most important ethnic stocks in the future American population. Hitherto all groups had, for a generation at least, continued to attract fellow countrymen. But the French religious emigration seems to have come to a definite standstill, except in so far as their coming to America was a remigration from other lands in which they or their parents had at first taken refuge. It may be that all who could or cared to leave France had departed immediately after the adoption of the policy of repression. Another possible cause should be mentioned. They were not welcome.

In the popular colonial mind the fact that the Huguenot was a Protestant was overshadowed by the more evident fact that he was a Frenchman. National intolerance was as characteristic of the period of wars between 1689 and 1713 as it has been of any later era of wars. The colonists of that generation associated with the French the massacres on their frontiers, their economic difficulties, and all the hardships and restrictions of military service. Not only every stranger but even the most peaceful neighbor who spoke French was a possible spy and a potential accomplice of skulking savages. It was the opposition of the Rhode Islanders that destroyed plans for a colony of vine-growers in the Narragansett country. In Massachusetts Bay, when strange Frenchmen were noted walking at large in the town of Boston, the council ordered that all such must report to the sheriff to give an account of themselves, and all loyal subjects were strictly forbidden to harbor them.[21] The Province of New York compelled the French who lived towards the frontier to retire to more settled areas,[22] and in Pennsylvania the people petitioned that greater surveillance would be exercised over the French living among them. Some were forced to give securities and others were detained in prison on suspicion only.[23]

That this attitude should be taken toward those French who were in daily contact with the Indians was natural. Whatever treatment was accorded them would probably have little influence on the future of migration. But when it was extended to the Huguenots, who were themselves fleeing from that monarch with whom the English were contending, the national prejudice was so evident that the refugees could not but be aware of how unwelcome they were. Those living in New York were obliged to protest because "a very infamous, pernicious, and detestable report is clandestinely and industriously spread abroad amongst the inhabitants" that they were in correspondence with France and

---

[18] R. A. Brock, "Documents relating to the Huguenot emigration to Virginia," *Collections of the Virginia historical society*, new series, V; "List of ye refugees," Va. hist. soc., *Collections*, n. s., VI, 65–67; *Huguenot society of the founders of Manakin in the colony of Virginia* (San Francisco, 1924), Yearbook No. 1.

[19] Charles E. Kemper, "Early settlers in the valley of Virginia," *William and Mary college quarterly historical magazine*, 2d series, V, 259–265.

[20] Hirsch, *Hug. col. S. C.*

[21] *Cal. st. p. col., 1702–1703*, 167.

[22] O'Callaghan, *Doc. hist. N. Y.*, II, 47.

[23] *Min. prov. coun. Pa.*, I, 436, II, 19, 170, 182, 385.

revealing the nature of the fortifications that protected the city. This rumor, they complained, " is of pernicious consequence to all the *French Refugees* in general, and disturbs their peace and quiet." [24]

The Virginia group fared little better. The officers who sought to collect the quit rents and other public levies demanded that these obligations be discharged in tobacco; and although they knew that the French produced no tobacco, refused to accept any other commodities.[25] Very often the Huguenots complained in petitions regarding the treatment that they received, and it was probably in exasperation that the council warned them that they should refrain from referring to themselves as the " French colony," directed that in the future all their communications should be presented in the English language, and instructed the secretary to inform the British Government with respect to their condition and ask them " to send no more." [26]

That it was only from the Huguenots that the French blood of 1790 was descended is the impression left by most discussions of the history of the stock. Undoubtedly they did contribute the largest proportions, but the other sources should be mentioned in order to suggest the lines of investigation that are necessary to complete the estimate.

Of direct emigration from France, other than that of religious refugees, there is little trace. The colonial system of Great Britain stifled the natural commercial connections which the difference in the economic resources of America and France would logically produce, so " commercial migration" is not marked. But the study of local history reveals, especially in the more settled and prosperous areas, the presence of professional men of French extraction which hints at the infiltration of a considerable number of doctors, professors, dancing masters, wigmakers, and the like. The medical element is especially worthy of treatment, the few almost chance findings telling of Doctor Chais, of New Haven; Doctor Forgue, of Fairfield; Louis Lauriatt, the Boston chemist; Lawrence Del Honde, French physician involved in several Massachusetts controversies; Doctor Jerauld, of Medfield, Mass.; Norbert Vigneron, of New Port, R. I.; Dr. Jean Harpin, of Guilford, Conn.; Nicholas de la Vergne, of Poughkeepsie; and Doctor Quilhot, of Kinderhook. Some of them had served in the French Army during the Revolution and remained to practice in the New World. [27]

It is beyond our limits to treat of the influx of Frenchmen who ministered to the intellectual and social needs of the colonists. Fortunately two studies have appeared which prove one point, that in the years immediately preceding and following the Revolution the French language and French tastes attained a vogue in American life which made necessary the presence of French professors and those who were competent to train the rising generation in the niceties of manners; and although these studies, being more interested in the results, do not attempt any numerical review, they do present evidence which

---

[24] O'Callaghan, *Doc. hist. N. Y.,* III, 259, 262.

[25] McIlwaine, *Ex. jour. col. Va.,* III, 345.

[26] *Id.,* II, 126, 261.

[27] Edward E. Atwater (ed.), *History of the city of New Haven* . . . (N. Y., 1887), 263; Hurd, *Hist. Fairfield Co.,* 31, 481; James G. Mumford, *A narrative of medicine in America* . . . (Phila., London, 1903), 46, 158; Joseph M. Toner, *Contributions to the annals of medical progress and medical education in the United States* (Wash., 1874), 25, 71; Gurdon W. Russell, *Early medicine and early medical men in Connecticut* (Hartford, 1892), 109; Theodore Diller, *Pioneer medicine in western Pennsylvania* . . . (N. Y., 1927), 57–68; Guy C. Bayley, *An historical address delivered before the Dutchess County medical society at its centennial meeting* . . . (Poughkeepsie, 1906), 32.

explains the appearance of many scattered French names on the census rolls of 1790.[28]

Probably of greater importance, though it is a subject upon which no historian has as yet had the courage to gather every scrap of information, was the commercial connection between American ports and the French islands in the West Indies. When shortly after 1790 revolution and anarchy descended upon these islands there was a mass exodus of the French inhabitants to the American mainland. No history of the times omits a description of this migration, but the earlier movements are overlooked, and it is only in local and family histories that traces may be found. It was in New England that the West India trade was most lively, and it is there that the Frenchmen of Caribbean origin are to be sought. The Decatur, De Wolf, and Marquand families of Rhode Island and Connecticut trace their descent from this source, and that the immigrants penetrated inland is illustrated by the La Croix family of Medway, Mass. Newburyport and New London each had an appreciable colony which even before 1790 was being increased by the arrival of refugees.[29]

As the English Colonies were flanked by the French on the north as well as the south the question naturally arises, Was there an admixture of French blood from Canada? The connection, however, is more pronounced in geography than in any other circumstance. Peaceful trading relations between two regions stimulates mutual infiltration, but the history of the relations between the English Colonies and Canada is a record of hostilities—military hostilities in four colonial wars and trading competition along the lakes and in the back country. Certain conditions of life were more desirable in the English than in the French colonies, and the French Government, which found it difficult at best to people the St. Lawrence region, opposed rigorously any loss which might contribute to the strength of its rival. Evidently there were those who sought to organize such a movement, for a decree of 1684 ordained death as the punishment for those "vagabond and loafing Frenchmen" who were trying to incite desertion, and all individuals who followed the lure were warned that if captured their punishment would be the galleys for life.[30] The result was a smaller accretion from this source than otherwise would have been expected.

But an analysis of the Maine population shows this geographical factor in operation. Between Maine and the Maritime Provinces there was a normal exchange—fish, furs, grain, and lumber. French families were already living in the Maine districts as early as the middle of the seventeenth century, but their fate in the devastation of the Indian campaigns is uncertain.[31] In the last quarter of the eighteenth century changes in New Brunswick and Nova Scotia, probably induced by the settlement of the loyalists, caused a southward drift, which, though slight, was large enough to form distinct communities of French-speaking inhabitants.[32] The same influence is illustrated by the two other main lines of communication between Canada and the south, the Con-

---

[28] Howard M. Jones, *America and French culture* . . . (Chapel Hill, N. C., London, 1927); Bernard Fay, *L'Esprit révolutionnaire en France et aux États-Unis à la fin du XVIII siècle* (Paris, 1925).

[29] William D. Parsons, *The Decatur genealogy* . . . (N. Y., 1921); Calbraith B. Perry, *Charles D'Wolf of Guadaloupe, his ancestors and descendants* . . . (N. Y., 1902); Hurd, *Hist. Fairfield Co.*, 292; Ephraim O. Jameson, *The history of Medway, Massachusetts* (Providence, c. 1886), 402; Frances M. Caulkins, *History of New London, Connecticut* . . . (New London, 1895), 579; John J. Currier, *History of Newburyport, Mass.* . . . (2 vols., Newburyport, 1906–1909), I, 115.

[30] O'Callaghan, *Docs. col. hist. N. Y.*, IX, 224.

[31] George W. Drisko, *Narrative of the town of Machias,* . . . (Machias, Me., 1904), 8.

[32] Jones, *Amer. & Fr. cul.*, 109.

necticut valley and the Champlain-Hudson route. In Greenfield, on the Connecticut River, lived Aaron Denio, "keeper of the Frenchmen's tavern,"[33] and in 1750, on both shores of Lake Champlain, were French villages. How many of these inhabitants survived the succeeding wars is problematical.[34] The list of Albany heads of families in 1697 marks several as "French," and further down the river, at Kingston, were several "Catholic French" (to distinguish them from the Huguenots) whose origin was probably Canadian.[35]

There was one other line of French communications—that to the West. The French "residue" in the Great Lakes region and in the Mississippi Valley is considered in another paper. Reference must be made, however, to a supplementary route which played a prominent part in colonial politics—the roads, rivers, and portages which connected Lake Erie with the Ohio River. Although primarily military posts, there may also have been civilian traders and farmers about the stations. The northern terminus was at Presque Isle, where in 1756, in addition to the troops, was a settlement of a hundred families. Although local historians make no reference to the continuation of this settlement through the two succeeding wars, it is logical to assume that, as in the posts of the West, the habitants continued their existence, little disturbed by the fate of the French empire in America.[36] The southern terminus, Fort Duvivors of the French régime. In 1790 there were a few French in Pittsburgh, but all those of whom we have positive evidence seem to be individual immigrants who came to America in one or the other of the above-mentioned movements.[37]

There remains now one final colonial source—the Acadians. The earlier histories, influenced by poetry and tradition, leave the impression that none of the eight or ten thousand exiles remained in the Atlantic colonies or survived the fevers and hardships. It is certain that the number of the exiles can not be used to gage the stock in 1790—many died, many went to Louisiana, some took refuge in France, and a much larger contingent than usually suspected returned to Acadia. But here and there, especially in those groups that were distributed among the inland towns, a family struck root, the strange names thereafter appearing in the town records of certain Anglo-Saxon communities, bearing witness to the presence and permanent settlement of the "neutrals."[38]

Without giving it much weight reference is made to the possibility of French troops remaining in America at the close of the Revolution. That some pro-

---

[33] Francis M. Thompson . . . *History of Greenfield, . . . Mass.* (2 vols., Greenfield, 1904), I, 429.

[34] Joseph A. Bedard, "Was the Lake Champlain region entirely lost to the French with the downfall of French dominion in America?" *Proceedings of the New York State historical association*, IX, 79–94.

[35] Munsell, *Ann. Albany*, IX, 81–89 ; "The Huguenots of Old Ulster," *Olde Ulster*, II, 132 ; note also in Roswell R. Hoes (ed.), *Baptismal and marriage registers of the old Dutch church of Kingston, Ulster County, New York . . . for one hundred and fifty years from their commencement in 1660* (N. Y., 1891), 520, "Jonas Larroy, born in Cubeck" (Quebec).

[36] Benjamin Whitman, *History of Erie County, Pennsylvania* . . . (Chicago, 1884), 191. quesne, was an outpost in hostile territory, and there is no record of any sur-

[37] Charles W. Dahlinger, *Pittsburgh, a sketch of its early social life* (N. Y., London, 1916), 46.

[38] For example : Thomas Weston, *History of the town of Middleboro, Mass.* (Boston. N. Y., 1906), 100 ; Thomas B. Wyman, *The genealogies and estates of Charlestown . . . Mass.* (Boston, 1879), 286 ; Daniel T. V. Huntoon, *History of the town of Canton, Norfolk County, Massachusetts* (Cambridge, Mass., 1893), 293 ; Wilson Waters, *History of Chelmsford, Mass.* (Lowell, Mass., 1917), 167 ; Samuel Orcutt, *A history of the old town of Stratford . . .* (2 vols., New Haven, 1886), I, 506, 507 ; Sidney Perley, *The history of Boxford, Essex County, Mass. . . .* (Boxford, Mass., 1880), 184 ; George F. Daniels, *History of the town of Oxford, Massachusetts . . .* (Oxford, 1892), 124 ; Silas R. Coburn, *History of Dracut, Mass. . . .* (Lowell, Mass., 1922), 115–116 ; Jedediah Dwelley and

fessional men and officers did so remain is recorded. That their ancestor was named de Estrées and that he was a "companion of Lafayette" is the boast of the Massachusetts Detray family and in the better-known names Toussard, Bernard, and L'Enfant we have reminders of other Revolutionary Frenchmen who contributed to the organization of the new Republic. But of the privates we know nothing, and their contacts were probably not such that personal associations would persuade them to remain, even if military discipline gave them any choice.[39]

This completes a survey of the various sources of immigration. The next step is the location of as many lists of these immigrants as possible.

Naturally, the Huguenots have been the object of prolonged investigation, and the most concise statement is found in the *Revised Edition of Huguenot Ancestors*.[40] But this compilation includes only those whose descendants are active members of the organization. There were Huguenot names recognizable in 1790 which have now vanished, and therefore local lists of original settlers provide a necessary supplement. In the *Memorial History of Boston* (vol. II, p. 553) is a brief discussion of French pioneers in Massachusetts and the anglicized forms in which their names appear historically, and similar information regarding Rhode Island is given in E. R. Potter's *Memoir Concerning the French Settlements and French Settlers in the Colony of Rhode Island.*[41]

In the State of New York in addition to the local histories already mentioned, the *Records of the Town of New Rochelle* (edited by J. A. Forbes) show in deeds, reports of town meetings, and tables of town officers the changing orthography of the first pioneers and give a clue for the identification of their descendants. A list of the inhabitants of the town of New Rochelle in 1710 shows the process already at work.[42] Much additional information, especially regarding the city of New York, is scattered through the three volumes of the *Genealogical Record of the St. Nicholas Society*, in Riker's *Harlem* and in Morris's *Memorial History of Staten Island*, especially the second volume. There is extant a list of signatures of members of the French church of New York in 1724.[43] Reference to the printed genealogies of leading Huguenot families (such as Jaudon, Du Pont, Caudebec, Eno, Decatur, Pelletreau, Strang, Monnet) reveals incidentally the origin of the lines with which they intermarried.

For New Jersey two articles in the *New York Genealogical and Biographical Record* provide the foundation.[44] Stapleton in his *Memorials of the Huguenots in America* and in an article entitled "The Huguenot Element in the Settlement of Berks County" disentangles the French from the German and Scotch-

---

John F. Simmons, *History of the town of Hanover, Mass.* . . . (Hanover, 1910), 244; Henry S. Nourse, *History of the town of Harvard, Mass.* (Harvard, 1894), 293; Abijah P. Marvin, *History of the town of Lancaster, Mass.* . . . (Lancaster, 1879), 252; Deloraine P. Corey, *The history of Malden, Mass.* . . . (Malden, 1899), 693; Darius F. Lamson, *History of the town of Manchester, Essex County, Mass.* . . . (Manchester, 1895), 347; Albert K. Teele (ed.), *The history of Milton, Mass.* . . . (Boston, 1887), 414; George K. Clarke, *History of Needham, Mass.* . . . (Cambridge, Mass., c. 1912), 555–558; etc.

[39] Joseph G. Rosengarten, *French colonists and exiles in the United States* (Phila., London, 1907), 64–77.

[40] "Revised edition of Huguenot ancestors," Hug. soc. Amer., *Proceedings*, VII.

[41] Potter, *R. I. hist. tr.*, No. 5.

[42] O'Callaghan, *Doc. hist. N. Y.*, III, 571, 572.

[43] *Ibid.*, 282, 283.

[44] Edwin Salter, "Huguenot settlers and land owners in Monmouth County, New Jersey," *N. Y. gen. & biog. rec.*, XX, 30–35; Josiah C. Pumpelly, "The Huguenot builders of New Jersey," *N. Y. gen. & biog. rec.*, XXIV, 49–59.

Irish stocks to which they are usually credited.[45] These sources, together with those mentioned above in connection with the Huguenot colonization of Virginia. cover the Middle States.[46]

As has been emphasized before, the southern Huguenots had their origin in South Carolina. In their identification dependence may be placed upon the names given in Hirsch's *Huguenots of Colonial South Carolina* and a *List of French and Swiss Protestants settled in South Carolina*. (Edited by D. Ravenel.)

Of those French who entered America through the medium of commerce and military service and in the slow movement of professional infiltration there are no compilations. Genealogy and local history are the only sources. The Acadian contingent is worthy of more prolonged study than has hitherto been bestowed upon it, as there are certain Canadian collections which record the names of families settled in Nova Scotia. If at the time of deportation the names and destinations of the exiles were reported, those reports are unfortunately not extant. In the confusion which attended the embarkation, however, it is likely that no systematic records were kept. Names which were common in Nova Scotia may be found in the signatures to the oath of allegiance in 1730;[47] and J. F. Herbin in his history of Grand Pré (p. 104) gives the family names current at Minas (from which the bulk of the exiles came) at the time of the deportation. Other clues may be discovered in various articles.[48] In the proceedings of almost all of the colonial legislatures can be discovered petitions from and references to the "neutrals," documents very valuable in tracing the changes in names.

In the light of this knowledge, the census rolls of 1790 become more intelligible. Heads of families may be positively identified as French, or from the background of nomenclatural usage and traditions safe deductions may be made. This has been done for the States for which the census lists are available. No attempt has been made to secure analysis by counties, as time has been wanting and use of the State indices considerably lightens the task. Securing State rather than county estimates also makes possible the employment of certain general sources in the "census-less" States. For New Jersey, for instance, we have the printed marriage records, 1665–1800.[49] They show, if anything does, the proportions of blood in the population of eighteenth century New Jersey, and the ratio thus obtained is applied to the 1790 totals. The best that can be obtained for Delaware is the muster rolls of the State militia during the Revolutionary era.[50] Instead of using the imperfect census records of Virginia an alternative is provided in the *List of the Revolutionary Soldiers of Virginia*.[51] Likewise, *Georgia's Roster of the Revolution* is available. The sources used for the Dutch in Tennessee and Kentucky and listed in the paper on that stock have also been employed in the case of the French.

[45] Amon Stapleton, "The Huguenot element in the settlement of Berks County," Hist. soc. Berks Co., *Transactions*, II, 386–401.

[46] There is a list of the refugees at Manal in in the *Cal. st. p. col., 1700,* 456–457.

[47] *Nova Scotia archives* . . . (2 vols., Halifax, 1869–1900), I, 84–85.

[48] Placide Gaudet, "Les Seigneuries de l'ancienne Acadie," *Le Bulletin des recherches historiques*, XXXIII, 343–347 ; Gaudet, "Acadian genealogy and notes," *Canada. Report of the public archives* . . . *1905*, II, Part III ; Pascal Poirier, "Des Acadiens déportés à Boston, en 1755 . . . .," *Proceedings and transactions of the royal society of Canada*, 3d series, II, Section I, 125–180.

[49] *Documents relating to the colonial history of the State of New Jersey* . . . (35 vols., Newark, 1880–1931), 1st series, XXII.

[50] *Delaware archives* . . . (Wilmington, 1911), II.

[51] Published by the Virginia State Library, 1912.

The total estimate of 54,900 is approximately half that of the Dutch and both absolutely and relatively higher than previous estimates.[62] That the stock is not easily recognizable is due to the conditions under which it was introduced and to the more uniform distribution which it received. But this blending with other nationalities is also an indication of a closer contact with the major forces shaping American society and an evidence of greater influence in that process than the members alone suggest.

---

[62] The estimate of 17,619 is given in *A century of population growth from the first census of the United States to the twelfth, 1790–1900* (Wash., 1909), 121.

CHAPTER IV

THE SWEDES

For two decades of the seventeenth century there existed in North America, contemporaneous with New France, New England, and New Netherland, a New Sweden. In 1655 these Swedish settlements along the Delaware were conquered by their Dutch neighbors, and a few years later (1664) these united colonies were conquered by Great Britain. But it was not until 1681 that comprehensive plans were made to plant English colonies on the Delaware, and when Pennsylvania was founded the compact settlements of the Swedes had struck such firm root that a century later (at the time of the Revolution) the Swedish tongue was still spoken, Swedish churches were maintained, and Swedish customs prevailed. The vitality and individuality of these communities were recognized by all observers of the eighteenth century. It is the purpose of this paper to estimate numerically the strength of this element in 1790.

The original settlement of New Sweden was accomplished by twelve " expeditions " sent out by the trading company at home, the first in 1637–1639 and the last in 1655–56.[1] But to adventure into such distant regions was at first not a popular project, the Swedes entertaining " a repugnance to the long sea voyage to the remote and heathen land ";[2] and even later it was reported that the soldiers had " a great dread of New Sweden."[3] But settlers were secured— soldiers, traders, company servants, young men guilty of evading military service, and many offending Finns whose proclivity to burn and destroy forests (it logically seemed) might be put to some profitable use in American. But owing either to a change of conditions in Sweden or to encouraging reports from the first emigrants popular sentiment changed, and when the ninth expedition was being recruited so many Finns applied for transportation that they could not be accommodated and caused the Queen to wonder " as there was enough land to be had in Sweden."[4]

To determine how many colonists were planted upon the banks of the Delaware is impossible. It is important to note, however, that their dispersion began at an early date. New Netherland and New Sweden had a reciprocal agreement to return all who fled from one jurisdiction into the other, and cases of such rendition are on record.[5] But when the Dutch had conquered their neighbors the departure of Swedes was accelerated. The officers were taken prisoners to New Netherland, and thence sent to Holland, but the common people remained in the country.[6] Probably fearing the political influence of racial concentration, the Dutch tried to persuade Swedes to remove to the banks of the Hudson, offering as an inducement the grant of fertile lands and a pair of oxen, and that this invitation was accepted by some is indicated by the 1,500

---

[1] The history of these expeditions is told in great detail in the two volumes by Amandus Johnson, *The Swedish settlements on the Delaware;* . . . (Phila., N. Y., 1911).

[2] C. T. Odhner, " The founding of New Sweden, 1637–1642," *The Pennsylvania magazine of history and biography,* III, 396.

[3] Johnson, *Swedish on Del.,* I, 268.

[4] *Ibid.,* 267.

[5] *Ibid.,* 454.

[6] Hazard, *Pa. reg.,* IV, 76.

Swedes in New York in 1790. But the movement to the South was greater, especially following the distress that resulted from the poor harvests of 1658, and the efforts made to secure the return of those refugees who were located in Maryland were unsuccessful.[7]

The seventeenth century Swedes, however, although they seem to have been more mobile than the Dutch, did not disperse as widely as the French. The Delaware River region, where the first colonists settled, remained the home of the bulk of their descendants. We are fortunate, therefore, in having a census of the Swedish inhabitants on the Delaware made in 1693 and printed in Israel Acrelius's *A History of New Sweden*.[8] This census shows a population of 942, the families totaling 188. Among them may be some Dutch, but in general the surnames in this census are the surnames borne by the Swedish stock of 1790, and their presence in any community is an indication of the presence of this element.

The original settlements of the Swedes on the Delaware were in three general localities, the first at Christiana (now Wilmington, Del.) ; the second at Tinicum and Wicaco (now parts of Philadelphia) ; and the third across the river at Raccoon Creek and Penn's Neck (now in Gloucester County, N. J). From these three original centers they followed natural lines of expansion :

1. From Wilmington settling Newcastle County, Del., and into Maryland.
2. From Philadelphia southward along the banks of the river and up the valley of the Schuylkill.
3. From Gloucester County, N. J., along the river and bay coast into Burlington, Cumberland, Salem, and Cape May Counties.

The Swedes were " river people." Their farms extended along the banks of the Delaware and its tributaries. The river was their highway and the canoe their vehicle.[9] This explains in part their distribution. But official policy also exerted an influence. The Swedes were in America for purposes of trade, and success in this enterprise depended upon the occupation of strategic points and the retention of the good will of the Indians. Therefore the company built its posts at places convenient for trade and in so doing provided a market for the farmers ; and the friendship of the Indians, which the Swedes were unusually successful in securing, prevented that Indian terror which cramped the expansion of New Netherland. Christiana controlled the entrance to the Delaware ; Tinicum and Wicaco guarded the Schuylkill, the direct route into the richest fur country ; and the settlements east of the Delaware, though in part a natural agricultural expansion, may have been an attempt to block the overland route to New Amsterdam. The Dutch watched this strategy with consternation and reported to Holland that the Swedes were even planning to proceed northward until they could cut Albany off from its supply of peltries.[10]

But such ambitions could never be achieved with the meager support received from Sweden. The Dutch conquered the Delaware and with exception of one vessel of emigrants who had been tempted to cross the Atlantic by the encouragement of successful predecessors the colonization of the Swedes was at an end.[11] Thereafter stray individuals occasionally appeared ; half a dozen school-

---

[7] O'Callaghan, *Docs. col. hist. N. Y.*, XII, 236, 249.

[8] First edition in 1759. Translated by William M. Reynolds in *Memoirs of the historical society of Pennsylvania*, XI, 190–193.

[9] Israel D. Rupp, *Histories of the counties of Berks and Lebanon* . . . (Lancaster, 1844), 80; " Swedish settlements on the Delaware," *Pa. mag. hist. & biog.*, I, 158.

[10] O'Callaghan, *Docs. col. hist. N. Y.*, XII, 372; Edmund B. O'Callaghan, *History of New Netherland;* . . . (2 vols., N. Y., Phila., 1846–1848), II, 80.

[11] Carl D. Arfwedson, "A brief history of the colony of New Sweden . . .," 25. This early sketch of the Delaware settlements, first published in 1825, is reprinted in *Proceedings and addresses . . . of the Pennsylvania-German society*, XVIII.

masters found their way to the settlement. But before the close of the seventeenth century, in the words of Acrelius "A newly arrived Swede was then a rare bird in the country." [12] The Swedes had been planted; and although many of the followers of Penn looked with covetous eyes upon the desirable lands of the Swedish settlers, Penn did not inquire into the validity of their titles but confirmed the possession of all who applied to him.[13] The distribution of the stock in 1790 shows a natural growth from these areas of original occupation.

Christiana was located in Newcastle County and the first line of Swedish expansion was up the Delaware River. The rocky and timbered interior was occupied at a later date, in part by the descendants of these first settlers, in part by the cosmopolitan immigrants of the eighteenth century.[14] But the county did not lose its original complexion and in 1790, although overshadowed by the other elements, the traces of the Swedes were marked. The intensity, however, varied from district to district. Unfortunately the census lists of 1790 are not extant, but assessment lists and lists of taxables in the various local divisions called "hundreds" are available. Most of these lists date from 1787; a few from 1804. But they are close enough to 1790 to give a clue to the general ratio of nationalities.[15]

Studying these lists in the light of our positive knowledge of the names borne by the Swedes, the results varied from 24 per cent in Christiana Hundred and 22 per cent and 20 per cent in most of the other northern hundreds to 6 per cent and 8 per cent in the southern parts of the county. But 20 per cent may be taken as the average for the county—a reasonable ratio in spite of the early start obtained by the Swedes, as during the early part of the eighteenth century Wilmington was as important a passenger port as Philadelphia and the Scotch and Irish immigrants bound for Pennsylvania and Maryland left a residue along their route. The population of the county in 1790 was 16,487, of whom 3,500 may be considered of Swedish blood.

The two other counties of Delaware are Kent and Sussex. They adjoin Maryland and received a large part of their population from Maryland and Pennsylvania.[16] A perusal of the tax lists shows this origin very clearly. Only occasionally is one of the Swedish names discovered, but they are spread so regularly that they indicate a general though small infiltration. But they would compose less than 2 per cent of the population of Kent and Sussex Counties; and of the totals, 300 in each may have been Swedes. This results in a total of 4,100 in Delaware.

There is no natural boundary between Delaware and Maryland, and one would expect to find in the latter evidence of expansion from the Swedish settlements, especially in the counties which are contiguous. The first of these is Cecil County. Two Swedish missionaries who visited the region in 1697 left record of a settlement on the Elk River, known as "Transtown." But an early and local historian has declared (without indicating his sources) that these settlers were Hollanders, who traded under a license from Sweden and spoke the Swedish language.[17] Applying the method indicated above to the heads of

---

[12] Acrelius, *Hist. New Sweden*, 352, 365. Quotation on 181.

[13] "A local incident of early colonial days, 1722–1723," *Pa. mag. hist. & biog.*, XXXVIII, 430.

[14] Henry C. Conrad. *History of the State of Delaware* . . . (3 vols., Wilmington, 1908), II. 451.

[15] Scharf, *Hist. Del.*, II, 851–852, 882–885, 902–903, 917–918, 934–935, 952–954, 966, 989–991, 1018–1019.

[16] Conrad, *Hist. Del.*, II, 579.

[17] Benjamin Ferris, *A history of the original settlements on the Delaware* . . . (Wilmington, 1846), 156.

families list in the census of 1790, of the white population, about 3 per cent, or 300, appeared Swedish.

In Kent County a Swedish post was established in 1653, but the English in Maryland looked upon them as interlopers. There were open hostilities, and most, if not all, of the Swedes returned to the Delaware.[18] Studying the names, it seems probable that 1 per cent may have been Swedish—about 75. Caroline County was also contiguous to the Swedish area in Delaware, but the census of 1790 gives little indication of Swedish settlement. The same is true with respect to the remainder of the State. Eastern Maryland was peopled by primary migration via the Chesapeake, and western Maryland by secondary migration from Pennsylvania. In the northern tier of counties there is accordingly a sprinkling of Swedes brought down from the Pennsylvania settlements, but the total for Maryland does not exceed 950.

The Swedish settlements on the banks of the Delaware crept up from Christiana and met settlements coming down the river from the posts at Tinicum and Wicaco (Philadelphia). The area of these original posts was later included in Philadelphia and Delaware Counties, but the Swedes were agricultural in their pursuits and their increase did not keep pace with the growth of population in the urban community of Philadelphia. In their search for agricultural land they struck toward the east into New Jersey and toward the west up the valley of the Schuylkill. By these last the most compact settlement was made in Montgomery County, but they were mixed in greater or less degree among the Scotch, Irish, and Germans in all the agricultural regions of Pennsylvania, especially south of the Schuylkill.

As the Pennsylvania census records are complete, it is not necessary to go into detail with the history of settlement. Perhaps less than 1½ per cent of the inhabitants of Philadelphia County were Swedish, and of a total of 51,916 whites about 750 may be so considered. The site of the neighboring city of Chester was originally a Swedish tobacco farm and the Swedish blood was diffused among the later comers, except the Quakers, who more strictly intermarried among their own group.[19] A study of the 1790 list yields 4 per cent in Delaware County, and consequently about 400 were Swedes.

The largest agricultural settlement of Swedes in Pennsylvania was made along the banks of the Schuylkill in Montgomery County. Place names are remains of this settlement, the geography of the county recording Swedes Ford, Swedesburg, and Matson's Ford.[20] But they occupied only a corner of the county; the Welsh and English were present in overwhelming proportions, and of the total population only 3 per cent, or about 700, may be accounted Swedes.

In the next county up the Schuylkill the Swedes planted one colony "and they did not wander away, remaining in the township almost entirely."[21] Traces of other settlements may be discovered in succeeding colonies, especially to the southwest. If the total of 3,325 for the State as a whole seems rather small, it must be remembered that Pennsylvania contributed largely to the Swedish colonization of New Jersey, and that Maryland, Virginia, and the South drew upon its rural population for its pioneers.

[18] George A. Hanson, *Old Kent; the eastern shore of Maryland;* . . . (Balto., 1876), 71.
[19] John H. Martin, *Chester (and its vicinity) Delaware County, in Pennsylvania;* . . . (Phila., 1877), 19; Henry G. Ashmead, *History of Delaware County, Pennsylvania* . . . (Phila., 1884), 327.
[20] S. Gordon Smyth, "Matson's ford," *Historical sketches. Historical society of Montgomery County, Pennsylvania,* IV, 62–72; G. W. Holstein, "Sketch of Swedes ford and its surroundings," Hist. soc. Mont. Co., *Sketches,* IV, 73–77; there is a general history of the Swedes in the county in Theodore W. Bean (ed.), *History of Montgomery County, Pennsylvania* (Phila., 1884), 1125–1129.
[21] Morton L. Montgomery, *History of Berks County in Pennsylvania* (Phila., 1886), 65.

Politically, the two original posts east of the Delaware (Raccoon and Penn's Neck) were unimportant; but when the Pennsylvania settlements began to expand New Jersey rapidly became the seat of the most flourishing Swedish communities. As mentioned before, the Swedes avoided the heavily timbered interior and located along the river and bay shores where the soil was easily cleared and there was an abundance of natural meadows. In these respects the New Jersey shore was ideal. There is a tradition that the conquest of New Sweden by Stuyvesant caused many to flee from his jurisdiction and they sought refuge in the Jersey wilds.[22] True or not, it is a fact that during the second half of the century all the desirable coast spots in southern New Jersey had been seized by Swedish pioneers and in the next hundred years their descendants moved into the interior as families grew and less desirable locations had to be occupied.

But it would be incorrect to assume that the Swedes were the only original settlers. Long Islanders and New Englanders from Connecticut engaged in whaling activities in the Deleware Bay region and their stations, at first merely fishing villages, gradually became the nuclei about which agriculturists settled. About one-fifth of the old family names of New Haven and Cape May are similar—an indication of this original connection.[23] The vigorous methods of colonization adopted by the proprietors of west Jersey brought in many directly from Europe, and long before 1790 the Swedes were in a minority.[24]

A numerical allocation of these elements is difficult, as the New Jersey census lists of 1790 are missing and there are no printed tax lists. Therefore it has been necessary to use company rolls from the Revolution and the other sources indicated in the paper on the Dutch. The result is a confirmation of the historical evidence. The Swedes are concentrated in the south and west of the State, more than 5,000 of the total 6,650 being located in 5 of the 13 counties. But their presence is also evident in those regions tributary to New York City— an indication that the efforts made to lure the conquered Swedes to the vicinity of New Amsterdam were not without results.

These efforts, the natural attraction of a metropolis, and the Swedish element among the colonizers of New Netherland can explain the 1,500 found in the State of New York.[25] The trade between New England and the Delaware accounts for the Swedes discovered in the commercial cities of the North. But their strength in Virginia and the Carolinas is somewhat surprising, and local history has not yet provided us with sources which interpret their presence. But they are unmistakably there, as familiar Delaware region surnames and the equally significant given names of "Hance" and "Mounce" clearly indicate. They prove that the Dutch conquerors of New Sweden, who complained that their new subjects would all flee to the south, were not expressing imaginary fears.[26] In determining the number in the South and West, use has been made of the sources enumerated in the paper on the Dutch.

The total of 21,500 Swedes in 1790 is reasonable. Acrelius gives the Swedish population of the Delaware region as 942 in 1693, and Rev. Andrew Rudman, then a minister in the Colony, reported in 1697 that there were about 1,200 per-

[22] Maurice Beesley, *Sketch of the early history of Cape May County, to accompany the geological report of the State of New Jersey* . . . (Trenton, 1857), 165.

[23] Lewis T. Stevens, *The history of Cape May County, N. J.* . . . (Cape May City, 1897), 30.

[24] Cushing and Sheppard, *Hist. Gloucester, Salem, Cumberland Cos.*, 510–518.

[25] John O. Evjen, *Scandinavian immigrants in New York 1630–1674;* . . . (Minneapolis, 1916).

[26] O'Callaghan, *Docs. col. hist. N. Y.*, II, 115.

sons who spoke the Swedish tongue.[27] This may have included some of other nationalities. If the total seems a little large it must be remembered that it includes the decendants of those who had already left the Delaware before the enumerations were made and of others who were original colonizers along the Hudson.

State and counties	White population	Dutch	Swedes	French
Maine	96, 107	100	0	1, 200
New Hampshire	141, 112	100	0	1, 000
Vermont	85, 072	500	0	350
Addison	6, 383	50		
Bennington	12, 173	150		
Chittenden	7, 264	100		
Orange	10, 485	25		
Rutland	15, 558	75		
Windham	17, 514	50		
Windsor	15, 695	50		
Massachusetts	373, 187	600	75	3, 000
Barnstable	16, 970	0		
Berkshire	29, 940	350		
Bristol	30, 966	0		
Dukes	3, 230	0		
Essex	57, 007	25		
Hampshire	59, 205	125		
Middlesex	42, 177	0		
Nantucket	4, 521	0		
Plymouth	29, 013	25		
Suffolk	43, 803	50		
Worcester	56, 355	25		
Connecticut	232, 236	600	25	2, 100
Fairfield	35, 173	150		
Hartford	37, 498	50		
Litchfield	38, 119	150		
Middlesex	18, 492	25		
New Haven	29, 882	125		
New London	31, 605	50		
Tolland	13, 111	25		
Windham	28, 356	25		
Rhode Island	64, 670	250	50	500
Bristol	3, 013	25		
Kent	8, 439	25		
Newport	13, 174	75		
Providence	23, 518	50		
Washington	16, 526	75		
New York	314, 366	55, 000	1, 500	12, 000
Albany	72, 087	15, 750		
Clinton	1, 583	50		
Columbia	25, 811	5, 000		
Dutchess	42, 981	6, 000		
Kings	3, 021	1, 500		
Montgomery	28, 223	3, 500		
New York	29, 619	5, 000		
Ontario	1, 058	50		
Orange	17, 315	4, 000		
Queens	12, 886	2, 000		
Richmond	2, 945	750		
Suffolk	14, 310	500		
Ulster	26, 295	8, 000		
Washington	14, 028	400		
West Chester	22, 204	2, 500		
New Jersey	169, 954	35, 000	6, 650	4, 000
Bergen	10, 108	7, 500	300	
Burlington	17, 270	1, 200	1, 400	
Cape May	2, 416	100	200	
Cumberland	7, 990	500	800	
Essex	16, 454	2, 000	50	

[27] Tomas Campanius Holm, *A short description of the province of New Sweden* . . ., 102. A translation of this early description (first published in 1702) is given in Hist soc. Pa., *Memoirs*, III.

State and counties	White population	Dutch	Swedes	French
New Jersey—Continued.				
Gloucester	12, 830	750	1, 800	----------
Hunterdon	18, 661	2, 000	100	----------
Middlesex	14, 498	4, 000	200	----------
Monmouth	14, 969	4, 500	250	----------
Morris	15, 532	750	250	----------
Salem	9, 891	200	1, 000	----------
Somerset	10, 339	8, 250	200	----------
Sussex	18, 996	3, 250	100	----------
Delaware	46, 310	2, 000	4, 100	750
Kent	14, 050	600	300	----------
Newcastle	16, 487	1, 200	3, 500	----------
Sussex	15, 773	200	300	----------
Pennsylvania	423, 373	7, 500	3, 325	7, 500
Allegheny	10, 032	100	100	----------
Bedford	13, 052	150	150	----------
Berks	29, 928	125	150	----------
Bucks	24, 374	1, 200	75	----------
Chester	27, 141	100	200	----------
Cumberland	17, 779	100	75	----------
Dauphin	17, 886	75	100	----------
Delaware	9, 133	75	400	----------
Fayette	12, 990	300	50	----------
Franklin	15, 057	100	50	----------
Huntingdon	7, 491	100	0	----------
Lancaster	35, 192	150	75	----------
Luzerne	4, 868	400	0	----------
Mifflin	7, 461	75	0	----------
Montgomery	22, 365	600	700	----------
Northampton	24, 086	1, 500	75	----------
Northumberland	16, 971	600	25	----------
Philadelphia	51, 916	600	750	----------
Washington	23, 617	250	50	----------
Westmoreland	15, 852	300	100	----------
York	36, 182	600	200	----------
Maryland	208, 649	1, 000	950	2, 500
Allegany [1]	4, 539	75	50	----------
Ann Arundel	11, 664	0	25	----------
Baltimore	30, 878	200	100	----------
Calvert [1]	4, 211	0	0	----------
Caroline	7, 028	0	25	----------
Cecil	10, 055	125	300	----------
Charles	10, 124	0	50	----------
Dorchester	10, 010	0	25	----------
Frederick	26, 937	150	75	----------
Harford	10, 784	75	50	----------
Kent	6, 748	150	75	----------
Montgomery	11, 679	25	50	----------
Prince Georges	10, 004	0	0	----------
Queen Anne	8, 171	50	25	----------
St. Marys	8, 216	0	0	----------
Somerset [1]	8, 272	0	0	----------
Talbot	7, 231	0	0	----------
Washington	14, 472	150	50	----------
Worcester	7, 626	0	50	----------
Virginia	442, 117	1, 500	2, 600	6, 500
North Carolina (districts)	289, 181	800	700	4, 800
Edenton	33, 568	100	100	----------
Fayette	28, 112	75	25	----------
Halifax	37, 955	25	100	----------
Hillsborough	45, 820	100	150	----------
Morgan	30, 687	150	50	----------
New Bern	38, 800	100	125	----------
Salisbury	58, 425	200	100	----------
Wilmington	15, 814	50	50	----------
South Carolina (districts)	140, 178	500	325	5, 500
Beaufort	4, 364	50	0	----------
Camden	29, 242	0	25	----------
Charleston	15, 402	100	50	----------
Cheraw	7, 418	125	0	----------
Georgetown	8, 878	0	25	----------
Ninety-six	62, 462	200	150	----------
Orangeburg	12, 412	25	75	----------
Georgia	52, 886	100	300	1, 200
Kentucky	} 93, 046	1, 200	500	{ 1,500 } 2,000 { 500 }
Tennessee				
Total	3, 172, 444	106, 750	21, 100	54, 900

[1] Census schedules missing.

Annex C.—THE POPULATION OF THE AMERICAN OUT-LYING REGIONS IN 1790

By Marcus L. Hansen

The "native stock" in the present-day United States is descended not only from those ancestors listed in the first census but also from pioneers who were living in areas not covered by that census or in territories which have become American since 1790. Specifically, the region known as the Old Northwest was practically unorganized and no enumeration was made; and Florida and the entire trans-Mississippi West have been secured by purchase or cession subsequent to that date. To make the appraisal of the native stock complete it is, therefore, necessary to supplement the official figures with an estimate of the number and composition of the contemporary population in these "outlying" regions. The task is twofold: First, to estimate the number of the inhabitants and, second, to allocate them to the various stocks. The term "Americans" refers to people descended from colonists originally settled on the seaboard and whose blood would be of the same composite nature as that exhibited by the Americans living in these older areas.

THE OLD NORTHWEST

The region historically known as the "Old Northwest" is now included in the States of Ohio, Indiana, Illinois, Michigan, and Wisconsin. In 1790, the machinery of government was so feeble and all public and private enterprises so paralyzed by the Indian war, that an enumeration, although planned, was never carried out. The following year a current magazine reported the population of the region in 1790 as 4,280,[1] and this figure has been quoted, exactly or approximately, as the results of a census or official estimate.[2] But whether official or not, it was not complete, figures for only a part of the known settlements appearing. There are, however, two estimates which carry more authority. Early in 1789, Congress was informed that the inhabitants numbered 7,000[3] and in the winter of 1795-96, Gvernor St. Clair and Judge Turner, who had just returned from a tour through the settled parts, jointly reported a population of 15,000 as their best opinion.[4] But the seasons of 1789 and 1790 witnessed a large immigration so that the actual number will be greater than the first figures quoted. On the other hand, the cessation of Indian hostilities brought a renewal of the movement in 1794 and 1795 so that the second figure will be too high. The population in 1790 was somewhere between the two. Although estimates for the region as a whole are scanty, considerable information exists regarding the particular settlements, and the safest method will be to consider each locality by itself and deduce the total from these local figures.

---

[1] *The American museum or universal magazine* . . . (Philadelphia, 1787–1792), IX, 8.

[2] Frederick A. Ogg, *The old northwest;* . . . (New Haven, 1919), 98 ; John B. McMaster, *History of the people of the United States* . . . (7 vols., N. Y., 1913), II, 575.

[3] *Annals of Congress* (2 vols., Wash., 1834), I, 412.

[4] Jacob Burnet, *Notes on the early settlement of the Northwestern Territory* (Cincinnati, 1847), 31.

The French era in the history of the Old Northwest left no population within the bounds of the present State of Ohio. Its permanent settlement began in the closing years of the Revolution—a desultory, individual, and (according to the land laws) an illegal movement which is necessarily difficult to gage. As early as 1785 the settlers comprised probably a hundred families and although their illegal homes were destroyed by American troops that year undoubtedly most of the squatters returned as John Mathews, who in 1786 was a member of the party engaged in surveying the Seven Ranges, speaks in his journal of the Mingo Bottom as being "considerably settled" and records social functions and the presence of social institutions that presuppose a considerable community.[5] Others, driven out by the Indians, were refugees in the cities on the left bank of the Ohio where, not being permanent, they were not included in the census; and several were held as captives by the tribes.[6] All together these squatters and refugees must have numbered at least 500.

More definite information is extant regarding the organized and legal settlements which were made in the years 1788, 1789, and 1790. The town of Marietta was founded in 1788 as the metropolis of the Ohio Company Purchase. The first group of settlers numbered only 47, but in the year 1789 the arrivals were numerous enough to make possible an extension into the back country. It is not likely, however, that they totaled more than 200 families.[7] Definite figures may be obtained from a return of men available in January, 1791, for the protection of Marietta. This return reports 264 militia, 8 civil officers, and 29 old men—a total of 301.[8] There were, perhaps, some isolated settlers not enrolled in the militia, but as this force included all boys above 16, the total of 301 represents a population that could hardly be greater than 1,000. This is, in fact, the number of inhabitants ascribed to the company's lands in the contemporary magazine article referred to above.[9] The geographer, Jedediah Morse, reported the population in 1792 as 2,500;[10] but the campaign against the Indians which began in 1791 was conducted from Marietta and the years 1791 and 1792 undoubtedly witnessed a considerable influx.

Lying between the Little and Big Miami Rivers was a group of settlements usually referred to as "Colonel Symmes' Settlements" of which the most important were Cincinnati and Columbia. In May, 1790, the number of men capable of bearing arms totalled 410.[11] A newspaper item of the same date states that in the town of Columbia there were 500 residents of whom 150 were of military age.[12] This would allow slightly over 3 inhabitants for each member of the militia and give to the entire area a population of about 1,350. But

[5] Charles A. Hanna, *Historical collections of Harrison County, in the State of Ohio.* . . . (N. Y., 1900), 51–53; Archer B. Hulbert (ed.), *Ohio in the time of the confederation* (Marietta, Ohio, 1918), 201, 210. John Matthew's journal is printed in this latter volume. Other references to these squatters may be found in the *Ohio archaeological and historical publications* (13 vols., Columbus, Ohio, 1900–1909), VII, 169, VIII, 231; Henry Howe, *Historical collections of Ohio* . . . (2 vols., Columbus, Ohio, 1890–91), I 314, 325; Journal of Col. John May, of Boston, relative to a journey to the Ohio country, 1789, *Pa. mag. hist. & biog.* XLV, 144.

[6] *American state papers. Documents legislative and executive of the congress of the United States.* . . . *Indian affairs* (Wash., 1832–1861), I, 87; Beverley W. Bond, jr. (ed.), *The correspondence of John Cleves Symmes* . . . (N. Y., 1926), 129.

[7] Howe, *Hist. coll. O.,* II, 778–782; Clement L. Martzolff, Big Bottom and its history, *Ohio archaeological and historical quarterly,* XV, 2–4.

[8] Rufus Putnam, *The memoirs of Rufus Putnam* . . . (Boston, N. Y., 1903), 113.

[9] *The Amer. museum,* IX, 8.

[10] Jedidah Morse, *The American geography,* . . . (London, 1794), 457.

[11] Beverley W. Bond (ed.), Dr. Daniel Drake's memoir of the Miami County, 1779–1794, *Quarterly publication of the historical and philosophical society of Ohio,* XVIII, 80.

[12] *New York daily advertiser,* May 25, 1790.

in the summer of 1790 there was a considerable accretion; Symmes wrote in November that the population of Cincinnati had doubled in the preceding nine months,[13] and to credit the region with 1,500 souls is not an exaggeration.

A third colony introduced the only non-American elements. Gallipolis was founded and peopled by revolutionary refugees from France. In the summer there arrived emigrants whose numbers have been variously estimated at from 500 to 800.[14] The latter is probably nearer the truth as in the main group there came 600[15] and other contingents followed. There were also in this colony Americans who had been hired to perform the pioneer work of clearing the township.[16] Morse's estimate for 1792 is 1,000.[17] After 1790 there is no record of a further immigration and the natural increase was certainly offset by the marked mortality. Therefore, it is logical to adopt the figure 1,000 for 1790 and divide the total into 750 French and 250 Americans. Combining these local summaries the total population of Ohio in 1790 was 4,000 of whom 3,250 were Americans and 750 French.

The American settlement of Indiana did not begin in earnest until after the close of the Indian war in 1795 and its inhabitants in 1790 were grouped around the old French posts on the Wabash. Of these the most important was Vincennes. When Governor Hamilton captured the post in 1778 the inhabitants numbered 621[18] and in 1787 General Harmar reported a population consisting of " about " 900 French and 400 Americans.[19] But his estimate of the French is somewhat exaggerated. Symmes, who passed through the community in the summer of 1790, without venturing a figure, states that the reports current as to its population could not be believed from its appearance and that there had been a considerable emigration to the Spanish territory beyond the Mississippi.[20] Most reliable is the evidence available from Catholic sources which indicates a parish of about 700.[21] General Harmar's statement regarding the Americans, however, is undoubtedly correct. The American infiltration into the town was very marked; John Filson found 60 American families already there in 1785; and 400 is a reasonable estimate.[22]

North of Vincennes was Fort Quiatanon, of uncertain size, but described in 1769 as consisting of 12 heads of families.[23] When General Scott destroyed it in 1791 he found there 70 houses and reported that " many of the inhabitants " were French.[24] There was also another large village at Miamitown (the later Fort Wayne), General Harmar reporting in the fall of 1790 that he had burned its 300 log houses and wigwams. Nowhere is definite information regarding the number of French traders at this post recorded, but from the journal of

[13] Bond, *Symmes corr.*, 135.

[14] John L. Vance, The French settlement and settlers of Gallipolis. O., arch. & hist. *Publications*, III, 49; Laurence J. Kenney, The Gallipolis colony, *The Catholic historical review*, IV, 433.

[15] Bond, *Symmes corr.*, 267.

[16] Howe, *Hist. coll. O.*, I, 673.

[17] Morse, *Amer. geog.*, 457.

[18] Account of the expedition of Lieut. Gov. Hamilton, *Pioneer collections . . . of the pioneer and historical society of the State of Michigan* (39 vols., Lansing, 1877–1915), IX, 495.

[19] William H. Smith, *The St. Clair papers* . . .(2 vols., Cincinnati, 1882), II, 27.

[20] Bond, *Symmes corr.*, 287.

[21] Herman J. Alerding, *A history of the Catholic church in the diocese of Vincennes* . . . (Indianapolis, 1883), 60, 63.

[22] Samuel P. Hildreth, *Pioneer history; being an account of the first examinations of the Ohio Valley, . . .* (Cincinnati, N. Y., 1848), 156; Beverley W. Bond, jr. (ed.), Two westward journeys of John Filson, 1785, *Mississippi Valley historical review*, IX, 320–330.

[23] Jacob P. Dunn, *Indiana and Indianans* . . . (Chicago, N. Y., 1919), 94.

[24] *Amer. st. p. Ind. aff.*, I, 131.

Henry Hay, who spent the winter of 1789–90 at the place, and who mingled freely in the rather boisterous society, one would judge there may have been a score of households. Hay also mentions the coming and going of traders stationed at scattered posts (if a cabin or two may be so described), so the total French population in Indiana may be placed at a thousand.[25]

To the Americans at Vincennes should be added a hundred at " Clark's grant " in the corner of the State, the settlement of which began in 1783 but which grew very slowly.[26] No allowance need be made for scattered groups. None could exist. Vincennes was practically isolated, messengers and travelers reaching it only by passing through a gauntlet of ambushed savages.[27] Indiana may be credited with 1,500 inhabitants, 1,000 French, and 500 Americans.

There is extant an exact census of the Illinois settlements in 1787, the French numbering at:

Kaskaskia	191
Prairie du Rocher	79
St. Philipp	11
Cahokia	239
Total	[28] 520

But from a report of General Harmar who quotes these figures, it is evident that they refer only to males.[29] Therefore, this number should be doubled to ascertain the total French population. This would result in approximately a thousand in 1787. In the three succeeding years there would be a slight decrease due to emigration across the Mississippi, but as there was a French settlement at Peoria (seven traders who were living there are named by a traveller of 1790)[30] and as there may have been a family or two at Chicago[31] the figure of a thousand may stand as the estimate of Illinois French. At the time when the above mentioned census was taken there were in the American settlements 62 men and 35 male children enrolled.[32] The figure 300 would cover all Americans of both sexes in Illinois in 1790.

In 1782, a census of Detroit and its immediate environs revealed the presence of 2,021 whites. A list of the 321 heads of families is extant.[33] This would mean about six persons per family. Forty of these heads of families have names clearly Anglo-American and they may be credited with accounting for a population of about 250. This would leave the French element at 1,750.

In the eight years that followed the growth of the community was slow. As the military posts were retained by the British, there was no incentive for American immigration, and the uncertainty of its future status checked internal development. Two settlements were, however, made in the vicinity. In 1784, about a hundred French families, some from Canada, some from Detroit, founded Frenchtown on the River Raisin, a community that spread with considerable rapidity. But the first evidence of Americans among them ap-

[25] *Ibid.*, 104 ; M. M. Quaife (ed.), A narrative of life on the old frontier, *Proceedings of the state historical society of Wisconsin . . . 1914*, 208–261.

[26] Lewis C. Baird, . . . *History of Clark County, Indiana* (Indianapolis, 1909), 25, 44.

[27] *New York daily advertiser*, August 23, 1790, (letter from Vincennes dated June 23, 1790) ; *Amer. st. p. Public lands,* I, 289.

[28] Clarence W. Alvord (ed.), . . . *Kaskaskia records, 1778–1790 . . .* (Springfield, Ill., 1909), 449.

[29] Smith, *St. Clair pap.,* II, 31.

[30] Milo M. Quaife (ed.), Hugh Heward's journal from Detroit to the Illinois; 1790, *The John Askin papers . . .* (Detroit, 1928–), I, 339–360, 359.

[31] Helen Troesch, The first convent in Illinois, *Illinois Catholic historical review,* I, 359.

[32] Alvord, *Kaskaskia rec.,* 421–423.

[33] *Mich. pioneer coll.,* X, 601–611.

pears in 1793.[34] During the same years the lands bordering the River Clinton were being occupied and by 1790 more than 60 families had arrived. The names that have survived are principally French with a sprinkling of Anglo-American.[35] Assuming as in Detroit, six members in each family, these 160 families on the Raisin and Clinton Rivers would number about a thousand souls.

Until 1796, Michigan was under the actual jurisdiction of Canada, and a letter among the papers of Governor Simcoe of Upper Canada reveals that in 1794 the population of the Detroit area was estimated at 3,000.[36] This agrees well with the local information recorded above and may be taken as an estimate for the year 1790—of the total, 2,600 being French and 400 Anglo-American.[37]

On the opposite side of the Peninsula, at St. Joseph, there existed until 1781 a French post of about 50 persons. But it was destroyed in the Revolution and its inhabitants scattered among the other settlements.[38] Mackinac, on the upper peninsula, was the center of an extensive Indian trade. The first figures available are those recorded in the census of 1800. At that time there were resident at Mackinac 251 whites and about 300 boatmen and traders made it their headquarters. There was no change in this upper country in the decade from 1790 to 1800, and these statistics may be used safely for the earlier date. In nationality they were overwhelmingly French and the total may be divided: French, 500; Americans, 50.

The summary for Michigan reveals a total of 3,550 of whom 3,100 were French and 450 Americans.

For those settlements which are now in the State of Wisconsin, the census of 1800 ascribes 50 white inhabitants to Green Bay and 65 to Prairie du Chien. How stationary Wisconsin's population was in these years is illustrated by the fact that in 1785 Green Bay had a white population of 56.[39] In Wisconsin, also, there were boatmen in the woods and perhaps traders at Milwaukee, Portage, and LaPointe. But in any case the total population of Wisconsin in 1790 did not exceed 150 French.

Recapitulation of the Old Northwest in 1790

	Americans	French	Total
Ohio	3,250	750	4,000
Indiana	500	1,000	1,500
Illinois	300	1,000	1,300
Michigan	450	3,100	3,550
Wisconsin		150	150
	4,500	6,000	10,500

THE LOUISIANA PURCHASE

Louisiana was acquired by purchase from France in 1803. Its boundaries were indefinite and there was even more uncertainty as to the number of its

---

[34] Talcott E. Wing (ed.), *History of Monroe County, Michigan* . . . (N. Y., 1890), 37–45.

[35] M. A. Leeson, *History of Macomb County, Michigan* . . . (Chicago, 1882), 200–213.

[36] E. A. Cruikshank (ed.), *The correspondence of Lieut. Governor John Graves Simcoe* . . . (4 vols., Toronto, 1923–1926), II, 358.

[37] Reference must also be made to an estimate of 4,000 for the Detroit region in 1789. William R. Riddell, *The life of William Drummer Powell* . . . (Lansing, Mich., 1924), 73.

[38] Clarence W. Alvord, The conquest of St. Joseph, Michigan, by the Spaniards in 1781, *Missouri historical review*, II, 195–210.

[39] Augustin Grignon, Seventy-two years' recollections of Wisconsin, *Collections of the state historical society of Wisconsin* (reprint edition, Madison, 1903–1908), III, 241.

inhabitants.   A pamphlet entitled *Information regarding Louisiana* was published officially in 1804.   It contains an estimate of population, and this estimate being reprinted in the *American State Papers* has received wide currency and is usually quoted as authoritative in any discussion of Louisiana in 1803.[40] The source of the figures is not given, except the uncertain "taken from the latest returns"; but it is admitted that they are "manifestly incorrect, the population being underestimated."   The first official American figures were obtained by a census of the "Territory of Orleans" (Louisiana) taken in 1806 and revealed the presence of 25,493 whites.[41]   A possible method of estimating the numbers in 1790 would be to project these figures back to the earlier date, but in view of the shifts in population taking place in these 15 years, this is considered a dangerous procedure and therefore reliance is placed upon the Spanish sources nearest in time to 1790.

The last general Spanish census of both upper and lower Louisiana dates from 1788.   These figures may be taken as providing a basis for the calculation of the population in 1790.   Although detailed figures are given for the individual parishes, unfortunately these figures do not distinguish between whites and blacks.   This makes an entirely satisfactory analysis impossible, as the proportion varies from parish to parish and it is chiefly through our knowledge of the history of these parishes that the division into nationalities must be made.   But three years before, in 1785, there had also been a count and this provides the desired information as to race.   It may be assumed that three years later the proportion was approximately the same except in certain of the Mississippi River communities into which we have record of American infiltration.[42]

Even a superficial acquaintance with population conditions in Louisiana reveals that the bulk of the people were of French descent.   Policy during the French régime did not encourage the settlement of other stocks and no general Spanish colonization was undertaken after the transfer of the province in 1763.   But Spaniards did come in (officials, traders, and adventurers); Americans crossed the river; a few British merchants established themselves in New Orleans; and the descendants of a unique German colony were present in considerable numbers.   Therefore the simplest and most reasonable method will be to estimate the size of these stocks and by subtraction to secure a figure which may be taken as representing the number of French.

Contemporaries who considered the matter grouped the inhabitants geographically under three headings.   In "lower Louisiana" were included the settled areas near the mouth of the river, along the coast of the Gulf and the scattered posts on the Arkansas.   "Upper Louisiana" was composed of St. Louis and its environs; and "west Florida" (interpreted generously) was used to designate such varied places as Natchez, Mobile, and Pensacola.

The element easiest to isolate is the German.   There was German blood in the American stock that entered, but an estimate must also be made for a group of original colonists.   Prominent in early Louisiana topography are the two German "coasts" of the Mississippi River.   Their inhabitants are the descendants of colonists brought out during the John Law régime and other

---

[40] *Amer. st. p. Miscellaneous*, I.

[41] 11th Congress, 3d session, *Message from the President of the United States transmitting a report of the secretary of state . . . February 5, 1811.* This census, it seems, has never been reprinted.

[42] The census of 1785 is printed in *An account of Louisiana, being an abstract of documents in the office of the departments of state, and of the Treasury* (Wash., 1803), 45. That of 1788 is in François-Xavier Martin, *The history of Louisiana . . .* (New Orleans. 1882), 251.

Germans who drifted in.[43] Until the time of annexation these colonists had retained their language and many peculiar customs. It may be assumed that they also retained their blood. There were reported to be a few French mixed with them [44] but this infiltration was probably balanced by emigration to neighboring parishes. There is no sign of American settlers. Therefore the total of the white population of these two coasts may be put down as German. In 1785 this white population amounted to 1,275 or 40 per cent of the total. In 1788 the population is returned as 3,740 and assuming the same ratio of whites to blacks this would mean 1,500 Germans in 1788. But the whites probably did not increase as rapidly as the negroes and therefore, 1,500 may be taken as the estimate for 1790.

Two communities usually described together constituted settled parts of southwest Louisiana. In Opelousas and Attakapas the original settlers were Spaniards and Acadians. In the published lists of pioneers, however, Germans are also to be found. In point of fact, the river Teche which flows through the length of the area derives its name through various corruptions from the word " deutsch," and the region was a natural field of expansion for the Germans.[45] But their measurement must, of necessity, be somewhat arbitrary. The white population in 1785 was only 1,200; if it held the same ratio in 1788, their number then was 1,700. Of these, it would seem, 250 might reasonably be considered German. As there is no trace of direct German settlement in any other part of Louisiana, 1,750 may be taken as their number in 1790.

The second problem to be solved is the determination of the number of Spaniards. As no areas were colonized during the Spanish period, it is evident that it is in the commercial centers that this nationality will be found. The lower part of the Mississippi (from New Orleans to the mouth) was entirely French,[46] but in the city the best contemporary estimate places the number of Spaniards at one-fourth of the whites.[47] In 1785 the whites had composed not quite three-fifths of the population. In 1788 this total was 5,338, of whom, therefore, approximately 3,000 were white. One-fourth of this would place the number of Spaniards at 750, and there is no reason to believe that they increased appreciably during the next two years. In the districts of Opelousas and Attakapas, traces of Spaniards may be found, the region occupying a natural position with respect to Spanish expansion along the coast of the Gulf.[48] The same figure assigned to the Germans may also be given to them—250. Part of the city of Baton Rouge to this day retains the name of " Spanish Town," a remainder of a colony of Spaniards living at Galveztown. A return for this settlement in 1788 numbers 268, so for 1790 an estimate of 300 is reasonable, allowing also for a few in Baton Rouge.[49]

Along the upper Red River, centered about the post of Natchitoches, were some stray hunters, trappers, and traders, and a few farmers. Having been so long on the border between the French and Spanish possessions, these two nationalities predominated, as the names of prominent eighteenth century

[43] John H. Deiler. *The settlement of the German coast of Louisiana and the creoles of German descent* (Phila., 1909).

[44] *Amer. st. p. Mis.*, I, 348.

[45] William H. Perrin (ed.), *Southwest Louisiana; biographical and historical* (New Orleans, 1891), 33–36.

[46] *Amer. st. p. Mis.*, I, 348.

[47] François Marie Perrin du Lac, *Voyage dans les deux Louisianes* . . . (Paris, 1805, 390.

[48] H. L. Griffin, The vigilance committees of the Attakapas country : or early Louisiana justice. *Proceedings of the Mississippi Valley historical association*, VIII, 146–159.

[49] William O. Scroggs, Rural life in the lower Mississippi Valley about 1803, Miss. vall. hist. assn., *Proceedings*, VIII, 262–277, 265.

settlers indicate.[50]   The village itself was composed of 40 or 50 families, mostly French.[51]   But there were a few Americans and of the 500 whites, an estimate of 200 Spaniards is a liberal apportionment.   Undoubtedly there was a sprinkling of settlers of this nationality on the upper Mississippi about St. Louis, but the roster of the militia company reveals only one or two who gave their birthplace as Spain.[52]   Therefore any estimate other than the allowance made for them under "American" may be omitted.

It is more difficult to gage the Spanish proportion among the whites in the west Florida area.   Contemporaries did not know.   At the time of the cession of Florida proper in 1819 it was a debated question.[53]   But among the claimants to land about Mobile and Pensacola the proportion is overwhelmingly Spanish.[54] Natchez, on the other hand, was reported in the fall of 1790 to be " an English settlement, subject to the Spaniards." [55]   If then, the inhabitants of the latter place may be considered entirely American, the former may be placed in the Spanish column and the total white population of approximately a thousand (Mobile, Pensacola, and the Tombigbee region) ascribed to this nationality.

From these scattered estimates we derive a total of 1,500 Spaniards in the Louisiana Purchase area and 1,000 in that part of Florida which was included in the census of 1788.

Estimating Americans involves a difficulty of its own.   Many of them were adventurers, coming and going, and this fluctuation is especially annoying as the years before and after 1790 were characterized by many vague plans for conquest and colonization.   But none of these materialized; Americans were not welcomed by the Spanish officials; and it is only as individuals that they established themselves in Louisiana.[56]   Therefore, the number will be smaller than the geographical position of the Province would suggest.   It has already been determined to classify the 2,000 whites at Natchez as Americans.   The only other point at which they would be liable to congregate in any numbers was New Orleans.   In 1806 the number of whites in the city who were neither French nor Spanish amounted to a little more than a fourth of the total.[57]   But following the cession there had been a large immigration; in 1790 the proportion was not as high; and out of the 3,000 in the city it is likely that about 500 were American.   Some allowance must be made for scattered individuals.   The parish of Rapides on the lower Red River was evidently wholly American.[58]   There were also some at Ouachita [59] and along the Arkansas.[60]   But 250 would cover all.

In the decade beginning 1790 there was a large movement across the Mississippi from the Territory of the United States into the Missouri region of Upper

---

[50] *Biographical and historical memoirs of northwest Louisiana* . . . (Nashville, Chicago, 1890), 297.

[51] Amos Stoddard, *Sketches, historical and descriptive, of Louisiana* (Phila., 1812), 187.

[52] Louis Houck (ed.), *The Spanish régime in Missouri* (2 vols., Chicago, 1909, I. 184–189.

[53] The population of Florida is discussed in James G. Forbes, *Sketches, historical and topographical, of the Floridas* (N. Y., 1821), 142; *East Florida Herald* (St. Augustine), July 26, 1823; *Pensacola Gazette,* May 13, 1826; *The Floridian* (Pensacola), August 17, 1822.

[54] *Amer. st. p. Public lands,* IV, 186–189.

[55] Letter from New Orleans, June 27, in *The Pennsylvania packet and daily advertiser* (Philadelphia), November 16, 1790.

[56] Houck, *Spanish in Mo.,* I, 233.

[57] John S. Kendall, *History of New Orleans* (3 vols., Chicago, N. Y., 1922), I, 85.

[58] Stoddard, *La. sketches,* 186.

[59] Claude C. Robin, *Voyages dans l'interieur de la Louisiane* . . . (3 vols., Paris, 1807), II, 328, 332.

[60] *Amer. st. p. Mis.,* I. 348, 382; Josiah H. Shinn, *Pioneers and makers of Arkansas* . . . (4 vols., 1908), I, 41–45; *Amer. st. p. Public lands,* VIII, 343–344, 355–357.

Louisiana. By the time of the transfer of the Province in 1803 it was believed that at least two-fifths of the inhabitants were of that origin.[61] But in 1790 the movement had hardly begun. The white population was concentrated in St. Louis and St. Genevieve and the most reliable evidence indicates that these two settlements were almost wholly French.[62] Col. George Morgan was busy with his plans for a great colony at New Madrid but in the summer of 1790 the inhabitants certainly numbered less than a hundred.[63] If the white population of upper Louisiana is taken at a little more than 2,000, the number of Americans may be considered about 150. This gives a total of 2,900 Americans in the region under survey.

The census of 1788 revealed the white population of the entire Province as 19,455. In 1790 it may be estimated at 20,000. This was, according to the above analysis, composed of:

Germans	1,750
Spanish	2,500
Americans	2,900
French	12,850

EAST FLORIDA

In 1790 Florida was, in general, a wilderness. There were two centers of settlement: Pensacola and its hinterland in the west, and St. Augustine and its hinterland in the east. The probable population of the former has been considered as a part of Louisiana. There remains the latter, or "East Florida."

A study of the settlement of Florida gives little clue to the number and nationality of its inhabitants. The first Spanish period was characterized by wars with the French and English, and massacres by the Indians. The English period saw comprehensive schemes of colonization, but they did not materialize and most of the many thousands of refugees from the revolting English colonies departed when the colony was returned to Spain in 1783.[64] A unique element was made up of several hundreds of Greeks and Minorcans who were settled at New Smyrna in 1767 by Dr. Andrew Turnbull and many of whom survived the disasters that usually attend projects of this sort.[65]

An official report dealing with the condition of east Florida in 1787 reveals a total white population (excluding officials and troops) of 908. Of the total, 31 were natives of Spain, 25 of the Canary Islands, 62 Floridians, 448 "Minorcans, Italians. Greeks," and 342 "British." [66] The first three groups may be consolidated as Spaniards and the last two as "Americans." It is hardly feasible to arrange a separate category for Doctor Turnbull's colonists and their inclusion among the Americans will merely provide a little more diversification in the "all other" group. The British were loyalists and as American as their former neighbors whom they deserted. The total, accordingly, would be Spaniards 118, Americans 790. Three years later the total may be considered 1,000, divided: Spaniards, 125; Americans, 875.

---

[61] *Amer. st. p. Mis.*, I, 348.

[62] Jonas Viles. Population and extent of settlement in Missouri before 1804, *Mo. hist. rev.*, V, 189–213.

[63] In the spring of 1789 seventy men settled at New Madrid. Letter from New Madrid in *The Amer. museum*, VI, 69–71.

[64] George R. Fairbanks, *History of Florida* . . . (Phila., Jacksonville, 1871), 239, 244.

[65] Caroline M. Brevard, *A history of Florida* . . . (2 vols., Deland, Fla.), I, 4. A footnote provides an extensive bibliography on this colony.

[66] Report of Vicente Martinez Cespedez, dated St. Augustine, April 15, 1787, in the Brooks Transcripts of the Library of Congress.

THE SPANISH SOUTHWEST

The term " Spanish Southwest " refers to those parts of the present United States which in 1790 were Provinces of the Spanish Empire—the States of Texas, New Mexico, Arizona, California, Utah, Nevada, and part of Colorado. The great storehouse for information regarding conditions in this area is the series edited by H. H. Bancroft: *History of the Pacific States of North America.* Whatever statistics of population are extant are collected in these volumes and although few of them happen to pertain directly to the year 1790, our estimates can be derived from those which are chronologically the nearest.

According to a Spanish report of 1782 the number of soldiers and settlers in Texas numbered 2,600, " though this would seem an exaggeration." [67]   Granting that it was an exaggeration, that the growth from 1782 to 1790 was slow and that soldiers ought to be omitted, the figure 2,500 would be a conservative estimate for the latter year.   Modern Texas includes what was then known as the " El Paso district " which was in 1793 reported as being inhabited by 3,622 whites.[68]   The growth in the three years was undoubtedly slow and 3,500 for 1790 would probably be safe.   This would give a total of 6,000 for modern Texas.

Judging from the geographical position of Texas, it seems possible that among these 6,000 whites there would be a considerable number of Americans and French.   But such was not the case.   In 1804 a list of foreigners in the jurisdiction of Nacogdoches was made and they totaled only 68.   Almost all of these had settled in the years immediately preceding.   Being on the frontier of the Spanish Empire, it was in this jurisdiction that the largest number of non-Spanish whites would be found.[69]   The 6,000 may be considered Spanish.

The New Mexico pueblo region was the center of the most extensive colonization in the Spanish Southwest.   A report of 1793 places the number of Spaniards at 16,156.[70]   For 1790 the number may be placed at 15,000.   For Arizona, there are no figures available until 1845—the eve of the American occupation.   The estimated population was then 2,000.[71]   But the settlements were old and 1,000 were probably there in 1790.

The white population of present-day California was estimated in 1800 at 300 in the southern district, 518 in the Monterey district, and 460 in the San Francisco district—a total of 1,278.[72]   A round thousand would, on this basis, be the estimate for 1790.   This agrees with the statement that in 1790, according to official reports, the white population was 970.[73]   It may be considered entirely Spanish as at that time the extent of the foreigners' trade on the Pacific coast and the policy of the Spanish Empire were not such as to make the settlement of foreigners likely.

The population of the Spanish southwest in 1790 was, accordingly, 23,000, all Spanish.

---

[67] Hubert H. Bancroft, . . . *North Mexican states* . . . (Vol. X, *Hist. Pac. st. N. Amer.,* San Francisco, 1883–89), I, 633.

[68] Bancroft, . . . *History of Arizona and New Mexico, 1530–1888* (Vol. XII, *Hist. Pac. st. N. Amer.*), 279.

[69] Mattie A. Hatcher, Conditions in Texas affecting the colonization problem, 1795–1801, *The Southwestern historical quarterly,* XXV, 81–97.

[70] Bancroft, *Hist. Ariz. & N. M.,* 279.

[71] *Ibid.,* 382.

[72] Bancroft, . . . *History of California* . . . (Vols. XVII–XIV, *Hist. Pac. st. N. Amer.*), I, 648, 676, 693.

[73] Charles E. Chapman, *The founding of Spanish California* . . . (N. Y., 1916), 428; Irving B. Richman, *California under Spain and Mexico* . . . (Boston, N. Y., 1911), 452.

Summary of the outlying regions

	Americans	French	Spaniards	Germans	Total
Old northwest	4, 500	6, 000			10, 500
Louisiana purchase	2, 900	12, 850	2, 500	1, 750	20, 000
East Florida	875		125		1, 000
Spanish southwest			23, 000		23, 000
Total	8, 275	18, 850	25, 625	1, 750	54, 500

INDEX TO REPORT OF COMMITTEE ON LINGUISTIC AND NATIONAL STOCKS IN THE POPULATION OF THE UNITED STATES[1]

Compiled by JOHN J. MENG, Ph. D.

A

A collection of papers read before the Bucks County historical society, note 375.

Aberdeen County, Scotland, 212.

Acadia, source of French immigration, 121, 387.

Achenbach, 287.

Acrelius, Israel, *A history of New Sweden,* 392.

Adam, 213 ff.

Adams, 137 ff., 216, 278.

Adams, Sherman W., *The history of ancient Wethersfield, Conn.,* note 382.

Adams, Mass., 271.

Adkins, 216.

Africa, French power in, 380.

Aggregates, in American nomenclature, 158–159.

Aitken, 213 ff.

Alaska, note 109.

Albany, N. Y., French in, 1697, 387; originally Fort Orange, 367; population of, 1698, 364–365.

Albany County, N. Y., Dutch in, 1698, 120.

Albert, 284.

Albrecht, 282–322.

Albright, 287–322.

Albrite, 319.

Alderchurch, 256.

Alein, 152.

Alerding, Herman J., *A history of the Catholic church in the diocese of Vincennes,* note 400.

Alexander, 137, 213 ff.

Allan, 152, 211 ff.

Allegheny Co., Md., Dutch in, 376.

Allen, 137–216.

Alt, 319.

Alvord, Clarence W., " The conquest of St. Joseph, Mich., by the Spaniards in 1781," note 402; . . . *Kaskaskia records, 1778–1790* . . ., note 401.

America, Celtic Irish in, 232–255; commerical connections, 385–386; Dutch in, 120, 366–367, 378; English contribution to, 164–196; English surnames, 177; French migration to, 121, 380–390; German contributions to, 271–305; minor stocks, 360–397; names, adoption, 200,

America—Continued.

affinities, 206, classification, 135–150, 154, codification, 158, currency, 144–264, evolution, 134, interpretations, 135, 248–251, modification, 146, origin, 113, 136, usage, 199–261, variants, 207, 223; national stocks, 126–296, 306–310, Celtic Irish, 232–255, English, 113, 164–205, German, 271–296, Scotch, 206–231, Ulsterite, 256–270, Welsh, 113; nomenclature, evolution, 147–148, foreign influence, 208, interpretation, 147; population, coherent whole, 197, East Florida, 406, English contributions, 169–199, expansion, 380–381, German, 271–305, groups of, 360, Irish, 249–264, list by States and counties, 396–397, Louisiana Purchase, 402–406, Scotch, 229–230, Old Northwest, 398–402, outlying regions, 398–408, Spanish Southwest, 407–408; racial strains, 126; surnames, 125; Swedes in, 391–397. *See also* Population, American.

American Colonies, movement of population in, 361; relations with Canada, 386.

American Council of Learned Societies, committee on linguistic and national stocks, 107–109.

American historical magazine, The, note, 378.

American Irish, by province of origin, 270.

American museum or universal magazine, The, note, 398.

American nomenclature. *See* Nomenclature.

American state papers. Documents legislative and executive of the congress of the United States. . . . Indian affairs, note 399.

American States. *See* States.

Americans, in E. Florida, 406; in Louisiana Purchase, 405–406; in outlying regions, 408; in Texas, 407.

Amweg, 319.

An account of Louisiana, being an abstract of documents in the office of the Department of State and of the Treasury, note, 403.

Analogy, name changes based on, 320.

Ancestry, evidence of, in names, 131.

Anderson, 135 ff., 210 ff.

[1] Titles of special studies referred to in Annex A are listed in separate bibliography, pages 325–359. All other titles are included here.

Fox, 279 ff.

Frailick, 311.

Fraise, 282.

France, emigration from, 121, 127, 381–385; influence on American life, 121; military rosters, 148–149; religious refugees, 381.

Franck, 279.

Frank, 279.

Frankfort, Me., 271.

Franklin, Benjamin, conception of American people, 127; on Pa. Germans, 292.

Franks, 279.

Frans, 281.

Fransse, 281.

Frantz, 281.

Fraser, 207 ff.

Frazer, 221.

Frazier, 224.

Frederic, 281.

Frederick, 281.

Frederickse, 281.

Freeland, 256.

Freese, 282.

French, 137.

French, as minor stock, 110, 127, 380; colonial attitude towards, 384; denationalization of, 381; dispersion of, 121, 381; from Canada, 386–387; in America, 121, 300–310, 360, 396–397, New York, 364–365, eastern states, 382–390, western states, 400–408; language in American life, 385–386; majority Huguenot, 381; migration of, 380, 386; names in CPG, 110; number, 127, 381–382; professional men in America, 385; tastes, in American life, 385–386. *See also* Huguenots.

French United States, national and linguistic stocks, 122, 124–125.

French West Indies, American commercial connection with, 386.

Frenchtown, Mich., settlement of. 401–402.

Frequencies, comparative study of, 144–146.

Frey, 279.

Friche, 283.

Friderich, 281.

Fries, 282 ff.

Frisch, 284.

Frith, 283.

Fritsch, 284.

Fritz, 282 ff.

Froehlich, 311.

Fry, 279.

Fuchs, 279 ff.

Fuller, 137.

Fullerton, James N., "Squatters and titles to land in early western Pennsylvania," note 376.

Funck, 131, 282 ff.

Fundamentals, in nomenclatural evolution, 276–277.

Funk, 285 ff.

Furbush, 224.

G

Gaelic names, by origin, 155.

Gallagher, 239 ff.

Gallipolis, Ohio, settlement of, 400.

Galloway County, Scotland, 212.

Galveztown, La., Spanish settlement at, 404.

Gamble, 222.

Gannon, 239 ff.

Gardiner, 216.

Gardner, 137, 213 ff.

Garver, 131, 294.

Gaudet, Placide, "Acadian genealogy and notes," note 389; "Les Seigneuries de l'ancienne Acadie," note 389.

Gaul, 311.

Geach, 282.

Gebbie, 283.

Gebhart, 288.

Gebhert, 282 ff.

Gedge, 282.

Geiger, 282 ff.

Genealogical record of the St. Nicholas society, 388.

Genealogy, New England, Dexter, Holmes and Savage on, 152; use of in investigating Census of 1790, 128–129.

Geographical factors, in German contributions to U. S., 300–301; in name origins and codification, 146, 160.

George, 279.

Georgia, Dutch in, 120, 378; English and Welsh in, 114, 123, 197–199, 203; French in, 121; Germans in, 119, 271, 296–299, 304, 305; Huguenots in, 384; Irish in, 118, 251–253, 270; name currency in, 164; national and linguistic stocks, 122, 124–125, 307; population, 110, 378; records for 1790 missing, 197; Scotch in, 113, 115, 230–231; Scotch-Irish in, 267; Swedes in, 122.

Georgia's Roster of the Revolution, 389.

Geraghty, 239 ff.

Gerber, 273 ff.

Gerbert, 283.

Gergainus, 309.

Gerhard, 279.

German, contributions, to America, 119, 271–307, 375, 408, states of missing records, 296–297, to outlying regions, 408, to the States. 294–296, 301, 375, La., 403–406, New England, 302–305, N. J., 372, N. Y., 368, of missing records, 304–305, Pa., 131, 291-294, 375; emigration, 363; families in South Africa, 363; national stock, 110, 112, 118–119, 127, 296–297.

German names, currencies, 110, 118, 277–278, 283–290, 301; Heintze on, 142, 148; in New England, 302–303, 118, 162, 272–274, 282, 311–316; study of, 271–305; usage, 119, 162, 271–305, 318–324; variants, 118–119, 146, 285–287, 299, 311–312, 318–324.

Hoppman, 281.

Horcheild, 303.

Horn, 278 ff.

Horton, 137.

Houch, 279.

Houck, Louis (Ed.), *The Spanish régime in Missouri,* note 405.

Hough, 159, 283.

Houghtalen, 140.

Hover, 136, 286 ff.

Howard, 137.

Howe, Henry, *Historical collections of Ohio,* note 399.

Howell, George R. and Jonathan Tenney (Eds.), *Bi-centennial history of Albany. History of the county of Albany, N. Y.,* note 368.

Huber, 136, 274 ff.

Hubert, 283.

Hudson River, artery of New Netherland, 368; colonized by Dutch, 361–364; English settlement along, 367.

Huff, 159, 287 ff.

Hughes, 155 ff., 269.

Huguenots, at New Rochelle, N. Y., 365; colonial prejudice towards, 384–385; immigration, 381–382; in South Africa, 363; in States, 382–389; in Suffolk Co., N. Y., 365; in York Co., Pa., 375; majority of French settlers, 381; migration, 121; names, 388; principal settlements, 382–384; settlement at New Paltz, 369. *See also French.*

Huguenot society of America, Proceedings, note 382.

Huguenot society of the founders of Manakin in the colony of Virginia, yearbook, note 384.

Huhn, 321.

Hulbert, Archer B. (Ed.), *Ohio in the time of the confederation,* note 399.

Humble, 283.

Hummel, 282 ff.

Hunt, 137.

Hunter, 211 ff.

Hunterdon County, N. J., German settlement in, 271; muster rolls, note 372.

Huntingdon County, England, 216.

Huntoon, Daniel T. V., *History of the town of Canton, Norfolk County, Mass.,* note 387.

Huntting, Isaac, *History of Little Nine Partners . . . of Duchess County,* note 369.

Hurd, Duane H. (Comp.), *History of Fairfield County, Conn.,* note 373.

Hutchinson, 217.

Hutchison, 213 ff.

Hutto, 309.

Hyland, 238 ff.

Hynes, 279.

I

Illinois, in Old Northwest, 398; population, 401.

Illinois Catholic historical review, note 401.

Immigrant names, classification of, 135–136.

Immigration, and name patterns, 125; currents of, 127; date of, effect on names, 152; Dutch, 363, 378; English, 151; Federal records of, 126; French, 121; German, 118–119; history of, 109; Irish, 117; national origins plan, 107; quantity of, bearing on nomenclature, 151–153; quotas, 107–108; U. S. policy, 107. *See also* Emigration, Migration.

Index of wills, inventories, etc., State of N. J., note 372.

Indexes, of families, classified in CPG by states, 193; of names, English indicator, 193.

Indian trade, profit of, 364.

Indiana, French in, 400–401; in Old Northwest, 398; population and settlement of, 400–401.

Indicator names, Cambrian, 174; Irish, composition of classes of, 238–239, selection of, 236–240; proportion of in England and Wales, 177; requirements to be met, 173; Scotch, 206–208; selection of, 173–176.

Information regarding Louisiana, 403.

Ingall, 217.

Ingle, 217.

Inglis, 213 ff.

Interpolation, for States of missing record, 197–198, 209–210, 230, 251–252, 266–267, 296–297, 304–305; for Delaware, 198; Germans, 296–297, 304–305; for Irish, 251–252; for New Jersey, 198; for Scotch, 209–210, 230; for Scotch-Irish, 266–267; for Virginia, 198–199.

Intolerance, in America, 384.

Inverness County, Scotland, 211–212.

Ireland, contributions, to America, 117, 233–234, 252–255, 270, to States of missing records, 251–252; emigration, 115–117; names, British by-usage, 179, common, 111–115, 135, 235–236, currency, 115, 173–174, 240, 265–269, distinctive, 116, 248, indicator, 209–210, 236–240, non-distinctive, 116, patterns, 112, Scotch, 117, usage, 115, 214; population, 232–233, 252; Scotch-Irish in, 151; southern origins of emigrants, 269–270.

Irish, Episcopalians, 256; important national stock, 110–112, 118, 127; in America, 116, 232–255, 264–270, 306–307; number and distribution, 1890, 240; of Ulster, 266–268; Presbyterians, 256; Quakers, 256; Scotch-Irish among, 264–268; study outline, 232–233.

Irish names, 110, 116, 143–145, 232–255; affinities, 206–207; classification of, 233–240; Connaught, 240; currency, 115–116, 248, 251; importance of, 237; in America, 117, 246–249, 255, 262; in New England, 246; indicator, 236–239; Leinster, 240; method of study, 232–234; Munster, 240; origins, 252; Scotch names shared with, 220–222; types, 115; Ulster, 240, 256–270; usage, 233, 240–248; variants, 146.